of Immigration Virginia. Board, Jediah Hotchkiss

# Virginia

A geographical and political summary : embracing a description of the state, its geology, soils, minerals and climate ; its animal and vegetable productions ; manufacturing and commercial facilities; religious and educational advantages

of Immigration Virginia. Board, Jediah Hotchkiss

**Virginia**

*A geographical and political summary : embracing a description of the state, its geology, soils, minerals and climate ; its animal and vegetable productions ; manufacturing and commercial facilities; religious and educational advantages*

ISBN/EAN: 9783337373764

Printed in Europe, USA, Canada, Australia, Japan

Cover: Foto ©Andreas Hilbeck / pixelio.de

More available books at **www.hansebooks.com**

# GEOGRAPHICAL AND POLITICAL SUMMARY,

EMBRACING

A DESCRIPTION OF THE STATE, ITS GEOLOGY, SOILS, MINERALS AND CLIMATE; ITS ANIMAL AND VEGETABLE PRODUCTIONS; MANUFACTURING AND COMMERCIAL FACILITIES; RELIGIOUS AND EDUCATIONAL ADVANTAGES; INTERNAL IMPROVEMENTS, AND FORM OF GOVERNMENT.

PREPARED AND PUBLISHED

UNDER THE SUPERVISION OF THE BOARD OF IMMIGRATION,

AND BY AUTHORITY OF LAW.

RICHMOND, VIRGINIA:
R. F. WALKER, SUPERINTENDENT OF PUBLIC PRINTING.
1876.

GEO. W. GARY, PRINTER. L. LEWIS, STEREOTYPER.

# PREFATORY.

The change in the labor system and the loss of capital in Virginia, resulting from the late war, having thrown large bodies of land out of cultivation and suspended or crippled many industrial enterprises and occupations, the General Assembly of the State, responding to the wishes of the people, have adopted various measures to promote immigration and induce the introduction and investment of means. As early as March, 1867, resolutions were adopted by that body inviting "all classes of men, from all countries, to Virginia, to settle the surplus lands and engage in all the great industrial pursuits."

At a later day the same body passed an act creating a Board of Immigration, and reciting in the preamble to the act that "in order to the restoration and improvement of our agriculture, the development of our numerous mineral resources, the introduction and support of manufacturing industry, and the fixed and permanent establishment of a population corresponding with the capacity of our vast and sparsely settled territory, it is eminently expedient to invite the migratory population of other States, both American and European, to fix their homes and invest their capital among us;" and to this end, they instructed the Board of Immigration to have prepared "a geographical and political summary, setting forth the numerous advantages of climate, soil and productions which are here offered to foreigners seeking settlement in new countries."

The Board of Immigration so created was composed of the Governor, the Lieutenant-Governor, the Secretary of the Commonwealth, the Adjutant-General and the Treasurer of the State. In the execution of the duty devolved upon them, they selected for the preparation of the summary Major JED. HOTCHKISS, of Staunton. They were led to select this gentleman, as they stated in their report to the Legislature, "because, in the pursuit of his calling as a topographical and mining engineer, he had devoted much time to acquiring accurate knowledge of the geography, the varied physical elements, the internal improvements and capabilities, the agricultural, manufacturing and general industrial condition and resources of the State, and was believed to possess greater experience and aptitude for the work than any person known to the Board."

The work in its successive stages was submitted to the Board, and underwent their careful supervision and criticism. When it was completed they gave it their endorsement in the following language, embraced in their report to the Legislature: "The Board feel warranted in saying that the work will prove itself, upon examination, to be of the very highest value and interest to the State; that it embodies and exhibits in accurate, lucid and comprehensive form complete information upon all the important topics treated; and that it constitutes a repository of most valuable information not to be found in any existing publication. The statistical tables comprise the results of laborious research through many scattered sources of information, and exhibit facts as to the actual production and the varied industrial capabilities of the State, which are instructive and gratifying. Maps accompany the work, prepared specially for its illustration; and the section which treats of the geological and mineral characteristics of each grand division presents, in a carefully condensed form, the results of the geological survey made by Professor Wm. B. Rogers, with the additional information obtained by Major Hotchkiss, through his investigation in the same field."

This work is now submitted to the public in the following pages.

# TABLE OF CONTENTS.

## PART I.—GEOGRAPHICAL SUMMARY.



## PART II.—POLITICAL SUMMARY.

# VIRGINIA.

## *PART I—GEOGRAPHICAL SUMMARY.*

CHAPTER I—GENERAL DESCRIPTION OF THE STATE.

CHAPTER II—GEOLOGICAL.
- SECTION 1. THE FORMATIONS.
- SECTION 2. THE SOILS.
- SECTION 3. THE MINERALS.

CHAPTER III—THE CLIMATE.

CHAPTER IV—THE PRODUCTIONS.
- SECTION 1. ANIMAL.
- SECTION 2. VEGETABLE.

CHAPTER V—MANUFACTURES.
- SECTION 1. RESULTS.
- SECTION 2. FACILITIES.

CHAPTER VI—COMMERCE.
- SECTION 1. RESULTS.
- SECTION 2. ADVANTAGES.

# VIRGINIA.

## PART I—GEOGRAPHICAL SUMMARY.

### CHAPTER I.

#### A GENERAL DESCRIPTION OF THE STATE.

Location.—Virginia is one of the Middle Atlantic States* of the United States of America, lying midway between Maine on the north and Florida on the south. It is also in the belt of Central States, across the continent from east to west. Its latitude is from 36° 31′ to 39° 27′ N., corresponding to Southern Europe, Central Asia, Southern Japan, and California. Its longitude is from 75° 13′ to 83° 37′ west from Greenwich. It extends 2° 57′ north and south, and 9° 24′ east and west.

Boundaries.—On the south it adjoins North Carolina for 326 miles, and Tennessee for 114 miles, making the line of the State from the Atlantic west 440 miles; on the west and northwest, Kentucky for 115 and West Virginia (by a very irregular line) for 450 miles, form the boundary. Maryland is northeast and north, separated by the Potomac and Chesapeake bay for 205 miles from Virginia (to which these waters belong), and by a line of 25 miles across the Eastern Shore. East and southeast it is bordered by the Atlantic for 125 miles. The boundary lines of the State measure about 1,400 miles: on the northwest they are mostly mountain ranges; on the northeast and east, water.

Dimensions.—The longest line in the State, from the Atlantic southwest to Kentucky, is 476 miles; the longest from N. to S. is 192 miles. The longest line in England (N. E. to S. W.) is 372 miles, and the longest from N. to S. is 360 miles.

---

* Guyot classes New York, New Jersey, Pennsylvania, Delaware, Maryland, Virginia and West Virginia as Middle Atlantic States. Maury follows the same classification.

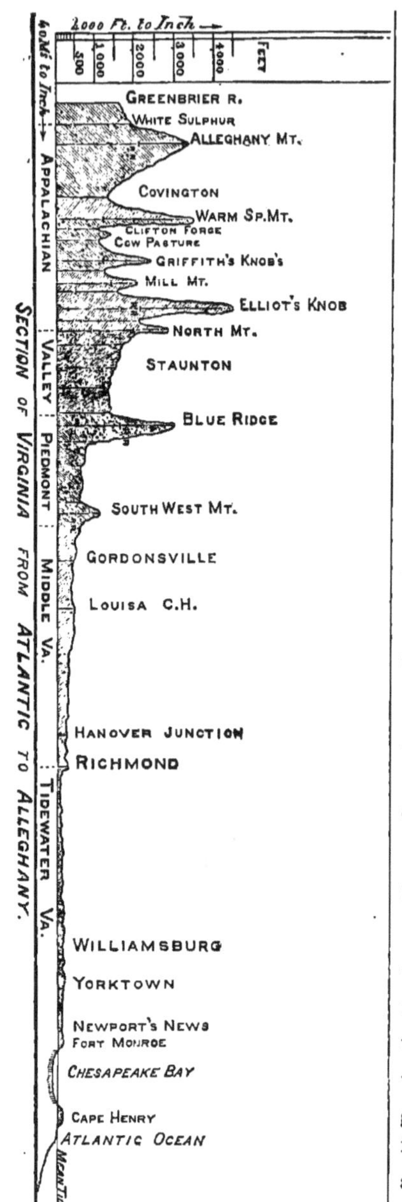


SECTION OF VIRGINIA FROM ATLANTIC TO ALLEGHANY.

NATURAL DIVISIONS.—There are six great Natural Divisions of the territory of Virginia; belts of country extending across the State from northeast to southwest, as a general direction, nearly parallel to each other, and corresponding to the trend of the Atlantic coast on the east, and of the ranges of the Appalachian system of mountains on the northwest.

These Grand Divisions are, taken in the order of succession from the ocean northwest across the State:

1st. The TIDEWATER Country, or TIDEWATER.

2nd. The MIDDLE Country, or MIDDLE VIRGINIA.

3rd. The PIEDMONT Country, or PIEDMONT.

4th. The BLUE RIDGE Country, or THE BLUE RIDGE.

5th. The GREAT VALLEY OF VIRGINIA, or THE VALLEY.

6th. The APPALACHIAN Country, or APPALACHIA.

These Divisions not only succeed each other geographically, as shown upon the map, but they occupy different levels above the sea, *rising to the west* like a grand stairway, as shown by the section.* They differ geologically also; therefore they have differences of climate, soil, productions, &c., and require a separate consideration, in every respect, in a description of the State.

*Copied by permission from Scribner's Magazine—article on Virginia by Jed. Hotchkiss, December, 1872.

## GROUPING OF COUNTIES IN NATURAL GRAND DIVISIONS OF VIRGINIA.

| GRAND DIVISIONS OF STATE. | NATURAL SUB-DIVISIONS. | | COUNTIES. |
|---|---|---|---|
| (1). TIDEWATER | The *first peninsula*, or "THE NORTHERN NECK." | | King George.<br>Westmoreland.<br>Richmond.<br>Northumberland.<br>Lancaster |
| | The *second*, or MIDDLESEX PENINSULA, | | Essex.<br>Middlesex. |
| | The *third*, or GLOUCESTER PENINSULA. | | King & Queen.<br>Mathews.<br>Gloucester. |
| | The *fourth*—the KING WILLIAM or PAMUNKEY PENINSULA | | Caroline.<br>King William. |
| | The *fifth*, or "THE PENINSULA". | | Hanover.<br>New Kent.<br>James City.<br>York.<br>Warwick.<br>Elizabeth City. |
| | The *sixth*—RICHMOND or CHICKAHOMINY PENINSULA | | Henrico.<br>Charles City. |
| | The *seventh*, or SOUTHSIDE PENINSULA, | | Prince George.<br>Surry.<br>Sussex.<br>Southampton.<br>Isle of Wight.<br>Nansemond. |
| | The *eighth*, or NORFOLK PENINSULA. | | Norfolk.<br>Princess Anne. |
| | The *ninth* peninsula—"THE EASTERN SHORE" | | Accomac.<br>Northampton. |
| 2). THE MIDDLE COUNTRY. | NORTHSIDE GROUP. | POTOMAC BASIN | Fairfax.<br>Alexandria.<br>Prince William.<br>Stafford. |
| | | PAMUNKEY BASIN. | Spotsylvania.<br>Louisa. |
| | | JAMES BASIN. | Fluvanna.<br>Goochland. |
| | SOUTHSIDE GROUP. | JAMES-APPOMATTOX BASIN. | Buckingham.<br>Cumberland.<br>Powhatan.<br>Chesterfield.<br>Appomattox. |
| | | APPOMATTOX BASIN | Prince Edward.<br>Amelia. |
| | | NOTTOWAY BASIN | Dinwiddie.<br>Nottoway. |
| | | MEHERRIN BASIN | Lunenburg.<br>Brunswick.<br>Greensville. |
| | | ROANOKE BASIN | Campbell.<br>Charlotte.<br>Pittsylvania.<br>Halifax.<br>Mecklenburg. |
| (3). THE PIEDMONT COUNTRY | POTOMAC WATERS | | Loudoun.<br>Fauquier. |
| | RAPPAHANNOCK WATERS | | Culpeper.<br>Rappahannock.<br>Madison.<br>Greene.<br>Orange. |
| | JAMES WATERS | | Albemarle.<br>Nelson.<br>Amherst. |
| | STAUNTON WATERS | | Bedford.<br>Franklin. |
| | DAN WATERS | | Henry.<br>Patrick. |

| GRAND DIVISIONS OF STATE. | NATURAL SUB-DIVISIONS. | COUNTIES. |
|---|---|---|
| (4). THE BLUE RIDGE......... | NEW RIVER PLATEAU........................ | Floyd.<br>Carroll.<br>Grayson. |
| (5). THE VALLEY OF VIRGINIA ........................ | THE SHENANDOAH VALLEY............... | Frederick.<br>Clarke.<br>Warren.<br>Shenandoah.<br>Page.<br>Rockingham.<br>Augusta. |
| | THE JAMES RIVER VALLEY................ | Rockbridge.<br>Botetourt. |
| | THE ROANOKE VALLEY....................... | Roanoke. |
| | THE NEW RIVER OR KANAWHA VALLEY.................................................. | Montgomery.<br>Pulaski.<br>Wythe. |
| | THE HOLSTON OR TENNESSEE VALLEY. | Smyth.<br>Washington. |
| (6). APPALACHIA................ | SOURCES OF JAMES............................ | Highland.<br>Bath.<br>Alleghany.<br>Craig. |
| | NEW RIVER COUNTRY....................... | Giles.<br>Bland. |
| | CLINCH RIVER COUNTRY.................... | Tazewell.<br>Russell.<br>Scott.<br>Lee. |
| | SOURCES OF SANDY RIVER, OF TRANS-APPALACHIA...................................... | Buchanan.<br>Wise. |

AREAS AND POPULATION.—Before describing these Divisions, or even the State as a whole, it is best to present the facts of area and population, so that proper ideas may be formed of the relative size and present condition of each and of the whole; also comparative statistics concerning other well known countries.

## TABLE I—AREAS AND POPULATION.

| | COMBINED NATURAL AND POLITICAL AREAS, &C. | | | | | | NATURAL AREAS. | |
|---|---|---|---|---|---|---|---|---|
| | Square Miles. | Statute Acres. | Population, 1870. | Population to Square Mile. | 45-ths of State. | 1,000-ths of State. | Areas of Natural Divisions.—Sq. miles. | 1,000-ths of State. |
| Tidewater.................................... | 11,350 | 5,664,000 | 346,305 | 30.5 | 11 | .252 | 11,350 | .252 |
| Middle......................................... | 12,470 | 7,980,800 | 363,932 | 29.2 | 12 | .277 | 12,470 | .277 |
| Piedmont...................................... | 6,680 | 4,276,200 | 207,204 | 32.5 | 7 | .149 | 6,000 | .133 |
| Blue Ridge.................................... | 1,230 | 787,200 | 28,558 | 23.2 | 1 | .027 | 2,500 | .056 |
| The Valley.................................... | 7,550 | 4,832,000 | 197,967 | 26.2 | 8 | .168 | 5,000 | .111 |
| Appalachia.................................... | 5,720 | 3,660,800 | 81,197 | 14.2 | 6 | .127 | 7,680 | .171 |
| Virginia.............................. | 45,000 | 27,201,000 | 1,225,163 | 27.2 | 45 | 1.000 | 45,000 | 1.000 |

The area of Tidewater includes 2,500 square miles of tidal waters; that of Piedmont all the eastern slope of the Blue Ridge; in that of the Blue Ridge, only the southwestern expansion of this mountain range is included; that of the Valley embraces the western slope of the Blue Ridge, and a strip along the western side of the Valley from Appalachia; the latter does not include the strip just named; in short, the first column gives the area of each section, as nearly as may be, as the aggregate of its counties. In the last two columns an effort is made to give the areas of each according to *natural bounds*. The first is given because all the statistics are gathered for counties, and must be so used in comparisons. The fifth column gives an approximation of relative areas, the Blue Ridge being the unit of comparison. The sixth column gives the actual proportion of the divisions as used in this summary. The sections, arranged by *natural* areas in 100-ths, would stand: 1st. Blue Ridge, 6; 2nd. Valley, 11; 3rd. Piedmont, 13; 4th. Appalachia, 17; 5th. Tidewater, 25; 6th. Middle, 28. So nearly one-fourth of the State is mountain region, and one-fourth is Tidewater, leaving one-fourth for the plains of the Middle Country, and one-fourth for the rolling regions of the Valley and Piedmont.

As presented in this summary, one-fourth of the State is Tidewater, over one-fourth Middle, nearly one-seventh Piedmont, over one-thirty-third Blue Ridge; one-eighth is Appalachian, and one-sixth Valley country. Tidewater and Middle are each nearly twice the size of Appalachia or Piedmont.

COMPARISONS.—The following table presents some of the same facts in regard to other states and countries:

TABLE II.

| STATE. | Square Miles. | Population. | Population to Square Mile. |
|---|---|---|---|
| England | (2) 50,922 | (4) 22,704,108 | 445.8 |
| Scotland | (2) 38,720 | (4) 3,358,613 | 86.7 |
| Belgium | (1) 11,372 | (5) 4,984,500 | 438.2 |
| Holland | (1) 12,680 | (6) 3,552,700 | 280.2 |
| New York | (3) 47,000 | (3) 4,382,759 | 93.3 |
| Pennsylvania | (3) 46,000 | (3) 3,521,551 | 76.6 |
| Massachusetts | (3) 7,800 | 1,457,351 | 186.8 |
| Connecticut | 4,750 | 537,454 | 113.2 |
| Saxony | 5,779 | (7) 2,426,200 | 419.3 |
| Brunswick | 1,425 | (7) 303,401 | 212.9 |
| Würtemberg | 7,532 | (7) 1,778,500 | 236.1 |
| Maryland | 11,124 | (3) 780,894 | 70.2 |
| Switzerland | 15,722 | 2,510,494 | 159.6 |

(1) Guyot; (2) Reynolds; (3) U. S. Census 1870; (4) in 1871; (5) 1865; (6) 1866; (7) 1867.

Table II. shows that Tidewater and Belgium, Middle and Holland, Piedmont and Würtemberg, Blue Ridge and Brunswick, The Valley and Massachusetts, Appalachia and Saxony do not differ much in area, although very materially in density of population. If Virginia were peopled like England, it would have 19,600,000 inhabitants, one-half the present (1870) population of the United States;—it has a capacity for production equal to their support.

SURFACE.—(1). TIDEWATER VIRGINIA is divided by the waters of Chesapeake bay and the large tidal rivers that flow into that great estuary, into nine principal and a large number of secondary peninsulas. This is mainly an alluvial country, a portion of the Tertiary, Atlantic tidewater plain, and its surface, composed of sands and clays, is thrown into low flat ridges forming the water-shed of the peninsulas, succeeded by terraces and plains down to the water's edge, where they meet the swamps and salt marshes that always accompany well developed, land-locked, tidal waters. But little of this section is as much as 100 feet above the sea. This is the clay, marl and sand region.

(2). The MIDDLE COUNTRY is a wide, undulating plain, crossed by many rivers that have cut their channels to a considerable depth, and are bordered by alluvial bottom lands. Sandstones and granitic rocks abound.

(3). PIEDMONT is a diversified region, with many broken ranges of hills and mountains, enclosing valleys of many forms, or with streams bordered by narrow bottom lands winding among them; its hills are generally rounded in outline. In many places there are extensive plains. The crumbling greenstone and granite occur here.

(4). The BLUE RIDGE is a many-branched mountain range, expanding into plateaus or rising into domes, extending across the whole length of the State and forming one of its most prominent features. This is ribbed with hard sandstones and soft epidotic rocks.

(5). THE VALLEY is a portion of the Great Central Appalachian Valley that extends for hundreds of miles from Canada to Alabama—a broad belt of rolling country, enclosed between lofty mountain ranges, diversified by hills and valleys, with many winding streams of water. The Blue Ridge is on the east, and the Kitatinny, or "Endless Mountains," on the west. This is a region of limestone rocks, shales, slates and clays.

(6). The APPALACHIAN COUNTRY is made up of a number of parallel mountain chains, with trough-like valleys between them, the mountains often running for fifty or more miles as an unbroken, single, straight, lofty ridge, with an equally uniform valley alongside: sometimes the mountains die out and the valleys widen. Some of the mountain ranges and valleys are of sandstone, some of slates and shales, others of limestone; so there is here great variety of surface.

Some portions of the State are but little above the sea level; others are wide table lands, over 2,000 feet above the sea. No country can have more variety of surface.

INLAND WATERS.—The State has two systems of inland waters—(1) the Atlantic, and (2) the Ohio or Mississippi.

(1). The waters of the State, from Tidewater, Middle, Piedmont, the eastern slope of the Blue Ridge and the central part of the Valley, flow southeast to Chesapeake bay and Albemarle sound, following the inclination of the "Atlantic slope;" those from the northern portions of the Valley and Appalachia follow the mountain ranges northeast to the Potomac, which river follows the southeasterly course before mentioned.

(2). The waters from the southwestern part of the Blue Ridge, the middle of the southwestern half of the Valley and Appalachia, flow northwest and north to the Ohio; those of the southwestern portions of the Valley and Appalachia flow southwest to the Tennessee. So the waters of the State flow in all directions.

PRINCIPAL RIVERS AND BRANCHES.—The waters belonging to the Atlantic system drain six-sevenths of the State. The principal streams of this system are: the Potomac, with its large branches—the Shenandoah and the South Branch, and its prominent smaller ones—Potomac creek, Occoquan river, Broad Run, Goose, Kittoctin and Opequon creeks—draining a large area of each of the sections of the State; the Rappahannock, with its Rapid Anne and numerous other branches flowing from the Blue Ridge across Piedmont, Middle and Tidewater, irrigating a large territory; the Pianketank, draining only a portion of Tidewater; the York, with its Pamunkey and Mattapony branches, and many tributaries flowing from a considerable area of Middle and Tidewater; the James, with the Chickahominy, Elizabeth, Nansemond, Appomattox, Rivanna, Willis', Slate, Rockfish, Tye, Pedlar, South, Cowpasture, Jackson's, and many other inflowing rivers and streams of all kinds, gathers from a large territory in all the Divisions, draining more of the State than any other river. All these flow into Chesapeake bay. The Chowan, through its Blackwater, Nottoway and Meherrin branches and their affluents, waters portions of Middle and Tidewater. The Roanoke receives the Dan, Otter, Pig and many other streams, from the Valley, Piedmont and Middle Virginia, and then flows through North Carolina to Albemarle sound, joining the Chowan. The sources of the Yadkin are in the Blue Ridge.

The waters of the Ohio, a part of the Mississippi system, drain the remaining seventh of the State; but they reach the Ohio by three diverse ways. The rivers are: The Kanawha or New River, that rises in North Carolina, in the most elevated portion of the United States east of the Mississippi, flows through the plateau of the Blue Ridge, from which it receives Chestnut, Poplar Camp, Reed Island and other creeks, and Little river; across the Valley, where Cripple, Reed and Peak's creeks join it; across Appalachia, from which Walker's, Sinking, Big and Little Stony and Wolf creeks, and East and Bluestone rivers flow into it; and then through West Virginia into the Ohio, having cut through the whole Appalachian system of mountains except its eastern barrier, the Blue Ridge. The Holston, through its South, Middle and North Forks, Moccason creek, &c., drains the southwestern portions of the Valley and Appalachia; and the Clinch, by its North and South Forks, Copper creek, Guest's and Powell's rivers, and many other tributaries, waters the extreme southwest of the Appalachian country. These flow into the Tennessee. A portion of the mountain country gives rise to the Louisa and Russell's Forks of the Big Sandy river, and to some branches of the Tug Fork of the same river, the Tug forming the Virginia line for a space: these flow into the Ohio by the Big Sandy.

These are but a few of the thousand or more named and valuable streams of Virginia. They abound in all portions of the State, giving a vast quantity of water power, irrigating the country, furnishing waters suited to every species of fish, giving channels for tide and inland navigation, and enlivening the landscapes. Springs are very numerous, many of them of large size. Nearly every portion of the State is well watered.

## THE NATURAL GRAND DIVISIONS.

(1). TIDEWATER VIRGINIA is the eastern and southeastern part of the State that on the south borders North Carolina 104 miles; on the east has an air-line border of 120 miles along the Atlantic; on the west is bounded by 150 miles of the irregular outline of the Middle country, (this would be 164 miles if it took in the mere edge of Tidewater along the Potomac up to Georgetown). The shore line of the Potomac and Chesapeake bay for 140 miles, and a line of 25 miles across the Eastern Shore, separate it from Maryland on the north. The whole forms an irregular quadrilateral, averaging 114 miles in length from north to south, and 90 in width from east to west, making an area of some 11,350* square miles, including some 2,500 square miles of valuable tidal waters.

The latitude is from 36° 30′ to 38° 54′ north, corresponding to that of the countries bordering on the northern shores of the Mediterranean in Europe; to Asia Minor, China and Japan in Asia; and to the central belt of States—Kentucky, Missouri, California, &c.—in the United States. The longitude is from 75° 13′ to 77° 30′ west from Greenwich—that of Maryland, central Pennsylvania and New York in the United States, and Ontario in Canada on the north, and of North Carolina, the Bahamas, Cuba, &c., on the south.

This is, emphatically, a *Tidewater* country, since every portion of it is penetrated by the tidal waters of Chesapeake bay and its tributary rivers, creeks, bays, inlets, &c., which cover some 2,500 square miles of surface, and give nearly 1,500 miles of tidal shore line. The united waters of nearly all this section, with those that drain 40,000 more square miles of country, or the drainage of 50,000 square miles (an area equal to that of England), flow out through the channel, 12 miles wide, between capes Charles and Henry—the "Virginia Capes"—into the Virginian Sea of Captain John Smith, along the eastern border of which, 50 or 60 miles from the land, runs the ever-flowing Gulf Stream, that great highway of the Atlantic, bearing the waters and inviting the commerce of Virginia to the British Isles and Western Europe.

The size of Tidewater Virginia is about the same as the State of Maryland or the Kingdom of Belgium; it would make 15 counties of the dimensions of Surrey in England. Belgium has a population of five millions, while this section has one-third of one. There were 30 people to a square mile in Tidewater in 1870, or over 31 acres for each: in Great Britain and Ireland in 1867 it was 250 to the square mile, and in Belgium in 1865 it was 438.

Tidewater is *naturally divided* into *nine principal peninsulas*, and these are subdivided into a great number of smaller ones, giving a wealth of outline not even surpassed by the famous Morea of Greece—in truth, there are here dozens of Moreas. These peninsulas are, *politically*, each divided into counties (thirty in all)—most of them laid out and named when this, the first settled portion of English-

* In the absence of actual surveys the areas can only be approximated.

speaking America, was a British colony—and the names given them were those of the counties or worthies of England, the "Mother Country," at the time.

The *first peninsula*—taking them from the north to the south—is THE NORTHERN NECK, 75 miles long and from 6 to 20 wide, extending southeast, from the Middle Country to the bay, between the Potomac and Rappahannock. Its counties are King George, Westmoreland, Richmond, Northumberland and Lancaster. This peninsula is almost surrounded by navigable waters.

The *second*, or MIDDLESEX PENINSULA, extends southeast for 60 miles, with a breadth of from 3 to 10, between the Rappahannock and the Pianketank rivers, including Essex and Middlesex counties. The Rappahannock is navigable all along one side and the Pianketank nearly half of the other. This is one of the short peninsulas succeeding a long one.

The *third*, or GLOUCESTER PENINSULA, reaches southeast from the Middle Country, between the Pianketank and the York and its extension, the Mattapony, some 70 miles to the Bay, where it is "forked" by the Mobjack bay. Its width is from 6 to 18 miles. It includes King & Queen, Mathews and Gloucester counties.

The *fourth*, the KING WILLIAM OR PAMUNKEY PENINSULA, a short one, extends 60 miles southeast, between the Mattapony and the Pamunkey (the streams that form the York). This is from 3 to 14 miles wide, and includes the counties of Caroline and King William, although the former extends across the neck of the *third* peninsula to the Rappahannock.

The *fifth*, a long one, is known as "THE PENINSULA," by way of eminence, as it was the first settled, and Williamsburg, its chief town, was the Colonial capital of Virginia. This stretches 100 miles to the southeast, with a width of from 5 to 15 miles, between the Pamunkey and its extension the York on the north and the Chickahominy and the continuing James on the south. This large peninsula extends from the Middle Country to the Bay, and looks out between "The Capes." Its counties are Hanover, New Kent, James City, York, Warwick and Elizabeth City.

The *sixth*, the short, RICHMOND or CHICKAHOMINY PENINSULA, between the Chickahominy and the James, is 50 miles long and from 5 to 15 wide, divided into Henrico and Charles City counties—the former contains Richmond, the capital of Virginia, a flourishing commercial and manufacturing city.

The *seventh*, or SOUTHSIDE PENINSULA, embraces all the country south of the James and between it and the Nansemond river and the North Carolina line. This is the last peninsula trending to the Southeast, which it does for 64 miles, with a width of from 35 to 40. Its counties are Prince George, Surry, Sussex, Southampton, Isle of Wight and Nansemond.

The *eighth* is the NORFOLK PENINSULA, including the counties of Norfolk and Princess Anne, the territory between the Nansemond river, Hampton Roads, Chesapeake bay and the Atlantic, some 30 by 35 miles in extent, protruding northward.

The *ninth*, THE EASTERN SHORE, is the peninsula extending to the south between Chesapeake bay and the Atlantic, divided between the large counties of Accomac and Northampton.

The last two are the UPPER TERTIARY PLAIN, raised but from twenty to thirty feet above the sea level, composed of north and south-lying belts of smaller peninsulas and islands, with the "pocoson" ends of the other peninsulas, forming the *first step* of the ascending stairway, or terraces of Virginia, to the westward. The shifting sands of its ocean shore are often elevated into dunes more than a hundred feet high.

The seven other peninsulas, with all their masses extended southeast and northwest, rise up as the *second* and *third* steps. The second step, corresponding in the main to the *Middle Tertiary Formation*, attains an elevation of from 80 to 120 feet above the sea. This is the widest tidewater terrace, gashed and broken by the broad estuaries that flow through it. The *third step* has its eastern edge just west of the meridian of 77°, and attains an elevation of from 90 to 150 feet above the sea, occupying the belt of *Lower Tertiary* country. Beyond this rises the *fourth step*, the border of granite and sandstone elevated from 150 to 200 feet above the sea, forming the rocky barrier over which the waters of the Middle or "upper country" fall, and up to which the tides of the "*low country*" come, making the "head of tide" for the Atlantic slope, and furnishing sites for manufacturing and commercial cities, where water power for manufacturing and tide power for commerce are found side by side. Here, half in Tidewater and half in Middle, on the *fourth* step and on the level of the first, on the hills and below them, are Petersburg, Richmond, Fredericksburg and Alexandria.

THE TIDEWATER PLAIN, then, has an average width of nearly 100 miles, and rises in three successive terraces to an elevation of about 150 feet. An inspection of the map will give a better idea of the many-shaped, lobed, gashed, notched and sea-penetrated character of this plain than words can convey. It is a fine, rolling, low country, with a surface diversified by salt water marshes and meadows, river bottoms, plains, upland, slopes and ridges, with a moderate proportion of "pocoson" or swamp country.

(2). The MIDDLE COUNTRY extends westward from the "head of tide" to the foot of the low, broken ranges that, under the names of Kittoctin, Bull Run, Yew, Clark's, Southwest, Carter's, Green, Findlay's, Buffalo, Chandler's, Smith's, &c., mountains and hills, extend across the State southwest, from the Potomac, near the northern corner of Fairfax county, to the North Carolina line, near the southwest corner of Pittsylvania, forming the eastern outliers of the Appalachian System, and that may, with propriety, be called the Atlantic Coast Range.

The general form of this section is that of a large right-angled triangle, its base resting on the North Carolina line for 120 miles; its perpendicular, a line 174 miles long, extending from the Carolina line to the Potomac, just east of and parallel to the meridian of 77° 30′ west, is the right line along the waving border of Tidewater which lies east; the hypothenuse is the 216 miles along the Coast Range, before mentioned, the border of Piedmont, on the northwest—the area of the whole, including the irregular outline, being some 12,470 square miles, or about the same as the Kingdom of Holland. Holland had in 1866 over three and a half million people; Middle Virginia in 1870 a little over one-third of a million—not 30 to the square mile in Middle Virginia, but 280 in Holland.

The latitude of this section is from 36° 30′ to 39°; the longitude 70° to 79° 40′ west. So its general situation and relations are nearly similar to those of Tidewater.

The Middle Country is a great, moderately undulating plain, from 25 to 100 miles wide, rising to the northwest from an elevation of 150 to 200 feet above tide, at the rocky rim of its eastern margin, to from 300 to 500 along its northwestern. In general appearance this is more like a plain than any other portion of the State. The principal streams, as a rule, cross it at right angles; so it is a succession of ridges and valleys running southeast and northwest, the valleys often narrow and deep, but the ridges generally not very prominent. The appearance of much of this country is somewhat monotonous, having many dark evergreen trees in its forests. It needs a denser population to enliven it. To many portions of the Middle Country the mountain ranges to the west, of the deepest blue, form an agreeable and distant boundary to the otherwise sober landscape. There are a few prominences like Willis', Slate River and White Oak mountains farther east, only prominent because in a champaign country.

There can be but little natural grouping of the *political divisions* of the Middle Country, since there are but few great natural landmarks, unless James river, which crosses this section at right angles nearly midway, be considered as one, and the 25 counties of Middle Virginia be grouped as Northside and Southside ones. Many of these counties were laid out, named and settled in Colonial times also, and some of the oldest settled portions of the State are here.

The Northside counties are Fairfax, Alexandria, Prince William and Stafford, bordering on the Potomac; Spotsylvania between the Rappahannock and the North Anna, Louisa on the south of the North Anna (portions of Caroline, Hanover and Henrico properly belong here), Fluvanna and Goochland on the James—making 8 northside counties.

The 17 Southside counties are Buckingham, Cumberland, Powhatan and Chesterfield, between the James and Appomattox rivers; Appomattox on the James, Prince Edward, Amelia and Dinwiddie south of the Appomattox, and the two latter between it and the Nottoway—Nottoway is north of the river of that name; Campbell between the James and Staunton (or Roanoke) rivers, Charlotte north of the Roanoke, Lunenburg between the Nottoway and Meherrin, Brunswick and Greensville extending from the Nottoway (see Map) across the Meherrin to the North Carolina line—a portion of the latter county is in Tidewater; Pittsylvania and Halifax reach from Staunton across the Banister and the Dan to the North Carolina line, and Mecklenburg extends from the Meherrin across the Roanoke to the same boundary.

Portions of Fairfax, Prince William, Stafford, Spotsylvania, Caroline, Fauquier, Culpeper, Hanover, Henrico, Goochland, Powhatan, Chesterfield, Buckingham, Cumberland, Prince Edward, Campbell and Pittsylvania, which are on the Triassic, or New Red Sandstone formation, differ considerably in appearance from the rest of the Middle Country which is on the Eozoic, or granite, gneiss, &c., rocks.

This section is essentially the same as the rest of the Eozoic belt that extends from the Alabama river to the St. Lawrence, embracing large portions of the best sections of Alabama, Georgia, South Carolina, North Carolina, Maryland, Pennsylvania, New York and all the New England States. The cities of Atlanta, Raleigh, Petersburg, Richmond, Fredericksburg, Alexandria, Washington, Baltimore, Philadelphia, New York, New Haven, &c., are situated, in whole or in part, on these rocks.

(3). PIEDMONT VIRGINIA is the long belt of country stretching for 244 miles from the banks of the Potomac and the Maryland line southwest, along the eastern base of the Blue Ridge mountains, and between them and the Coast Range, to the banks of the Dan at the North Carolina line; it varies in width from 20 to 30 miles, averaging about 25; its approximate area is 6,680 square miles.

Its latitude corresponds with that of the State 36° 30′ to 39° 27′ north; its longitude is from 77° 20′ to 80° 50′ west.

This Piedmont country is the *fifth step* of the great stairway ascending to the west; its eastern edge, along Middle Virginia, is from 300 to 500 feet above the sea; then come the broken ranges of the Coast Mountains, rising as detached or connected knobs, in lines or groups, from 100 to 600 feet higher. These are succeeded by the numberless valleys, of all imaginable forms, some long, straight and wide, others narrow and widening, others again oval and almost enclosed, locally known as "Coves," that extend across to and far into the Blue Ridge, the spurs of which often reach out southwardly for miles, ramifying in all directions. Portions of Piedmont form widely extended plains. The land west of the Coast ranges is generally from 300 to 500 feet above the sea, and rises to the west, until at the foot of the Blue Ridge it attains an elevation of from 600 to 1,200 feet. The Blue Ridge rises to from 2,000 to 4,000 feet above the sea; at one point near the Tennessee line, it reaches a height of 5,530* feet: its general elevation is about 2,500, but its outline is very irregular.

Numerous streams have their origin in the heads of the gorges of the Blue Ridge, and most of them then flow across Piedmont to the southeast until near its eastern border, where they unite and form one that runs for a considerable distance along and parallel to the Coast mountains, and takes the name of some of the well known rivers that cross Middle and even Tidewater Virginia, like the Roanoke or Staunton, and the James. Some of these rivers break through the Blue Ridge from the Valley, making water gaps in that formidable mountain barrier, as the Potomac, the James and the Roanoke; but they all follow the rule above given in their way across this section.

This is a genuine "Piedmont" country—one in which the mountains present themselves in their grand as well as in their diminutive forms—gradually sinking down into the plains, giving great diversity and picturesqueness to the landscape, with its wealth of forms of relief as varied as those of outline in Tidewater. Few countries surpass this in beauty of scenery and choice of prospect, so it has always been a favorite section with men of refinement in which to fix their homes. Its population is 31 to the square mile, giving some 21 acres for each.

The *political divisions* of Piedmont are fourteen. Some of its counties have long been settled, and are highly improved. There are no natural groupings possible for these counties; they all, with three exceptions, run from the summit of the Blue Ridge across this belt of country. Taking them from the Potomac, the counties are: Loudoun, watered mostly by Goose and Kittoctin creeks and the Potomac; Fauquier, drained by the Rappahannock waters, to which river it extends; Rappahannock and Culpeper, on the southwest side of the same stream, Culpeper reach-

---

*Guyot's measurements.

ing to the Rapid Anne, as does also Madison; Greene and Orange, southwest of the Rapid Anne; Albemarle, drained by the Rivanna and Hardware branches of James, and reaching to the James; Nelson and Amherst, bounded by the Blue Ridge and the James, Amherst by that river, both southeast and southwest; Bedford and Franklin, southwest of the James, and drained chiefly by waters of the Roanoke or Staunton; Patrick and Henry, next the North Carolina line, furnishing many branches to the Dan. An inspection of the map will show that every portion of this section is penetrated by water courses. Every portion of it is well supplied with unfailing, bright, pure water, from springs and mountain rivulets.

(4). THE BLUE RIDGE, for two-thirds of its length of 310 miles, is embraced in the Valley and Piedmont counties that have their common lines upon its watershed; it is only the southwestern portion of it, where it expands into a plateau, with an area of some 1,230 square miles, that forms a separate political division: still the whole range and its numerous spurs, parallel ridges, detached knobs and foot hills, varying in width from 3 to 20 miles, embracing nearly 2,500 square miles of territory, is a distinct region, not only in appearance but in all essential particulars. The river, in the gorge where the Potomac breaks through the Blue Ridge, is 242 feet above tide. The Blue Ridge there attains an elevation of 1,460 feet. Mt. Marshall, near and south of Front Royal, is 3,369* feet high: the notch, Rockfish Gap, at the Chesapeake and Ohio Railroad, is 1,996 feet, and James river, where it passes through the Ridge, is 706 feet above tide, or more than twice as high as the Potomac at its passage. The Peaks of Otter, in Bedford county, are 3,993† feet, and the Balsam mountain, in Grayson, is 5,700† feet, and in North Carolina this range is nearly 7,000 feet above the sea level. These figures show that this range increases in elevation as we go southwest, and every portion of the country near rises in the same manner. At a little distance this range is generally of a deep blue color. The whole mountain range may be characterized as a series of swelling domes, connected by long ridges meeting between the high points in gaps or notches, and sending out long spurs in all directions from the general range, but more especially on the eastern side, these in turn sending out other spurs, giving a great development of surface and variety of exposure.

The *political* divisions upon the plateau of the Blue Ridge are the counties of Floyd, Carroll and Grayson, all watered by the Kanawha, or New river, and its branches, a tributary of the Ohio, except the little valley in the southwest corner of Grayson, which sends its water to the Tennessee. The population of this romantic section is 23 to the square mile.

(5). The GREAT VALLEY OF VIRGINIA is the belt of limestone land west of the Blue Ridge, and between it and the numerous interrupted ranges of mountains, with various local names, that run parallel to it on the west at an average distance of some 20 miles, that collectively are called the Kitatinny or North Mountains. This valley extends in West Virginia and Virginia for more than 330 miles from the Potomac to the Tennessee line, and 305 miles of this splendid country are within the limits of Virginia. The county lines generally extend from the top of the Blue Ridge to the top of the second or third mountain range beyond the Valley proper,

---

*U. S. Coast Survey measurements. †Guyot's measurements.

so that the political Valley is somewhat larger than the natural one, which has an area of about 6,000 square miles, while the former has 7,550, and a population of 26 to the square mile. The latitude of the Valley is from 36° 35′ N. to 39° 26′; its longitude is from 77° 50′ to 80° 16′ W.

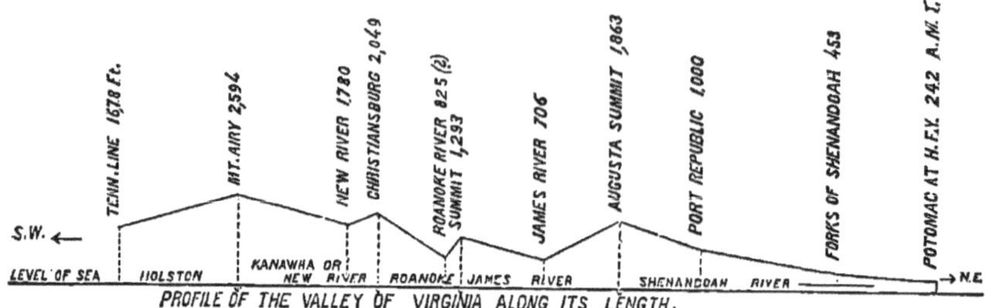

PROFILE OF THE VALLEY OF VIRGINIA ALONG ITS LENGTH.

While this is one continuous valley, clearly defined by its bounding mountains, it is not the valley of one river, or of one system of rivers, but of five; so that it has four water-sheds and four river troughs in its length, as shown in the above profile, *along* the Valley from the Potomac to the Tennessee line. These valleys and their length in the Great Valley are, from the northeast—

| | |
|---|---|
| 1st. The Shenandoah Valley, - - - - - - - - | 136 miles. |
| 2nd. The James River Valley, - - - - - - - - | 50 " |
| 3rd. The Roanoke River Valley, - - - - - - - - | 38 " |
| 4th. The Kanawha or New River Valley, - - - - - | 54 " |
| 5th. The Valley of the Holston or Tennessee, - - - - | 52 " . |
| | 330 miles. |

This profile shows that as a whole the Valley rises to the southwest, being 242 feet above the tide where the Shenandoah enters the Potomac and the united rivers break through the Blue Ridge at Harper's Ferry, and 1,678 feet where the waters of the Holston leave the State and pass into Tennessee. The entire Valley appears then as a series of ascending and descending planes, sloping to the northeast or the southwest. That of the Shenandoah rises from 242 to 1,863 feet along the line of its main stream, in 136 miles, looking northeast; those of the James slope both ways, from the Shenandoah summit to the southwest, and from the Roanoke summit to the northeast, and so on, as shown in the profile. This arrangement gives this *seventh* great step a variety of elevations above the sea from 242 to 2,594 feet, or even to 3,000, in a great enclosed valley, sub-divided into very many minor valleys, giving "facings" in all directions; for the whole Valley has a very decided southeastern inclination, to be considered in this connection, its western side being from 500 to 1,000 feet in surface elevation above its eastern, presenting its mass to the sun, giving its streams a tendency to flow across it toward the east, as the result of its combined slopes, and making the main drainage way hug the western base of the Blue Ridge. A moment's reflection and an inspection of the map will show that this is a well watered country, having a wealth of water power and drainage and irrigation resources almost beyond estimate.

The aspect of this region is exceedingly pleasant. The great width of the Valley; the singular coloring and wavy but bold outline of the Blue Ridge; the long, uniform lines of the Kitatinny mountains, and the high knobs that rise up behind them in the distance; the detached ranges that often extend for many miles in the midst of the Valley, like huge lines of fortifications—all these for the outline, filled up with park-like forests, well cultivated farms, well built towns, and threaded by bright and abounding rivers, make this a charming and inviting region.

The fifteen counties of the Valley—its *political* divisions—are naturally grouped by the river basins, to which their lines generally conform.

The noted SHENANDOAH VALLEY has, in Virginia, in the northeast Frederick and Clarke counties, reaching from the North Mountains to the Blue Ridge across the Valley, watered by the Opequon creek and the Shenandoah river and branches; Shenandoah county, extending from the mountains west to the Massanutton range, that for 50 miles divides the Valley into two, one watered by the North and the other by the South Fork of the Shenandoah; Warren, that lies at the confluence of these forks and between the Massanutton and the Blue Ridge, and Page county, between the same mountains and intersected by the South Fork; Rockingham, a large and noted county, reaching across the whole Valley, and holding the sources of the North Fork; and Augusta, the largest county, also occupying the width of the Valley, and containing the head springs of the Shenandoah. These seven counties occupy the whole of this well-known, fertile and wealthy valley.

In the *valley of the James* are Rockbridge and Botetourt, two fine counties in the heart of the valley, both extending across it, the former watered by the North and South rivers of the James, and that river and other tributaries, and the latter by the much-developed James river and Catawba, Craig's and other creeks. The mountain scenery of Rockbridge is especially noted.

In the *valley of the Roanoke* is the small but rich county of the same name: portions of Botetourt and Montgomery are drained by that river also.

The *Kanawha* or *New River valley* has Montgomery, Pulaski and Wythe counties, famous ones for grazing and stock, that reach from mountain to mountain. This is the most elevated portion of the Great Valley, and many people foolishly continue to call the water-shed between the Roanoke and New river, where that "divide" crosses the Valley, the Alleghany Mountain—saying that Christiansburg is *on the top of the Alleghany*—when there is no mountain there, only a "water divide" in the continuous limestone valley—because, *before* anything was known of the country or its peculiarities, it was supposed that the Alleghany Mountain wound its way everywhere, *over* and *under* mountains and valleys, to keep the waters of the Mississippi from those of the Atlantic. The Alleghany Mountain, as every well informed person knows, is a single, well-defined range, that begins just south of the White Sulphur Springs and runs northeast to and beyond the Potomac.

In the *valley of the Holston* or *Tennessee* are the two fine counties of Smyth and Washington, with soils of rare fatness.

(6). APPALACHIAN VIRGINIA, or APPALACHIA, succeeds the Valley on the west. It is a mountain country, traversed its whole length by the Appalachian or Alleghany System of mountains. It may be considered as a series of comparatively narrow, long, parallel valleys, running northeast and southwest, separated from each other by mountain ranges that are, generally, equally narrow, long and parallel, and quite elevated. In crossing this section to the northwest, at right angles to its mountains and valleys, in 50 miles one will cross from 6 to 10 of these mountain ranges, and as many valleys. As before stated, a strip of this region is embraced in the Valley counties, as they include the two or three front ranges that have drainage into the Valley; so that some 900 square miles of Appalachia are politically classed with the Valley, leaving 5,720 square miles to be treated of here. This, in Virginia, is an irregular belt of country 260 miles long, varying in width from 10 to 50 miles. Its waters, generally, flow northeast and southwest, but it has basins that drain north and northwest, and south and southeast. The heads of the valleys are generally from 2,000 to 2,800 feet above tide, and the waters often flow from each way to a central depression—that is, from 600 to 1,200 feet above sea level—before they unite and break through the enclosing ranges. The map shows this arrangement, as in the case of Potts' creek and the Cow-pasture river. Potts' creek heads in Giles county, at 2,698 feet of altitude, flows northeast 42 miles, a portion of the way as Jackson's river, to 1,036 feet of elevation at Clifton Forge, where the river turns southeast: the Cow-pasture has its sources in Highland county, at an elevation of about 3,000 feet, and flows southwest 48 miles to near the same point, where it unites with Jackson's river and forms the James. The remarks made concerning the slopes of the Great Valley apply also to this section, except that the Appalachian valleys are straighter.

The twelve counties of this section group very well as follows:

1st. The James River Group, the waters from which flow into that river, including Highland, on the water-shed of the James and Potomac, the South Branch of the latter having several of its sources there, with the Cow-pasture and Jackson's river branches of the former; Bath, crossed by the same branches of the James; Alleghany, through a portion of which the same rivers flow, and in which they unite, meeting the waters of Dunlap's and Potts' creeks from the southwest; and Craig, drained by Johns', Craig's and Barber's creeks, flowing from the southwest. Sinking creek of New river flows southwest from this county. All these waters but the last run into the James before it crosses the Valley.

2nd. The Kanawha or New River Group includes Giles, which is intersected by New river, into which flow from the northeast Sinking and Big and Little Stony creeks, and from the southwest Walker's and Wolf creeks; Bland, on the head waters of Walker's and Wolf creeks, just mentioned, and having also some of the springs of the Holston, that flows southwest.

3rd. The Tennessee River Group, on the waters of that river, embraces Tazewell, on the divide of New and Tennessee, (the lowest gaps of which are 2,116 feet above tide); Wolf creek, Bluestone and East rivers run from this county northeast into New river, while the North and the Maiden Spring Forks of Clinch flow southwest: Russell is southwest of Tazewell, and the Clinch and its Copper and Moccason creek branches run through it to the southwest: Scott is next, on the southwest, and the same streams pass through it from Russell, and the North Fork of the Holston besides, all running southwest: Lee is southwest of Scott, Powell's river and its numerous branches flowing southwest from it to the Clinch. All these

.aters unite in the State of Tennessee, and form the river of that name. The land of the counties of this group is exceedingly fertile, large portions of it being limestone, and its exposure to the southwest, and the situation and elevation of its surrounding mountains, secure to it a *very mild* climate.

4th. The SANDY RIVER GROUP includes Buchanan county, drained by the Tug, Louisa and Russell's Forks of the Big Sandy, flowing northwest; and Wise county, drained by Russell's and Pound Forks of the same river, and a portion by the Guest's river branch of the Clinch, and some head springs of Powell's river. These two counties really belong to the TRANS-APPALACHIAN country, the great plain that slopes from the parallel ranges of mountains to the northwest, from which the waters have eroded their deep channels. They cover Virginia's part of the Great Carboniferous formation, and give her a most valuable coal field.

Appalachia is noted as a grazing country, its elevation giving it a cool, moist atmosphere, admirably adapted, with its fertile soil, to the growth of grass and the rearing of stock of all kinds.

## CHAPTER II.

# THE GEOLOGY OF VIRGINIA.

### SECTION I.—THE GEOLOGICAL FORMATIONS.

The Geology of Virginia was determined by Professor William B. Rogers, the distinguished Geologist of the State, in a survey conducted for that purpose from 1835 to 1840, and much of the brief outline here given is condensed from his reports. The accompanying geological map of the Virginias was most kindly colored by Professor Rogers especially for this work.

The geological formations found in Virginia, like its geographical divisions, succeed each other in belts, either complete or broken, nearly parallel to the coast of the Atlantic. In fact the geographical divisions of the State that have already been given correspond in the main to the different geological formations, and have been suggested by them; hence those divisions are *natural.*

The formations developed in Virginia, taken in the order in which they succeed each other and cover the surface, or form the rocks found with the surface, from the Atlantic at the Virginia Capes to the northwest across the State, are as follows:

GEOGRAPHICAL ORDER OF FORMATIONS.

| | |
|---|---|
| TIDEWATER. | 1. Quaternary.<br>2. Upper Tertiary.<br>3. Middle Tertiary.<br>4. Lower Tertiary. |
| MIDDLE. | 5. Triassic and Jurassic.<br>6. Azoic and Granitic. |
| PIEDMONT. | 7. Azoic, Epidotic, &c. |
| BLUE RIDGE. | 8. Azoic and Cambrian. |
| THE VALLEY. | 9. Cambrian and Silurian. |
| APPALACHIA. | 10. Sub-Carboniferous and Devonian.<br>11. Silurian.<br>12. Devonian and Sub-Carboniferous.<br>13. Great Carboniferous. |

The GEOLOGICAL ORDER OF THESE FORMATIONS, arranged according to the recognized age of the rocks, from the newest to the oldest, is this:

| Era | Formations | Region |
|---|---|---|
| Cenozoic, or TERTIARY. | 1. Quaternary (and Alluvium?)<br>2. Upper Tertiary.<br>3. Middle Tertiary.<br>4. Lower Tertiary. | *Tidewater.* |
| Mesozoic, or SECONDARY. | 5. Triassic and Jurassic (and Cretaceous?) | *Middle.* |
| Paleozoic, or TRANSITION. | 6. Great Carboniferous Series.<br>7. Sub-Carboniferous.<br>8. Devonian. | *Appalachia.* |
| | 9. Silurian and Cambrian. | *Valley and Appalachia.* |
| Eozoic, or PRIMARY. | 10. Azoic, Granitic, &c. | *Middle, Piedmont and Blue Ridge.* |

The chief Geological Sub-Divisions shown on the accompanying map,* are:

(1). The Upper Tertiary, passing into Quaternary.

(2). The Middle and Lower Tertiary.

(3). The Triassic and Jurassic Beds.

(4). The Great Carboniferous, down to the base of the Seral Conglomerate.

(5). The Sub-Carboniferous, including Umbral limestones, shales and slates, and at the base Vespertine sandstone, having coal in some places.

(6). The Devonian sandstones, slates and shales, from top of Meridian to top of Ponent.

(7). The Cambrian and Silurian—Primal to top of Meridian.

(8). The Azoic and Granitic Group—Syenite; Mica, Talc and Hornblende Slates, Argillaceous Slates, Auriferous Quartz, &c.

Professor William B. Rogers, in his Reports on the Geology of Virginia, described the formations of the State as follows†:

( 1). Tertiary. Miocene=(*The Middle Tertiary*). Eocene=(*The Lower Tertiary*).

( 2). Middle and Upper Secondary=(*The Triassic and Jurassic*).

( 3). Primary and Metamorphic Rocks (including beds of limestone)=(*The Azoic and Granitic Group*).

|  |  |  |
|---|---|---|
| ( 4). | Formation No. I. | *(The Cambrian and Silurian).* |
| ( 5). | Formation No. II. | |
| ( 6). | Formation No. III. | |
| ( 7). | Formation No. IV. | |
| ( 8). | Formation No. V. | |
| ( 9). | Formation No. VI. | |
| (10). | Formation No. VII. | |
| (11). | Formation No. VIII. | *(The Devonian).* |
| (12). | Formation No. IX. | |
| (13). | Formation No. X. | *(The Sub-Carboniferous).* |
| (14). | Formation No. XI. | |
| (15). | Formation No. XII. —Coarse Sandstones. | *(The Great Carboniferous).* |
| (16). | Formation No. XIII. —Lower Coal Group. | |
| (17). | Formation No. XIV. —Lower Shale and Sandstone Group. | |
| (18). | Formation No. XV. —Upper Coal Group. | |

* As named and colored by Professor William B. Rogers.

† The equivalents of the map are given in italics in parentheses.

The various geological formations have received different names, and been differently classified in various states and countries, and as it is desirable, for many reasons, to know the equivalent names, those of the more important systems are here given.

SYSTEMS OF GEOLOGICAL CLASSIFICATION COMPARED.

| Early Writers | Eras. | Ages. | | Periods. | | New York System. | Pennsylvania and Virginia Names—H. D. & W. B. Rogers. | Names used in Virginia Reports—W. B. Rogers. |
|---|---|---|---|---|---|---|---|---|
| Tertiary. | Psychozoic. | Age of Angiosperms and Palms. | Age of Man. | Quaternary. | | | | |
| | Cenozoic Time. | | Age of Mammals. | Tertiary. | | | | Pliocene.<br>Miocene.<br>Eocene. |
| Secondary. | Mesozoic Time. | | Age of Reptiles. | Cretaceous. | | | | |
| | | Age of Cycads. | | Jurassic. | | | | |
| | | | | Triassic or New Red Sandstone. | | | | Middle and Upper Secondary. |
| Transition. | Paleozoic Time. | Age of Coal Plants, Amphibians & Acrogens. | | Permian. | | | | |
| | | | | Carboniferous. | | Lower Carboniferous. | Seral.<br>Umbral.<br>Vespertine. | Formations No. XV. to No. X. inclusive. |
| | | Age of Fishes, Algae & Acrogens. | | Devonian or Old Red Sandstone. | | Catskill.<br>Chemung.<br>Hamilton.<br>Corniferous. | Ponent.<br>Vergent.<br>Cadent.<br>Post-Meridian. | Formations No. IX. and No. VIII. |
| | | Age of Mollusks and Algae. | | Silurian. | Upper. | Oriskany.<br>Helderberg.<br>Salina.<br>Niagara........... { | Meridian.<br>Pre-Meridian.<br>Scalent.<br>Surgent.<br>Levant. | Formations No. VII. to No. I. inclusive. |
| | | | | Cambrian. | Lower. | Hudson.<br>Trenton.<br>Potsdam. | Matinal.<br>Auroral.<br>Primal. | |
| Primitive. | Azoic Time, or Eozoic. | | | Metamorphic. | | Taconic or Huronian.<br>Laurentian. | Crystalline Schists.<br>Azoic. | Metamorphic.<br>Primary. |

The *first* "*dry land*" of the State that appeared was the country between the western base of the Blue Ridge and the eastern side of the Middle country at the head of tide; its borders were the shores of the ocean east and west. So Middle, Piedmont and Blue Ridge Virginia are the *oldest* portions of the State; they are based on Granite, Gneiss and Syenite; Mica, Talc and Hornblende Slates, Argillaceous Slates, Auriferous Quartz, &c.; *the region is Eozoic or Primary.*

The *second formed land* was the Great Valley, a broad belt of seacoast along the shore of a subsiding ocean, where corals were abundant, making it a limestone region—the Cambrian and Lower and Upper Silurian—a country with sandstones and limestones of many varieties, together with slates and shales: a part of the *Transition* or Paleozoic period. So the Valley is the second oldest country in the State. These are followed by the Devonian rocks as third, and these in turn by the Sub-Carboniferous and Carboniferous as fourth and fifth, all in Appalachia. The sixth, the Triassic or New Red Sandstone, is only found as detached masses, deposits in depressions of the Primary, in the Middle country. The seventh, the *last formed* portion of the State, is the Tertiary, the entire Tidewater region, if we except the alluvium now forming on the shores.

TIDEWATER.—This is what the geologists call a Tertiary or lately formed region, one where the remains of plants and animals found in the rocks and soils do not differ greatly from the plants and animals now living—they belong to the same families. The beds of mineral substances here found are rarely converted into real rocks, but lie as beds of sand, gravel, clay, &c., much the same as when they were deposited in shallow waters by the ocean and inflowing rivers.

1st. *The Quaternary or Post-Tertiary** formation is the sandy shore, the mere margin, of the Atlantic and the Bay; it is like the shore land of Lincolnshire and other eastern counties of England.

2d. *The Upper Tertiary or Pliocene** is the *first step* or terrace of the State above the ocean; it is the low plain of the Eastern Shore and Norfolk peninsulas, where the surface is composed of "*light-colored sands and clays, generally of a fine texture,* and never enclosing pebbles of large dimensions."† This is, geologically, a similar country to most of Suffolk in England, to the hills of Rome in Italy, and the territory around Antwerp in Belgium. *Underneath* this are found the other formations, in order, and their valuable marls can be reached, at no great depth, by going through this. The immense piles of shells found along the shores, and the refuse fish, furnish fertilizers adapted to the soils of this section.

3d. *The Middle Tertiary,‡ or Miocene,* is the surface of the *second* step of country, extending from the western border of the last described formation, where this passes *under* that, to a line running southward from Mathias Point, on the Potomac, to Coggin's Point on the James—a line just west of the meridian of 77°; from the

---

* These are together called Alluvium, in the recently published Statistical Atlas of the United States, by Professors Hitchcock and Blake.

† Rogers.

‡ The Middle and Lower Tertiary are together called Tertiary in the United States Statistical Atlas.

James south it inclines to the west. This formation, generally, descending from the surface, consists of the following materials:

1. Beds of coarse sand and gravel just under the soil, sloping in position.

2. Horizontal beds of sand and clay.

3. Yellow marl, underlaid by a conglomerate of fragments, with shells nearly entire but water-worn.

4. Yellow marl with friable shells and tenacious clay.

5. Upper blue marl—a clay, bluish, of fine texture, rich in shells.

6. Lower blue marl—clay with more sandy materials, more shells and more varieties.

7. A thin band of pebbles, with ferruginous matter: the bottom of the formation.

In some parts of Tidewater some of these strata harden into a sort of limestone, or into sandstones, very good for building purposes. Of course the Lower Tertiary *underlies* this as this underlies the Upper, and is overlapped by it. This formation covers a large portion of the Atlantic plain and of the lower Mississippi valley of the United States; it is the formation of the valley of the Columbia in Oregon and of the valleys of California; in Europe it forms the Gironde and Landes of France and the basin of Vienna; in England it is the New Forest region of Hampshire and Dorset, the country around Portsmouth and Southampton.

4th. *The Lower Tertiary or Eocene.* This formation underlies both the others and forms the surface of the remainder of Tidewater west of the line already described as forming the western boundary of the Middle Tertiary: it is a strip of country some 15 miles wide along the "head of tide." The fossils found in this are more unlike the forms now existing. This *greensand* marl formation on the east pushes its headlands into the Middle Tertiary, and on the west fills up the ravines between the headlands of sandstone, granite, &c., that protrude into it from the Middle country.

The following section,* from the banks of the Potomac, below Aquia creek, will give an insight into the composition of this group of "rocks":

(1). The soil.
(2). 20 feet of yellow clay, impregnated with sulphates.
(3). 5 feet of sulphur-colored clay, containing shells.
(4). 3 feet of rock, resembling marl in color and composition.
(5). 12 feet of yellowish gray marl, specked with greensand and abounding in shells.

40 feet, the level of the Potomac.

In some places the marl of this Eocene contains so much carbonate of lime from the shells distributed through it, it has become a *limestone.* Here are also beds of *blue marl*, *shell-rock*, *gypseous* and acid clays, dark bluish clay and sand containing sulphates of iron and lime. There are also beds of sand and gravel, coarse and often cemented by iron. In all of these there is great variety of color and composition. The strata are slightly inclined, generally to the southeast. This is the formation on which the most of Essex, Middlesex, Kent, &c., counties around London in England, are situated—the region of the noted London clay. (The same

* As before stated, the data here used are from Professor Rogers' Reports.

material abounds in Virginia.) The Isle of Wight, Dorset, Wilts, Hants, Suffolk, Norfolk, Cambridge and Lincoln counties, the most productive in England, are in the Lower Tertiary; the cities of Liverpool and Paris are also on it.

5th. *The Triassic or New Red Sandstone* is sometimes found as transported fragments from that formation, (which forms a part of the western boundary of this section,) scattered over the surface of some of the peninsulas southeast from where this rock is found in place.

6th. *The Azoic or Primary Rocks*, which underlie all the others and also form part of this western border, are sometimes found as headlands thrust into the Tertiary or as islands in its surface.

MIDDLE COUNTRY.—The larger portion of this region is Azoic,* or Primary. The rocks contain no organic remains; they are crystalline in their character, generally stratified, dip at a high angle either to the southeast or the northwest, or are nearly vertical, rarely horizontal, and their exposed edges, or "strike," run northeast and southwest. The strata vary in thickness from the fraction of an inch to many feet.

The rocks of this formation are: *Gneiss*, (a name given to any crystalline, stratified rock composed of quartz and felspar, mixed with smaller quantities of hornblende, mica, or other simple minerals,) the most abundant, which along the east side of the Middle country is a gray rock, consisting of quartz, felspar and black mica, with some spangles of white, and grains of hornblende—this is the fine Richmond granite. In some of the layers of this rock the felspar predominates, and the rock crumbles on exposure. The finer grained gneiss is generally called granite, the coarser Syenite, or Syenitic granite; the former are quartzose, the latter felspathic. Next, going westward, are other varieties of gneiss more slaty in structure, containing more felspar and hornblende, (quartz is the *flint* rock, felspar is softer and duller in color, hornblende is dark green or black,) and are more decayed, sometimes into beds of porcelain clay or kaolin. These are succeeded, on the western border of this section, by a broad belt of *micaceous, talcose* and *argillaceous* slates, according to the ingredient predominant in the rock, whether mica, talc or soapstone, or alumina. The rocks on the east side of this slaty belt are most micaceous on the west talcose. In these belts are some beds or small tracts of chloritic gneiss, slate, steatite, serpentine, &c., making spots noted for fertility like the Green Spring country in Louisa county. In the more argillaceous part of this belt, the western side next to Piedmont, some of the slates become so sandy they pass as sandstones or conglomerates, (gneissoid sandstones,) and among these are found roofing slates and a fragmentary belt of limestone. Through the centre of this region runs the "gold belt," where gold is found in quartz veins, interstratified with the other rocks; here are also veins of various kinds of iron and copper ores. This formation covers large areas of valuable country in all parts of the world.

In this Middle section, as before stated, laid over the other rocks, (the granitic ones,) or filling depressions in them, are a number of patches of the Triassic† and Jurassic, or New Red sandstone rocks, sometimes called the Middle Secondary, and

---

* Called Eozoic in the U. S. Statistical Atlas of 1874.

† Classed with the Cretaceous as Mesozoic in U. S. Statistical Atlas.

generally known as "*brown stone.*" The localities of this are: (*a*) the "Richmond coal-field," a large oval area in Chesterfield, Powhatan, Goochland and Henrico counties, inside Middle Virginia; (*b*) a small oval territory bordering Tidewater between Ashland and Milford stations on the Richmond and Fredericksburg railroad, and nearly divided by it; (*c*) a long, narrow strip, bordering Tidewater from several miles south of Fredericksburg, on, along the west bank of the Potomac, to near Mount Vernon; (*d*) a large wedge, nearly 600 square miles, resting for some twenty miles on the Potomac and extending southwest, between the Middle and Piedmont sections, to its apex on the Rapid Anne near Orange Courthouse, with a small outlying portion near that place, and extending beyond it towards Gordonsville; (*e*) a curved portion of land extending from Hampden Sidney College north through Farmville to Willis' river, and northeast along that river to near Cumberland Courthouse; (*f*) a narrow belt along James river from Scottsville, some 15 miles to the southwest; (*g*) a band of country some 60 miles long, extending from a point southeast of Campbell Courthouse southwest to the North Carolina line near Danville.

These rocks are of the kind known as sedimentary—composed of particles of sand and earth, and of pebbles derived from other rocks, and deposited by water where they now are. They are in strata, some of coarse conglomerate, with very large pebbles; others of finer material, making sandstones, slates and shales, generally *dark brown or red* in color, but sometimes gray, brownish gray or yellow, and greenish gray. They generally dip but little, being nearly horizontal. The "brecciated marble" of the Potomac is from this formation, as is also the "brown stone" from Manassas. In this formation are found remains of plants, as lignite or coaly matter, and of fishes; and in the Richmond, Danville and Farmville portions are valuable beds of rich bituminous coal.

PIEDMONT is in the same region of Primary, Azoic or Transition rocks as Middle, but they differ much in their characteristics.

The *gneiss* of Piedmont, from the Blue Ridge to the Southwest Mountain, is usually of a darker color and coarser texture than that of Middle Virginia, and it has much more variety in its structure and composition. Generally it contains more or less talce, or chlorite, not much mica, and very often hornblende and iron pyrites, the latter a powerful agent in decomposing rocks, and with hornblende giving a red tinge to the soil; so that this is often called the "Red-land" district. Near the base of the Blue Bidge are belts of granitic gneiss: also belts of micaceous, chloritic, argillaceous and talcose slates, generally narrow, with bands and patches of limestone. The *epidotic*, or greenstone rocks, form the chief mass of the broken Southwest Mountain, or Coast Range Chain, the eastern border of Piedmont. These rocks are of a greenish hue, with crystals of epidote and quartz. They weather into a yellowish soil that changes into orange and red, and is always fertile. Bands of iron ores of various kinds, slates, soapstone, &c., are found throughout this section.

THE BLUE RIDGE is the border land between the Azoic, Primary or Transition rocks, and the fossiliferous ones. Generally its eastern flank and summit, and sometimes a good portion of the western slope, are composed of the *epidotic* rocks before mentioned, more highly epidotic than even those of Piedmont; and so it acquires peculiar geological characteristics. The epidote is found there compact, with quartz imbedded, as amygdaloid, &c. Here are also beds of epidotic granite, of whitish granite and of Syenite, with sandstones and slates of various kinds; but *epidote* is here more abundant than elsewhere, and this by decomposing makes the wonderful soil of this mountain range.

The western flank of the Blue Ridge is composed of the rocks of the Cambrian, Potsdam Sandstone, Primal, or Formation I. of Professor Rogers; for by all these names is known the "close-grained white or light gray sandstone," with beds of coarse conglomerate, brown sandstones and brownish olive-colored shales here found, that once made the eastern shore of a great *ocean*. In this formation are bands of specular iron ore and beds of hematite.

The VALLEY is the region of Cambrian and Lower Silurian rocks—Formations I., II. and III., of Rogers, or from Potsdam to Hudson River formations, of New York, inclusive—a country mainly of *limestone*, slate and shale rocks, with a fertile soil and undulating surface. The section across the Valley through Staunton gives some 30 alternating bands of slates and limestones of various kinds, some magnesian, others silicious, or rich carbonates; some compact, others flaggy or slaty, &c. Among these are beds of chert, iron ore, umber, lead, zinc, &c. This formation extends northward, and forms the rich Cumberland, Lebanon, and other valleys of Maryland, Pennsylvania and New Jersey, the Hudson and Mohawk valleys of New York, and the Champlain valley of Vermont. Southwest it becomes the valley of East Tennessee, and extends into Alabama, making a great Central Valley, some 1,500 miles in length, of unsurpassed fertility and productiveness. This formation underlies a large portion of Scotland, especially the southern and central parts; much of the area of Wales, and large districts in the west, southwest and northwest of England. It covers an extensive tract in Russia; is found in Spain, &c. The most fertile portions of New York, Ohio, Indiana, Kentucky, Wisconsin and Missouri are also underlaid by this rock.

*Belonging to the Valley counties* (the lines of which extend to the summit of the Blue Ridge, and cross, often, several ranges of the mountains west), of course we have the half of the summit and all the western slope of the Blue Ridge, already described. To it also, politically, will belong parts of the Upper Silurian and Devonian Systems, that are more especially referred to in the account of the Appalachian Country. These form long ridges that rise up and run for great distances in the Valley, like the Massanutton and other mountain ranges—making barriers that divide the Valley lengthways into two parallel valleys. The rocks of the Valley generally dip to the southeast at a high angle. In some places there runs an axis through the Valley from which the rocks dip both ways, to the southeast and to the northwest, making an anticlinal. The upturned edges of the rocks strike, or run, northeast and southwest with the Valley.

Fragments of the Sub-Carboniferous formation are found along the western margin of the Valley, sometimes containing valuable beds of semi-anthracite coal, as in Montgomery, Augusta and other counties. This formation consists of conglomerates, shales, sandstones, &c

The APPALACHIAN Country, beginning with the mountains on the west side of the Great Valley, is occupied chiefly by the Upper Silurian and Devonian rocks from IV. to IX. inclusive. It also shows narrow outcrops of Lower Silurian and important areas of Carboniferous rocks, comprising sandstones, slates, limestones, coal seams, &c. The sandstones hold up the high, parallel ridges or chains of mountains that run unbroken for such long distances; the slates and limestones form the rich valleys between. In these rocks are great continuous bands of hematite and fossil iron ores, among the most abundant and valuable in the world.

The DEVONIAN Rocks (or Old Red Sandstone—Rogers' VIII. and IX.; the Corniferous, Hamilton, Chemung and Catskill groups of New York) are found among those that have already been described, the convulsions of nature having exposed in successive ridges and valleys the different formations. Formation VIII. is composed of slates and slaty sandstones that often appear as low serrated ridges; the slates are black, olive, green and reddish, sometimes with calcareous bands; some of the shales contain copperas, alum and iron ore. Formation IX. is known by its red slates and sandstones alternating with green, yellow, brown and dark gray shales and slaty sandstones, with some iron ore.

The SUB-CARBONIFERIOUS Rocks in Virginia, formations X. and XI., are confined to narrow belts made up of conglomerates, slates, shales and limestones, running along the southeast flanks of the North mountains. It is in Formation X. (Vespertine) that Rogers locates the coal of Augusta, Botetourt, Montgomery, &c. Formation XI. is very calcareous, and is the repository of the Gypsum and Rock-salt of Southwest Virginia (Rogers). This is the equivalent of the *Carboniferous limestone* of England. Great down-throws and upheavals of the rocks have brought the Carboniferous and Silurian formations in the southwestern portion of Appalachia side by side, and all the intervening formations are often wanting. Iron ore of good quality is found in the shales of this group.

The CARBONIFEROUS or true coal-bearing rocks, Rogers' XII. to XV., cover but a moderate area in Virginia, when compared with that occupied by the other formations; still the State has nearly a thousand square miles of territory that belongs to the great Carboniferous, in the Southwest, in that portion of it lying north of the Clinch river and drained by its western branches, and in the Virginia territory drained by the Sandy river, with some small adjacent areas. This formation is a group of sandstones, slates, bands of limestone and seams of coal that together make the great Appalachian coal field—one of the most remarkable in the world for the number, thickness, quality and variety of its seams of bituminous coal, and for their accessibility above water level.

The formations of Appalachia *are the same* as those that cover large portions of the States of New York, Pennsylvania, Ohio, Indiana, Michigan and Iowa. In Europe this formation occupies the Lowland region of Scotland, the country of

Edinburg and Glasgow, also the Cromarty and Caithness region; in England it underlies large areas in the northwest and southwest and in Wales.

## Section II.—The Soils of Virginia.

The Character of the Soils of Virginia, as of other countries, is dependent on its geology: that understood, this becomes easy of comprehension.

Tidewater is a Tertiary region; its soils are the alluvial deposits, the sands and clays peculiar to that formation. The soil of the low, flat, sandy shores and islands is, naturally, thin, light and soft: at the same time it is warm, and under the influences of a mild climate, a near ocean and bay, and the dense crops of wild bent-grass, magothy bay-beans, &c., that grow and decay upon it, it becomes very productive and "*quick.*" The salt-marshes of this region are rich in the elements of fertility, as is evidenced by the crops of grass they produce. The soil of the Eastern Shore peninsula is like that already described, only it rests upon a stiff clay, and so retains fertilizers applied to it and is easily improved. The soils of the Norfolk peninsula also belong to this class; they are light, warm, easily tilled, and respond quickly to the influence of fertilizers—all these may be characterized as *garden* soils, adapted to the hoe. In all this Upper Tertiary country there is much salt marsh and swamp land that, when properly drained, becomes exceedingly productive.

In every portion of Tidewater along the streams are "*first*" or alluvial bottoms, composed of mixed materials, the sediment of the waters—these, where above tide, or where protected by embankments, have a perpetual fertility.

The *second* bottoms, or second terrace above the waters, are called the "rich lands" of the country—they "are composed of loams of various qualities, but all highly valuable, and the best soils are scarcely to be surpassed in their original fertility and durability under severe tillage."* The subsoil is a dark red or yellow clay—the yellow becoming of a chocolate color on exposure—lying not very deep. These soils are drier and stiffer than those of the first bottom; sometimes they are sandy, but all are susceptible of improvement.

In some places there are spots of "shelly" soil, where the remains of oysters, mussels, &c., have decomposed and mingled with the loam and sand. These are permanently fertile, bringing forth abundantly. "Shelly" soils could be made anywhere in this region, for Providence has bountifully supplied the means by which this "hint" may be taken advantage of.

The *first* and *second* bottoms are not far above the water level, and form a comparatively small portion of the country. They are succeeded by the "slope," the incline that reaches back to the ridge or water-shed of the peninsulas. The soil of these slopes—compared with that on the flat ridges—"is of a higher grade of fertility, though still far from valuable," * * "generally more sandy than the poorer ridge land,"* and, when exhausted by injudicious cultivation, inclined to wash

---

*Edmund Ruffin's Calcareous Manures.

during rains. "The washing away of three or four inches in depth exposes a sterile sub-soil." Sometimes these soils are productive, but as a rule, do not wear. That they are not wanting in some of the elements of fertility, is well shown by the dense growth of pine trees that speedily covers them when abandoned by severe cultivation. Though thin, sandy and poor, and considered as almost valueless, these lands have been made fertile by using the marls and shells that are near by. The same can be done again. There is a large area of this land.

"The *ridge* lands are always level, and very poor, sometimes clayey, more generally sandy, but stiffer than would be inferred from the proportion of silicious earth they contain, which is caused by the fineness of its particles."* These evils "vary between sandy loam and clayey loam." Numerous shallow basins are found in these soils, which are filled with rain water in winter, and are dry in summer. The quantity of land in all the Tidewater country that pertains to the "slopes" and "ridges" is very large, but Mr. Ruffin has shown, by his cultivation and experiments, using the marls of the country as fertilizers, that they can be readily made productive.

Captain John Smith observes of the soil of Tidewater, which he knew when in a state of nature, in 1607: "The vesture of the earth in most places doth manifestly prove the nature of the soyle to be lusty and very rich." * * "Generally for the most part it is a blacke sandy mould, in some places a fat shiney clay, and in other places a very barren gravell."

The soils of the MIDDLE Country vary of course as the rocks do which they overlie. In the recently published Geology of New Jersey, speaking of a similar region in that State (page 68), it says: "Hitherto the country in which they† are found, has been considered poor and little capable of improvement. But gradually the farmer has been encroaching upon them, and turning these unpromising hills into fruitful fields. It is observed that the rocks are in many places subject to rapid decay, and that in such localities *the soil is susceptible of high cultivation.*" This report then gives an analysis of three varieties of felspar, common in the composition of the rocks there, and also in Middle Virginia, with the following results:

| | Soda Felspar. | Potash Felspar. | Soda and Lime Felspar. |
|---|---|---|---|
| Silica | 68.6 | 64.6 | 62.1 |
| Alumina | 19.6 | 18.5 | 23.7 |
| Soda | 11.8 | ...... | ...... |
| Potash | ...... | 16.9 | ...... |
| Lime | ...... | ...... | 14.2 |
| | 100.0 | 100.0 | 100.0 |

It has been found that the soda, and the soda and lime felspars, are more easily decomposed than the potash ones. It will readily appear that a soil containing the ingredients shown in the table must have the elements of fertility, and since there are numerous and wide belts of these in this section, we find here, upon these, fertile and productive soils. Along the streams, also, the transported materials of these easily decomposed rocks have been deposited, giving everywhere rich soils in the "bottom" lands. Where the beds of gray or light brown slate occur, the soil is not

* Ruffin. † The Azoic rocks.

productive, but it has been found that lime renders the soil from these fertile. Wherever the rocks contain epidote, they decompose into a very fertile soil of a deep red hue. Sometimes these rocks cover considerable areas, and we find these noted for their fertility, like portions of Louisa, Buckingham, and the other counties of this section. There are also calcareous soils found in various portions of the Middle Country, where the patches of limestone before mentioned occur. These are always fertile. Some of the red soils of this section are derived from gneiss rocks containing sulphuret of iron, *but not epidote.* Such soils are as noted for sterility as the epidotic ones are for fertility.

The soils of the Triassic or New Red Sandstone belts are generally fertile, and easily worked. The composition of these rocks in New Jersey shows what they furnish to make a good soil. The Red Shale of the Triassic at Brunswick, N. J., gave, by analysis,* the following results:

| | |
|---|---|
| Silicic acid and quartz | 73.00 |
| Peroxide of iron | 10.00 |
| Alumina | 3.20 |
| Lime | 4.93 |
| Magnesia | 0.90 |
| Potash | 0.73 |
| Soda | 0.97 |
| Sulphuric acid | a trace |
| Water | 1.00 |

Other analyses of other rocks from this formation indicate the presence of a considerable percentage of lime, potash, soda, sulphuric acid, alumina, silica, &c., &c., all valuable ingredients of fertile soils. As a rule, the soils on the areas of this formation are among the best in this section.

The soils of Piedmont, and of its Southwest Mountain border, as remarked in Section I., are much more epidotic in their character, and therefore naturally more fertile than most of those farther east.

The red or chocolate colored soils of this section, formed from the decomposed, dark, greenish-blue sandstone here found, is generally considered the most fertile. This sandstone contains several per cent. of carbonate of lime. The other soils of this region are grayish or yellowish. These are by no means as fertile as the darker soils; but there are red soils here, as in Middle Virginia, that are also poor ones, and for the same reasons. The epidote rocks, from which the best soils of this region are formed, often contain, says Rogers, 24 per cent. of lime. Hornblende, in decomposing, forms a red soil also that is very fertile, but it contains magnesia, and less lime and alumina.

The soils of Piedmont are, many of them, undoubtedly among the most fertile known, and can be made to produce a great variety and abundance of crops. They are loose and easily worked, but care must be exercised in their management, since they are easily washed away by heavy rains. If neglected, they are soon covered by a growth of underbrush.

The Blue Ridge is composed of much the same materials as Piedmont, only

*State Report.

they are richer in their abundance of greenstone rocks, which impart to the soils of this much expanded mountain range a wonderful fertility, and adapt them to the growth of rich grasses, vines, orchards and all the usual crops of the country wherever the character of the surface admits of cultivation.

The soils in the sandstone belt of the western slope of this range are sandy and poor.

The soils of the GREAT VALLEY are quite numerous; they are generally called limestone soils, as this is a limestone region. The prevailing soil is a stiff, clayey loam, a durable and fertile soil well adapted to the growth of grass and grain. In the slaty belts the admixture of the decomposed aluminous rocks makes a lighter and warmer soil. There are also belts of sandy or gravelly soil that are *cold* and require cultivation and fertilizers to make them productive, but once redeemed they yield very well. Much the larger portion of the Valley has, naturally, a good soil, rich in the elements of fertility. The soil, like the rocks, runs in belts, with the Valley, and the *lean* ones are the smaller number. The streams, as in all limestone regions, are very winding, so there is here a considerable area of *bottom* lands. Washington* said of this section that "in soil, climate and productions, and in my opinion will be considered, if it is not considered so already, as the Garden of America."

The soils of the APPALACHIAN region are very marked in their character; the sandstone ridges and mountains are very poor, while those made up of limestones and some of the shales are very rich; some of the slate valleys have a thin and poor soil, others on limestone or certain red sandstones are very rich: indeed, the natural exuberant fertility of some of these broad ridges and narrow valleys is something wonderful. Some of the little valleys are appropriately called "gardens." This region is so penetrated by streams that it has everywhere alluvial lands.

Thus it appears that there are soils of every variety, in Virginia, suited to all kinds of productions.

IN TIDEWATER: *peat-bottom*, or *swamp* and *savanna* lands, for cranberry culture; *salt marshes and meadows* for grass and cheap grazing; *river marshes* that reclaimed are fine hemp lands; *plains* with soft and warm soil for great market gardens and the rearing of delicate fruits; *river bottoms*, marly alluvial lands, excellent for cotton, corn, wheat, oats or meadows; thin, *sandy uplands*, for great sheep pastures and for forest planting.

IN MIDDLE: *clay soils* that produce the finest of wheat; *mixed sand and clay* well suited to general agriculture; *thin lands*, where fruit-growing would be remunerative; *river low-grounds*, where great crops of Indian corn and rank tobacco grow from year to year without exhausting their fertility; *light soils*, where the finer kinds of tobacco are produced; lands for Swedes, Mangolds, &c., and improved sheep husbandry.

IN PIEDMONT: *rich upland loams*, unsurpassed as wheat or tobacco lands, and producing heavy crops of cultivated grasses; *low grounds*, where the corn crop is always good, and where heavy shipping tobacco comes to perfection; *lighter soils*, where the vine and the apple produce abundantly; the best of lands for dairies and for sheep and cattle rearing.

---

*Letter to Sir John Sinclair, 1796.

In the Blue Ridge, where the natural grasses invite to sheep and cattle grazing, and the rich, warm soil and sunny exposures are adapted to fruit culture on lands that elsewhere would be too valuable for the plow.

In the Valley: the natural *blue grass lands*, the home of the stock-raiser and dairyman; the *heavy clay lands*, fat in fertilizing ingredients, always repaying the labor spent on them in crops of corn or wheat; the *lighter slaty lands*, famous for wheat crops; the poorer *ridge lands*, where sheep rearing should be followed.

In the Mountain Region are great cattle ranges—lands where grass grows naturally as soon as the trees are cleared away and the sunlight admitted; rich meadow lands in the valleys well suited to dairying; fat corn or tobacco lands along the streams; lands for root crops along the slopes and on the plateaus.

## Section III.—The Minerals of Virginia.

The Mineral Resources of Virginia are very great, though as yet mostly undeveloped. They comprise gold, iron, copper, lead and zinc; semi-bituminous and bituminous coals; granite, limestone, marble, freestone, greenstone and brownstone; brick and fire-clays, glass sand, plumbago, manganese, gypsum, salt, &c., &c.

The Tidewater Country can hardly be called a mineral region, and yet it abounds in agricultural minerals, which to it, a country so well adapted to agriculture, are invaluable. The use of these can make this region everywhere fertile.

Among the Agricultural Minerals, the *greensand marl* is first in importance. This mineral, so rich in carbonate and sulphate of lime, alumina, potash, &c., is found in extensive deposits in the Lower Tertiary formation, very accessible and convenient to navigation and railway transportation. The use of marls in the State of New Jersey has revolutionized its agriculture. More than a million tons of it were there applied in 1868.

The *blue marl* is hardly less valuable, containing often 40 per cent. of carbonate of lime; it is full of decomposed shells. This abounds everywhere in the Middle Tertiary, its beds being found near the level of the rivers. *White*, chalky-looking *marl* is abundant in portions of the Middle Tertiary. This is rich in calcareous matter, sometimes containing 75 to 95 per cent. of carbonate of lime. *Yellow marls* are also common. These are valuable for some soils. The iron in these often cements them into a kind of limestone. The noted "phosphate beds" of South Carolina are in a formation similar to that on the shores of Virginia, and such may yet be found here. *Peat*, valuable as a fuel and fertilizer, exists in the swampy plains.

The Architectural Minerals of Tidewater are: the best of *clay* for brick making, like the London clay, found in all sections; *shell marl*, often in beds hard enough for building purposes, and that can be easily wrought; Tertiary *limestones* are frequent, and furnish a very good building material; the *ferruginous sandstones* are sometimes used. The materials for *concrete*, sand and pebbles, and shells for lime, are in all parts. The gray *granites*, at the head of tide, are among the best known. The *brownstone* is also on the border. These can be shipped directly from the quarries to all parts of this water-penetrated region.

5

Some bands of iron ore are found among the strata of the marls, &c., in various parts of Tidewater, some of them a foot thick. A specimen from Surry county yielded Professor Rogers 72.4 per cent. of peroxide.

The *architectural* minerals of the MIDDLE Country are the fine gray *granite*, found in its eastern border at the head of tide, at Richmond, Petersburg, Fredericksburg and elsewhere. This is of an even texture, easily wrought to a smooth surface, can be obtained in large slabs or blocks, is strong and durable, and has a pleasant tint. The trade in this fine building stone is increasing. It is being used in the construction of public buildings at Washington and elsewhere. The *brown-stone* of the Triassic is an esteemed building material, and is extensively used locally. Where that formation is crossed by the Midland railroad near Manassas, this rock is quarried and shipped to market. The *Potomac* or *brecciated marble*, found not far from Leesburg, is used for inside columns and ornamental work. A modified variety of this is found in Fauquier and other counties. *Greenish* and *bluish slates*, compact and separating into slabs suitable for building, are also found in this Triassic in Culpeper and elsewhere. In numerous localities, interstratified with the gneiss, are beds of soapstone, as in Amelia, valuable for hearths, furnaces, &c. *Clays* for brick are found in very many localities, and *kaolin* for fire bricks is often met with, as in Prince Edward, Cumberland, &c. Granite, stratified and unstratified, exists throughout the region. Gneiss, of a granitic character, laminated so that it is easily split into slabs, is found, as at the valuable quarries at Columbia on the James. A wide belt of this runs through the country. A *syenite*, found in Campbell county, is used for mill-stones, cut out in a single piece. *Asbestus*, used in making a fire-proof roofing, is found in Pittsylvania and elsewhere. *Roofing slate*, of the very best quality, is found in great abundance in Buckingham and other counties. Several companies are engaged in quarrying it. In the western border of this section, in Albemarle, &c., is a fine *slate* for mantels, hearth-stones, &c., being soft and easily cut. *Mica* is obtained in Hanover, Goochland, Louisa, &c., of a quality suitable for stove windows. A great variety and abundance of building materials are found everywhere.

The *agricultural minerals* of the Middle Country are the beds of *limestone*, disposed in lenticular masses along its western border, and the *epidotic* rocks, that extend through its whole territory. Both of these can be used to great advantage on the lands here.

The *ores and metals* of Middle Virginia are: *gold*, which is found in a belt some 15 or 25 miles in width, that runs for 200 miles through this section from Washington city to Halifax Courthouse. This is known as the "Gold Belt" of Virginia. It is composed of a series of granitic, syenitic, steatitic, chloritic and other rocks peculiar to this section, striking northeast and southwest with the belt, and dipping at high angles, or standing nearly vertical. Stratified with these are numerous veins of gold-bearing quartz, seams of magnetic, specular, hematite and other ores of iron, trap dykes, &c. The gold found in these materials varies in value from $1.30 to $1,000 to the ton; an average 100 tons, from the surface downward, is estimated as worth $939.32.* Assays of samples from the Franklin mine, in Fauquier county, made

* Report of Richmond Chamber of Commerce for 1871. Article on "Gold Belt."

by R. D. Irving, of New York, in 1870, gave for 200 pounds of materials from the veins, as an average value, in one sample, $46.40 of gold and $1.48 of silver; in another, $72.55 of gold and $0.41 of silver, while another gave but $2.32 of gold. The mean value of the assays of 10 samples was $24.44 to the ton of 2,000 pounds. Large numbers of mines have been opened along the "belt," notably in Fauquier, Culpeper, Spotsylvania, Orange, Fluvanna and Buckingham counties, and from these and gatherings from the surface and soils, $1,662,627 worth of gold had reached the U. S. Mint up to June 30th, 1871.* If the same skill and capital were employed here as in California, these mines, in the opinion of practical miners, would yield as well as those of that noted gold-producing State. *Silver* is associated with some of the gold-bearing rocks above named, especially the chloritic slate. *Copper* pyrites are *abundant* in all the "gold belt;" carbonate of copper is also found. The excellent character of the sulphurets of copper of this region is becoming known, and large quantities of this ore are now shipped from Tolersville in Louisa county. An analysis of a sample of the Tolersville pyrites, by Pattinson, of Newcastle-on-Tyne, England, gave—

| | | |
|---|---|---|
| Sulphur | 43.00 | per cent. |
| Copper | 5.89 | " |
| Silicious Matter | 8.73 | " |
| Moisture | 0.38 | " |

Another analysis, by Gibb, of Jarrow, gave—

| | | |
|---|---|---|
| Sulphur | 48.25 | per cent. |
| Copper | 0.60 | " |
| Silica | 5.60 | " |

*Plumbago*, of good quality, occurs in Halifax, Amelia and other counties. *Iron* ores are found in great plenty, and the first successful furnaces in America were on the hematite beds of this section. In the "gold belt" are seams of *specular iron ore*, from 10 to 15 feet in thickness, extending with the belt. *Sulphuret of iron* is very plentiful in the same range, and extensive deposits of *brown hematite* ores are well known, both in the belt and along its eastern border. *Magnetic* iron ores are found in thick veins in many localities, as in Buckingham, Spotsylvania, &c. It may be stated as a general fact, that any section across the 200 miles of the length of Middle Virginia will embrace a dozen valuable seams of iron ore—including *limonites or hydrous peroxides, magnetites, chromates, sulphurets, micaceous, specular*, &c., where the ores are abundant and can be easily mined. The introduction of cheap coal, now inaugurated, will bring these into use. Prof. Rogers gives the following analyses of ores here found:

| LOCALITY. | COUNTY. | Composition in 100 Parts. | | | | | Per Cent. Metallic Iron. |
|---|---|---|---|---|---|---|---|
| | | Peroxide of Iron. | Alumina. | Silica, &c. | Water. | Loss. | |
| 1. Ross Furnace | Campbell | 81.11 | 0.28 | 6.54 | 11.10 | 0.97 | 56.77 |
| 2. Stonewall Creek | Appomattox | 76.00 | 0.50 | 13.00 | 10.00 | 0.50 | 53.20 |
| 3. Elk Creek | ........ | 84.00 | 0.85 | 7.60 | 7.10 | 0.45 | 58.80 |
| 4. Falling River | Campbell | 84.20 | 0.56 | 4.50 | 10.00 | 0.74 | 58.94 |
| 5. New Canton | Buckingham | 72.00 | 1.33 | 16.47 | 10.04 | .... | 50.40 |
| 6. Chesterfield County | ........ | 85.15 | 4.00 | 4.20 | 6.50 | .... | ..... |

* Merchants and Bankers Almanac, 1872.

*Bituminous coal* and *natural coke* are found in extensive beds in the Triassic or New Red Sandstone—especially in the "Richmond coal field" portion, where the coal-bearing rocks cover 150 square miles of surface. Over a million* tons were taken from this field in the 20 years, from 1822 to 1842. It has been longer known and worked than any other field in America, but never to the extent that the value of its coals would seem to justify.

† "In the part of this field upon the north side of James river five seams of coal have been opened, varying in thickness from two and a half to eight feet, giving an aggregate of more than 20 feet, as at Carbon Hill. On the south side of the river, at Midlothian, three seams have been opened, varying in thickness from 4 feet to 40, making from 50 to 60 feet of coal. One of the seams on the north side, from two and a half to six feet thick, is a natural coke (the coal having been coked by the intrusion of a trap dyke), known as carbonite; the other seams are coking coals, highly bituminous, as they should be, for they are young coals, and therefore fat, as the adage says, and admirably adapted to gas making. For this purpose the mines are extensively worked.

"Professor Hull, in the last edition of his work on the 'Coal-Fields of Great Britain,' says: 'The Richmond coal-field contains several beds of valuable coal, one of which is from thirty to forty feet in thickness, highly bituminous, and equal to the best coal of Newcastle.'

"These mines are admirably located for commercial purposes, and the coals are highly commended by all that have used them."

The analyses of these coals, by Prof. Rogers, give from 55.20 to 70.80 per cent. of carbon, from 22.83 to 38.60 of volatile matter, with from 2 to 22.60 per cent. of ash (most of the samples contain a small percentage of ash). A recent analysis ‡ (1873) made in Glasgow, Scotland, gives the following results from seven analyses of samples from different seams and localities:

Volatile matter, 14.26 to 34.57 per cent.

Coke { Fixed Carbon, 56.23 to 81.61 per cent.
Sulphur, 0.04 to 1.10 per cent.
Ash, 2.24 to 8.88 per cent.

Water (at 212° Fahr.), 0.82 to 1.80 per cent.

Dry Coke, per ton of Coal, 12 cwt. 3 qrs. 13 lbs. to 16 cwt. 3 qrs. 10 lbs.

Coke, per cent., 64.33 to 84.18.

Sulphur in volatile matter, 1.14 to 0.78, or in all 0.18 to 1.83.

Heating power calculated, 8.35 to 11.04.

Specific gravity, 1.219 to 1.321.

Weight of a cubic foot, 77.6 to 82.3 pounds.

Weight per inch per acre, 123 to 133 tons.

The most important element in coals is the fixed carbon, and Dr. Wallace says: "In this respect the whole of the coals are of excellent quality, and are considerably superior to the average of the Newcastle coal, which, in many respects, they resemble." The *Carbonite*, or natural coke, the same authority says, "is a material admi-

* R. C. Taylor—Statistics of Coal.

† Address of Maj. Jed. Hotchkiss before Society of Arts, London, 1873.

‡ Dr. William Wallace's.

rably adapted for stoves,* having a high heating power, and containing very little ash or sulphur." The census of 1870 reports 61,803 tons mined. Dana† says: "The coal is of good quality, and resembles the bituminous coal of the Carboniferous era;" and Macfarlane‡—"This oldest of our coal fields is yet to see its best days." And why should it not, when it has a capacity for an annual production of millions of tons, is but a few miles from tidewater, and can be water-borne to all the Atlantic cities. The Triassic coal has been partially opened in the field near Farmville; also, in the one near the North Carolina line. It is not likely that it is worth mining to any extent in the other Triassic beds—they are too shallow.

PIEDMONT has, for *architectural* purposes, an abundance, in all portions of it, of the best of *brick clay;* good *roofing* and heavier *slates* are found in Amherst and other localities; *soapstone* is found in Madison and elsewhere; *variegated marble* in Fauquier, and *kaolin* in numerous localities. The various *gneissoid* rocks, *greenstone*, &c., afford excellent and beautiful building stones.

For *agricultural* purposes this, like Middle Virginia, has the epidote rocks, the decay of which constantly renews its fertility.

The ores of Piedmont are very valuable; its beds of *magnetic iron ore* are numerous throughout its extent, notably in Nelson, Amherst, Albemarle, &c.

The quantity of magnetic ore, of the best quality, in this section, is very large, and now that coal is accessible, these most valuable ores must come into use, especially for mixing with other ores of iron. Prof. Rogers mentions the S. W. Mountain and Buffalo Ridge, its prolongation S. W., as containing deposits of this, with *micaceous iron ore.*

Recent§ operations in Amherst and Nelson counties, along James river and between it and Buffalo Ridge, have exposed some 25 parallel veins of iron ore, varying in width from 5 to 60 feet. The ores are the specular, magnetic, brown hematite, micaceous and manganiferous. The following analyses of these ores indicate fully their character:

*Analysis of Magnetic and Specular Ores from Virginia, made by Prof. F. A. Genth, Dec., 1874.*

| | No. 1. Specular. | No. 3. Magnetic. | No. 5. Blue Magnetic. | No. 6. Specular. | No. 10½. Magnetic. | No. 11. Magnetic. | No. 16. Magnetic. | No. 19. Specular. | No. 14. Brown Hematite. |
|---|---|---|---|---|---|---|---|---|---|
| Silicic Acid (Quartz) | 30.86 | 4.10 | 14.67 | 3.04 | 16.60 | 11.32 | 3.29 | 25.09 | 24.02 |
| Titanic Acid | 0.20 | 0.15 | 0.22 | 0.10 | 0.18 | 0.22 | Trace | 0.43 | ..... |
| Phosphoric Acid | 0.37 | 0.02 | 0.08 | 0.11 | 0.54 | 0.70 | 0.08 | 0.55 | 0.93 |
| Ferric Oxide | 55.04 | 90.74 | 82.38 | 91.39 | 75.69 | 81.86 | 95.24 | 64.40 | 62.29 |
| Manganic Oxide | 0.17 | 0.11 | 0.32 | 0.17 | 0.29 | 0.20 | 0.09 | 0.27 | 0.19 |
| Alumina | 10.24 | 4.43 | 1.96 | 4.20 | 3.76 | 3.06 | 0.53 | 7.07 | 3.03 |
| Magnesia | 0.88 | 0.12 | 0.06 | 0.15 | 0.25 | 0.18 | 0.07 | 0.45 | 0.10 |
| Lime | 0.97 | 0.29 | 0.23 | 0.20 | 1.29 | 1.38 | 0.04 | 0.71 | 0.20 |
| Water | 1.27 | 0.04 | 0.18 | 0.64 | 1.40 | 1.08 | 0.66 | 1.04 | 9.24 |
| | 100.00 | 100.00 | 100.00 | 100.00 | 100.00 | 100.00 | 100.00 | 100.00 | 100.00 |
| Metallic Iron | 38.53 | 65.71 | 57.68 | 63.97 | 52.98 | 57.30 | 66.32 | 45.08 | 43.60 |
| Phosphorus | 0.16 | 0.009 | 0.035 | 0.048 | 0.237 | 0.307 | 0.035 | 0.24 | 0.41 |

* Meaning those of blast furnaces.

† Manual of Geology—1871.

‡ Coal Regions of America—1873.

§ Report of Iron Company.

The manganiferous ore here found was also analyzed by Prof. Genth, with the following results:

| | |
|---|---|
| Silicic Acid | 2.74 |
| Phosphoric Acid | 0.76 |
| Binoxide of Manganese | 66.91 |
| Binoxide of Cobalt | 0.79 |
| Ferric Oxide | 18.34 |
| Alumina | 1.50 |
| Magnesia | 0.40 |
| Lime | 0.93 |
| Water | 5.00 |
| Baryta | 2.63 |
| | 100.00 |
| Manganese | 42.34 |
| Phosphorus | 0.33 |

A comparison of these analyses with those of the ores of Lake Superior and other portions of the United States, and with those of Europe, is very favorable to these ores, and shows that some of them, from their freedom from impurities, are especially adapted to the manufacture of Bessemer steel and the most valuable grades of iron. The best Lake Superior ores contain from 50.40 to 65.94 per cent. of metallic iron, 0.03 to 0.22 per cent. of phosphorus, and from 0.01 to 0.35 per cent. of sulphur. The magnetic ores of New York contain from 58.31 to 64.31 per cent. of metallic iron, from 0.022 to 0.723 per cent. of phosphorus, and from 0.002 to 1.502 per cent. of sulphur.

A test of the strength of pig iron recently made by the United States showed that the iron from No. 11 of above table resisted a pressure of 20,600 pounds to the square inch, while that of the Thomas Iron Company, of Pennsylvania, stood but 18,000, and that of the Cold Spring Furnace, of Hudson, New York, 17,000 pounds.

The President of the Virginia Midland Railway, Col. J. S. Barbour, in his report* to the State in 1874, mentions the opening of deposits of magnetic ore, for 30 miles along his railway, in Albemarle and Nelson counties. Some ore from Albemarle is "regarded as suitable for the manufacture of Bessemer pig iron." Deposits of ore have also been opened in Orange county, and a vein of specular ore, that has been traced for 30 miles through Culpeper, Orange and Albemarle, has been found to contain over "60 per cent. of metallic iron, and to be free from sulphur and phosphorus." This ore is of an excellent quality for making steel, and is so situated that it can be cheaply mined and transported to Pennsylvania and other Atlantic States, where it is needed to mix with local ores to produce the best results.

In Franklin county, Prof. Rogers mentions a bed of magnetic oxide from 4 to 6 feet thick, and another in Patrick from 3 to 6 feet wide—"a fine-grained, generally black ore." These ores yield from 70 to 72.4 per cent. of metallic iron, noted for purity and tenacity. *Specular*, *magnetic* and *hematite* and other iron ores exist in ex-

*Report of Virginia Board of Public Works for 1874, page 31.

tensive beds throughout Piedmont. Green *carbonate of copper* is found in small quantities in several counties, but little is known concerning it. *Lead* has been mined in Nelson county, the ore yielding some 52 per cent. of metallic lead and forty-five dollars worth of silver to the ton; lead is also found in Franklin and other counties. Brown oxide of *titanium* is known near Lynchburg. *Manganese* is extensively mined in Nelson county, and evidences of its existence in other localities are numerous.

The Blue Ridge has beautiful *greenstones* and some *granitic* rocks that answer for building stones, though, as a rule, these rocks are too soft or decay too readily, making good soil but poor walls; the reliance for the latter must be on the harder sandstones of the western slope. Where the greenstones are hard, nothing is prettier, or more agreeable in color for building purposes.

Mention has been made several times of the valuable properties of the *epidote* of this mountain range for enriching the soil. Prof. T. Sterry Hunt (formerly of the Geological Survey of Canada), in a recent article,* speaking of the southwestern portion of the Blue Ridge, says: "The traveler from New England, who expects ledges of rock, beds of sand and gravel, and huge boulders scattered over the land, the marks of what is called glacial action, is surprised to find nothing of all this here. *The hills to their very summits are covered not only with dense forests, but with a deep and strong soil,* which is, however, very unlike the layers of clay and loam with which he is familiar. *The rocks* themselves, although of gneiss and mica slate, like that which prevails over so great a part of New England, *have undergone a process of decay* which has rendered them so soft that *they may be readily cut by a spade or pick,* although retaining all the veins and layers which marked their original stratification. Without having been broken or ground up, *these hard rocks have moldered into a soft clayey mass, forming a soil* 20 *feet, and* often much *more, in depth,* which from its peculiar structure has a natural drainage, and possesses, moreover, great fertility." These observations could be made in regard to nearly all the 300 miles of the length of this most fertile region.

The *ores* of the Blue Ridge are: *copper*, more or less, the whole length of the range, as *carbonates, sulphurets,* &c., chiefly in the latter form. In Floyd, Carroll and Grayson, a dozen mines were once opened and several thousand tons of ore, yield- from 6 to 30 per cent. of metal, were sent to market. Prof. T. S. Hunt, at the 1872 meeting of the American Science Congress, called attention to these Blue Ridge mines as sources from which abundant supplies of copper and sulphur could be obtained. Stating that England imports from Spain sulphurets of iron for sulphuric acid with which to treat the South Carolina phosphates, and we bring native sulphur from Sicily for the same purpose, "while the mountains of the Blue Ridge contain deposits of sulphur ore as abundant as those of Spain." England draws annually a half million tons of sulphurets from Spain, and 5 to 6,000 tons of Sicily sulphur are yearly used at Charleston, S. C.

In a letter to the Eng. and Mining Journal, of N. Y., Aug. 12th, 1873, Prof. Hunt states that he traced a belt of copper in Carroll county 7 miles N. E. and S. W.; it was from 20 to 200 feet wide—adding, "The supply of sulphur ores which

---

* In New York Tribune.

the region could be made to supply is enormous—only 17 miles, by good road, to near Meadows* Station." Some of the ore yields 26 to 29 per cent. of copper.

The manufacture of alkalies, soda-ash, &c.—one of the most important of industries, but not found in the whole United States—is dependent upon such sulphurets. The salt, the coal, and the copper ores of Southwest Virginia, offer the finest field in the world for this industry. More than half the copper furnished to the world comes from the 6 to 8 per cent. ores of Chili. Space forbids more on this important subject.

*Iron ores* of great value are found in these same Blue Ridge counties. Prof. Rogers says of some iron ore in Grayson county, that it often yields, "by the usual smelting process, a metal having all the qualities of steel." *Limonite* the *yellow*, *hematite* the *red*, and *magnetite* the *black* iron ores, are found in this region, though it has been poorly explored. Heavy strata of *specular iron ore*, many feet thick, are often found on the western flanks of this range, near the dividing line of the Azoic and Potsdam formations—it gives from 30 to 40 per cent. of iron, and is valuable for mixing with the richer ores near by.

The following analysis of specular ore from this range, in Augusta county, is by Prof. Mallett, of the University of Virginia:

| | |
|---|---|
| Peroxide of iron | 2.64 |
| Sesquioxide of iron | 51.33 |
| Alumina | 1.73 |
| Magnesia | 1.93 |
| Silicic acid, as fine quartz | 42.69 |
| Trace of magnetite. | |
| Metallic iron | 37.98 |

Among the foot-hills at the western base of the Blue Ridge, in the red shales of the Potsdam, or Formation I., often adjacent to the Valley limestone itself, is the remarkable deposit of *brown hematite* or *hydrated peroxide of iron*, that for nearly 300 miles offers its *great beds, of the best quality*, of this valuable ore to the manufacturer. This ore is often found in beds from 10 to 100 feet thick, and these, especially to the southwest, often extend unbroken for miles. The quantity and quality of this ore is a constant theme of remark in Prof. Rogers' Reports. These ores often yield, as the "run of the furnace," some 60 per cent. of metallic iron, noted for its general excellence. The following analysis, by Booth and Garrett, in 1868, of ore from the Fox Mountain bank, of Hon. Wm. Milnes, Page county, shows the character of these ores:

| | |
|---|---|
| Peroxide of iron | 79.77 |
| Oxide of manganese | Trace. |
| Silica | 6.75 |
| Alumina | .80 |
| Magnesia | .05 |
| Lime | None. |
| Sulphur | .17 |
| Phosphoric acid | .13 |
| Water | 12.85 |
| Metallic iron | 55.84 |
| Phosphorus | .06 |

*Max Meadows, Atlantic, Mississippi and Ohio Railroad, Wythe county.

The analysts state that this ore is noteworthy—(1), for its percentage of iron; (2), for the small amount of silex, with ample alumina to slag it off; (3), for the small percentage of sulphur and phosphorus; (4), for containing one-eighth water, making it more reducible in the bosh of the furnace; and from the proportion the small amount of sulphur and phosphorus bear to each other, they should neutralize the respective cold and hot short properties they impart to iron. They consider this adapted to making Bessemer steel. The furnace that used this ore, a common cold-blast charcoal one, from June 18 to Dec. 19, 1866, made 799 tons (2,240 lbs.) of pig iron, from 3,300,194 lbs. of ore, 367,500 lbs. of limestone, and 104,125 bushels of charcoal—a yield of over 54 per cent. of metallic iron. Fine beds of manganese are found in the Blue Ridge also.

The GREAT VALLEY has many varieties of *limestone*—magnesian, silicious, flaggy, coralline, &c., for building purposes, and it is difficult to find better, all things considered; the best of lime, both common and hydraulic, is burned from them; there are also excellent *freestones*. *Clay*, for brick making, of good quality, abounds; and beds of *kaolin* are common near the foot of the Blue Ridge. Several varieties of *marble*, most of them dark or mottled, are often found.

The limestone gives a choice for almost any quality of lime for agricultural purposes; calcareous marls are plentiful in the beds of the smaller streams; the caves, which are numerous, are rich in nitrous earth.

*Iron ores*, brown hematites, are found in "pockets" in all portions of the Valley. These can supply large quantities of fine ores. *Umber* exists in many places. In the mountain ranges that rise up in the Valley are very extensive beds of several varieties of iron ore. The Valley limestones make an excellent *flux* for iron; they are carried east for that purpose. *Lead** is found in many parts of this region. The mines in Wythe county have been worked since 1763, and some 25,000,000 pounds have been taken from them. The crude ore, sulphuret and carbonate generally, is found in veins in the limestone, and gives an average yield of 5 per cent. of metal, though some ores produce from 12 to 15 per cent. This metal could be mined here very extensively. *Zinc*, sillicate and carbonate mostly, and sulphuret, abounds in the same locality in Wythe county. The ores are shipped to other States for smelting at present. Zinc is found co-extensive with the lead. *Fine sand* is abundant along the eastern side of the Valley. The large deposit of pure *kaolin* in Augusta has been used in the manufacture of "stone china" and "Rockingham" wares, and is now made into terra-cotta pipes and tiles, fire bricks, &c. *Barytes* are mined extensively in Smyth.

Beds of semi-anthracite or semi-bituminous coal are found all along the western side of the Valley throughout its whole extent. These are detached and broken fragments of what some call the *proto-carboniferous*, and others the false *coal-measures* (overlying the old red sandstone it is said), brought into these topographical relations by a great downthrow of the higher formations. These fragments are generally of small extent, yet they furnish two or more seams of good semi-anthracite coal, but so disturbed and crushed as to be of little value. In the New river basin is found, on the contrary, a very well developed coal-field of this era,

* Most of the lead is now (1875) made into shot at the mines.

containing, among others, two very accessible seams of good coal, varying in thickness from two to three and a half, and from six to nine feet. The better part of the field is thought to be the thirty miles of the length of it lying north of New river in Montgomery county; hence the whole is often spoken of as the Montgomery coal field, but very good openings have been made through 100 miles in length of a somewhat narrow belt along the west side of the Valley. These coals have only been used for domestic purposes, but the proximity of the great hematite iron deposits must soon lead to their trial for manufacturing purposes. The profitable area of this field may be roughly estimated at 100 square miles. Professor Rogers gives this analysis of the Montgomery county coal:

| | |
|---|---|
| Carbon | 80.20 |
| Bitumen, &c | 13.60 |
| Ash | 6.20 |

And adds: The combustible value or calorific power of 100 parts of this coal is equivalent to that of 92.5 parts of carbon.

A sample from Botetourt county gave:

| | |
|---|---|
| Carbon | 78.50 |
| Bitumen | 16.50 |
| Ash | 5.00 |
| Calorific power | 89.04 |

The Dora mines are in these measures in Augusta county.

The APPALACHIAN region has a great variety and abundance of excellent *building stones* in the numerous seams of limestone, sandstone, freestone, &c., extending through it. The beautiful variegated *brown marbles*, known as "Tennessee," are found in Scott county. In other localities *encrinal marbles*, having a great variety of colors, are found. The limestones are, many of them, easily wrought, and have a pleasant tint. The heavy, fine-grained sandstones are highly esteemed for the construction of furnaces. *Brick clay* is found in all the limestone valleys, and *fire clay* in connection with the extensive ranges of iron ore deposits.

The limestones of this region are of the best character for burning into *agricultural* lime. Marls are found along the streams of the numerous limestone valleys; and in the caves and fissures of the limestone ridges *nitrous earths* are abundant.

This Appalachian Country includes the great "*iron belt*" of Virginia, in which are found vast quantities of the *red* and *brown* iron ores, *limonites*, *hematites*, and some that resemble *magnetites*, spoken of as *red* or *brown hematites*, *fossil* ore, *red shale* ore, *dyestone* ore, &c. Professor Rogers says: "Of the twelve rocks, each marked by certain distinctive characters, composing the mountains and valleys of this region, it has been determined that at least *eight are accompanied by beds of iron ore.* Each ore has distinctive marks by which it may be recognized, and peculiarities of composition, fitting it for certain uses to which others would be less happily adapted. Thus, in the quantity and variety of this material in all its valuable forms, our State is now proved to have no rival."* * * Again, speaking of smelting iron with *raw coals*, (now, 1873, being done)—"Should these improvements be brought into extensive operation, as in process of time they most assuredly will, the prosperity of this vast and almost forgotten portion of the State will outstrip anything that the imagination of its present inhabitants can conceive."* Speaking† of For-

*Report of 1836. †Report of 1837.

mation No. VII.: "Indeed this part of it, throughout a large portion of the Appalachian region, is the repository of *continuous beds of iron ore of immense extent*, which often replace the sandstone for a great depth." In the first ranges of the mountains west of the Valley, called by various names, Little North Mountain, &c., but as a range known as the Kitatinny, on their eastern and western slopes are found solid masses of *brown hematite iron ore*, presenting the appearance of a thick stratum between the sandstone and limestone rocks that form the mountains and dip, generally, at a considerable angle. *These ores extend to unknown depths between these rocks, and often stand out as huge bluffs, along the sides of the ridges, from* 10 *to* 50 *feet high.* As the same formation is repeated in a number of successive ranges of mountains, so, also, is the deposit of this ore. The following analyses, by O. J. Heinrich, of two samples from the largest bluff deposits, at Elizabeth Furnace, in Augusta county, show the general character of these ores:

| | | |
|---|---|---|
| Water | 10.33 | 14.656 |
| Peroxide of iron | 73.33 | 83.310 |
| Oxide of alumina | 2.00 | .500 |
| Oxide of lime | 1.00 | ......... |
| Oxide of magnesia | .30 | .066 |
| Silicic acid | 12.20 | 1.466 |
| Carbonic acid | .83 | ......... |
| Loss | .01 | .002 |
| | 100.00 | 100.000 |
| Metallic iron | 51.33 | 58.32 |

Analyses by Britton, of hematite ores from Callie Furnace, near Clifton Forge, Alleghany county, give a yield of 58.60 per cent. of metallic iron.

The *manganese* found in some of these ores gives them a special value for use in the manufacture of Bessemer steel.

In the same ranges of mountains the poorer, but, for many purposes, not less valuable, *red shale* ores are found; their seams are not as thick, but they are very abundant.

The *Fossil-ore* of Formation V.—the Clinton ore of New York and the *Paint or Dyestone* ore of Tennessee—is notably developed in the southwestern portion of this region, where it runs for a hundred miles or more in persistent strata, some of them from two to five feet in thickness; these ores are generally found in low ridges. At Cumberland Gap the Dyestone seam, in Poor Valley Ridge, a low range in Virginia, parallel to the Cumberland Mountain, is from 24 to 30* inches thick, regularly stratified and quarried in blocks. Prof. Rogers gives this analysis† of the ore at Cumberland Gap:

| | |
|---|---|
| Peroxide of iron | 76.60 |
| Alumina | 7.60 |
| Carbonate of lime | 1.00 |
| Water | 3.00 |
| Silica and insoluble matter | 11.30 |
| Loss | 0.60 |
| | 100.00 |
| Metallic iron | 53.55 per cent. |

It also contained traces of oxide of manganese and of magnesia.

* Safford—Geology of Tennessee. † Report of 1840.

This* ore, when *pure*, can yield 70 per cent. of metallic iron. As the formation in which this ore is found is repeated in many parallel ridges, so, in like manner, the beds of ore are multipled. This ore, in the southwest of Appalachia, has the advantage of being within 8 or 10 miles, sometimes nearer, of the eastern edge of the great Appalachian coal field, as in Lee, Scott, Russell and Tazewell counties.

It is difficult to find another belt of country, 300 *miles long* and averaging 15 *miles in width*, that is as well supplied with immense deposits of numerous kinds of the ores of this most valuable metal as this *Appalachian iron belt* of Virginia.

*Gypsum*, or *plaster* (sulphate of lime), is found in beds that have been opened for more than twenty miles along the North Fork of Holston river, in Washington and Smyth counties. In some places shafts have been sunk in the plaster for 500 feet without going through it. The width of the deposit is unknown—often over 50 yards—giving a quantity of this most valuable specific manure almost beyond calculation. An analysis of two specimens, made at the Virginia Military Institute gave 78.86 and 76.81 per cent. of sulphate of lime in this plaster; *pure* sulphate would contain 79.07, showing the excellent quality of the Holston plaster. This plaster is sold at the mines at $2.50† per ton; it reaches market by the railroad from Saltville. "Its† virtues are well known and highly prized. It *doubles* the grass crop and grain, and greatly improves corn. One bushel of 100 pounds is sown to the acre."

*Salt* is found in the same region with the plaster, at Saltville, on the North Fork of Holston; brine is drawn from Artesian wells about 200 feet deep, the water rising to within 40 feet of the surface. This brine comes from a *solid bed of rock salt*, 200 feet below the level of the Holston, and borings have been made into it 176 feet without passing through it. The supply of brine is not affected by any operations yet carried on, and at one time, during the Confederate war, 10,000 bushels of salt were made there each day for some six months. The present yield is about 360,000‡ bushels a year, using wood for fuel. When improvements contemplated bring the coal, that is but 40 miles off, to these works, there will be a very large amount of salt made here, as it has the advantage by being so far inland. The copper ores of Floyd, before mentioned, make it possible to here locate, successfully, alkali works.

Professor Lesley, in the report before referred to, mentions the fact that a salt well has been bored in Tazewell county, and adds: "It must be borne in mind that the salt wells of Eastern Kentucky get their water from the conglomerate at the base of the Coal Measures. There must, therefore, be a salt water bearing formation several hundred feet below the coal bed at the bottom of this well."

Salt has been made at works in the southeastern part of Lee county, on the waters of Clinch river. There is, no doubt, an abundance of brine throughout this region in the formation above named.

---

* Safford—Geology of Tennessee

† Prof. Lesley—1871—Report on this Region to Am. Phil. Soc.

‡ Lesley—1871.

The following table, from the Report of the Superintendent of the New York Salt Works, at Syracuse, for 1854, gives the character of the Saltville salt, compared with that from other localities:

| | | Chloride of Sodium. | Sulphate of Lime. | Sulphate of Magnesia. | Chloride of Calcium. | Chloride of Magnesium. | Oxide of Iron. | Water. |
|---|---|---|---|---|---|---|---|---|
| **Brine.** | Saltville ............... | 98.39 | 1.22 | 0.39 | ...... | ...... | Trace. | ...... |
| | Syracuse, N. Y. ........... | 95.86 | 2.54 | ...... | 0.90 | 0.69 | 0.004 | ...... |
| | Kanawha, W. Va. ......... | 79.45 | ...... | ...... | 1.52 | 0.85 | Trace. | ...... |
| | Cheshire, Eng. ........... | 98.07 | 1.57 | ...... | 0.13 | 0.23 | ...... | ...... |
| **Manufactured Salt.** | Saltville......... | 91.18 | 0.27 | 0.05 | ...... | ...... | ...... | 0.40 |
| | Syracuse....... | 97.95 | 0.04 | ...... | 0.04 | 0.03 | ...... | 1.94 |
| | Kanawha....... | 91.31 | ...... | ...... | 1.26 | 0.43 | ...... | 7.00 |
| | Cheshire ....... | 98.53 | 1.26 | ...... | Trace. | 0.01 | ...... | 0.20 |
| | Turk's Island. | 96.76 | 1.56 | 0.64 | ...... | 0.14 | ...... | 0.90 |

*Barytes*, *lead* and some other minerals are found in a number of localities.

*Bituminous coal* is found in the counties of Tazewell, Russell, Scott, Lee, Buchanan and Wise, in the southwest, where a portion of the Great Appalachian coal field of the United States crosses Virginia territory, giving it nearly 1,000 square miles of this remarkable deposit of fossil fuel. Nowhere else in the Union do we find the same condition of things as that existing here, where "the limestones of the Lower Silurian, holding the brown hematite ores, directly abut against the coal beds of the carboniferous and sub-carboniferous era"*—the result of great upheavals and down-throws, that have brought the richest farming and grazing lands and the most valuable ores of iron alongside the coals, *without an intervening mountain barrier.* The line of the fissure, where these formations meet, is *in* the valley of the Clinch river, so that the branches of that stream from the west flow from the coal measures *"for about 70 *miles* along the valley of the Clinch; any railroad descending the Clinch, from Jeffersonville to the mouth of Guest's river, in Wise county, may have *as many collieries* alongside of it as it pleases. Short streams, from five to eight miles long, flow into the Clinch from the north, *cutting the coal beds at water level.* There are thirteen or fourteen of these streams on which to establish collieries, and up which to turn in branch coal roads, from half a mile to three miles long, with ascending gradients of twenty to thirty feet in the mile. In one case a six and a half foot coal bed underlies the river bottom flats at a depth of 300 feet. The coal beds thus open * * are the *lower coals of the carboniferous system*, occupying the position of the coal beds at Cresson on the Pennsylvania railroad, at Blossburg and Towanda in northern Pennsylvania, and at Kittaning and Brady's Bend on the Alleghany river. They

* Lesley—Report on Region. Prof. L. is high authority on coal and iron.

yield a highly bituminous coal, deposited in benches of different constitution and value, some of which furnish a fuel pure enough to be coked and used for smelting iron ore." Prof. Lesley also says: "On Crab Orchard creek is a fine six-foot bed of rather handsome flaming coal, solid enough to wagon over rough roads, and not making much ashes or clinker in the grate. It is at least equal to the general run of the Lower Coal Measure coals in the Bituminous Coal Basins of the Susquehanna West Branch and the Conemaugh." Again of the 6-foot seam in Wise county: "At one place, where the bed has been dug a little into, it yields the best kind of bituminous coal, fat and caking, but friable, with no appearance of sulphur and making no clinker. It is good blacksmith coal, and no doubt will make good coke. A piece of ill-made coke from what is, perhaps, the same bed, near Gladesville, shows that the best coke can be got from it." There are four or five good seams of coal, well known in the Lower Measures—these are all accessible along the east border of this field. Going northwestwardly, through Buchanan and Wise, the section would cross the *Lower* Coal Measures and enter the *Middle* series, which is so well developed where cut through by New river and its continuation—the Great Kanawha in West Virginia. This series, with its 30 to 50 feet of workable thickness of *gas, shop, splint, cannel*, and other varieties of coal, will, no doubt, be found as complete in Virginia territory as it has been in the adjacent portions of Kentucky and West Virginia. So Virginia has a most valuable bituminous coal field, favorably situated, and that can yield her millions of tons of the best of these coals.

The mineral resources of the State may be summed up as consisting—

IN TIDEWATER—of several kinds of marls, greensand, &c., highly esteemed as fertilizers; of choice clays, sands and shell-limestones, for building purposes.

IN MIDDLE—of fine granites, gneiss, brownstone, sandstone, brick-clays, fire-clays, soapstones, marble, slates, &c., for building materials; epidote in various forms and limestone for fertilizing uses; gold, silver, copper; specular, magnetic, hematite and other ores of iron in abundance; bituminous coal, &c.

IN PIEDMONT—granitic building stones, marbles, sandstones, brick and fire clays; epidotic rocks and limestone, for improving the soil; magnetic, hematite and other ores of iron; barytes, lead, manganese, &c.

IN THE BLUE RIDGE—various and abundant ores of copper; immense deposits of specular and brown hematite and other iron ores; greenstone rocks, rich in all the elements of fertility; sandstones and freestones; glass sand and manganese; brick and fire-clays.

IN THE VALLEY—limestones of all kinds, for building and agricultural uses; marbles, slates, freestones and sandstones; brick and fire-clays, kaolin, barytes; hematite iron ores, lead and zinc in abundance; semi-anthracite coal, travertine marls, &c.

IN APPALACHIA—limestones, marbles, sand and freestones; slates, calcareous marls, brick clays, &c.; various deposits of red, brown and other ores of iron, plaster, salt, &c., and a large area of all varieties of bituminous coal.

In conclusion, it may truthfully be stated, that in the *abundance and variety* of building stones and mineral building materials; of fertilizing minerals; of the ores of the most useful metals and of mineral fuel, Virginia occupies the front rank.

Virginia is so situated in respect to the Great Appalachian Coal Field that fronts her entire western border, in West Virginia, as to command all the advantages of cheap fuel of excellent quality, offered by that vast deposit of bituminous coal; her railways and canals can place it beside her ores at prices that will enable the manufacturer to defy competition in the production of iron. The geological map presents this fact very forcibly.

## CHAPTER III.

### THE CLIMATE OF VIRGINIA.

Man is so dependent, in all the essentials of his existence, upon the climatic conditions of the country he inhabits, a knowledge of the phenomena of climate is of the utmost importance. The length and safety of a voyage to or from any country; the cultivation of crops, not only in the questions of seed-time and harvest, but also the selection of kinds; the returns that may be looked for in the agricultural operations of a series of years; the conditions of health; the precautions necessary to guard against sickness and the destruction of the fruits of industry—all these, and many other things that affect human comfort and happiness, depend on the character of the meteorology of the region inhabited.

Virginia, as a whole, lies in the region of "middle latitudes," between 36° 30′ and 39° 30′ north, giving it a climate of "*means*" between the extremes of heat and cold incident to States south and north of it.

If Virginia were a plain, the general character of the climate of the whole State would be much the same; but the "*relief*" of its surface varies from that of some of its large peninsulas not more than 10 or 15 feet above the sea-level, to that of large valleys more than 2,000 feet above that level. Long ranges of mountains, from 3,000 to 4,000 feet in height, run entirely across the State, and the waters flow to all points of the compass. So diversified are the features of the surface of the State, within its borders may be found all possible exposures to the sun and general atmospheric movements. It follows, from these circumstances, that here must be found great variety of temperature, winds, moisture, rain and snow-fall, beginning and ending of seasons, and all the periodical phenomena of vegetable and animal life depending on "the weather."

*The winds* are the great agents nature employs to equalize and distribute temperature, moisture, &c. Virginia lies on the eastern side of the American Continent, and on the western shore of the Atlantic ocean; it extends to and embraces many of the ranges of the Appalachian system of mountains that run parallel to that ocean shore; therefore it is subject not only to the *general movement* of winds, storms, &c., *from west to east*, peculiar to the region of the United States, but to modifications of that movement by the great mountain ranges; it is also subject to the great atmospheric *movements from the Atlantic* that, with a rotary motion, come up from the tropics and move along the coast, extending their influence over the Tidewater and Middle regions of the State, *sometimes* across Piedmont *to* the foot of the Blue Ridge, but rarely ever over or beyond that range; it has also *surface winds*, usually from the southwest, that follow the trend of the mountains, and bring to them and their enclosed parallel valleys the warmth and moisture of the Gulf that clothes them all with an abundant vegetation.

The same causes that produced the magnificent forests of the Carboniferous Era, and furnished the materials for the vast deposits of coal in the 60,000 square miles of the great Appalachian Coal Field that flanks Virginia on the west, still operate and clothe the surface of the same region with an abundant vegetation. The laws of the winds make one region fertile and another barren. America owes its distinction as the Forest Continent* to the situation of its land masses in reference to the prevailing winds.

TEMPERATURE is the fundamental phenomenon of climate. †"The distribution of heat is the controlling influence of all climates." "The knowledge of the extremes of heat and cold at any one point, in any one year, is of the greatest importance. An extremely hot week, or even a hot day, has a very marked effect on human life; an extremely cold day or week is equally destructive."

In the State of New Jersey‡ it has been noted that the difference of 3 or 4 degrees of *mean spring temperature* found between the northern and southern portions of that State, makes a difference of from 10 to 14 days in the ripening of strawberries; and a similar difference of *mean summer temperature* enables the farmer, in the southern part of the same State, to grow profitably and successfully sweet potatoes, melons and other sub-tropical products that will not ripen in the northern part.

§The following table presents the *maximum*, the *minimum*, and the *mean*, for each month of two years, from the Spring of 1869 inclusive, to that of 1871, for ten stations, in different divisions of the State, grouped in *seasons*, with the *means* for the seasons and the years. The stations are selected so that, as far as possible, they may be representative ones for each section of the State. No observations are recorded from the Blue Ridge or from Appalachia, consequently we have no stations there. These *highest* and *lowest* indications of the thermometer (Fahrenheit's), show the extremes of the temperature, but the *means* of the seasons furnish the data for arriving at conclusions as to the adaptability of the climate for different productions, &c. The observations were made at 7 A. M., 2 and 9 P. M. of each day.

* Guyot.

† Statistical Atlas of the United States.

‡ Geology of New Jersey, 1868.

§ The meteorological tables of the Smithsonian Institution are the authority in preparing this article. The world is largely indebted to Prof. Henry for contributions to the meteorological science of the country; his labors have made possible the valuable "Probabilities" of the weather of the United States Signal Service, the "certainties" of which are so highly valued by all.

# TABLE I.

## Maximum, Minimum and Mean Temperature of Virginia, by Seasons.

| TIMES | | TIDEWATER. | | | | | | | | | | | | MIDDLE. | | | PIEDMONT. | | | | | | VALLEY. | | | | | | | | |
|---|---|---|---|---|---|---|---|---|---|---|---|---|---|---|---|---|---|---|---|---|---|---|---|---|---|---|---|---|---|---|---|
| | | JOHNSONTOWN. | | | HAMPTON. | | | BACON'S CASTLE. | | | COMORN. | | | VIENNA. | | | PIEDMONT S'N. | | | LYNCHBURG. | | | STAUNTON. | | | LEXINGTON. | | | WYTHEVILLE. | | |
| | | Maximum. | Minimum. | Mean. | Maximum. | Minimum. | Mean. | Maximum. | Minimum. | Mean. | Maximum. | Minimum. | Mean. | Maximum. | Minimum. | Mean. | Maximum. | Minimum | Mean. | Maximum. | Minimum. | Mean. | Maximum. | Minimum. | Mean. | Maximum. | Minimum. | Mean. | Maximum. | Minimum. | Mean. |
| SPRING. | Mar.—1869.. | 67 | 18 | 43.2 | 68 | 18 | 44.0 | 75 | 19 | 46.9 | 73 | 17 | 45.0 | .... | .... | ...... | .... | .... | ...... | 67 | 18 | 47.6 | 67 | 14 | 40.7 | 73 | 17 | 45.0 | ‡76 | —1 | 40.6 |
| | April....... | 80 | 35 | 54.1 | 66 | 33 | 56.1 | 91 | 36 | 53.6 | 87 | 32 | 56.7 | .... | .... | ...... | .... | .... | ...... | 77 | 32 | 55.7 | 79 | 29 | 51.8 | 87 | 32 | 56.7 | 80 | 26 | 55.5 |
| | May........ | 87 | 47 | 56.8 | 96 | 47 | 63.8 | 96 | 47 | 65.8 | 92 | 43 | 62.6 | .... | .... | ...... | .... | .... | ...... | 84 | 46 | 59.9 | 84 | 39 | 60.5 | 92 | 43 | 62.6 | 85 | 41 | 58.9 |
| Means......... | | .... | .... | 51.4 | .... | .... | 54.6 | .... | .... | 57.1 | .... | .... | 53.8 | .... | .... | ...... | .... | .... | ...... | .... | .... | 54.3 | .... | .... | 51.0 | .... | .... | 54.8 | .... | .... | 51.7 |
| SUMMER. | June...... | 91 | 57 | 73.8 | 94 | 60 | 76.6 | 100 | 60 | 79.8 | 96 | 52 | 73.9 | .... | .... | ...... | .... | .... | ...... | 88 | 55 | 73.2 | 90 | 58 | 72.2 | 96 | 52 | 73.9 | 87 | 51 | 68.9 |
| | July...... | 94 | 64 | 76.9 | 99 | 65 | 80.0 | 104 | 66 | 82.9 | 101 | 62 | 79.0 | .... | .... | ...... | .... | .... | ...... | 92 | 63 | 77.6 | 93 | 60 | 75.8 | 101 | 62 | 79.0 | 92 | 54 | 72.5 |
| | August ... | 95 | 59 | 75.2 | 98 | 62 | 77.5 | 100 | 64 | 81.0 | 104 | 56 | 78.4 | .... | .... | ...... | .... | .... | ...... | 95 | 56 | 77.5 | 92 | 58 | 75.0 | 104 | 56 | 78.4 | 95 | 49 | 73.1 |
| Means ... ..... | | .... | .... | 75.3 | .... | .... | 78.1 | .... | .... | 81.2 | .... | .... | 76.7 | .... | .... | ...... | .... | .... | ...... | .... | .... | 76.1 | .... | .... | 74.3 | .... | .... | 77.1 | .... | .... | 71.5 |
| AUTUMN. | Sept...... | 90 | 50 | 69.6 | 92 | 46 | 70.5 | *90 | 44 | 69.2 | 86 | 53 | 70.2 | 66 | 42 | 68.8 | .... | .... | ...... | 82 | 45 | 66.5 | 82 | 44 | 64.1 | 90 | 41 | 67.4 | 82 | 36 | 61.5 |
| | Oct. ...... | 82 | 36 | 54.8 | 78 | 34 | 55.2 | 80 | 33 | 54.6 | 77 | 33 | 52.6 | 77 | 34 | 52.3 | .... | .... | ...... | 69 | 33 | 53.7 | 69 | 30 | 48.1 | 73 | 31 | 52.3 | 68 | 25 | 47.1 |
| | Nov....... | 64 | 27 | 43.4 | 64 | 27 | 43.5 | 66 | 26 | 42.1 | 65 | 28 | 41.7 | 66 | 27 | 41.2 | 62 | 22 | 38.5 | 61 | 29 | 43.4 | 63 | 28 | 40.2 | 70 | 20 | 40.8 | 65 | 18 | 36.3 |
| Means......... | | .... | .... | 55.9 | .... | .... | 56.4 | .... | .... | 55.3 | .... | .... | 54.8 | .... | .... | 54.1 | .... | .... | ...... | .... | .... | 54.5 | .... | .... | 50.8 | .... | .... | 53.5 | .... | .... | 48.3 |
| WINTER. | Dec....... | 60 | 23 | 43.4 | 61 | 24 | 42.5 | 63 | 24 | 44.4 | 68 | 23 | 39.8 | 57 | 25 | 38.5 | 64 | 18 | 35.8 | 58 | 27 | 41.2 | 56 | 21 | 37.4 | 60 | 16 | 39.1 | 53 | 13 | 34.0 |
| | Jan.—1870. | 66 | 23 | 45.7 | 70 | 22 | 45.8 | 71 | 22 | 47.1 | 72 | 16 | 42.5 | 69 | 14 | 41.0 | 70 | 10 | 36.1 | 66 | 18 | 44.8 | 66 | 18 | 41.5 | 74 | 13 | 43.0 | 60 | 6 | 37.3 |
| | Feb....... | 60 | 17 | 39.7 | 65 | 16 | 41.5 | 69 | 18 | 42.2 | 60 | 14 | 37.1 | 55 | 8 | 36.0 | 56 | 1 | 30.7 | 55 | 17 | 40.4 | 57 | 11 | 36.1 | 70 | 0 | 40.0 | 54 | 5 | 34.7 |
| Means......... | | .... | .... | 42.9 | .... | .... | 43.3 | .... | .... | 44.6 | .... | .... | 39.8 | .... | .... | 38.5 | .... | .... | 34.2 | .... | .... | 42.1 | .... | .... | 38.3 | .... | .... | 40.7 | .... | .... | 35.3 |

| | | | | | | | | | | | | | | | | | | | | | | | | | | | | | | | |
|---|---|---|---|---|---|---|---|---|---|---|---|---|---|---|---|---|---|---|---|---|---|---|---|---|---|---|---|---|---|---|---|
| SPRING. | Mar. ...... | 61 | 28 | 43.5 | 66 | 28 | 43.3 | 64 | 26 | 44.1 | 64 | 27 | 42.2 | 67 | 23 | 40.3 | 67 | 16 | 39.2 | 64 | 30 | 44.2 | 60 | 19 | 39.1 | 71 | 19 | 43.1 | 60 | 10 | 37.3 |
| | April...... | 78 | 36 | 52.9 | 84 | 38 | 55.1 | 84 | 40 | 56.6 | 83 | 35 | 55.3 | 86 | 36 | 54.8 | 91 | 32 | 52.4 | 82 | 39 | 55.9 | 80 | 34 | 52.7 | 86 | 38 | 55.7 | 80 | 36 | 52.5 |
| | May...... | 81 | 52 | 63.7 | 90 | 52 | 66.0 | 88 | 48 | 67.2 | 82 | 52 | 65.5 | 86 | 48 | 67.6 | 85 | 42 | 63.4 | 83 | 48 | 66.6 | 81 | 49 | 62.7 | 91 | 48 | 66.1 | 84 | 40 | 61.5 |
| Means ........ | | .... | .... | 53.4 | .... | .... | 54.8 | .... | .... | 56.0 | .... | .... | 54.3 | .... | .... | 54.2 | .... | .... | 51.7 | .... | .... | 55.6 | .... | .... | 51.5 | .... | .... | 55.0 | .... | .... | 50.4 |
| SUMMER. | June...... | 94 | 58 | 74.6 | 98 | 64 | 76.5 | 98 | 64 | 78.5 | 92 | 64 | 76.0 | 91 | 60 | 73.6 | 94 | 58 | 72.9 | 90 | 58 | 73.4 | 89 | 56 | 71.8 | 99 | 58 | 74.5 | 86 | 56 | 68.0 |
| | July ...... | 94 | 67 | 79.5 | 100 | 67 | 81.4 | 98 | 72 | 83.1 | 94 | 66 | 79.7 | 93 | 63 | 77.4 | 95 | 62 | 76.6 | 91 | 66 | 78.5 | 89 | 64 | 75.1 | 99 | 66 | 79.5 | 86 | 57 | 74.1 |
| | August ... | 95 | 64 | 77.7 | 98 | 64 | 79.0 | 100† | 65 | 81.9 | 90 | 64 | 78.2 | 90 | 57 | 75.1 | 93 | 60 | 74.7 | 90 | 64 | 76.3 | 87 | 61 | 72.4 | 98 | 60 | 77.2 | 84 | 62 | 72.3 |
| Means ........ | | .... | .... | 77.3 | ... | .... | 79.0 | .... | .... | 81.2 | .... | .... | 78.0 | .... | .... | 75.4 | .... | .... | 74.7 | .... | .... | 76.1 | .... | .... | 73.1 | .... | .... | 77.1 | .... | .... | 71.4 |
| AUTUMN. | Sept...... | 85 | 56 | 71.0 | 86 | 56 | 71.7 | 91 | 53 | 73.1 | 86 | 54 | 71.3 | 78 | 58 | 69.7 | 86 | 50 | 66.9 | 82 | 53 | 69.8 | 78 | 47 | 64.3 | 85 | 50 | 66.8 | 80 | 45 | 64.2 |
| | Oct. ...... | 80 | 42 | 61.9 | 82 | 45 | 62.3 | 90 | 39 | 63.2 | 82 | 47 | 62.7 | 71 | 43 | 57.0 | 78 | 34 | 56.0 | 76 | 44 | 60.5 | 73 | 39 | 55.0 | 78 | 34 | 54.8 | 71 | 34 | 54.3 |
| | Nov...... | 76 | 28 | 50.0 | 72 | 25 | 49.9 | 78 | 20 | 49.4 | 71 | 31 | 49.2 | 69 | 32 | 46.8 | 69 | 20 | 41.8 | 68 | 31 | 49.2 | 66 | 29 | 41.9 | 66 | 18 | 41.3 | 66 | 20 | 41.9 |
| Means ........ | | .... | .... | 61.0 | .... | .... | 61.3 | .... | .... | 61.9 | .... | .... | 60.7 | .... | .... | 57.8 | .... | .... | 54.9 | .... | .... | 59.8 | .... | .... | 54.7 | .... | .... | 54.3 | .... | .... | 53.5 |
| WINTER. | Dec. ...... | 66 | 9 | 38.7 | 65 | 6 | 38.7 | 71 | —4 | 38.2 | 61 | 6 | 35.9 | 59 | 8 | 34.8 | 64 | 2 | 32.3 | 62 | 9 | 38.1 | 60 | 5 | 32.3 | 65 | —2 | 31.2 | 60 | —4 | 31.4 |
| | Jan.—1871. | 64 | 18 | 38.2 | 64 | 18 | 38.6 | .... | .... | ...... | 66 | 14 | 35.3 | 65 | 12 | 37.3 | 69 | 8 | 32.4 | 62 | 20 | 40.4 | 60 | 21 | 35.7 | .... | .... | ...... | 62 | 17 | 35.7 |
| | Feb. ...... | 74 | 16 | 41.8 | 78 | 16 | 44.3 | 74 | 12 | 44.4 | 66 | 13 | 38.3 | 69 | 12 | 37.5 | 70 | 6 | 36.0 | 63 | 20 | 42.9 | 69 | 10 | 39.2 | 64 | —3 | 37.5 | 60 | 14 | 40.5 |
| Means ........ | | .... | .... | 39.6 | .... | .... | 40.5 | .... | .... | ...... | .... | .... | 36.5 | .... | .... | 36.5 | .... | .... | 33.6 | .... | .... | 40.5 | .... | .... | 35.7 | .... | .... | ...... | .... | .... | 35.9 |
| YEARLY MEANS. | 1869-'70.... | .... | .... | 56.4 | .... | .... | 58.1 | .... | .... | 59.5 | .... | .... | 56.3 | .... | .... | ...... | .... | .... | ...... | .... | .... | 56.7 | .... | .... | 53.6 | .... | .... | 56.5 | .... | .... | 51.7 |
| | 1870-'71.... | .... | .... | 57.8 | .... | .... | 58.9 | .... | .... | ...... | .... | .... | 57.4 | .... | .... | 55.9 | .... | .... | 53.7 | .... | .... | 58.0 | .... | .... | 53.7 | .... | .... | ...... | .... | .... | 52.8 |

* Zuni substituted—Bacon's Castle wanting.

† Surry Courthouse substituted for rest of table.

‡ Near Wytheville for March.

The Tidewater stations are, probably, none of them as much as 100* feet above the sea. JOHNSONTOWN is in Northampton county, on the "Eastern Shore" peninsula, and gives the conditions for that almost insular region, where the influence of the ocean is most felt in preserving a mean temperature and equalizing the seasons. The *extremes* and *average* temperature are decidedly less than at the other stations—even much less than at Hampton, on the opposite side of the Bay, but more inland. HAMPTON, in Elizabeth City county, is open to the sea on one side only; it gives the type of climate for the interior or bay-coast line; its *extremes* and *means* are greater than those of Johnsontown. BACON'S CASTLE in Surry and ZUNI in Isle of Wight county, stations not far apart, give the representative climate for the midland of Tidewater, especially for the Southside peninsula, where the season temperatures are greater than in any other portions of the State, making this the cotton belt. COMORN, in King George county, is still farther from the sea; it represents the western portion of the Tidewater plain, as Hampton does the eastern: and, of course, has greater *extremes* and lower *means*. Taking the averages for the year 1869–'70 at these Tidewater stations; that is—

| | |
|---|---|
| Johnsontown | 56°.4 |
| Hampton | 58 .1 |
| Bacon's Castle, &c. | 59 .5 |
| Comorn | 56 .3 |
| Average | 57°.6 |

We have 57°.6 as the mean temperature of that year. VIENNA, in Fairfax county, compared with Comorn, shows how small the differences of temperature are between western Tidewater and eastern Middle Virginia; Vienna is probably some 350 to 400 feet higher than Comorn above the sea, and, by the rule that each 333 feet of difference in elevation diminishes the temperature one degree for the higher place, we find that Vienna has, generally, this element lower than Comorn. LYNCHBURG, in Campbell county, though grouped in Piedmont, is the representative of the higher western portion of the Middle country, as it is 575 feet above tide; it is far inland, and its *means* are higher than those of Vienna. PIEDMONT STATION, in Fauquier county, some 650 or 700 feet above the sea, shows the temperature of northeastern Piedmont; its lower season *means* indicate the more elevated country and the proximity of the mountains. STAUNTON is 1,400 feet above the sea, in a valley bounded on each side by high mountain ranges, the western the higher, and the *means* and *extremes* of its temperature are those peculiar to the central portions of the Great Valley; the spring and summer *means* approximate, remarkably, those of Johnsontown by the seashore; those of autumn differ more, but they are more alike again in winter. LEXINGTON is not as elevated as Staunton; it represents the depressed portion of the Valley near the "troughs" of the rivers and the water-gaps of the Blue Ridge; its *means* are greater than those of Staunton, but it offers the same resemblances. WYTHEVILLE is 2,300 feet above the sea, and fairly typifies the elevated southwest of the Valley and Appalachia; its summer temperature is lower than that of the other meteorological stations, so are also its yearly means—results due not only to

*The elevations given are those of the stations of observations, as near as can be ascertained.

its elevation, but also to its interior location and the lofty character of the enclosing mountain ranges.

In the following table the Season Means of Table I. are brought together:

*TABLE II.—Mean Temperatures of Virginia for Two Years, by Seasons.*

| | TIDEWATER. | | | | MID. | MID. & PIED. | | VALLEY. | | |
|---|---|---|---|---|---|---|---|---|---|---|
| | Johnsontown. | Hampton. | Bacon's Castle. | Comorn. | Vienna. | Lynchburg. | Piedmont S'n. | Staunton. | Lexington. | Wytheville. |
| 1869-'70.—Spring ......... | 51.4 | 54.6 | 57.1 | 53.8 | ...... | 54.3 | ...... | 51.0 | 54.8 | 51.7 |
| Summer....... | 75.3 | 78.1 | 81.2 | 76.7 | ...... | 76.1 | ...... | 74.3 | 77.1 | 71.5 |
| Autumn....... | 55.9 | 56.4 | 55.3 | 54.8 | 54.1 | 54.5 | ...... | 50.8 | 53.5 | 48.3 |
| Winter... ..... | 42.9 | 43.3 | 44.6 | 39.8 | 38.5 | 42.1 | 34.2 | 38.3 | 40.7 | 35.3 |
| Yearly Means......... | 56.4 | 58.1 | 59.5 | 56.3 | ...... | 56.7 | ...... | 53.6 | 56.5 | 51.7 |
| 1870-'71.—Spring ......... | 53.4 | 54.8 | 56.0 | 54.3 | 54.2 | 55.6 | 51.7 | 51.5 | 55.0 | 50.4 |
| Summer....... | 77.3 | 79.0 | 81.2 | 78.0 | 75.4 | 76.1 | 74.7 | 73.1 | 77.1 | 71.4 |
| Autumn....... | 61.0 | 61.3 | 61.9 | 60.7 | 57.8 | 59.8 | 54.9 | 54.7 | 54.3 | 53.5 |
| Winter......... | 39.6 | 40.5 | ...... | 36.5 | 36.5 | 40.5 | 33.6 | 35.7 | ...... | 35.9 |
| Yearly Means......... | 57.8 | 58.9 | ...... | 57.4 | 55.9 | 58.0 | 53.7 | 53.7 | ...... | 55.8 |

The mean temperature of the State, deduced from the above, was 56°.1 in 1869-'70, and 56° in 1870-'71.

The years 1869-'70 were selected for these tables, because they include the year for which and that in which the census of 1870 was taken, and the results of that census are used for various purposes in these pages. The census was taken June 1st, 1870—therefore its "crop" returns must be for the season of 1869.

Guyot, in the "Map Showing the Distribution of the Temperature of the Air and the Course of the Annual Isothermal Lines," in his recently issued Physical Geography, locates Virginia between the curves of 50° and 60° of mean annual temperature (the result reached by the tables already given), the belt that includes Cincinnati, St. Louis and San Francisco in the United States, the south of England and Ireland, the whole of France, the most of Portugal, Spain and Italy, the valley of the Danube, including Vienna, Constantinople and most of Turkey, in Europe; Pekin and the Hoangho Valley in China, and the island of Yeddo in Japan, in Asia.

The Statistical Atlas of the United States, published by the authority of Congress, has a Temperature Chart, Plate VII., "Showing the distribution by Isothermal Lines of the Mean Temperature for the year," constructed under the direction of Professor Henry, of the Smithsonian Institution, one of the ablest living meteorologists.

This chart shows that the *isotherm*, or mean annual temperature line of 60°, runs through Eastville on the Eastern Shore, and then southwest by Hicksford to Montgomery in Alabama. All the region to the southeast of this line in Virginia has a mean annual temperature between 60° and 64°. This is the cotton producing zone; it includes nearly half of North and South Carolina, much of Georgia, &c.

The line of 56° enters the United States through the mouth of Delaware bay, runs by a south curving line west to and through Washington, then southwest between Middle and Piedmont Virginia, passing west of Danville, on to Atlanta in Georgia. All the country between this line of 56° and that of 60°, before described, is the belt of 56° to 60° of mean annual temperature. In this zone tobacco is a prominent staple.

The isothermal curve of 52° enters the United States about midway of New Jersey, south of the latitude of New York, then runs west by Trenton to the Cumberland Valley of Pennsylvania, then curving southward through Cumberland in Maryland and Staunton in the Shenandoah Valley, crossing the Blue Ridge in Augusta county, it passes along the eastern foot of the Blue Ridge into Georgia, where it curves to the northwest, and returns and runs along the eastern side of the Great Central Valley in Tennessee; continuing northeast, its course is along the western side of the Great Valley of Virginia to the vicinity of the James, where it bears more to the west and runs north to the Potomac near New Creek in Maryland, whence by boldly curved lines it extends westward through the central portions of Ohio, Indiana, Illinois, &c. So the zone of mean temperature of from 52° to 56° embraces all of Piedmont, the less elevated portions of the Valley and much of Appalachia—especially the southwestern portion of it. It includes much of the grass and small grain country.

A narrow belt of the elevated portions of the State is in the zone of 48° to 52°—the one that includes East Massachusetts, all of Rhode Island and Connecticut, much of New York, New Jersey, Pennsylvania, Ohio, &c. It is the grazing region especially.

The scale of this map is so small, its delineations can only be accepted for general results; these would locate—

Tidewater in the zones of 60° to 64° and 56° to 60°;

Middle in the zones of 56° to 60° and 52° to 56°;

Piedmont in the zone of 52° to 56°;

The Valley in the zones of 52° to 56° and 48° to 52°; and

Appalachia in the zones of 48° to 52° and 52 to 56°.

All these facts present the temperature of Virginia in a most favorable light, and show its perfect adaptedness to the growth of the productions of both the cool and the warm-temperate climates of the earth—it has the *medium means*.

The *average temperatures of January and July*—the representative months of winter and summer—are often taken as guides for determining the character of the temperature of any given locality. The following table gives these averages for a number of places in all parts of the historic world, compared with those of the selected stations in Virginia, furnishing the data for selecting a situation for any specified *mean* of this most important climatic element:

*TABLE III.—Average Winter and Summer Temperature of Places, as Determined by the Averages of January and July.*

| IN VIRGINIA.—1870. | JAN. | JULY. | IN UNITED STATES. | JAN. | JULY. | IN EUROPE. | JAN. | JULY. | IN ASIA, AUSTRALIA. | JAN. | JULY. |
|---|---|---|---|---|---|---|---|---|---|---|---|
| Johnsontown | 45° | 79° | Oregon City | 40° | 72° | Edinburg | 36° | 58° | Smyrna | 53° | 82° |
| Hampton | 45 | 81 | San Francisco | 50 | 58 | Dublin | 38 | 61 | Jerusalem | 48 | 77 |
| Bacon's Castle | 47 | 83 | Salt Lake City | 27 | 81 | London | 37 | 65 | Delhi | 54 | 84 |
| Comorn | 42 | 79 | St. Paul, Minn. | 14 | 73 | Paris | 38 | 66 | Calcutta | 69 | 85 |
| Vienna | 41 | 77 | St. Louis | 33 | 77 | Madrid | 45 | 76 | Canton | 52 | 83 |
| Piedmont Station | 36 | 76 | New Orleans | 54 | 80 | Brussels | 35 | 64 | Sydney* | 72 | 50 |
| Lynchburg | 44 | 78 | Cincinnati | 33 | 76 | Berlin | 18 | 68 | Melbourne* | 65 | 48 |
| Staunton | 41 | 75 | Charleston, S. C. | 48 | 80 | Vienna | 29 | 71 | Hobart Town* | 62 | 44 |
| Lexington | 43 | 79 | Washington, D. C. | 34 | 78 | Rome | 46 | 76 | Auckland* | 68 | 49 |
| Wytheville | 37 | 74 | New York | 30 | 75 | Constantinople | 41 | 74 | Peking | 25 | 81 |
| Fairfax Courthouse | 38 | 82 | Boston | 25 | 72 | Odessa | 26 | 73 | Shanghai | 40 | 83 |
| | | | Eastport, Maine | 22 | 62 | St. Petersburg | 16 | 63 | Manila | 77 | 80 |
| | | | Fort Snelling | 13 | 73 | Moscow | 14 | 76 | | | |
| | | | Natchez | 52 | 81 | Stockholm | 24 | 64 | | | |
| | | | IN N. A. | | | Bergen | 35 | 60 | | | |
| | | | Montreal | 15 | 73 | Cairo, Egypt | 56 | 86 | | | |
| | | | Havana | 65 | 85 | | | | | | |
| | | | Bermudas | 32 | 84 | | | | | | |

* These are in South Latitude, so seasons are opposite.

The averages of Virginia are from Smithsonian observations; the others from Guyot's Physical Geography.

It is not a perfectly fair comparison to take the *means* of one year and compare them with the average of a number of years; still the results are approximate, and are the best that can now be had.

These tables of temperature suggest the *possibilities* of production in Virginia, and show that it has a wide range of *annual* temperatures from which selections may be made.

The United States Signal Service contributed to the atlas before mentioned a chart "showing the mean temperature at 4.35 P. M. of the hottest week of 1872, and at 7.35 A. M. of the coldest week of 1872 and 1873," compiled from the abundant data of that most important office. On this chart the mean of 90° occupies the same position as the isotherm of 60° just described, passing from the Eastern Shore southwest across North and South Carolina, and around, south of the Appalachian system of mountains, and back northeast nearly through Ohio, and on to the west and northwest. A small portion of country near Washington and the Potomac is also in an area of 90°, but some 95 per cent. of the State is between 85° and 90° in the *hottest* week. The curve of mean *cold* for the coldest week was 20°, which passed southwest across Tidewater, and through North Carolina, Tennessee, Alabama, Mississippi, &c. The 10° of cold passed through New York city west, by Wheeling, Cincinnati, into Arkansas. The 0°, or zero, ran through New York, Michigan, Illinois, Missouri, Kansas, &c. These facts also show the medium character of the Virginia climate.

The Rain-fall is next in importance to the temperature in the climate of a country, for heat and moisture are the two great requisites for abundant production when a fertile soil is present.

*Guyot, a standard authority, says: "North America has in the eastern half a greater amount of rain than either of the other northern continents in similar latitudes." * * "The great sub-tropical basin of the Gulf of Mexico sends up into the air its wealth of vapors to replace those lost by the winds in crossing the high mountain chains. Hence the eastern portions—the great basins of the Mississippi and the St. Lawrence and the Appalachian region—which, without this source of moisture, would be doomed to drought and barrenness, *are the most abundantly watered, and the most productive portions of the continent.*" "In the *eastern half* of the United States the southwesterly winds which prevail in the summer spread over the interior *and the Atlantic plains* an abundant supply of vapors from the warm waters of the Gulf. Frequent, copious showers refresh the soil during the months of greatest heat, which show a maximum of rain. *Thus the dry summers of the warm-temperate region disappear*, and with them the periodical character of the rains so well marked elsewhere in this belt."

These quotations show the advantages Virginia has, in this respect, over the warm-temperate regions of Europe and elsewhere.

The "Rain Chart" accompanying the census of 1870, and forming Plate V. of the Statistical Atlas (also by Professor Henry), shows the mean precipitation in rain

---

*Physical Geography.

and melted snow for the year in the United States—the mean average of numerous observations, by isohyetal lines—that is, lines connecting places that have the same average annual rain-fall. Virginia lies mostly in the belt of country where the annual amount of precipitation is from 32 to 44 inches. One curve of 40 inches runs through Washington city, then nearly west to Warrenton and Woodstock, and on to Charleston, West Virginia; another passes eastward from the mouth of the Greenbrier river to Richmond, where, by a bold curve, it turns southwest through Hicksford and on to Greensboro', North Carolina. Parallel to and west of the last named is a curve of 36 inches of fall; another curve, that of 44 inches, lying northeast of the latter and parallel to it, includes a belt of country reaching across the State from Rockingham county to Norfolk. To sum up the results of this chart—

*Tidewater* is in the belt of 32 to 44 inches of *fall, except* the Southside, Richmond, Williamsburg, Pamunkey and Gloucester peninsulas, which are in that of 44 to 56 inches—a strip northwest from the opening of Chesapeake bay.

*Middle* is in the belt of 32 to 44, except the part between the Rappahannock and the Pamunkey, or North Anna, which is in the 44 to 56 inch belt—the extension of the same from Tidewater.

*Piedmont, Blue Ridge* and the *Valley* are all put down in the region of 32 to 44, except that a portion of the belt of 44 to 56, just mentioned, continues across northwest, including Rockingham and part of Augusta counties, to the west side of the Valley.

*Appalachia* is entirely in the district of 32 to 44 inches of deposition—the one in which most of the great Central States of the Union, east of the Mississippi, are situated.

The following table gives the inches of rain and melted snow that fell in Virginia, for the seasons of the period embraced in the temperature table and for the same stations:

| | | Tidewater. | | | | Mid. | Pied. | Valley. | | |
|---|---|---|---|---|---|---|---|---|---|---|
| Seasons, &c. | | Johnsontown. | Hampton. | Zuni. | Comorn. | Vienna. | Piedmont S'n. | Staunton | Lexington. | Wytheville. |
| 1869-'70. | Spring | 8.60 | 9.20 | ..... | 7.59 | ..... | ..... | 10.84 | 12.14 | 8.46 |
| | Summer | 7.85 | 12.60 | ..... | 6.10 | ..... | ..... | 3.75 | 5.15 | 6.20 |
| | Autumn | 7.90 | 6.10 | 10.07 | 12.08 | 10.51 | ..... | 8.04 | 9.99 | 8.50 |
| | Winter | 8.25 | 9.95 | 10.84 | 6.12 | 12.10 | 12.25 | 10.83 | 12.33 | 9.45 |
| Year | | 32.60 | 37.85 | ..... | 31.89 | ..... | ..... | 33.46 | 39.53 | 32.61 |
| 1870-'71. | Spring | 12.78 | .3.50 | 14.81 | 8.03 | 13.90 | 15.90 | 13.47 | 13.41 | 9.40 |
| | Summer | 7.05 | 12.60 | 8.80 | 8.53 | 13.90 | 10.85 | 13.80 | 11.31 | 15.90 |
| | Autumn | 5.60 | 7.50 | 6.97 | 5.28 | 9.50 | 13.65 | 14.93 | 20.52 | 5.65 |
| | Winter | 8.34 | 8.85 | ..... | 4.82 | 10.30 | 7.70 | 8.81 | ..... | 6.60 |
| Year | | 33.77 | 42.45 | ..... | 26.66 | 46.60 | 48.10 | 50.51 | ..... | 37.55 |
| Irregular Year | | ..... | ..... | 37.42 | ..... | ..... | ..... | ..... | ..... | ..... |

The table on next page presents the *monthly precipitation*, the totals of which are embraced in the preceding table.

| SEASONS, &c. | | TIDEWATER. | | | | MID. | PIED. | VALLEY. | | |
|---|---|---|---|---|---|---|---|---|---|---|
| | | Johnsontown. | Hampton. | Zuni. | Comorn. | Vienna. | Piedmont St'n. | Staunton. | Lexington. | Wytheville. |
| SPRING. | March—1869 | 2.60 | 3.00 | .... | 1.95 | .... | .... | 5.06 | 3.78 | 3.15 |
| | April | 1.10 | 1.50 | .... | 2.20 | .... | .... | 1.71 | 3.42 | 1.29 |
| | May | 4.70 | 4.70 | .... | 3.44 | .... | .... | 4.07 | 4.94 | 4.02 |
| | | 8.60 | 9.20 | .... | 7.59 | .... | .... | 10.84 | 12.14 | 8.46 |
| SUMMER. | June | 3.80 | 2.80 | .... | 3.05 | .... | .... | 1.40 | 2.60 | 2.88 |
| | July | 3.85 | 6.30 | .... | 2.44 | .... | .... | 1.70 | 1.02 | 1.38 |
| | August | 0.20 | 3.50 | .... | 0.61 | .... | .... | 0.65 | 1.58 | 1.94 |
| | | 7.85 | 12.60 | .... | 6.10 | .... | .... | 3.75 | 5.15 | 6.20 |
| AUTUMN. | September | 2.20 | 1.10 | 3.68 | 3.29 | 3.71 | .... | 3 84 | 4.73 | 4.20 |
| | October | 3.45 | 3.80 | 4.97 | 6.98 | 5.30 | .... | 3.14 | 3.88 | 2.70 |
| | November | 2.25 | 1.20 | 1.42 | 1.81 | 1.50 | 1.80 | 1.06 | 1.38 | 1.60 |
| | | 7.90 | 6.10 | 10.07 | 12.08 | 10.51 | .... | 8.04 | 9.99 | 8.50 |
| WINTER | December | 2.55 | 3.55 | 4.53 | 2.90 | 7.10 | 6.40 | 5.13 | 5.47 | 4.10 |
| | January—1870 | 2.60 | 3.30 | 3.04 | 1.71 | 2.90 | 3.30 | 3.40 | 4.65 | 2.35 |
| | February | 3.10 | 3.10 | 3.27 | 1.51 | 2.10 | 2.55 | 2.30 | 2.21 | 3.00 |
| | | 8.25 | 9.95 | 10.84 | 6.12 | 12.10 | 12.25 | 10.83 | 12.33 | 9.45 |
| SPRING. | March | 4.08 | 2.70 | 3.61 | 1.78 | 3.70 | 5.35 | 3.66 | 3.50 | 4.30 |
| | April | 3.00 | 5.50 | 3.61 | 2.10 | 5.50 | 5.25 | 3.92 | 4.51 | 2.80 |
| | May | 5.70 | 5.30 | 7.59 | 4.15 | 4.70 | 5.30 | 5.89 | 5.40 | 2.30 |
| | | 12.78 | 13.50 | 14.81 | 8.03 | 13.90 | 15.90 | 13.47 | 13.41 | 9.40 |
| SUMMER. | June | 3.20 | 7.70 | 5.02 | 4.75 | 4.70 | 7.70 | 6.73 | 3.60 | 5.90 |
| | July | 3.40 | 2.55 | 1.78 | 2.97 | 7.70 | 0.80 | 4.33 | 4.56 | 2.50 |
| | August | 0.45 | 2.35 | 2.00 | 0.81 | 1.50 | 2.35 | 2.74 | 3.15 | 7.60 |
| | | 7.05 | 12.60 | 8.80 | 8.53 | 13.90 | 10.85 | 13.80 | 11.31 | 15.90 |
| AUTUMN. | September | 1.05 | 3.70 | 1.68 | 1.25 | 2.20 | 9.55 | 11.24 | 15.88 | 1.30 |
| | October | 2.55 | 2.25 | 2.75 | 3.09 | 5.00 | 2.10 | 2.13 | 2.87 | 2.80 |
| | November | 2.00 | 1.55 | 2.54 | 0.94 | 1.30 | 2.00 | 1.56 | 1.77 | 1.55 |
| | | 5.60 | 7.50 | 6.97 | 5.28 | 8.50 | 13.65 | 14.93 | 20.52 | 5.65 |
| WINTER. | December | 2.15 | 2.50 | 3.80 | 0.99 | 3.40 | 2.30 | 2.05 | 2.04 | 1.40 |
| | January—1871 | 2.19 | 2.60 | .... | 1.49 | 3.70 | 3.00 | 2.81 | .... | 2.35 |
| | February | 4.00 | 3.75 | .... | 2 34 | 3.20 | 2.40 | 3.45 | 4.18 | 2.85 |
| | | 8.34 | 8.85 | .... | 4.82 | 10.30 | 7.70 | 8.31 | .... | 6.60 |

These tables show that the precipitation is well distributed among the seasons and throughout the State, confirming the statement of Professor Guyot, just quoted, in regard to the rains of this portion of the United States.

The amount of rain-fall at Piedmont, Staunton and Lexington in September, 1870, is very many times more than the normal quantity. It was the result of an unprecedented storm that poured out its waters in a flood over a limited area at the sources of the Shenandoah and the James. It will be noted that the spring and winter rains are more abundant than those of fall and summer. Generally the rain-fall is moderate in April and early May, the *planting and sowing* time; in late May and early June more abundant, the *growing* season; less in late June and in July for the *harvest* time; still less in August and September, for thoroughly drying the already cut wheat, and giving it the character so highly prized in the markets, and for maturing Indian corn. The autumn seeding is done in September and October, and the later rains then follow.

Guyot's tables give the mean annual rain-fall of a number of places as follows, in English inches and hundredths, viz: In the United States—Richmond, 38.29; Fortress Monroe, 47.04; Washington city, 41.05; Cincinnati, 44.87; Memphis, 45.46; New York, 44.59. In Europe—Edinburg, 19; London, 19; Paris, 23; Vienna, 18; Berlin, 23; Naples, 31. In Australia—Sydney 83, and Auckland (N. Z.) 48.

The "comments"* on the weather, &c., at the stations selected in Virginia often give a better idea of the actual condition of things than the "means" of tables. Extracts from these will be given for the months taken in the order of the tables:

March, 1869.—At Johnsontown strawberries bloomed the 17th, peaches the 28th; at Hampton, hyacinths 15th, peaches 22d, wild plum 24th; at Bacon's Castle, daisy 8th, plum and peach 23d, Indian corn planted 25th, martins appeared 27th; at Zuni, cloudy but favorable to farmers; at Comorn, colder than January or February, but no thick ice; at Lexington peas planted 4th, potatoes 12th, and oats sown 18th; at Wytheville, cold and wet. Elsewhere in the United States: in Maine sleighing the whole month, temperature below zero on 6 days; in Vermont snow 4 or 5 feet deep, and ice on Connecticut river 2 feet thick on 31st; in New York good sleighing at Buffalo until 22d; in Tennessee snow at Memphis 11th, and rain froze in gauge 15th; in Ohio 5 inches of snow at Kelley's Island 22d; and in Minnesota sleighing at St. Paul until the 23d.

April.—There were hard frosts in Virginia 11th and 15th; at Johnsontown cherry and plum in bloom 6th; at Comorn apple in blossom the 24th; corn-planting at Lexington 25th. Elsewhere: snow left Amherst, Massachusetts, 20th; ice still in Buffalo harbor, New York, 30th, and six snows there during the month; at Toledo, Ohio, four snows, and peaches blossomed the 30th; at Milwaukee, Wisconsin, frost 25th; in Nebraska "grasshoppers by millions" the 7th, and peaches in bloom 28th. Frost in all the Southern States, and snow and ice in the Northern.

May.—At Johnsontown a frost on 9th killed tender vegetables, locust bloomed 13th and *rye 15th;* at Bacon's Castle *peanuts were planted 4th to 14th*, slight frost and hail 3d, *cherries were ripe 26th*; at Comorn locust in bloom 18th, *strawberries ripe 24th;* at Lexington frost 8th and 18th, and at Wytheville several times, but locust bloomed 29th. Elsewhere: Buffalo, New York, ice in harbor 16th, apple in bloom 29th—35 *days later than at Comorn;* mean temperature of spring at Memphis, Tennessee, 58°.05 and rain-fall 16.90 inches; frosts in North Carolina 7th, 8th and 20th; at Kelley's Island, Ohio, peaches bloomed 10th (41 *days after those at Johnsontown*), and apples 24th; at Winnebago, Illinois, cherry flowered 12th (36 *days later than* at Johnsontown); at Dubuque, Iowa, cherry in bloom 9th; at Nebraska city frost 17th; storms and frosts all the month at Milwaukee.

June.—At Bacon's Castle *haying began* 16th, *blackberries were ripe* 27th; *wheat harvest* began at Comorn 21st, Lexington 28th, and Wytheville 23d; clover hay cut at Lexington 21st and strawberries ripe 1st. Elsewhere: no harvesting was done in any of the Northern or Western States, except in Missouri 17th, and some barley in southern Pennsylvania 24th, and southern Indiana 30th; no haying done but in New Jersey 16th, southern Indiana 18th, and Pennsylvania 28th; strawberries were ripe at Buffalo, New York, the 21st (28 days later than at Comorn and 20 later than at Lexington); frosts in Kansas and Nebraska 5th.

---

* In Smithsonian Reports, published by U. S. Department of Agriculture.

July.—The hottest at Hampton in 22 years, and vegetation suffered some, but rains revived it; same remarks apply to Zuni and Bacon's Castle; very dry at Lynchburg, Lexington and Wytheville. Elsewhere: cold and dry in Northern and Northeastern States; wheat harvest began in southern Pennsylvania 2d (11 days later than at Comorn), and in New Jersey 5th; oat harvest began in Pennsylvania 22d; Texas had continuous rains and floods; heavy, cold rains in the West and some frosts; haying in Wisconsin 23d (37 days *later* than at Bacon's Castle); harvest began in Iowa 19th (27 *days later* than at Wytheville).

August was hot and dry in Virginia until the last of the month, when rains came; there was a frost that did no damage, at Lexington, on the 8th, and Wytheville 9th—the same killed corn in Maine, buckwheat in Pennsylvania, and formed ice in Wisconsin, where wheat harvest began 6th (*only* 46 days after Comorn); heavy rains and high waters throughout the West.

September was very dry in Virginia until 25th, with *slight* frosts 28th and 29th at Johnsontown, Zuni, Bacon's Castle, Comorn and Lexington, and heavy at Wytheville; also slight one at Lexington 3d and at Wytheville 2d, 3d and 4th. The frost of the 28th extended over the whole United States north of the latitude of Central Alabama; it froze the ground and formed ice in many parts of the North and West, damaging the corn. At Johnsontown it was 143 days between frosts, and at Monticello, Iowa, 111.

October brought killing frosts at Johnsontown 17th, Hampton 18th, Zuni 16th, Bacon's Castle 14, Comorn and Vienna 25th, Lexington and Lynchburg 14th. At Bacon's Castle it was 188 days between frosts; the first ice formed 27th at Johnsontown, Zuni, Lynchburg and Vienna, and at Bacon's Castle 14th; the first slight snow was 30th in Tidewater, 28th at Vienna and 20th at Wytheville. Elsewhere: eight inches of snow at Buffalo, New York, 25th, killing frost in Mississippi 16th, skating in Michigan 26th and twenty-three inches of snow. Generally reported as the coldest October ever known in the West. Floods numerous, with ice and snow, in the North.

November was calm and cold, but pleasant in Tidewater; the month was unusually cold, with severe snow-storms and loss of life in the Northwest; the farmers in many parts of the North and West did not succeed in getting their potatoes dug, the snow having covered the ground so early.

December did not give a flake of snow at Hampton, and roses were in bloom out of doors at Zuni on New Year's day. The mean temperature at Zuni for 1869 was 58°.54, and the rain-fall 37.78 inches; at Piedmont snow lay on the ground from 18th to 26th; it was cold at Wytheville. Elsewhere it was damp and cloudy, but not very cold. The mean temperature of 1869 at Hillsboro', Central Ohio, was 50°.24 and the rain-fall 38 inches; at Milwaukee, Wisconsin, it was 44°.44 and 37.81 inches, and in December it was 26°.37 and 2.79 inches; at Leavenworth, Kansas, for 1869, the temperature was 50°.35 and the rain 43.35 inches.

January, 1870.—At Johnsontown peaches in flower 31st; at Hampton weeping willow in leaf 31st; at Zuni red maple in bloom 26th; at Bacon's Castle gangs of robins 9th, daisy blooms 21st and alder 24th; at Comorn plowing was done all the month; at Piedmont birds began to sing 12th and plowing commenced 22d; at Lynchburg peas were sown 14th and were up 24th, when potatoes were planted.

A great gale on the 2d, and storm of wind, rain and snow on 16th and 17th, extended over the west—the one of the 2d reached Wytheville as a deep snow; teams crossed the Mississippi on the ice, in Illinois, on the 18th; snow was two feet deep in Minnesota 31st; ice on rivers in Nebraska, fifteen inches thick, 23d; at Leavenworth, Kansas, 16th it was 50° degrees at noon and —1° at 8 P. M., killing peach buds.

FEBRUARY.—At Johnsontown violets in bloom and frogs croaking 17th, and some snow 23d; at Hampton hyacinths in flower 10th, ground froze 9th, frosts 21st and 22d, plowing began again 25th; at Bacon's Castle elms and filberts in blossom 5th; at Comorn plowing done the whole month; at Vienna light snow 8th and 28th, blue birds 3d, wild geese 8th; at Piedmont ground frozen 24th; at Lynchburg snow 7th and 8th, ice 22d, robins 13th, and frogs 26th; at Wytheville wheat looking well, people making maple sugar. Many and deep snows, ice and cold weather in all the Northern and Western States; at Pittsburg, Pennsylvania, ice five inches thick on river last of month; frost and ice even in Florida and Texas 21st, and in New Orleans 18th to 20th. The mean of January at Belvidere, Illinois, 22°.98 and of the winter 22°.66; at Nebraska city ground frozen twenty inches deep on the 18th.

The same comments for the next year, 1870–71, would show nearly the same condition of things. Corn-planting began in Tidewater April 13th, and on the 17th the temperature in Kansas and Nebraska was below freezing all day. Rye "headed" at Johnsontown May 1st and wheat at Piedmont 22d. May was so dry in Texas that water sold for a dollar a barrel at Lavacca, and the drouth extended over all the Northwest. Harvest began at Piedmont June 24th. In Illinois the temperature in some places, in June, was over 100° for a week. Peaches were ripe at Surry court-house July 13th. The average rain-fall for July, for twenty-one years, at Comorn, was 3.88 inches. The mean temperature for July, for sixteen years, at Cleveland, Ohio, 72°.61 and 3.26 inches of rain—this year 10.15 of rain. At Iowa city the *mean temperature* was 84.68 from 13th to 27th of July. At Lawrence, Kansas, it was above 90° on twenty-two days of July, and at Holton, in same State, over 100° on nine days; at Chico, California, every day above 90° and twenty-one over 100°, and much the same at Visalia. The mean for the summer was, at New York 76°.43, Winnebago, Illinois, 72°.56. At Deer Lodge City, Montana, the squirrels went into winter quarters August 10th, and snow came 18th. At Lawrence, Kansas, there was a *heated term* of fifty days, the heat above 90° on forty-six. The first frost in Virginia was at Vienna September 12th, when a killing one was general in the North; there was none at Wytheville until the 21st, and none in Tidewater.

The renowned Captain John Smith, one of the first royal governors of Virginia, sums* up the climate of Tidewater Virginia, the only part he knew, by saying: "The temperature of this country doth agree well with English constitutions, being once seasoned to the country." "The summer is hot as in Spain; the winter cold as in France or England. The heat of summer is in June, July and August, but commonly the cool breezes assuage the vehemency of the heat. The chief of winter is half December, January, February and half March. The cold is extreme sharp, but here the proverb is true, that '*no extreme long continueth.*' From the southwest came the greatest gusts, with thunder and heat. The northwest wind is

---

*History of Virginia, vol. 1, p. 113.

commonly cool and bringeth fair weather with it. From the north is the greatest cold, and from the east and southeast, as from the Bermudas, fogs and rains."

Thomas Jefferson, President of the United States, whose residence was on Monticello, in the Southwest Mountain range, the barrier between Middle and Piedmont Virginia, made the following observations* after giving this table of the winds:

| | N. E. | S. E. | S. W. | N. W. | Total. |
|---|---|---|---|---|---|
| Williamsburg | 127 | 61 | 132 | 101 | 421 |
| Monticello | 32 | 91 | 126 | 172 | 421 |

"By this it may be seen that the southwest wind prevails equally at both places, that the northeast is, next to this, the principal wind towards the sea coast, and the northwest is the predominant wind at the mountains. The difference between these two winds to sensation, and in fact, is very great. The northeast is loaded with vapor, insomuch that the salt makers have found that their crystals would not shoot while that blows; it brings a distressing chill, is heavy and oppressive to the spirits: the northwest is dry, cooling, elastic and animating. The eastern and southeastern breezes come on generally in the afternoon." The more extended observations that have been quoted can be studied to advantage aided by these comments.

The direction from which the winds† at Staunton blew for a year, from October, 1868, were as follows:

| WIND—FROM | 7 A. M. | 2 P. M. | 9 P. M. | Total. |
|---|---|---|---|---|
| North | 10 | 19 | 19 | 48 |
| Northwest | 21 | 31 | 23 | 75 |
| East | 8 | 14 | 15 | 37 |
| Southeast | 128 | 76 | 77 | 281 |
| South | 32 | 28 | 22 | 82 |
| Southwest | 63 | 92 | 83 | 238 |
| West | 11 | 24 | 21 | 56 |
| Northwest | 102 | 79 | 90 | 271 |

This table shows that the prevailing winds are from the "*south quadrants.*" It is more than likely, from the location of the place of observation, that southwest winds were often changed to southeast by the near high hills.

* Notes on Virginia. † MS. records of D. D. & B. Inst.

The direction of the winds* for the year 1857, at a number of places in Virginia, was as follows, viz:

| | TIDEWATER. | | | MIDDLE. | | PIED. | VAL. | AP. |
|---|---|---|---|---|---|---|---|---|
| | Portsmouth. | Smithfield. | Rose Hill. | Alexandria. | Crichton's Store. | Rougemont. | Berryville. | Wirt C. H. |
| From North | 131 | 101 | 89 | 113 | 251 | 84 | 86 | 13 |
| From between North and East | 192 | 118 | 134 | 169 | 55 | 44 | 88 | 42 |
| From East | 56 | 95 | 54 | 33 | 34 | 80 | 56 | 2 |
| From between East and South | 95 | 62 | 77 | 71 | 29 | 14 | 101 | 98 |
| From South | 81 | 184 | 84 | 235 | 163 | 267 | 130 | 25 |
| From between South and West | 228 | 160 | 182 | 99 | 325 | 118 | 169 | 375 |
| From West | 100 | 112 | 66 | 72 | 117 | 223 | 195 | 9 |
| From between West and North | 207 | 112 | 76 | 271 | 77 | 70 | 205 | 260 |
| Calm or Variable | 1 | 0 | 158 | 2 | 20 | 45 | 33 | 202 |
| TOTALS | 1,091 | 944 | 920 | 1,065 | 1,071 | 945 | 1,063 | 1,026 |

Portsmouth is in Norfolk, Smithfield in Isle of Wight, and Rose Hill in Essex counties, Tidewater; Alexandria is in Alexandria, and Crichton's Store in Brunswick counties, Middle Virginia; Rougemont, in Albemarle, is in Piedmont; Berryville, in Clarke county, is in the Valley, and Wirt courthouse, in West Virginia, stands for Trans-Appalachia, and shows "how the wind blows" there. A comparison of the numbers of the table will give the prevailing winds of each section, and show how they differ. The Signal Service chart,† showing the annual means of the barometer for 1872–3, shows that the mean barometer 30.05 crossed the State near the parallel of 37° 30′. The same chart gives the results of the winds—or total movement of the air for the same year—by diagrams, which show that the prevailing winds of the State are from the west and northwest—and that they are moderate in velocity. There are but few "high winds" in Virginia.

At Staunton, Augusta county, in the Valley, the following observations‡ were made for the year beginning October, 1868: At 7 A. M. the sky was without clouds 91 times, entirely overcast 61 times, partly cloudy 204 times; at 2 P. M. it was entirely clear 60, entirely cloudy 63, and partially cloudy 243 times; at 9 P. M. it was clear 167, cloudy 51, and partially cloudy 148 times. There were 42 days without a cloud. These results show that most of the time the weather is what would be called "clear"—and this is rendered more apparent by the record of the rain and snow fall for the same period, during which 32.1 inches of rain and

* Smithsonian results. † Plate X. of Statistical Atlas.

‡ By Deaf, Dumb and Blind Institute, from the manuscripts.

melted snow fell at 61 different times, or on that many different days, 51 being rain and 10 snow. The whole depth of snow fall for the year was 38.5 inches.

In 1858*, for the year, at Portsmouth, Norfolk county, the mean cloudiness was 3.60—that is, 360 times out of 1,000 the sky was overcast; at Smithfield, Isle of Wight county, it was 5.28; at Crichton's Store, Brunswick county, 5.07; at Rougemont, Albemarle county, 5.48. These figures will give a good general idea of the state of "the face of the sky" in Virginia.

The Signal Service office furnished the data for a chart of the United States, showing the Frequency of Storm Centres—published as Plate VI. of the Statistical Atlas. This chart shows the number of storm centres, of areas of low barometer that passed over any given district from March, 1871, to February, 1873, inclusive. It is said in the Statistical Atlas: "This chart is of interest in connection with all statistics bearing on the security of navigation, and on the habitability of a country, and the diseases that originate in the sudden changes of weather that attend storms." Tidewater, except that part of it north of a line from Richmond city to Point Lookout, is in the belt of country over which from 5 to 10 storms passed—the same belt extends for 150 miles or more out to sea along the Virginia coast—it is the belt which embraces much of the States of Pennsylvania, West Virginia, Kentucky, Indiana, Missouri, &c., and all of Ohio. All the remainder of Virginia, Middle, Piedmont, Blue Ridge, Valley and Appalachia, are in the belt of the fewest number of storms—only from 1 to 5—a result that might have been expected by any one familiar with the State. Most of the New England States, large portions of New York, Michigan, Wisconsin, Illinois, Iowa, &c., are in the belt of from 10 to 15—and large areas of New England and of the States near the Great Lakes, including Canada, &c., are crossed by the belts of 15 to 20; 20 to 22.5 and of over 22.5. The effects of these storms are evident in the "disease" and "death rate" maps and statistics of the country.

The advantages of the climate of Virginia may be summarized thus:

1*st.* It is a *dry* climate, that is, while it has an *abundance* of moisture, it is nowhere *damp.*

2*nd.* It is a *mild* climate, for, while it is sometimes very cold or very warm, neither of these last long—the general temperature is a medium one.

3*rd.* It is a climate *favorable to agricultural operations;* the *length of its growing* season; the *distribution of its rain throughout the year;* the *shortness and mildness of the winter;* the *long periods adapted to seeding and harvesting,* &c., are all well attested facts.

4*th.* It is a *very healthy climate:*—in no part of the world is there a more general state of health or a more long-lived and vigorous people, as proven by the statistics—and in no country in the temperate zone do the inhabitants, from choice, stay more in the open air and open their houses to the "weather."

5*th.* It has a *great variety of climate* from that of the low sea coast plains, through all gradations, up to that of great valleys and table lands thousands of feet above the sea:—this provides localities for a widely varied production and for the choice of a habitation.

---

* Smithsonian results.

# CHAPTER IV.

## THE PRODUCTIONS OF VIRGINIA.

### Section I.—Animal Products.

The climate of Virginia is favorable for the growth and the products of its soil for the sustenance of animal life, consequently it has an abundant and vigorous native fauna on its land and in its waters. All the varieties of domestic animals reared in temperate climates have here found a congenial habitation, and excellent breeds of horses, mules, milch cows, working oxen, beef cattle, sheep, swine, goats, and poultry, abound in all sections of this State.

Before presenting the facts of production in Virginia, most of which are drawn* from the census of 1860, it may be of interest to present, from the same census, the statements in regard to the "*Lands*" *of the State*, the *Value* of the same, and of the farming implements and machinery in use:

| SECTIONS. | Acres of Land. | | | Cash Value of Land. | Value of Farming Implements and Machinery. |
|---|---|---|---|---|---|
| | Improved. | Woodland. | Total. | | |
| Tidewater.................. ......... | 2,034,399 | 2,216,990 | 4,139,389 | 59,993,096 | 1,701,909 |
| Middle......... ......... ............. | 2,882,525 | 3,148,376 | 6,030,901 | 63,105,528 | 1,985,196 |
| Piedmont ........................... | 1,951,427 | 1,840,149 | 3,791,576 | 65,870,771 | 1,638,127 |
| Blue Ridge............................ | 162,567 | 413,944 | 576,501 | 3,322,761 | 133,799 |
| The Valley............................. | 1,520,873 | 1,810,512 | 3,331,385 | 63,249,035 | 1,691,459 |
| Appalachia... ........................ | 539,913 | 1,708,987 | 2,248,900 | 17,695,383 | 358,830 |
| Totals.................... | 9,091,694 | 11,128,958 | 20,417,752 | $273,236,274 | $7,419,611 |

A comparison of these figures with those of areas, &c., in Chapter I., will give a good idea of proportional amounts of cleared land, woodland, &c., in each section.

*By direction of the Board of Immigration.

Virginia had more acres of cleared land than any of the States of the Union, except Illinois, New York and Pennsylvania, which had, in round numbers, 13, 14 and 10 million acres respectively. She was the eighth in the quantity of unimproved land, having about the same quantity as Kentucky or South Carolina, and nearly twice as much as California, Iowa, New York or Pennsylvania. The cash value of Virginia lands placed her in the 7th rank, the order being, 1st New York, 2d Ohio, 3d Pennsylvania, 4th Illinois, 5th Indiana, and 6th Kentucky, the last being but a little in advance of Virginia.

The following table shows the *Number, and Size in Acres, of the Farms* in Virginia in 1860:

| SECTIONS. | Number over 3 and under 10 Acres. | Over 10 and under 20. | Over 20 and under 50. | Over 50 and under 100. | Over 100 and under 500. | Over 500 and under 1000. | 1000 Acres and over. | No. of Farms of all sizes. |
|---|---|---|---|---|---|---|---|---|
| Tidewater ................ | 385 | 845 | 2,929 | 3,325 | 5,331 | 667 | 148 | 13,630 |
| Middle.................. .... | 255 | 543 | 2,016 | 2,928 | 7,905 | 1,032 | 202 | 14,881 |
| Piedmont................. | 165 | 355 | 1,909 | 2,423 | 5,435 | 602 | 135 | 11,024 |
| Blue Ridge................ | 28 | 109 | 628 | 670 | 574 | 13 | 2 | 2,024 |
| The Valley... ..... ..... | 102 | 320 | 1,616 | 2,624 | 5,484 | 296 | 57 | 10,499 |
| Appalachia ............. | 132 | 4[illegible]8 | 1,440 | 1,330 | 1,703 | 74 | 33 | 5,130 |
| TOTALS......... | 1,067 | 2,590 | 10,538 | 13,300 | 26,432 | 2,684 | 577 | 57,188 |

*Milch Cows* and *Dairy Products* are of the first importance in the estimation of the husbandman—and the physical vigor of any people is largely dependent upon their abundance.

The number of milch cows, and the butter and cheese produced in the several sections of Virginia, in 1860, are shown in the following table:

| SECTIONS. | No. of Milch Cows. | Butter. (Pounds.) | Cheese. (Pounds.) | Pounds of Butter to each Cow. | Cows to each 100 People. |
|---|---|---|---|---|---|
| Tidewater ...... ................ | 43,876 | 1,085,671 | 755 | 22.4 | 13 |
| Middle.. ................ ............ | 63,564 | 1,911,902 | 4,274 | 30.0 | 17 |
| Piedmont.......................... | 46,681 | 2.816,054 | 10,190 | 60.3 | 22 |
| Blue Ridge........................ | 6,805 | 269,416 | 15,030 | 39.5 | 28 |
| The Valley......................... | 44,643 | 2,463,400 | 78,316 | 55.0 | 23 |
| Appalachia ......................... | 25,090 | 776,505 | 40,707 | 39.4 | 32 |
| TOTALS. ...................... | 230,[illegible] | 9,322,948 | 149,272 | 40.4 Av. | 20 Av. |

The statistics of other portions of the United States, for 1860, give these results:

| | Pounds of Cheese to each Cow. | Pounds of Butter to each Cow. | Cows to each 100 People. |
|---|---|---|---|
| New England States | 32 | 75 | 21 |
| Middle States | 25 | 87 | 24 |
| Western States | 10 | 58 | 27 |
| Southern States | $\frac{5}{16}$ | 22 | 29 |
| Pacific States | 5 | 15 | ... |
| United States—average | 16 | 53 | 27 |
| England, in 1874 | ... | ... | 9 |

The production of butter was very creditable to Virginia, when it is considered that dairying was not at that time one of the established industries of the State as in New England and the Middle and Western States; it was only incidental to the rearing of cattle for market, especially in the Blue Ridge, Valley and Appalachian sections—in fact, at that time, butter and cheese were rarely produced for market in all the southwestern portions of the State.

The cost of producing a given quantity of butter and cheese is much less in Virginia, owing to its milder climate and longer seasons, than in many other States of the Union. The statistics of production show the effects of elevation above the sea of portions of the State, giving them more adaptability to natural grasses and to the dairy business. The production of cheese by the "factory" system has of late been undertaken in Piedmont. The "Old Dominion Cheese Factory," in Loudoun county, reports, for 1871:

Milk received from May 6th to September 8th........378.138 pounds.
Cheese manufactured from above........36,625 "
Milk consumed for one pound of cheese........10.3 "
Average net price received for cheese, deducting boxes, freight and all expenses but manufacturing........12⅞ cts. per lb.
Value of 36,625 pounds of cheese, @ 12⅞ cents per pound........$4.715.47.
Average number of cows milked........125.
Charges for manufacturing, curing, boxing, furnishing materials (except boxes), selling, collecting and dividing among partners in proportion to milk furnished and cheese made, 2½ cents per pound........$915.62.
Giving for each cow a return of........$30.39.

It was ascertained that the milk used in making one pound of butter would make three pounds of cheese.

This company, in 1874, manufactured 174,143 pounds of milk into 16,152 pounds of cheese, averaging one pound of cheese to 10.78 of milk: the average price received for cheese was 15 cents per pound.

It was estimated by the officers of the above mentioned company that the entire cost of a factory, in working order, for manufacturing into cheese the milk of from 400 to 600 cows, would be about $3,000. They also conclude that generally cheese can be made with profit during six or eight months of the year, and that the article produced is as good as any made in the United States; results to be expected when all the circumstances are known.

A farmer (J. K. Taylor) in the same county gives the following results of dairying in 1871, with eight cows:

2,640 pounds of cheese made from May 6th to September 8th, or 80 pounds a month to each cow.

| | |
|---|---|
| Received for cheese (10½ cents per pound net) after deducting all expenses...... | $272 00 |
| Received for 320 gallons milk, @ 11 cents per gallon, from September 8th to December 1........................ | 36 19 |
| Received for 120 pounds butter, @ 25 cents per pound, from September 8th to December 1, expenses deducted........................ | 30 00 |
| Value of 7 calves reared........................ | 49 00 |
| Profit, averaging $48 39 for each cow........................ | $387 19 |

The value of a thoroughbred calf, $100, was not included.

Another farmer (T. R. Smith) in the same county, reported for 1871, from 10 cows kept:

| | |
|---|---|
| 2,610 pounds of cheese, worth........................ | $273 81 |
| 970 pounds of butter, worth........................ | 297 14 |
| 10 calves, worth........................ | 61 40 |
| | $632 25 |
| Deduct 3 tons of mill feed consumed........................ | 60 00 |

Averaging $57.23 to the cow, but making no deduction for cost of making butter.

E. J. Smith, from the same county, reports for an average of 10½ cows:

| | |
|---|---|
| For 2,730 pounds of cheese, net value........................ | $288 30 |
| For 765 pounds of butter, @ 30⅞ cents per pound........................ | 236 05 |
| For calves........................ | 33 50 |
| | $557 85 |

Or $46.03 per cow, with no deduction for making the butter.

These facts from Loudoun county give a fair estimate of the profits of the dairyman in Piedmont Virginia, and as the conditions of the Blue Ridge, Valley and Appalachia are much the same, it may be taken as an average for the sections named, the advantages of nearness to market in some districts being compensated for by diminished cost of production in others. A cheese factory has been operated in Smyth county.

The butter produced in Virginia in 1860 was 7.6 pounds to the person. In the dairy States it was 21.5. When the location of Virginia is considered, so near to the large cities of the Atlantic, the great consuming centres of dairy products, in conjunction with its extensive pasture lands covered by nutritious natural grasses, where pure water abounds and the climate is genial, it will appear that it offers superior attractions to the dairy farmer.

*Sheep* have always thriven in Virginia, and the *wool* here grown has an established reputation for excellence of quality. Wherever the business of rearing sheep, for wool or for mutton, has been judiciously conducted, it has proven remunerative. Few States have as many special adaptations for sheep husbandry:—extensive areas of cheap, elevated lands, covered with natural grasses; broad plains suited for root culture; short winters and a comparatively dry climate, with nearness to markets.

The following table presents the statistics of sheep in 1860:

| SECTIONS. | Number of Sheep. | Number of Sheep to each Person. | Pounds of Wool Produced. | Pounds of Wool to each Sheep. |
|---|---|---|---|---|
| Tidewater | 84,125 | 0.24 | 192,028 | 2.28 |
| Middle | 153,066 | 0.41 | 310,380 | 2.02 |
| Piedmont | 120,399 | 0.57 | 377,283 | 3.13 |
| Blue Ridge | 29,223 | 1.19 | 55,819 | 1.91 |
| The Valley | 124,746 | 0.64 | 337,177 | 2.70 |
| Appalachia | 79,466 | 1.07 | 164,149 | 2.06 |
| TOTALS | 590,935 | Av. 0.48 | 1,436,863 | Av. 2.43 |

The following similar statistics, for 1860, furnish comparative data:

| | Number of Sheep to each Person. | Pounds of Wool to each Sheep. |
|---|---|---|
| New England | 0.56 | 3.62 |
| Middle States | 0.53 | 3.28 |
| Western States | 0.88 | 2.82 |
| Southern States | 0.54 | 1.95 |
| Pacific States | ...... | 1.68 |
| United States | 0.71 | 2.68 |
| Great Britain, in 1874 | 1.20 | |
| Spain | 1.33 | ...... |
| France | 0.44 | |
| Australia* | 33.00 | ...... |

* The number of sheep in Australia more than doubled from 1862 to 1874.

It will be seen that the average production per sheep for Virginia is but little below that for the United States as a whole, while Piedmont is nearly equal to New England, the most productive section of the country in this particular, and where sheep husbandry is extensively carried on. It should also be borne in mind, that in Virginia the lands are cheap and the winters short, two essentials, when the soil and climate are favorable, for the cheap rearing of sheep and production of wool.

The United States imported, between 1860 and 1870, over 500,000,000 pounds of wool, at an average price of 15.7 cents, gold, per pound—a fact proving that here is an excellent field for the business of sheep rearing.

Experience has shown that lambs can be raised in Virginia, in the spring, and sent to the great northern markets long before they can be put there from the farms nearer; consequently good prices can be realized. The low priced lands of Tidewater and Middle Virginia are especially well situated for thus supplying early lambs, and large areas there are well adapted to the growing of swedes, mangolds, and other crops that are so extensively cultivated in England and elsewhere for fattening sheep.

*Angora Goats* have been successfully and profitably raised in Piedmont and Middle Virginia, furnishing large fleeces of the valuable Cashmere wool.

*Bees* find in the sections of this State an abundant flora, and the long and comparatively dry seasons are peculiarly favorable for apiculture—especially does this seem to be the case in Piedmont, where large profits are reaped by those that have given some attention to this pleasant home industry.

The production in 1860 was:

| SECTIONS. | Honey. (Pounds.) | Beeswax. (Pounds.) | Pounds to each Person. |
|---|---|---|---|
| Tidewater | 69,976 | 7,037 | 1/6 |
| Middle | 253,502 | 20,635 | 2/3 |
| Piedmont | 326,518 | 24,251 | 1 1/2 |
| Blue Ridge | 29,947 | 2,725 | 1 1/5 |
| The Valley | 161,847 | 9,040 | 4/5 |
| Appalachia | 166,442 | 10,656 | 2 1/16 |
| TOTALS | 1,008,232 | 74,374 | Av. 2/3 |

Virginia produced 1-23rd of the honey crop of the Union in 1860. This profitable industry ought to be a leading pursuit on the slopes of the Blue Ridge and other mountain ranges of Virginia, where experience has shown that the quantity and quality of the honey produced surpass that of almost any known region. The average production of the United States in 1860 was about two-thirds of a pound to the inhabitant; that was, very nearly, the average of New York, the State producing the largest quantity.

*Swine* are easily and cheaply raised in all portions of Virginia, especially in the portions abounding in forests, where they subsist much of the year on the nuts of the beech, oak, chestnut, and other trees, at no cost to their owners; in fact they are often fattened entirely on "mast." These animals can be reared more cheaply here than in almost any other part of the country; consequently they are kept in large numbers, and "Virginia bacon" has a valuable reputation in the markets. The climate is credited with aiding in the "cure" of hog meat. The table presents the statistics of swine in Virginia in 1860:

| SECTIONS. | Number of Swine. | Number of Swine to each 100 People. |
|---|---|---|
| Tidewater | 345,814 | 100 |
| Middle | 291,902 | 80 |
| Piedmont | 228,101 | 109 |
| Blue Ridge | 36,924 | 150 |
| The Valley | 229,358 | 118 |
| Appalachia | 130,608 | 170 |
| TOTAL | 1,262,707 | Av. 103 |

At the same period the number to each 100 people was:

| | |
|---|---|
| In New England | 10 |
| In Middle States | 31 |
| In Western States | 149 |
| In Southern States | 175 |
| In Pacific States | 101 |
| In the United States | 106 |
| In Great Britain, in 1874 | 9¼ |
| In Norway | 5⅔ |

Virginia had 1-24th of all the swine in the United States. There can be no question but that it would be better for the people and the State to raise sheep rather than swine for animal food.

*Stock* and *Beef Cattle*—the "other cattle" of the census—including all horned cattle, except milch cows and working oxen, are reared in large numbers in all parts of Virginia, but especially in Piedmont, the Blue Ridge, the Valley and Appalachia, where stock raising is an important and profitable branch of husbandry. Large numbers of fat cattle are annually sent to the Eastern markets from the rich grass lands of the sections named, especially from the portions where the nutritious and fattening "blue grass" grows. Many young stock cattle are also sold to the farmers of the country near the large cities, where they are stall fed. The table on next page is the return of "other cattle" for Virginia in 1860.

| SECTIONS. | Number of Cattle. | Number of Cattle to each 100 People. |
|---|---|---|
| Tidewater | 74,741 | 21 |
| Middle | 93,605 | 25 |
| Piedmont | 96,764 | 46 |
| Blue Ridge | 10,528 | 43 |
| The Valley | 95,361 | 49 |
| Appalachia | 51,644 | 67 |
| TOTAL | 422,643 | 34 Av. |

In Great Britain, in 1874, there were about 15 "other cattle" to each 100 of the inhabitants.

There are vast tracts of mountain land in Virginia that furnish a "range" for young cattle, enabling the grazier to rear them at but little expense. These tracts of land are covered by a growth of timber, more or less heavy, beneath which is an undergrowth of rich-weed, wild grasses, &c., that are highly nutritious, and on which cattle can subsist from April to November. The stock raising capacity of the State can hardly be estimated, so great is it.

*Working Oxen* are favorite "plow cattle" in many portions of Virginia, experience having proven that they are very efficient for all ordinary farm team labor, while they are valuable for beef after their activity is lost. The figures of the census indicate that in the Valley, where the heavy, limestone clay soil abounds, fewer oxen and more horses are used than where the soils are lighter and looser. Oxen are more numerous, in proportion to the farming population, in Tidewater, than in any other section of the State.

The working oxen in 1860 were distributed as follows:

| SECTIONS. | Number of Oxen. | Number of Oxen to each 100 People. |
|---|---|---|
| Tidewater | 28,487 | 8 |
| Middle | 27,519 | 7 |
| Piedmont | 14,222 | 6 |
| Blue Ridge | 1,896 | 7 |
| The Valley | 3,378 | 2 |
| Appalachia | 3,601 | 4 |
| TOTAL | 80,103 | 7 Av. |

The *Cattle used for Human Food*, including milch cows, sheep, swine and "other cattle," already enumerated separately, may be summed up as below:

| SECTIONS. | Number of All Kinds. | Number to each 100 People. | Value of Animals Slaughtered. |
|---|---|---|---|
| Tidewater | 577,043 | 1.6 | 2,379,683 |
| Middle | 629,756 | 1.7 | 2,147,580 |
| Piedmont | 505,077 | 2.1 | 2,004,078 |
| Blue Ridge | 85,376 | 3.4 | 199,161 |
| The Valley | 497,486 | 2.5 | 1,734,486 |
| Appalachia | 290,409 | 3.9 | 699,163 |
| TOTALS | 2,586,047 | 2.1 Av. | $9,365,151 |

The number of animals slaughtered for food of course depends upon the population. This accounts for the large numbers slaughtered in Tidewater, Middle and Piedmont, since in those sections are located the large cities of the State.

The *Scale and Shell Fish* of Virginia furnish not only a large portion of the animal food of thousands of the people of Virginia, especially in the Tidewater country, but immense numbers are taken from the waters of this and shipped to other States.

The thousands of square miles of Virginia territory covered by tidal waters abound, in the proper seasons, in shad, herring, rock, perch, sturgeon, sheepshead, bass, chub, spots, hogfish, trout, tailor, Spanish mackerel and other fish, besides crabs, lobsters, terrapins, &c. Not less than $1,000,000 worth of the fishes enumerated are annually taken. The fishing season opens early, and while the waters near New York, Philadelphia, and other cities, in a higher latitude, are yet frozen, the shad and other spring fish can be caught in Virginia waters and sent to northern and northwestern markets, where they command high prices. Many of the fresh water streams of the State abound in many kinds of fish, and both the State and the United States authorities are stocking them with other varieties. No country has more or better streams for fish breeding.

*Oysters* are found in all the tributaries of Chesapeake bay and along the Atlantic coast, giving to Tidewater an extensive territory where this valuable shell fish grows naturally and where it can be propagated and reared in almost any desired quantity. It is estimated that more than 15,000,000 bushels of oysters are annually taken from the beds of Tidewater, valued at from twelve to fifteen million dollars. In 1869 over 5,000 small boats and 1,000 vessels of over five tons burthen, were employed in taking these oysters from the water, and 193 State and 309 other vessels, of 18,876 tons aggregate burthen, were engaged in conveying them to market. It is well known that the published statistics come far short of the actual numbers ot scale and shell fish taken in Virginia. A correspondent of the Richmond Dispatch, in a letter from Chincoteague island, (August 1875), states that there are annually sent from that island—which is 7 miles long and averages 1½ miles in width—to market 500,000 bushels of oysters, "at prices ranging from 65 to 90 cents, while the cost of planting, gathering and marketing does not exceed 30 cents a bushel." There should be added to the "value of animals slaughtered" from $15,000,000 to $20,000,000 for Tidewater, on account of fish of all kinds, swelling the *meat* production of Virginia to the dimensions of that of almost any State of the Union.

*Birds* for food are abundant, especially water fowl, in the great marshes and rivers of Tidewater, where canvas-back, mallard, creek, red-head, bald-face, teal and other ducks, geese, swans, sora, &c., swarm abundantly. In all portions of the State are found partridges or quails, pigeons, wild doves, grouse or pheasants, wild turkeys, and other game birds.

*Wild Deer* are found in all portions of the State, especially in Tidewater and the Middle and Mountain sections.

The statistics give Virginia most ample resources of *animal food*, sufficient for a population many times as numerous as she now has. Nowhere is this kind of food better or cheaper.

The *Working Animals* of any country furnish, by their numbers, a test of its agricultural industry. In 1874, there were in Great Britain about 8½, and in France, in 1872, 8 horses to each 100 of the inhabitants. The number in Virginia, in 1860, was 16½ horses to each 100 people. Virginia had, in 1860, of working animals, 330,452, or over 27 to each 100 of the population. The following table gives their distribution in the State:

| SECTIONS. | Number of Horses. | Number of Mules and Asses. | Number of Working Oxen. |
|---|---|---|---|
| Tidewater | 30,971 | 15,403 | 28,487 |
| Middle | 46,930 | 15,784 | 27,519 |
| Piedmont | 47,770 | 4,804 | 14,222 |
| Blue Ridge | 4,937 | 179 | 1,896 |
| The Valley | 51,518 | 1,953 | 3,378 |
| Appalachia | 19,807 | 1,318 | 3,601 |
| TOTALS | 201,933 | 39,441 | 79,103 |

This State has always been noted for the general excellence of the horses and mules bred in it, and it is well known that they can be reared cheaply in almost every section. Recently buyers from other States have found it to their interest to attend the sales of stock that usually take place in all the county towns on the monthly court days.

The *Value of the Live Stock* of Virginia, in 1860, was:

| SECTIONS. | Value. | To each Person. |
|---|---|---|
| Tidewater | 6,986,612 | 29 26 |
| Middle | 9,198,584 | 24 79 |
| Piedmont | 7,989,105 | 38 20 |
| Blue Ridge | 718,173 | 29 31 |
| The Valley | 7,489,675 | 38 59 |
| Appalachia | 3,046,660 | 30 61 |
| | $35,419,809 | $29 04 Av. |

The United States Department of Agriculture, in the Report for 1869, gives the following *Live Stock* statistics for Virginia, as of February 1st, 1870:

| | Number. | Average Price. | Value. |
|---|---|---|---|
| Horses | 220,500 | $ 89 59 | $19,752,300 |
| Mules | 32,400 | 114 33 | 3,704,292 |
| Oxen and other cattle | 295,000 | 20 42 | 6,023,900 |
| Milch Cows | 240,000 | 30 04 | 7,209,600 |
| Sheep | 557,000 | 2 58 | 1,437,000 |
| Swine | 904,400 | 5 42 | 4,901,848 |
| TOTALS | 2,249,300 | ......... | $43,029,030 |

These are not returns from actual inspections, but they are approximations from reliable sources of information. The increased value over 1860 is very considerable, notwithstanding the great losses to which this kind of property is especially liable during war times.

*Price* of Farm Stock in Virginia January 1st.*

| | 1874. | 1873. | 1872. | 1871. | 1870. | 1869. |
|---|---|---|---|---|---|---|
| Horses | $ 75 92 | $ 81 57 | $ 78 18 | $ 84 93 | $ 89 58 | $ 80 60 |
| Mules | 103 83 | 109 30 | 110 42 | 105 93 | 114 33 | 110 72 |
| Oxen and other Cattle | 17 20 | 16 87 | 17 21 | 21 34 | 20 42 | 20 39 |
| Cows | 22 00 | 23 69 | 24 93 | 29 09 | 30 04 | 28 76 |
| Sheep | 2 90 | 3 04 | 2 70 | 2 37 | 2 58 | 2 40 |
| Swine | 3 51 | 3 67 | 3 53 | 5 60 | 5 42 | 4 39 |

*Report of U. S. Department of Agriculture, 1873.

The following statement* of the number of horses, mules, asses, jennets, cattle, sheep, goats and hogs (swine), in the State of Virginia in 1874, and their value, is from the official returns of the assessors in the office of the Auditor of the State:

| SECTIONS. | Horses, Mules, Asses and Jennets. | | Cattle. | | Sheep and Goats. | | Hogs (Swine). | |
|---|---|---|---|---|---|---|---|---|
| | Number. | Value. | Number. | Value. | Number. | Value. | Number. | Value. |
| Tidewater............. | 38,251 | 2,276,993 | 93,549 | 1,016,865 | 38,297 | 79,001 | 138,919 | 309,148 |
| Middle................. | 48,357 | 2,828,420 | 130,725 | 1,432,907 | 53,609 | 129,544 | 126,914 | 278,850 |
| Piedmont.............. | 48,599 | 2,704,725 | 121,297 | 1,032,412 | 81,759 | 101,889 | 105,556 | 234,085 |
| Blue Ridge............ | 6,020 | 289,938 | 23,283 | 290,694 | 21,581 | 25,108 | 20,934 | 24,426 |
| Valley.................. | 58,104 | 3,388,261 | 126,739 | 1,894,253 | 85,992 | 176,193 | 113,739 | 272,369 |
| Appalachia............ | 23,668 | 1,224,275 | 78,716 | 837,734 | 78,488 | 86,047 | 65,717 | 88,818 |
| Totals.......... | 220,909 | $12,712,667 | 567,259 | $6,963,564 | 362,627 | $678,582 | 571,779 | $1,207,695 |

*Silk Cocoons* are reported from each section of the State in 1860. Considerable attention was once given to silk culture, and enough is known of the results to warrant the statement that the conditions of the climate are favorable. The mulberry flourishes.

## Section II.—Vegetable Productions.

Virginia has a rich and abundant native flora, and the introduced plants, the cereals, grasses and others, that in temperate climates are objects of cultivation, here have found favorable soils and congenial climates. Here grow and yield abundantly the "plants good for food" both for man and beast, and those employed in manufactures. Timber trees of many kinds abound in all sections of the State.

The *Cereals*, the furnishers of the larger portion of human food, hold the first place among vegetable productions. The following table gives the returns in bushels, of Virginia, in 1859 (census of 1860), of the four most important bread-grain cereals:

| SECTIONS. | Wheat. | Rye. | Indian Corn. | Buckwheat. |
|---|---|---|---|---|
| Tidewater ............................................ | 2,524,435 | 42,151 | 9,066,159 | 703 |
| Middle.................................................. | 2,941,641 | 42,906 | 7,299,421 | 13,108 |
| Piedmont............................................... | 2,295,596 | 186,629 | 5,823,289 | 14,381 |
| Blue Ridge............................................ | 117,393 | 69,476 | 428,835 | 28,353 |
| The Valley ........................................... | 2,621,535 | 272,788 | 4,973,919 | 41,646 |
| Appalachia ........................................... | 347,809 | 56,102 | 2,169,688 | 37,338 |
| Totals ........................................... | 10,848,499 | 670,052 | 30,361,352 | 135,549 |

* Furnished by Auditor Wm. F. Taylor, August, 1875.

These cereals aggregate 42,015,253 bushels of production, over 34.4 bushels to each of the population of the State—an abundant supply for seven times as many people. A comparison of the production of cereals with any other country presents Virginia in a most favorable light as a grain-producing region, while nearness to markets adds largely to the value of the products. The yield of these cereals in 1869, per capita, in round numbers, was:

| SECTIONS. | BUSHELS OF PRODUCTION TO EACH INHABITANT. | | |
|---|---|---|---|
| | Wheat. | Indian Corn. | All Four. |
| Tidewater | 7 | 28 | 35 |
| Middle | 8 | $19\frac{2}{3}$ | 28 |
| Piedmont | 11 | 28 | 40 |
| Blue Ridge | $4\frac{7}{8}$ | 18 | 26 |
| The Valley | $13\frac{1}{2}$ | $25\frac{1}{3}$ | $40\frac{2}{3}$ |
| Appalachia | $4\frac{1}{7}$ | $28\frac{2}{7}$ | 34 |

Indian corn is the staple bread grain of most sections of the State, except the Valley; the laboring rural population, in many portions, use it almost exclusively.

The United States Department of Agriculture, in its report for 1869, gives the following "*Table of the* CROPS *of* VIRGINIA *for* 1869," the results of its estimates gathered from all sources of information:

| | Crop of 1869. | Yield per Acre. | Acreage. | Value per Bushel, &c. | Total Value. | Cash Value per Acre. | Average Value per Acre. |
|---|---|---|---|---|---|---|---|
| Indian Corn—Bushels... | 17,500,000 | 15.5 | 1,129,032 | $ 0 91 | $15,925,000 | $14 10 | $12 66 in Illinois. |
| Wheat " ... | 8,642,000 | 10.5 | 823.047 | 1 21 | 10,456,820 | 12 70 | 13 02 in Minnesota. |
| Rye " ... | 800,000 | 9.3 | 86,021 | 0 91 | 728,000 | 8 46 | 13 40 in Georgia. |
| Oats " ... | 9,017,000 | 17.1 | 527,309 | 0 48 | 4,328,160 | 8 20 | 13 71 in Wisconsin. |
| Barley " ... | 28,000 | 17.3 | 1,618 | 0 87 | 24,360 | 15 05 | 14 61 in Virginia. |
| Buckwheat " ... | 75,000 | 10.7 | 7,009 | 0 87 | 65,250 | 9 30 | |
| Potatoes " ... | 1,188,000 | 50.0 | 23,760 | 0 69 | 819,720 | 34 50 | |
| Tobacco—Pounds....... | 65,000,000 | 418.0 | 155,502 | 10 30 cwt. | 6,695,000 | 43 05 | |
| Hay—Tons............. | 220,000 | 1.46 | 150,684 | 15 41 ton. | 3,390,200 | 22 49 | |
| | | | 2,903,982 | | $42,432,510 | $14 61 Av. | |

The following comparative table presents facts in regard to wheat production which show that Virginia compares favorably with the noted wheat-growing States. Illinois produced the largest and Iowa the next largest crops of the States in 1869. France had the largest wheat crop in the known world in 1872. England, by high cultivation, has reached an average of 28 bushels to the acre, but has only increased one-fifth of a bushel in one hundred years—still its average surpasses that of any other country:

| | Average Product of Wheat per Acre. Bushels. |
|---|---|
| * California, 1869 | 18.2 |
| Illinois, 1869 | 11.2 |
| Iowa, 1869 | 13.0 |
| United States, 1869 | 13.5 |
| † United States, 1873 | 12.7 |
| France, 1872 | 19.3 |
| Holland, 1872 | 25.3 |
| Austria, 1871 | 15.2 |
| Prussia, 1867 | 17.1 |
| ‡ England (average) | 28.0 |

In 1869* Pennsylvania produced the largest crop of rye, 17.7 bushels, average, per acre, and of buckwheat, 16.4 bushels; Missouri the largest crop of maize, averaging 30.6 bushels to the acre. In 1870† Norway produced 25.9 bushels of rye, and in 1867 Prussia had 16.7 bushels to the acre.

*Potatoes, Peas and Beans*, or *Tubers and Pulse*, are raised in considerable quantities in all portions of Virginia. The returns, in bushels, for 1859 (census of 1860), are as follows:

| SECTIONS. | Potatoes. | | Peas and Beans. |
|---|---|---|---|
| | Irish. | Sweet. | |
| Tidewater | 477,036 | 1,314,377 | 323,603 |
| Middle | 321,913 | 407,283 | 89,893 |
| Piedmont | 312,256 | 118,669 | 35,291 |
| Blue Ridge | 34,238 | 2,039 | 1,718 |
| The Valley | 300,519 | 23,736 | 8,177 |
| Appalachia | 96,930 | 26,652 | 24,154 |
| Totals | 1,542,892 | 1,892,776 | 482,836 |

*Department of Agriculture Report, 1869.
†Agricultural returns of Great Britain, 1874.
‡Times, January 11, 1875.

The total potato crop was 3,435,668 bushels, an average of 2.8 to each inhabitant of the State, and over 6 bushels to each in Tidewater, where both sweet* and Irish† potatoes are a staple crop, the former having a high reputation in market for their superior quality. The latter are sent to market very early in the season. Except in the Tidewater section, where market gardening has become a leading industry, potatoes, as a rule, are only raised in Virginia for family consumption; they are not fed to stock, nor, except from Tidewater, sent to distant markets. There is no question but that more use should be made of this prolific and easily raised article of human and animal food. The average potato crop of Holland‡ is 165 bushels to the acre: that of Michigan§ in 1869 was 155 bushels, and of the whole United States 109.5.

*Peas* and *Beans* are not cultivated in Virginia to the extent they should be when account is taken of the large areas so admirably adapted to their cultivation, so much more so than to the production of maize, that requires a strong soil, which it rapidly exhausts. Only in Tidewater and parts of Middle Virginia are peas and beans farm products. In European States, large crops of pulse are raised; the average yield in Holland‡ is 25.9 bushels to the acre.

The production of cereals, tubers and pulse, in Virginia, in 1859, was about forty-six million bushels, or 38.25 bushels to each of its inhabitants—enough for seven or eight times as many people.

*Oats* and *Barley*, cereals not used here for human food, are important Virginia crops, especially the former. Barley is only cultivated to a limited extent, though it always does well, and it could be most advantageously grown for exportation, since the climate would give it *generally* the quality it has only in *occasional* seasons in England, when it bears a high price. The productions of 1859 (1860 census), in bushels, were:

| SECTIONS. | Oats. | Barley. |
|---|---|---|
| Tidewater | 1,524,466 | 172 |
| Middle | 3,047,548 | 834 |
| Piedmont | 1,739,159 | 767 |
| Blue Ridge | 262,544 | 282 |
| The Valley | 1,372,823 | 6,012 |
| Appalachia | 591,090 | 430 |
| TOTALS | 8,537,630 | 8,497 |

The Middle country led in the production of oats, and was followed by Piedmont. The friable soils and early seasons of the lower country are well suited to

* Convolvulus batatas—the "long potato."

† Solanum tuberosum—the "round potato."

‡ Agricultural returns of Great Britain, 1874.

§ Department of Agriculture Report, 1869.

the growth of this crop. In 1869, by report of the Department of Agriculture, the average product per acre, in Virginia, of oats, was 17.1, and of barley, 17.3 bushels. In France, in 1872, the average for oats was 28.2, and for barley 21.5 bushels per acre.

The *entire crop* of cereals, tubers and pulse, of Virginia, in 1859, was more than 54 million bushels, over 45.3 bushels for each inhabitant.

The *Production of Wheat and Indian Corn* in bushels, per capita, in the various sections of the United States, by the returns of 1860, was:

| SECTIONS. | Wheat. | Maize. |
|---|---|---|
| New England | 0.34 | 2.92 |
| Middle States | 3.69 | 9.12 |
| Western States | 10.00 | 45.86 |
| Southern States | 3.50 | 31.49 |
| United States | 5.50 | 26.73 |

A comparison of the figures here given with those before presented for the sections of Virginia, shows that the Valley and Piedmont excelled any of the groups of States in the production of wheat per capita, while Middle and Tidewater were only surpassed by the Western States. Every portion of Virginia produced more than the great wheat growing Middle States. In the production of Indian corn nearly all sections of Virginia produced more than the average for the United States.

The *Products of Orchards and Market Gardens* in Virginia are large and valuable, much more so than is indicated by the returns of the census. Every portion of the State is remarkably well adapted to the growth of fruits of the warm-temperate and temperate climates.

The following table is from the census of 1860, but it must be regarded as *merely an approximation* to the value of the products of the orchards and market gardens of Virginia:

| SECTIONS. | VALUE OF PRODUCTS OF | |
|---|---|---|
| | Orchards. | Market Gardens. |
| Tidewater | 198,956 | 455,127 |
| Middle | 57,791 | 66,503 |
| Piedmont | 112,291 | 11,416 |
| Blue Ridge | 30,664 | 2,406 |
| The Valley | 113,595 | 4,321 |
| Appalachia | 53,080 | 695 |
| TOTALS. | $566,377 | $540,468 |

In Tidewater Virginia apples, pears, peaches, quinces, plums, cherries, nectarines, grapes, figs, strawberries, raspberries, gooseberries, currants, and other fruits, thrive and produce abundantly, the quality of the products being unsurpassed, as the awards of the American Pomological Society attest. The value of the *small fruits* alone, annually sent to market from Tidewater, is more than the sums for orchards and gardens above given. The trade in early strawberries is one of large proportions. Especial mention should be made of the wild Scuppernong grapes, peculiar to the Tidewater country near the sea, which spread over the forests and bear large crops of excellent fruit, from which a very palatable wine is made. The originals of the Catawba, Norton's Virginia, and other esteemed American grapes, grow wild in the forests of Virginia.

*All the fruits named above grow in every section of the State*, except, perhaps, figs. Piedmont, the Blue Ridge and The Valley are famous apple regions. Peaches flourish in all sections, but Middle and Tidewater may claim some precedence in adaptability. The Blue Ridge is entitled to the name of the "Fruit Belt," and its extensive area is yet to become the most noted wine and fruit producing section of the United States east of the Rocky Mountains; all the fruits of Virginia flourish there in a remarkable manner, and find special adaptations of soil, climate and exposure.

The *Market Gardens* of Tidewater shipped* from Norfolk alone, to other markets, in the spring of 1870, a million baskets of strawberries, 50,000 barrels of Irish potatoes, 40,000 barrels of green peas, 10,000 barrels of snap beans, 650,000 heads of cabbage, 20,000 barrels of cucumbers, 100,000 barrels of tomatoes, 5,000 barrels of squashes, 2,000 barrels of beets, 40,000 bunches of radishes, 100,000 cantelope melons, and 100,000 watermelons, valued at $1,043,000. This does not include $25,000 worth of apples, pears, peaches, &c., shipped during the same season. The shipments of 1872 were valued at $1,500,000. Shipments were made from *many other* places. This business is called "trucking." The products of the "truck patches," or market gardens of Tidewater, are mostly marketed from March to August.

No country can be better situated for market gardening than Tidewater Virginia:—it is from 14 to 36 hours, by water, from Baltimore, Washington, Philadelphia, New York and Boston, the centres of population of the Atlantic slope of the United States; at the same time its seasons are from one to two months earlier, giving an advantage of fully a double price for its garden products over the country in the vicinity of those cities.

The *Home Gardens* are not considered in any of the "returns" of the productions of Virginia, where potatoes, Irish and sweet, corn, peas, beans, onions, beets, parsnips, radishes, lettuce, celery, salsify, asparagus, melons and squashes of numerous kinds, carrots, okra, tomatoes, &c., &c., *are raised in the greatest abundance, and form a portion of the daily food of the entire population.*

The *Peanut* (*Arachis hypogæa*) is extensively cultivated in Tidewater. Isle of Wight county, it is reported, in 1872, sent 40,000 bushels to market, that sold for

*Estimates of Pomological Society.

$1.50 to $3 a bushel. In 1871–'2 there were received at Norfolk 351,120 bushels* of these *ground*-nuts. Sandy and light soils are suited to the growth of peanuts.

*Vegetable Sweets* are produced in Virginia from the sugar maple (*Acer saccharinum*), and the Chinese sugar cane (*Sorghum saccharatum*). The production from these sources was, in 1859:

| SECTIONS. | MAPLE— | | Sorghum Molasses. |
|---|---|---|---|
| | Sugar. Pounds. | Molasses. Gallons. | Gallons. |
| Tidewater | ........ | 192 | 50 |
| Middle | ........ | 286 | 201 |
| Piedmont | 352 | 178 | 213 |
| Blue Ridge | 20 | 752 | 144 |
| The Valley | 54,132 | 9,711 | 21,021 |
| Appalachia | 216,657 | 16,805 | 24,805 |
| TOTALS | 271,161 | 27,924 | 46,434 |

Sorghum flourishes in strong soils in all portions of the State, and the production of molasses from this source is from eight to ten times the quantity here given. The objection to its cultivation is that it matures simultaneously with Indian corn, and both crops demand attention at the same time. The sugar maple, or "sugar tree," as it is familiarly called, abounds on the rich lands of the mountain regions, and there, every spring, much larger quantities of delicious tree sugar and molasses are made than the State obtains credit for. This manufacture is an extensive and profitable one in many of the States, and could be made so here.

*Beet Root Sugar* ought to be made in Virginia in large quantities, as it has an abundance of rich bottom lands for growing the beets, and seasons highly favorable for the development of saccharine matter in them. In France, in 1872, more than 221 million hundred-weights of beets were raised for sugar; they occupied 856,176 acres of land—a quantity equal to that occupied by wheat in Virginia in 1869.

The *Wine* crop of Virginia is a small one compared with the extensive territory here found that is especially adapted to the growth of the vine both by the character of the soil and the conditions of the climate. Fully two million acres of land in Virginia have soils and exposures similar to those of the most noted wine producing sections of Europe, and the seasons are so long that the grape has ample time to fully mature and develop its natural juices, fitting them for the manufacture of pure wine. Experience has shown that the vines here grown are free from diseases, and that they may be relied on for abundant crops. The yield for 1859 is given on succeeding page; it was more than the figures indicate.

* Report of Merchants Exchange.

| SECTIONS. | Wine. Gallons. |
|---|---|
| Tidewater | 6,398 |
| Middle | 20,641 |
| Piedmont | 6,608 |
| Blue Ridge | 92 |
| The Valley | 4,562 |
| Appalachia | 139 |
| TOTAL | 38,440 |

The BLUE RIDGE offers great advantages for viticulture: one vineyard on it, in Warren county, of 75 acres, produces from 20 to 30,000 gallons of wine and from 6 to 10,000 gallons of brandy annually, the yield being from 300 to 500 gallons per acre. The "red lands" of the PIEDMONT section are famous for their fitness for this pleasant and profitable industry. There are many localities in the other sections of the State where the vine flourishes. Early grapes are sent in considerable quantities from Virginia to northern and eastern markets. Mention has been made of the Scuppernong grape of Tidewater, marvellous for the space a single vine will cover and the quantity of fruit and wine it will produce. There is no more inviting field for the vigneron than Virginia. France had in 1872 under cultivation in vines 6,455,627 acres, an area nearly equal to all of Tidewater, larger than the Valley and Blue Ridge combined. Virginia should have as many acres, because it has equal advantages, naturally, in every particular, combined with a virgin soil, in its "fruit belt." The value of the *plain* wines made in France averages $500,000,000 in gold annually; the average yield is 220 gallons per acre, and for the last 16 years the product has averaged 1,100,000,000 gallons yearly.*

*Tobacco* is a staple product of Virginia, and in 1859 it produced about one-third of the crop of the United States, being the leading State in production, making about 100 pounds to each of its inhabitants. The crop of the sections for that year is shown in the table:

| SECTIONS. | Tobacco. Pounds. |
|---|---|
| Tidewater | 8,893,092 |
| Middle | 84,333,419 |
| Piedmont | 24,148,461 |
| Blue Ridge | 450,449 |
| The Valley | 3,657,921 |
| Appalachia | 304,304 |
| TOTAL | 121,787,646 |

* London Times.

*Middle Virginia* produced 84½ million pounds, 228 to each of its population, figures attesting the industry of its people, because no cultivated crop requires as much care and labor to bring it to market in good condition.

The "Virginia Leaf" is noted the world over for its excellence, the result of manipulation as well as of soil and climate. *Piedmont* produced 120 pounds to the head. The soils of this and the *Middle* section are among the best for the growth of good tobacco; those of *Middle* produce the finest and most valuable. *Tidewater* is the region for Cuba and Latukiah varieties, while immense crops of coarse and heavy tobaccos are grown on the rich lands of the Blue Ridge, the Valley and Appalachia. Some idea may be formed of the value of this great staple, when it is stated that more than 20,000,000* pounds were manufactured in Richmond alone in 1872, employing the labor of 11,049 hands. The United States tax, collected on Virginia tobacco in 1869–'70† was $4,068,220, or one-seventh of that paid for the whole Union.

The price of tobacco in Richmond in June, 1870, was from $7 to $35 per 100 pounds for "lugs," and from $8.50 to $100 for "leaf," according to quality.

In 1869 Richmond exported tobacco as follows:

| | | | |
|---|---|---|---|
| To Bremen | 124.184 | pounds of | "leaf." |
| " " | 550.813 | " | "stems." |
| " Havre | 2,433.278 | " | "leaf." |
| " Trieste | 1,338.000 | " | " |
| " Fiume | 686.000 | " | " |
| " London | 1,591,163 | " | " |
| " Liverpool | 1,571.607 | " | " |
| " Halifax | 217.817 | " | " |
| | 8,5.2,862 | | |

It has been found that no known country can compete with Virginia in the growth and manufacture of the better kinds of "the weed:"—her soil and climate are "just right" for it.

It should be noted that tobacco culture is not an exclusive one in any part of Virginia—large crops of grain and roots are raised on the same plantations.

*Grass* is one of the abundant productions of Virginia, much of its territory being inside the limits of "natural grasses," and all of it is adapted to the vigorous growth of the "artificial" or cultivated ones, but the character of its climate does not require a large stowing away of hay, therefore it does not "figure" largely in the returns. A reference to the number of cattle in each section of the State makes the quantity of hay produced appear very small in proportion, but it shows that the pastures can be relied on for most of the year, owing to the mildness of the climate, greatly to the advantage of the stock feeder. It is true that a large quantity of long forage is obtained from the "tops, blades and stalks" of Indian corn, which, where this is a staple crop, take the place of hay for home consumption, and leave the hay for market, if desired.

---

* State Journal.

† Report of Richmond Chamber of Commerce.

The *Seeds of Clover, Grass and Flax* naturally claim attention along with grass, and the table shows the sectional production of these articles in Virginia for 1859:

| SECTIONS. | Hay. Tons. | Seeds.—Bushels. | | |
|---|---|---|---|---|
| | | Clover. | Grass. | Flax. |
| Tidewater | 45,246 | 186 | 298 | 496 |
| Middle | 49,689 | 783 | 3,104 | 1,528 |
| Piedmont | 58,945 | 4,906 | 10,439 | 7,331 |
| Blue Ridge | 8,553 | 301 | 837 | 2,917 |
| The Valley | 104,955 | 22,652 | 23,626 | 7,146 |
| Appalachia | 18,609 | 904 | 458 | 4,859 |
| Totals | 285,997 | 29,732 | 38,792 | 24,277 |

Fine crops of hay are made from cultivated grasses in all portions of the State, but the *natural* meadows are mostly in Piedmont, Blue Ridge, The Valley and Appalachia. The "Hay Map" of the Statistical Atlas of the United States shades these sections the same as it does most of Pennsylvania, West Virginia, Ohio, Indiana, Illinois, Missouri, &c., and as more productive than most of Tennessee and Kentucky. The Report of the Department of Agriculture for 1869 gives, as the average production of hay in Virginia, 1.46 tons per acre, worth $22.49, a larger yield than any of the New England States, and almost equal to the 1.54 of New York, the leading hay State, and worth more, its value being $19.49 per ton.

The perennial grasses of Piedmont, the Blue Ridge, The Valley and Appalachia, including the noted "blue grass," are famed for their nutritious and fattening qualities, and place these among the most highly favored grazing regions in the world. Nowhere, save on the great plains of Texas and the extreme West, or South America, can cattle be reared and fattened more cheaply than in these sections of Virginia, as has been proven by the investigations of the United States Department of Agriculture. The Valley leads in the production of hay and seeds: Piedmont follows. The meadows of the *low country* in Virginia have an advantage in the early "haying" time, and where not too remote from the great cities, much profit can be gained by being early in market. *Tidewater* and *Middle* Virginia have many fine alluvial meadows, and the *salt marshes* of the former yield fine crops of hay, and perpetual pastures.

The crops of clover and grass seeds are unusually large where they are made an object; the long seasons seem to give a larger yield of good seed. The first crop of clover, for the year, is generally cut for hay, it has so large a growth, and seed is taken from the less rank second growth.

*Flax* grows well in all portions of Virginia, though little attention is now given to its cultivation. The elevated mountain valleys suit it admirably.

*Castor Beans* (*Ricinus communis*) are raised in considerable quantities, especially on the Eastern Shore of TIDEWATER.

The raising of *Garden Seeds* upon a large scale has lately been introduced in TIDEWATER, the climate and soil of which appear to be very favorable to this industry. The seeds grown have given much satisfaction, as they are sure to be ripe. England annually obtains many of her seeds from Italy and other warmer climates.

The warm thin lands of TIDEWATER and the MIDDLE country offer many advantages for growing *Garden Herbs* and *Perfumery Plants* and *Shrubs* on an extensive scale—the requisite heat and dryness of climate can there be found.

*Hops* are only raised for domestic use, except in a few cases. When planted the vines grow luxuriantly and bear well. The returns were:

| SECTIONS. | Hops. Pounds. |
|---|---|
| Tidewater | 1,294 |
| Middle | 1,776 |
| Piedmont | 1,310 |
| Blue Ridge | 163 |
| The Valley | 2,284 |
| Appalachia | 179 |
| TOTAL | 7,006 |

Large areas of land, similar to the hop lands of Kent, in England, and to those of the State of New York, can be found in Virginia, and hop culture could be advantageously undertaken in many localities, to vary the industrial productions.

*Ramie** and *Jute*, most valuable textile plants, could, without doubt, be most advantageously and successfully cultivated on the deep and rich *second bottoms* and *reclaimed swamp* lands of Tidewater. Ramie is a perennial, and the stalks are cut three or four times in a year, and the crude ramie-staple is worth from £65 to £70 a ton in Europe, and more in America. Millions of bales of jute are now annually consumed in the manufacture of paper, gunny-bags, grain sacks, &c.

*Cotton*, *Flax* and *Hemp*, the vegetable textile or fibrous products, are grown in Virginia successfully and profitably, but by no means as extensively as circumstances would seem to warrant. *Cotton* is somewhat largely cultivated in portions of TIDEWATER, especially south of the James, in the Southside Peninsula, where the climatic† conditions are favorable. A planter in Greenesville county, in 1873, averaged two 400 pound bales to the acre, and others report equally gratifying results. Virginia has these 1860 census credits for 1859 production, in pounds:

* See Report of Department of Agriculture (U. S.) 1873.

† See chapter on Climates.

| SECTIONS. | Cotton. | Hemp. | Flax. |
|---|---|---|---|
| Tidewater | 4,104,800 | 10 | 5,454 |
| Middle | 850,400 | 148 | 33,357 |
| Piedmont | ........... | 15,961 | 60,003 |
| Blue Ridge | 4,000 | 653 | 31,907 |
| The Valley | 83,600 | 11,060 | 69,838 |
| Appalachia | 12,000 | 210 | 90,051 |
| TOTALS | 5,054,800 | 28,042 | 290,610 |

A usually well informed writer* estimated the cotton crop of Virginia for 1871–'2 as 110,439,200 pounds (341,080 bales), and for 1872–'3 as 173,433,200 pounds (433,583 bales). These differ widely from other estimates, but no explanation can be made from existing data.

The Report of the Bureau of Statistics of the United States Treasury, for September, 1874, page 128, gives the following statements:

| | 1869–'70. | 1870–'71. | 1871–'72. | 1872–'73. | 1873–'74. |
|---|---|---|---|---|---|
| Product of Bales of Cotton in Virginia | 203,931 | 339,175 | 276,098 | 433,583 | 505,876 |
| Total Crop of the United States | 3,114,592 | 4,347,006 | 2,974,351 | 3,930,508 | 4,170,388 |
| Manufactured at the South | 79,843 | 91,240 | 120,000 | 279,162 | 366,098 |

These figures convey a wrong impression—they can only mean that the number of bales credited to Virginia found their way to market *through* her ports, else she would be the third State in cotton production. The cultivation of cotton on small farms has of late been very successful, and the fine prices realized from the better cotton so raised has greatly stimulated production.

*Cotton Seeds* have recently become articles of commerce, and they are in demand in Great Britain and elsewhere for the oil they contain and for food for cattle, giving an additional value to the cotton crop. The seeds were worth† in 1873, in Liverpool, $40 a ton. They also make a most excellent manure. The production of cotton is one of the elements in a mixed husbandry (*the only one that can thrive in a thinly peopled region*), that should be fostered, especially in Tidewater.

*Hemp* is not a staple of Virginia, and yet there are many rich, moist, bottom lands that could not be put to a more profitable use than the growing of this plant.

*Flax*, as before stated, is grown for "domestic manufacture" only—a crop now and then supplies the home demand, so luxuriantly does it grow. The fibre of

*E. de Leon, Harpers' Magazine, January, 1874, who states that Virginia *produced* as given above.

† de Leon—supra.

Virginia flax is of a superior quality, and the climatic conditions, especially of the elevated valleys, are favorable for fitting the crop for market. Flax is cultivated in all sections of the State, but the quantity produced increases in going westward. Virginia produced one-seventeenth of the flax crop of the United States in 1860, and one-twenty-fourth of the flax seed.

*The Products of the Forests* of Virginia are large, varied and important, but it is difficult to establish quantities and values; so meagre are the published statistics, only local returns can be given.

The Statistical Atlas of the United States, published by order of Congress, (1874), contains a "*Woodland*" map, showing by five degrees of density of shading the forest distribution of the country. On this map Virginia is represented as having a portion of four classes. The northeast of Piedmont, near Washington and Alexandria, is shaded in the second class, as having from 40 to 120 acres of woodland to the square mile of 640 acres, an average of one-eighth of the surface. All of the Valley northeast of Augusta county and the portions of Piedmont, Middle and Tidewater northeast of and including the Rappahannock valley, the Eastern Shore, the basin of the James to Piedmont, the north part of the Norfolk peninsula, the valley of the Dan from the North Carolina line to Danville, and an extensive region around Lynchburg, are in the third class, having from 120 to 240 acres of forest to the square mile, or over one-fourth of the whole surface. The Valley from Rockingham to the New river "divide," Piedmont southwest of the Rappahannock basin, all the portions of Middle and Tidewater not mentioned before, and the southwest corner of the State, except the extreme southeast of the State on the waters of Albemarle sound, are in the fourth class, having from 240 to 360 acres to the square mile, or about one half of the country in woods. The Blue Ridge from the North Carolina line, and the Valley to Roanoke county, and all the Appalachian region, except the drainage ground of the Big Sandy and the North Fork of Clinch, are placed in the fifth class, having from 360 to 560 acres of forest to the 640, or over two-thirds of the whole surface. The Big Sandy and North Fork of Clinch basins, and a belt along the North Carolina line, from the Atlantic to the Roanoke, including the Dismal Swamp, are embraced in the sixth, or highest class, having 560 or more acres of forest to the square mile. These areas are determined from the returns of cleared land of the census, and may be accepted as fair generalizations; though they fail to give much idea of the *timber* resources of the State, still the general presentation puts Virginia among the most highly favored in woodlands.

In the memoir, by Prof. Brewer, of New Haven, accompanying the "Woodland Map," Virginia is placed, geographically, among the Middle States, which are stated to have from "100 to 105 species of trees, 65 to 67 of which sometimes reach 50 feet in height. The region was originally entirely wooded, over much of it the forests were very heavy, and there are still immense quantities of timber available. The forests of this region are usually made up of quite a number of species, in some places the broad-leaved species predominating, in others the Coniferae; but both kinds commonly grow together." Of the Appalachian forests Prof. Brewer says: "While the hard woods may not attain their greatest size, some of them, particularly white oak, white ash, and some of the hickories, are believed to attain their greatest perfection as regards strength and durability, or, at least, they are only equalled by the timber of the same species extended on the line of these ridges beyond this district in both directions. This is a matter of great importance in ship and boat building, and in the manufacture of railroad cars and of agricultural implements." "It is believed that the white oak attains its greatest development of strength in certain parts of Virginia and West Virginia."

Prof. Brewer remarks that we have above 300 species of native trees, 132, according to Gray, north of the Carolinas, while Central Europe has but about 60, France from 30 to 34, and Great Britain 29, only 15 of which become large trees.

The Richmond Chamber of Commerce reported that for the third quarter of 1868 there were officially measured, in that city, 2,331,542 feet, board measure, of lumber. This would give an annual trade of 9½ million feet, worth over $200,000. There were received* into the Richmond dock, during the year ending September 30th, 1871, 5,005,000 feet of lumber, 1,272,000 shingles, 338,616 staves, and 30,000 railroad ties. For 1871-'2 the receipts in the dock were 6,771,000 feet of lumber, 2,572,000 shingles, 371,700 hoop poles, &c. These would be but a portion of the total receipts.

The *bark* trade of Richmond for 1868 was valued at $100,000, and for 1871 at $750,000. This was chiefly oak bark, for tanning and dyeing purposes, of which this State has an almost inexhaustible supply that must before long be in demand at good prices, as the hemlock forests of the United States, the chief source of tan bark now, are being rapidly cut down. As an illustration of the value of tan bark, it may be stated that 100† tanneries, at Siegen, in Germany, are supplied with bark from oak *bushes*, cultivated for the purpose, that furnished 80,000 tons of bark in 1868 (averaging seven shillings and sixpence per hundred weight in value), with which 100,000 hides were manufactured into 32,000 hundred weight of sole leather having a great reputation for durability.

The sales‡ of lumber in Norfolk for the year 1871-'2 were over six million oak staves, forty-five million shingles, forty-seven million feet of sawed lumber, worth not less than $2,000,000.

The *Sumac* trade of Virginia is becoming a very important one from the wild shrubs. In 1870, over 1,900 tons of sumac, ground and crude, were shipped from Richmond, valued at over two and a half million dollars. In 1870 a mill at Winchester ground 800 tons of sumac, valued at $75,000. Analysis, made in Liverpool, gave twenty-seven per cent. of tannin in the Winchester sumac, and the article ranked high commercially. There are extensive areas in all parts of Virginia that could be profitably devoted to the cultivation of sumac, as in Sicily.

*Sassafras* roots are consumed by hundreds of tons in the manufacture of oil. This shrub, often tree in Virginia, grows abundantly in many sections of the State.

*Medicinal roots*, as ginseng, snake root, sarsaparilla, mandrake, &c., are gathered in large quantities in the mountains for exportation.

The products of the forests of Virginia, for the year 1869-'70 were worth from

* Richmond Dispatch. January 1st, 1873.

† British Blue Book—1869.

‡ Report of Merchants and Mechanics Exchange.

20 to $25,000,000. They were shipped from hundreds of points, and but a small portion of the trade passed through Richmond and Norfolk.

TIDEWATER has extensive forests of pine (the noted yellow Virginia), oak, cypress, cedar, locust, &c., from which large quantities of sawed lumber and timber, staves, heading, hoop-poles, shingles, railway ties, fire wood, &c., are constantly shipped, very often from the edges of the forests, since sailing vessels can penetrate all portions of the. section—directly to all the seaboard markets of the country. Sumac is here an abundant shrub.

The MIDDLE SECTION has large areas of superior hard pine, black, white and other oaks, hickory, locust, persimmon, gum, cedar, holly, and other trees, from which much excellent lumber, tan bark, &c., are sent over the railways and canals that penetrate and cross it to various markets. Sassafras and sumac are plentiful, and the former could advantageously be made a staple crop on the ridge lands.

PIEDMONT has considerable forest land with many varieties of oak, hickory, tulip-poplar, black walnut, locust, cedar, chestnut, pine, and other timber trees, but it can hardly be considered a source of supply for timber for exportation, save in a few localities. Sumac and sassafras abound.

The BLUE RIDGE is mostly covered with forests of oak, white, black, red, rock, &c., hickory, chestnut, locust, birch, some excellent yellow pines, and other trees. This section has furnished great quantities of charcoal for the manufacture of iron from the ores of its western margin, and it will long be a source of supply, so rapidly do its forests renew themselves. The timber supply of pine and other woods for the eastern part of the Valley is drawn from the Blue Ridge. Here is found much valuable hard wood, as hickory and oak for wagon and agricultural implement making. This is yet to become a most important source of supply for oak tanbark to convert into quercitron for exportation, or to be used in the country for tanning. Almost any quantity of oak bark can be obtained from this extensive range.

THE VALLEY has nearly half its surface covered by a growth of oaks, hickories and locusts, interspersed with black and white walnuts, yellow and other pines, all having a uniform age of 150 to 200 years. This timber, while not the largest, is of the very best quality, and no well settled portion of the Union can offer a larger quantity of timber suitable for wagon, carriage, railroad car, cabinet and other work, for which hard, sound and durable woods are required. The slaty lands abound in sumac.

APPALACHIA is both *rich* and *poor* in forestal wealth. On the sandstone mountain ranges, and in the slate and shale valleys, the trees are small but the growth is dense, consisting of oaks and other hard woods, pines, &c., good for charcoal, with larger trees in the hollows and more fertile spots. On the limestone ridges and adjacent valleys, as also in the calcareous and some shale valleys, on the other hand, the oaks, walnuts, white and yellow tulip-poplars, birches, beeches, locusts, cherries, sycamores, and other timber trees, are found of a sound growth and very large size, often several feet in diameter, straight and without a limb for fifty to eighty feet from the ground. Only portions of this region have been reached by railroads, and extensive forests of the best of timber for nearly all purposes await the progress of internal improvements and future demands. There are some extensive forests of white pine and of the more common varieties of the fir tribe, but generally the Coniferæ, suitable for timber, are not abundant in the forests of this section. It is fortunate that there is so much excellent coaling timber here in the vicinity of large deposits of the easily fused ores of iron. It is from these mountain forests that ginseng, snake root, sarsaparilla and other medicinal plants are obtained.

*Forest Fruits*, such as blackberries, whortleberries, cranberries, strawberries, dewberries, haws, persimmons, service berries, thorn and crab apples, wild plums and cherries, are found in boundless abundance in nearly all the unoccupied lands and in the forests of Virginia, where, in their season, they may be had for the picking by any one that is inclined to gather them. Not only are thousands of bushels of these wild fruits annually gathered for home use and sale in home markets, but they are dried or canned for exportation, furnishing important and valuable articles of commerce.

*Nuts* are found in all sections, embracing chestnuts, chinquapins, black walnuts, white walnuts or butter nuts, hickory nuts of several kinds, hazel nuts, beech nuts, acorns of many varieties, &c.

## CHAPTER V.

# MANUFACTURES.

### Section I.—Results of Manufacturing in Virginia.

In *Home Manufactures*, the results of the hand spinning wheel and loom, Virginia has always held a prominent position, a large portion of her rural population having an honest pride in the wearing of home-made clothing. The farmers and planters of all sections of the State were careful to have annual crops of the best flax and wool, and in some sections cotton, to be manufactured at home, not only for the wants of the family, but also for sale. The census of 1860 gives the following returns for the value of Virginia home manufactures:

| SECTIONS. | Value. |
|---|---|
| Tidewater | 149,403 |
| Middle | 332,779 |
| Piedmont | 168,507 |
| Blue Ridge | 62,010 |
| The Valley | 196,568 |
| Appalachia | 162,618 |
| TOTAL | $1,071,885 |

In proportion to population the sections stood, in the value of home manufactures, 1st Appalachia, 2d Blue Ridge, 3d Valley, 4th Middle, 5th Piedmont, and 6th Tidewater.

In *Manufactures* of various kinds, as *special branches* of industry, but a small portion* of the population of Virginia has engaged, and generally only to supply neighborhood demands.

The aggregate results were as follows in 1860:

| SECTIONS. | Number of Establishments. | Capital Invested. | Cost of Raw Material. | Number of Hands Employed. | | Annual Cost of Labor. | Annual Value of Products. |
|---|---|---|---|---|---|---|---|
| | | | | Male. | Female. | | |
| Tidewater | 966 | $6,096,490 | $9,480,391 | 9,908 | 277 | $2,555,868 | $16,019,801 |
| Middle | 1,233 | 7,442,934 | 9,571,826 | 10,170 | 2,480 | 2,630,602 | 15,685,012 |
| Piedmont | 688 | 2,091,452 | 2,761,759 | 2,674 | 321 | 545,538 | 4,010,422 |
| Blue Ridge | 62 | 157,515 | 124,741 | 170 | ...... | 37,644 | 198,457 |
| Valley | 1,220 | 3,500,191 | 3,316,550 | 3,590 | 120 | 868,214 | 5,303,216 |
| Appalachia | 122 | 230,063 | 292,803 | 215 | ...... | 55,720 | 421,091 |
| TOTALS | 4,291 | $19,5[illegible] | $25,548,070 | 26,727 | 3,198 | $6,693,585 | $41,637,999 |

* Less than 12 per cent. in 1870, while nearly 22 per cent. of the population of the U. S. were so engaged.

Comparing the totals here given with those for the entire United States, it appears that Virginia had, in round numbers, 1-35th of the manufacturing establishments, 1-50th of the invested capital, paid 1-40th of the cost of raw material used, employed 1-39th of the male and 1-90th of the female hands, paid 1-54th of the cost of labor, and the annual value of its products was 1-45th of the whole—a result highly creditable to the State.

The following tables present the details of manufacturing in each section, which, added, form the totals above given.

The Tidewater counties in 1860 were returned as having the following totals of the results of manufacturing:

| COUNTIES.* | Number of Establishments. | Capital Invested. | Cost of Raw Material. | Number of Hands Employed. | | Annual Cost of Labor. | Annual Value of Products. |
|---|---|---|---|---|---|---|---|
| | | | | Male. | Female. | | |
| Accomac | 17 | $ 3,465 | $ 9,260 | 47 | 4 | $ 13,812 | $ 29,285 |
| Caroline | 28 | 76,875 | 132,423 | 85 | 3 | 17,061 | 203,600 |
| Charles City | 15 | 33,550 | 56,890 | 45 | .... | 10,788 | 111,109 |
| Elizabeth City | 26 | 16,625 | 30,335 | 57 | .... | 12,429 | 56,995 |
| Essex | 5 | 8,900 | 3,000 | 23 | .... | 7,260 | 16,000 |
| Gloucester | 40 | 92,995 | 104,682 | 152 | 5 | 21,120 | 156,325 |
| Hanover | 37 | 40,700 | 63,507 | 64 | .... | 16,896 | 101,035 |
| Henrico | 320 | 4,637,030 | 7,815,431 | 7,418 | 171 | 2,002,812 | 12,926,949 |
| Isle of Wight | 9 | 89,400 | 44,200 | 68 | 40 | 19,368 | 90,500 |
| James City | 29 | 75,425 | 90,087 | 80 | 4 | 22,524 | 157,693 |
| King George | 30 | 84,160 | 53,193 | 145 | .... | 9,104 | 69,430 |
| King & Queen | 21 | 43,900 | 63,472 | 37 | .... | 7,916 | 87,469 |
| King William | 24 | 73,000 | 85,035 | 59 | .... | 16,044 | 121,675 |
| Lancaster | 14 | 37,050 | 64,680 | 45 | .... | 7,374 | 84,019 |
| Mathews | 11 | 28,500 | 38,517 | 20 | .... | 4,359 | 50,109 |
| Nansemond | 8 | 20,100 | 61,000 | 29 | .... | 5,140 | 81,500 |
| New Kent | 18 | 46,460 | 58,320 | 48 | 1 | 8,906 | 100,402 |
| Norfolk | 86 | 397,277 | 209,764 | 644 | 39 | 193,621 | 732,811 |
| Northampton | 6 | 10,750 | 10,920 | 40 | .... | 6,180 | 25,510 |
| Northumberland | 19 | 41,000 | 64,374 | 41 | .... | 7,456 | 90,732 |
| Prince George | 3 | 32,000 | 15,500 | 42 | 4 | 8,388 | 35,400 |
| Princess Anne | 14 | 2,950 | 11,350 | 26 | .... | 5,760 | 20,750 |
| Richmond | 3 | 1,500 | 3,000 | 15 | .... | 4,500 | 9,000 |
| Southampton | 20 | 9,361 | 5,630 | 45 | .... | 10,884 | 21,149 |
| Surry | 10 | 42,465 | 43,649 | 83 | 4 | 15,876 | 97,545 |
| Sussex | 39 | 89,300 | 116,435 | 96 | 2 | 18,597 | 182,535 |
| Warwick | 5 | 20,500 | 61,688 | 31 | .... | 10,200 | 132,856 |
| Westmoreland | 2 | 2,200 | 1,710 | 9 | .... | 2,880 | 5,600 |
| York | 119 | 90,053 | 58,270 | 356 | .... | 65,568 | 218,697 |
| TOTAL | 966 | $6,096,490 | $9,480,391 | 9,908 | 277 | $2,555,868 | $16,019,501 |

* There were no returns from Middlesex.

The manufacturing centres of Tidewater are: 1st, Henrico, including the city of Richmond at the lower falls of the James, *where three-fourths of the manufacturing of the section is done;* 2d, Norfolk, including the cities of Norfolk and Portsmouth; 3d, York, and 4th, Caroline counties. Most of the manufacturing of this section is done in and near Richmond and Norfolk.

The following table gives the details of manufacturing in Tidewater in 1860:

| KIND. | Number of Establishments. | Capital Invested. | Cost of Raw Materials. | Number of Hands Employed. | | Annual Cost of Labor. | Annual Value of Products. |
|---|---|---|---|---|---|---|---|
| | | | | Male. | Female. | | |
| Agricultural implements | 12 | $ 82,400 | $ 38,860 | 162 | .... | $ 57,660 | $ 188,100 |
| Blacksmithing | 48 | 17,646 | 33,374 | 120 | .... | 33,469 | 67,561 |
| Book-binding and blank books | 3 | 4,500 | 5,200 | 13 | 3 | 5,520 | 14,000 |
| Boots and shoes | 49 | 60,015 | 77,990 | 208 | 25 | 67,752 | 211,380 |
| Boxes—tobacco | 6 | 5,500 | 23,597 | 56 | .... | 19,200 | 54,180 |
| Brass founding | 1 | 8,400 | 325 | 3 | .... | 1,200 | 2,000 |
| Bread, crackers, &c | 6 | 7,000 | 83,675 | 62 | 6 | 24,660 | 133,000 |
| Brick | 21 | 103,750 | 58,583 | 336 | 5 | 31,788 | 119,500 |
| Carpentering | 29 | 52,750 | 86,345 | 182 | .... | 64,428 | 278,640 |
| Carriages | 47 | 114,375 | 95,459 | 404 | 5 | 119,192 | 343,010 |
| Cars | 1 | 37,000 | 39,150 | 45 | .... | 20,244 | 75,000 |
| Cigars | 9 | 13,200 | 17.220 | 37 | .... | 13,872 | 50,300 |
| Chemicals | 1 | 6,000 | 4,000 | .... | 3 | 1,080 | 8,000 |
| Clothing—ladies' cloaks, &c | 1 | 150 | 500 | .... | 5 | 1,200 | 2,330 |
| Clothing—ladies' hoop-skirts | 1 | 350 | 1,500 | .... | 15 | 2,400 | 4,670 |
| Clothing—men's | 21 | 47,250 | 70,050 | 39 | 100 | 34,452 | 133,000 |
| Coal—bituminous | 1 | 100,000 | 5,700 | 80 | .... | 19,200 | 47,000 |
| Confectionery | 15 | 3,300 | 18,985 | 13 | .... | 3,756 | 26,050 |
| Cooperage | 18 | 37,650 | 111,550 | 263 | .... | 80,505 | 232,850 |
| Copper-smithing | 1 | 14,000 | 2,650 | 10 | .... | 4,200 | 9,000 |
| Cordage | 1 | 500 | 3,000 | 6 | .... | 900 | 5,000 |
| Coffins | 2 | 800 | 700 | 4 | .... | 1,080 | 2,660 |
| Cotton goods | 2 | 55,000 | 38,000 | 40 | 40 | 12,000 | 62,795 |
| Cotton ginning | 1 | 1,000 | 1,000 | 2 | .... | 360 | 1,900 |
| Fire-arms | 2 | 1,500 | 1,000 | 8 | .... | 2,520 | 5,000 |
| Fisheries—shad, &c | 116 | 63,142 | 24,224 | 481 | .... | 50,484 | 104,157 |
| Fisheries—oyster | 25 | 40,850 | 26,590 | 124 | .... | 13,140 | 53,135 |
| Flour and meal | 192 | 1,415,750 | 3,655,518 | 501 | .... | 130,396 | 4,217,342 |
| Furniture—cabinet | 8 | 40,950 | 50,250 | 67 | .... | 23,784 | 103,490 |
| Gas | 1 | 83,000 | 2,295 | 3 | .... | 1,296 | 12,000 |
| Hardware—coach and saddlery | 1 | 800 | 920 | 4 | .... | 2,160 | 7,000 |
| Hardware—files | 1 | 1,200 | 2,070 | 10 | .... | 1,200 | 4,000 |
| Hardware—locks, &c | 2 | 3,500 | 1,950 | 9 | .... | 3,960 | 8,000 |
| Hats and caps | 4 | 5,500 | 11,900 | 12 | 1 | 7,536 | 28,200 |
| Iron—bar, sheet and railroad | 1 | 425,000 | 411,775 | 800 | .... | 307,200 | 1,000,000 |

## TABLE OF MANUFACTURES CONTINUED.

| KIND. | Number of Establishments. | Capital Invested. | Cost of Raw Materials. | Number of Hands Employed. Male. | Number of Hands Employed. Female. | Annual Cost of Labor. | Annual Value of Products |
|---|---|---|---|---|---|---|---|
| Iron—castings | 6 | $ 27,200 | $ 32,990 | 72 | .... | $ 27,000 | $ 87,750 |
| Iron—forging | 1 | 10,000 | 20,000 | 16 | .... | 7,200 | 42,750 |
| Jewelry | 1 | 300 | 1,000 | 2 | .... | 960 | 2,500 |
| Leather | 6 | 13,250 | 10,041 | 18 | .... | 2,410 | 18,000 |
| Lime | 2 | 3,150 | 8,017 | 7 | .... | 1,872 | 17,200 |
| Looking-glass and picture frames | 2 | 1,300 | 4,120 | 10 | .... | 2,424 | 8,500 |
| Liquors—distilled | 1 | 200,000 | 155,800 | 35 | .... | 12,600 | 225,000 |
| Liquors—malt | 1 | 10,000 | 5,000 | 7 | .... | 2,820 | 15,000 |
| Lumber—planed | 3 | 63,500 | 80,600 | 25 | .... | 10,560 | 103,300 |
| Lumber—sawed | 96 | 328,025 | 309,256 | 613 | 10 | 132,504 | 805,752 |
| Machinery, steam engines, &c | 12 | 252,600 | 146,004 | 513 | .... | 171,744 | 563,945 |
| Marble and stone work | 2 | 3,700 | 21,000 | 38 | .... | 7,440 | 41,300 |
| Medicines | 1 | 2,000 | 9,300 | 4 | 1 | 720 | 24,000 |
| Millinery | 2 | 710 | 3,500 | .... | 14 | 1,368 | 8,000 |
| Musical instruments, pianos, &c | 1 | 150,000 | 174,000 | 225 | .... | 30,000 | 213,750 |
| Nails and spikes | 1 | 2,000 | 800 | 12 | .... | 3,000 | 4,200 |
| Ornaments—plaster | 1 | 100 | 250 | 2 | .... | 720 | 1,225 |
| Painting | 1 | 100 | 500 | 2 | .... | 720 | 1,500 |
| Paper for printing | 1 | 41,000 | 40,000 | 24 | 12 | 9,000 | 75,000 |
| Plaster—ground | 4 | 9,500 | 16,700 | 4 | .... | 840 | 31,210 |
| Printing | 5 | 41,900 | 22,453 | 57 | .... | 13,920 | 40,044 |
| Plumbing and gas-fitting | 2 | 20,000 | 16,410 | 29 | .... | 10,200 | 35,000 |
| Pottery ware | 2 | 6,000 | 2,550 | 20 | .... | 5,400 | 15,000 |
| Pumps | 1 | 1,500 | 240 | 1 | .... | 720 | 1,500 |
| Regalia, banners, flags, &c | 1 | 2,000 | 600 | 3 | .... | 432 | 1,500 |
| Saddlery and harness | 21 | 31,975 | 40,919 | 87 | .... | 33,192 | 100,710 |
| Sails | 1 | 2,500 | 8,000 | 5 | .... | 1,800 | 12,000 |
| Sash, doors and blinds | 6 | 28,600 | 16,802 | 49 | .... | 16,596 | 50,700 |
| Saws | 2 | 8,000 | 13,200 | 16 | .... | 4,992 | 29,000 |
| Ship and boat building | 5 | 4,950 | 6,540 | 39 | .... | 9,960 | 23,700 |
| Soap and candles | 9 | 93,200 | 83,027 | 38 | .... | 11,340 | 140,012 |
| Springs—steel | 1 | 500,000 | 106,300 | 25 | .... | 9,600 | 225,000 |
| Stair-building | 1 | 500 | 300 | 3 | .... | 1,440 | 4,000 |
| Staves, shooks and heading | 3 | 500 | 5,600 | 15 | .... | 5,640 | 13,575 |
| Iron, copper and sheet-iron ware | 18 | 87,750 | 70,439 | 129 | .... | 40,376 | 175,200 |
| Tobacco—manufactured | 52 | 1,121,025 | 2,882,415 | 3,370 | 34 | 714,384 | 4,938,995 |
| Trunks, &c | 1 | 500 | 1,000 | 3 | .... | 1,296 | 2,600 |
| Wagons, carts, &c | 39 | 23,180 | 39,547 | 125 | .... | 33,945 | 105,007 |
| Willow ware | 2 | 300 | 585 | 3 | .... | 1,089 | 1,700 |
| Woolen goods | 1 | 130,000 | 96,000 | 100 | .... | 27,600 | 200,000 |
| TOTALS | 966 | $6,096,490 | $9,480,391 | 9,908 | 277 | $2,555,868 | $16,019,801 |

The agricultural implements were made in King William, Sussex and Henrico. Blacksmithing is only credited to one-third of the counties, giving none to the Northern Neck, save King George; none to the Middlesex, and only to Gloucester, of the Gloucester Peninsula; *none* to King William, New Kent, York, Warwick, Charles City, Prince George, Surry, Isle of Wight, Nanesemond, or Northampton; so that numerous shops, &c., were not reported. Boots and shoes were made in 13 counties, but Henrico produced 17-21ths of the whole, and Norfolk 2-21ths. Bread and crackers and bricks were made in Elizabeth City, Henrico and Norfolk. Carpentry was confined to James City and Henrico. Carriages were manufactured in 19 counties, Henrico having 14-34ths, Caroline 3-34ths and Norfolk 6-34ths of the whole product; the notable omissions are Hanover, New Kent, Isle of Wight and Nansemond. Men's clothing is 6-13ths of it credited to Norfolk and the same to Richmond. Cooperage is confined to Southampton, Norfolk and Henrico. Coffins are given to James and Elizabeth City. Isle of Wight and Henrico monopolized cotton goods, and cotton ginning was done in King William. The shad fisheries were in King George, York, Norfolk and Northampton, and the oyster in Gloucester and Norfolk. Flour and meal were ground in all but Westmoreland, Richmond, Essex, Middlesex, Prince George and the Eastern Shore—Henrico having 5-7ths of the whole product, followed by Caroline and Sussex each about 1-42d. Cabinet furniture was made in Henrico, Norfolk, Nansemond and Accomac, 74-103ds of all in Henrico and 25 in Norfolk. Iron castings were produced in Hanover, Henrico and Norfolk, 81-87ths of the product being credited to Henrico. Leather was tanned in Northumberland, Lancaster, Gloucester, Caroline, Henrico, Isle of Wight and Accomac, one establishment in each county named, except Northumberland, which had two. Saw mills were credited to all the counties but King George, Westmoreland, Richmond, Essex, Southampton and Accomac; Warwick was first in production with 12-80ths of the value, followed by York with 10-80ths, Prince George and Henrico each 7-80ths, these four sawing about half the product. Machinery and steam engines were made in Hanover, Henrico and Norfolk, 51-56ths of the production being from Henrico. Elizabeth City, by the census, was the only county that had any painting done. Plaster was ground in Henrico and King George, 30-31ths of it in the former. Printing, by the census, was confined to four establishments in Norfolk and one in James City, and no mention is made of Henrico, including Richmond, with its numerous newspaper, book and job printing establishments. Eleven counties had saddlery and harness shops, but 78-100ths of the annual product was from Henrico and 13-100ths from Norfolk. Sash, doors and blinds were made in Hanover, Henrico and Norfolk; 28-50ths of the production was from Henrico, and 20-50ths from Norfolk. Ship and boat building was carried on in York, Elizabeth City, Henrico and Isle of Wight, the production being nearly the same in each; the omission of Norfolk should be noted. Wagons, carts, &c., were manufactured in 12 counties, but 77-105ths of the production was in Henrico and 9-105ths in Hanover.

The following manufactures were carried on in *Henrico* county (including Richmond city) *alone*, viz: Making tobacco boxes, brass founding, ladies' clothing and hoop skirts, mining bituminous coal, confectionery, copper smithing, cordage, hardware, file and lock making, hats and caps, bar, sheet and railroad iron, iron forging, jewelry, lime, looking glass and picture frames, distilled and malt liquors, planed lumber, marble and stone cutting, medicines, millinery, nails and spikes, plaster ornaments, printing paper, plumbing and gas fitting, pottery ware, pumps, regalia, banners, &c., sails, saws, steel springs, stairs, tobacco manufacture, trunks, willow ware and woolen goods.

These industries were found only in Henrico and Norfolk counties, viz: Book binding and blank books, making cigars, fire arms, soap and candles, and tin, copper and sheet iron ware.

In Norfolk county (including Norfolk city, Portsmouth, &c.) *alone* were the following, viz: The making of cars, chemicals, gas, musical instruments, and staves, shooks and heading.

The manufactures of Richmond are numerous and important, and the following statistics* of value of products show that they are in a healthy condition, notwithstanding the depression in business during the years presented:

| PRODUCTS. | 1872. | 1873. | 1874. |
|---|---|---|---|
| Iron, nail, architectural iron, and railroad car works, and iron ware | $ 5,492,000 | $ 4,081,000 | $ 2,946,760 |
| Tobacco and cigars | 5,205,600 | 5,062,466 | 6,327,581 |
| Flour, meal and mill offal | 2,045,000 | 2,422,000 | † 2,214,683 |
| Agricultural implements | 368,000 | 323,600 | 435,300 |
| Furniture, mattresses and wooden ware, including barrels, buckets, brooms, &c | 378,965 | 352,400 | 306,514 |
| Leather, as boots, shoes, trunks, harness, belting, &c | 298,300 | 273,500 | 251,750 |
| Fertilizers, lime, sumac, dye-stuffs, oils, &c | 375,495 | 491,000 | 472,400 |
| Printers' types and material, paper, paper boxes and twine, lithographs, photographs, books, &c | 137,110 | 314,650 | 1,031,087 |
| Refined sugars | 803,858 | ‡ | ........ |
| Lager beer, ale, wines and liquors | 187,250 | 198,200 | 116,000 |
| Carriages, wagons, carts, &c | 95,300 | 121,300 | 126,520 |
| Cotton goods, clothing, &c | 528,000 | 865,900 | 682,500 |
| Sash, blinds, doors and mouldings | ........ | ........ | 113,375 |
| Miscellaneous manufactures, such as soap, candles, cakes, crackers, bread, candy, pumps, ship rigging, rope, tin ware, brushes, spirits, stone, earthen and marble wares, blank books, picture frames, &c | 285,000 | 344,520 | 632,250 |
| TOTALS | $16,199,870 | $14,581,136 | $17,746,720 |

The values for 1870 were $7,000,000, and for 1871, $14,840,146.

The gas works of the city of Richmond manufactured as follows, viz:

In 1872—66,260,700 cubic feet of gas from 273,687 bushels of coal.
In 1873—83,686,200 cubic feet of gas from 297,294 bushels of coal.
In 1874—81,812,600 cubic feet of gas from 288,345 bushels of coal.

* From the annual exhibits of the Richmond Dispatch.

† One of the largest flouring mills was burned in April, diminishing the product.

‡ This was the "panic" year, and the sugar refineries stopped early in the year.

The counties* of Middle Virginia, in 1860, were credited with these totals of manufactures:

| COUNTIES. | Number of Establishments. | Capital Invested. | Cost of Raw Materials. | Number of Hands Employed. | | Annual Cost of Labor. | Annual Value of Products. |
|---|---|---|---|---|---|---|---|
| | | | | Male. | Female | | |
| Alexandria | 96 | $357,250 | $403,659 | 732 | 149 | $193,350 | $761,290 |
| Amelia | 37 | 69,575 | 128,352 | 71 | .... | 16,374 | 158,545 |
| Appomattox | 17 | 42,900 | 24,920 | 57 | 2 | 13,356 | 51,542 |
| Buckingham | 28 | 92,480 | 118,416 | 82 | .... | 20,776 | 169,904 |
| Brunswick | 36 | 70,200 | 132,677 | 65 | .... | 13,932 | 176,820 |
| Cumberland | 33 | 41,600 | 23,795 | 55 | .... | 9,564 | 42,326 |
| Chesterfield | 50 | 2,372,624 | 1,539,895 | 1,208 | 497 | 373,350 | 2,686,870 |
| Campbell | 141 | 1,242,190 | 1,918,814 | 1,900 | 314 | 445,044 | 3,171,360 |
| Charlotte | 33 | 21,030 | 39,615 | 58 | .... | 13,404 | 64,765 |
| Dinwiddie | 78 | 1,133,795 | 2,091,187 | 2,150 | 961 | 626,168 | 3,570,855 |
| Fairfax | .. | ......... | ......... | .... | .... | ...... | ...... |
| Fluvanna | 58 | 148,940 | 185,475 | 304 | 35 | 64,136 | 300,455 |
| Goochland | 38 | 80,150 | 85,914 | 75 | .... | 15,756 | 126,683 |
| Greensville | 15 | 50,375 | 76,020 | 30 | 1 | 5,772 | 92,827 |
| Halifax | 55 | 155,145 | 84,128 | 207 | 10 | 42,390 | 189,213 |
| Louisa | 57 | 218,800 | 277,320 | 279 | 3 | 58,392 | 455,950 |
| Lunenburg | 14 | 40,450 | 49,201 | 20 | .... | 3,912 | 59,147 |
| Mecklenburg | 65 | 140,525 | 352,420 | 489 | 140 | 85,122 | 518,398 |
| Nottoway | 45 | 124,225 | 127,863 | 119 | 3 | 33,472 | 186,541 |
| Prince William | 47 | 166,480 | 160,836 | 108 | 5 | 26,268 | 235,927 |
| Powhatan | 20 | 66,800 | 15,150 | 34 | .... | 6,180 | 23,950 |
| Pittsylvania | 141 | 439,525 | 1,176,172 | 1,136 | 238 | 370,626 | 1,670,257 |
| Prince Edward | 24 | 91,325 | 193,459 | 261 | 52 | 63,820 | 299,917 |
| Stafford | 33 | 131,900 | 218,946 | 339 | 34 | 29,630 | 302,920 |
| Spotsylvania | 72 | 144,650 | 147,592 | 391 | 36 | 109,808 | 368,050 |
| TOTALS | 1,233 | $7,412,934 | $9,571,826 | 10,170 | 2,480 | $2,630,602 | $15,685,012 |

The manufacturing centres of Midland Virginia were: 1st, Dinwiddie, including most of Petersburg, at the falls of the Appomattox; 2d, Campbell, including Lynchburg, on the James; 3d, Chesterfield, including Manchester, at the falls of the James opposite Richmond; 4th, Pittsylvania, including Danville, on the Dan; 5th, Alexandria, on the Potomac; and 6th, Spotsylvania and Stafford, including Fredericksburg and Falmouth, on the Rappahannock at the falls.

*It is well to call attention to a statement in Chapter I. that all the counties are *not wholly included* in the Natural Divisions in which they are grouped, but they are placed where the larger portion of their area lies. The figures are taken from *county* returns, therefore they must follow the county in grouping. A census-taking by smaller political divisions would remedy these defects, but the general result would not vary much from that given, because of the compensation of areas.

The results of manufacturing in MIDDLE VIRGINIA, by the census of 1860, were:

| KIND. | Number of Establishments. | Capital Invested. | Cost of Raw Material. | Number of Hands Employed. | | Annual Cost of Labor. | Annual Value of Products. |
|---|---|---|---|---|---|---|---|
| | | | | Male. | Female | | |
| Agricultural implements | 15 | $ 54,300 | $ 34,272 | 107 | 1 | $ 31,800 | $ 110,349 |
| Bark, ground, sumac | 2 | 9,200 | 9,200 | 8 | .... | 1,920 | 14,000 |
| Blacksmithing | 140 | 45,370 | 29,858 | 279 | .... | 64,284 | 124,619 |
| Book-binding and blank books | 4 | 4,300 | 4,738 | 10 | .... | 3,444 | 11,000 |
| Bread, crackers, &c | 6 | 20,750 | 43,070 | 34 | .... | 7,740 | 67,500 |
| Brick | 19 | 55,950 | 16,345 | 201 | .... | 26,964 | 76,680 |
| Brooms | 1 | 500 | 700 | 3 | .... | 1,080 | 4,000 |
| Boots and shoes | 54 | 84,680 | 83,047 | 298 | 63 | 89,916 | 226,394 |
| Boxes—tobacco | 7 | 15,895 | 19,388 | 44 | .... | 16,728 | 46,649 |
| Coal—bituminous | 4 | 1,050,000 | 45,500 | 413 | 3 | 122,088 | 285,090 |
| Cars | 4 | 38,000 | 11,130 | 105 | .... | 35,440 | 62,100 |
| Chemicals | 1 | 100 | 500 | 2 | .... | 720 | 2,000 |
| Coffins | 1 | 500 | 300 | 1 | .... | 540 | 1,700 |
| Cigars | 4 | 2,800 | 5,350 | 7 | .... | 2,580 | 10,500 |
| Clothing—men's | 18 | 27,750 | 61,624 | 68 | 80 | 39,824 | 126,913 |
| Carriages | 31 | 64,125 | 50,687 | 253 | 1 | 91,416 | 190,770 |
| Confectionery | 40 | 36,700 | 51,950 | 29 | .... | 8,472 | 87,700 |
| Carpentering | 9 | 23,000 | 32,257 | 79 | .... | 29,064 | 90,160 |
| Cotton goods | 11 | 1,212,000 | 678,990 | 596 | 742 | 223,728 | 1,256,600 |
| Cooperage | 15 | 20,370 | 14,320 | 88 | .... | 13,620 | 37,585 |
| Cordage | 1 | 4,000 | 10,000 | 6 | 1 | 6,636 | 16,000 |
| Dyeing and bleaching | 1 | 100 | 300 | 1 | .... | 432 | 1,200 |
| Flour and meal | 279 | 1,444,675 | 3,624,239 | 518 | 2 | 124,240 | 4,300,588 |
| Furniture—cabinet | 27 | 67,300 | 31,621 | 121 | 1 | 42,888 | 105,771 |
| Fire-arms | 1 | 2,700 | 800 | 2 | .... | 720 | 2,000 |
| Fertilizers | 2 | 37,000 | 202,500 | 32 | .... | 10,800 | 223,000 |
| Fisheries—shad | 17 | 26,000 | 15,400 | 401 | 4 | 19,070 | 50,250 |
| Glue | 1 | 1,000 | 1,000 | 2 | .... | 480 | 1,550 |
| Gas | 1 | 70,000 | 5,000 | 5 | .... | 1,920 | 17,000 |
| Gold-mining | 2 | 87,000 | 9,000 | 33 | .... | 4,200 | 35,000 |
| Hats and caps | 4 | 3,800 | 2,765 | 8 | 1 | 2,580 | 7,275 |
| Iron castings | 17 | 183,100 | 88,413 | 221 | .... | 75,852 | 271,300 |
| Jewelry | 1 | 3,000 | 50 | 2 | .... | 1,080 | 1,200 |
| Leather | 38 | 95,900 | 113,299 | 116 | .... | 27,306 | 173,852 |
| Liquors—malt | 1 | 5,000 | 6,120 | 4 | .... | 1,200 | 9,000 |
| Liquors—distilled | 1 | 25,000 | 750 | 3 | .... | 432 | 1,800 |
| Lumber—sawed | 161 | 304,429 | 168,117 | 495 | 4 | 99,664 | 444,686 |
| Lumber—planed | 1 | 3,000 | 5,700 | 5 | .... | 1,200 | 7,360 |
| Locomotives | 1 | 20 000 | 120,700 | 30 | .... | 9,360 | 133,000 |

## TABLE OF MANUFACTURES CONTINUED.

| KIND. | Number of Establishments. | Capital Invested. | Cost of Raw Material. | Number of Hands Employed. | | Annual Cost of Labor. | Annu Value Produ |
|---|---|---|---|---|---|---|---|
| | | | | Male. | Female | | |
| Mineral waters | 1 | $ 300 | $ 150 | 2 | .... | $ 480 | [illegible] |
| Machinery, steam engines, &c. | 4 | 54,000 | 76,500 | 144 | .... | 89,900 | 14 |
| Marble and stone works | 5 | 15,700 | 22,000 | 72 | .... | 25,748 | 8 |
| Millinery | 4 | 17,775 | 18,775 | 16 | .... | 3,720 | 3 |
| Pipes—clay | 1 | 500 | 150 | 3 | .... | 684 | [illegible] |
| Pottery ware | 2 | 3,000 | 1,700 | 8 | .... | 3,552 | [illegible] |
| Plaster—ground | 6 | 26,400 | 20,885 | 16 | .... | 4,956 | 3 |
| Sash, doors and blinds | 2 | 18,200 | 17,275 | 25 | .... | 8,400 | 3 |
| Ship and boat building | 2 | 2,000 | 10,000 | 15 | .... | 1,584 | 1 |
| Spokes, hubs and felloes | 1 | 3,000 | 2,000 | 5 | .... | 1,080 | |
| Saddlery and harness | 35 | 49,625 | 51,529 | 112 | .... | 35,048 | 11 |
| Slate quarrying | 2 | 26,000 | 210 | 21 | .... | 7,860 | 1 |
| Soap and candles | 5 | 33,000 | 27,600 | 23 | 4 | 5,670 | [illegible] |
| Tin, copper and sheet iron | 20 | 37,250 | 51,148 | 84 | .... | 26,052 | 10 |
| Tobacco—manufactured | 134 | 1,993,265 | 3,617,894 | 7,851 | 1,452 | 1,196,164 | 6,2 |
| Wool carding | 4 | 5,000 | 10,600 | 7 | .... | 1,008 | 1 |
| Woolen goods | 1 | 22,500 | 5,990 | 12 | 5 | 2,796 | [illegible] |
| Wagons, carts, &c. | 61 | 35,625 | 18,150 | 141 | .... | 35,772 | [illegible] |
| TOTALS | 1,233 | $7,442,934 | $9,571,826 | 10,170 | 2,480 | $2,630,602 | $15,6 |

Most of the agricultural implements were made in Halifax, Spotsylvania, Cal bell and Alexandria. The sumac mills were in Spotsylvania and Alexand Blacksmithing is credited to all but Greensville, Brunswick, Prince Edward, P hatan, Buckingham, Spotsylvania and Fairfax. Book-binding was done in A andria, Spotsylvania, Dinwiddie and Campbell. Bread and cracker making limited to Alexandria and Campbell; brick making to Alexandria, Spotsylva Goochland, Chesterfield and Campbell. Brooms, chemicals, cigars, dyeing bleaching, malt liquors, mineral waters and clay pipes were only made in A andria. Boots and shoes were made in all the counties but Fairfax, Stafford, C berland, Powhatan, Lunenburg, Greensville and Mecklenburg; tobacco boxe Goochland, Campbell, Pittsylvania and Mecklenburg. The coal was mined in C terfield. Railroad cars were made in Alexandria and Campbell; coffins in Pitt vania; men's clothing mostly in Alexandria, Spotsylvania, Pittsylvania and Ca bell; carriages in 11 counties, more in Campbell and Dinwiddie than elsewh confectionery in Alexandria, Lynchburg, Fredericksburg and Petersburg. Car try was confined to Spotsylvania, Campbell and Pittsylvania. Cotton goods produced in Alexandria, Chesterfield, Stafford, Dinwiddie, Fluvanna and Meck burg. Cooperage was a considerable industry in Chesterfield, Campbell, Spo vania, &c. Cordage was made only in Dinwiddie; gas and fire arms in Campl ue in Alexandria; distilled liquors in Goochland; pottery in Alexandria and Din-iddie; ship and boat building in Fluvanna; locomotive making in Chesterfield; oolen goods in Prince William; jewelry and watch making in Halifax; lumber laning in Pittsylvania; shad fisheries in Alexandria and Stafford; hat and cap aking in Alexandria and Pittsylvania; sash, blind and door making in Alexandria nd Campbell; spokes, hubs and felloes in Prince William; fertilizers in Alexandria nd Dinwiddie; slate quarrying in Buckingham; gold mining in Stafford and Spot-lvania; millinery in Spotsylvania and Campbell. Cabinet furniture was made 10 counties, but largely in Alexandria and Campbell. Leather was made in 16 unties, but most extensively in Alexandria, Dinwiddie and Campbell. Wool rding was done in Campbell, Prince William, Louisa and Fluvanna; marble and one cutting in Alexandria, Fluvanna, Chesterfield, Dinwiddie and Campbell; plas-r grinding in Alexandria, Prince William, Fluvanna and Campbell. Tin, copper nd sheet iron ware were made in Alexandria, Spotsylvania, Prince Edward, Din-iddie, Greensville and Pittsylvania. Flour and meal were made in all the counties ut Fairfax, Alexandria and Spotsylvania, says the census, but it is well known iat all of these manufactured these articles on a large scale. Tobacco was manu-ctured in Spotsylvania, Louisa, Fluvanna, Chesterfield, Prince Edward, Dinwiddie, ampbell, Pittsylvania, Halifax and Mecklenburg—Dinwiddie leading, followed by ampbell and Pittsylvania. Saddlery and harness were made in all the counties ive Fairfax, Stafford, Goochland, Powhatan, Chesterfield, Appomattox, Greensville nd Halifax—all of which no doubt had many establishments; the leading county as Dinwiddie. Wagons and carts were manufactured in all but Fairfax, Stafford, owhatan, Prince Edward, Lunenburg and Brunswick—Pittsylvania leading. Soap nd candles were the products of Alexandria, Goochland and Dinwiddie; machinery f Spotsylvania, Fluvanna, Dinwiddie and Pittsylvania. Iron castings were made twelve counties—Campbell leading far in advance. Sawed lumber was produced every county but Fairfax and Alexandria—Pittsylvania leading.

It will be seen from the table on preceding page that the leading manufacture f the Middle Country was tobacco, producing 6–16ths of the whole; the second as flour and meal, yielding 4–16ths; and the third cotton goods—these three pro-ucing three-fourths of the value of the annual product.

Fredericksburg is a very important manufacturing town of Midland Virginia. ts woolen factory has acquired a wide reputation for the broad-cloths, cassimeres, erseys and blankets it manufactures. Its two cotton mills make cotton cloths, snaburgs, yarn, &c. The two foundries manufacture stoves, agricultural imple-ents, hollow-ware, water and steam machinery, &c. The three merchant flouring ills have a capacity for grinding 500,000 bushels of grain annually. Two sumac ills are in operation, one of them the first opened in Virginia. A paper mill, two nneries, two carriage and wagon manufactories, and a planing mill and sash, &c., ctory, three furniture, three saddle and harness, seven blacksmith, two gun and ocksmith, two jewelers, and a large number of boot and shoe shops, seven bakeries, ne brewery, two distilleries, one soap factory, and three newspaper printing offices, re among the reported* industries. It was estimated that in 1867 Fredericksburg

*See report of Fredericksburg Manufacturers and Mechanics Association, 1869.

sold, of its manufactures, for home consumption the value of $150,000, and to other markets $500,000.

The MANUFACTURING STATISTICS of PIEDMONT, by counties, for 1860, were as follows:

| COUNTIES. | Number of Establishments. | Capital Invested. | Cost of Raw Material. | Number of Hands Employed. | | Annual Cost of Labor. | Annual Value of Products. |
|---|---|---|---|---|---|---|---|
| | | | | Male. | Female. | | |
| Albemarle | 73 | $257,140 | $433,085 | 215 | 27 | $46,908 | $605,010 |
| Amherst | 45 | 51,916 | 76,474 | 84 | 2 | 20,264 | 112,245 |
| Bedford | 84 | 273,030 | 405,282 | 439 | 34 | 88,374 | 598,919 |
| Culpeper | 7 | 51,335 | 95,212 | 71 | 27 | 18,612 | 159,175 |
| Fauquier | 110 | 251,316 | 185,842 | 248 | 20 | 63,612 | 337,848 |
| Franklin | 85 | 346,470 | 345,984 | 476 | 81 | 73,964 | 485,233 |
| Greene | 22 | 14,800 | 31,841 | 34 | .. | 7,200 | 47,315 |
| Henry | 52 | 293,115 | 239,326 | 496 | 93 | 91,758 | 408,245 |
| Loudoun | 83 | 274,786 | 570,601 | 288 | 8 | 70,889 | 750,178 |
| Madison | 15 | 52,800 | 43,627 | 36 | .. | 9,120 | 57,080 |
| Nelson | 23 | 38,540 | 105,877 | 40 | .. | 9,294 | 132,165 |
| Orange | 45 | 69,855 | 108,677 | 90 | .. | 19,368 | 143,360 |
| Patrick | 10 | 74,700 | 44,070 | 95 | 29 | 14,607 | 70,790 |
| Rappahannock | 34 | 41,655 | 75,861 | 62 | .. | 11,568 | 102,959 |
| TOTALS | 688 | $2,091,452 | $2,761,759 | 2,674 | 321 | $545,538 | $4,010,423 |

These figures give this section *about* 1–7th of the number of establishments, 1–9th of the invested capital, 1–7th of the cost of raw materials, 1–10th of the males and females employed, 1–11th of the annual cost of labor, and 1–10th of the annual value of products, compared with those for the whole State.

The following table presents the DETAILS of the several MANUFACTURING INDUSTRIES then carried on in PIEDMONT:

| MANUFACTURING INDUSTRIES. | Number of Establishments. | Capital Invested. | Cost of Raw Material. | Number of Hands Employed. | | Annual Cost of Labor. | Annual Value of Products. |
|---|---|---|---|---|---|---|---|
| | | | | Male. | Female. | | |
| Agricultural implements | 7 | $20,150 | $10,585 | 39 | .. | $8,640 | $28,200 |
| Boots and Shoes | 43 | 28,771 | 25,567 | 115 | 15 | 29,772 | 74,749 |
| Blacksmithing | 68 | 28,190 | 16,703 | 139 | .. | 30,924 | 61,995 |
| Brick | 2 | 2,000 | 215 | 15 | .. | 1,380 | 3,290 |
| Cigars | 1 | 5,000 | 3,500 | 10 | .. | 2,400 | 7,500 |
| Cotton goods | 2 | 30,300 | 36,770 | 15 | 15 | 3,912 | 51,560 |
| Cooperage | 3 | 2,000 | 1,745 | 11 | .. | 2,676 | 5,920 |
| Carriages | 8 | 22,200 | 7,658 | 38 | 1 | 13,008 | 37,400 |
| Carpentry | 2 | 4,950 | 2,850 | 15 | .. | 4,080 | 15,500 |
| Copper ore | 1 | 15,000 | 1,800 | 9 | 2 | 4,968 | 9,000 |

TABLE OF MANUFACTURES CONTINUED.

| MANUFACTURING INDUSTRIES. | Number of Establishments. | Capital Invested. | Cost of Raw Material. | Number of Hands Employed. | | Annual Cost of Labor. | Annual Value of Products. |
|---|---|---|---|---|---|---|---|
| | | | | Male. | Female. | | |
| Clothing—men's | 4 | $ 2,910 | $ 8,120 | 6 | 5 | $ 2,400 | $ 12,146 |
| Dentistry | 3 | 2,200 | 1,400 | 3 | .. | 1,680 | 4,900 |
| Flour and meal | 212 | 675,765 | 1,604,668 | 278 | .. | 62,050 | 1,866,373 |
| Furniture—cabinet | 10 | 8,965 | 7,796 | 28 | .. | 6,482 | 16,311 |
| Gold mining | 1 | 10,000 | ..... | 8 | 1 | 1,032 | 1,200 |
| Hats and caps | 3 | 3,900 | 1,989 | 7 | 2 | 2,274 | 7,950 |
| Iron—pig | 3 | 124,000 | 35,687 | 121 | 5 | 29,670 | 77,000 |
| Iron—castings | 3 | 2,500 | 1,610 | 0 | .. | 1,212 | 4,100 |
| Iron—bar, &c | 1 | 10,000 | 7,200 | 15 | .. | 1,620 | 9,000 |
| Leather | 44 | 96,525 | 89,318 | 106 | 1 | 22,440 | 146,242 |
| Lumber—sawed | 106 | 130,845 | 61,448 | 251 | 5 | 48,780 | 222,844 |
| Liquor—distilled | 1 | 700 | 1,730 | 1 | .. | 180 | 3,200 |
| Matresses, beds, &c | 1 | 800 | 1,720 | 2 | .. | 720 | 2,700 |
| Plaster—ground | 24 | 27,000 | 31,770 | 23 | .. | 4,194 | 43,670 |
| Pottery | 2 | 600 | 300 | 6 | .. | 984 | 1,900 |
| Printing | 3 | 4,100 | 550 | 9 | .. | 3,360 | 5,060 |
| Saddlery and Harness | 16 | 8,405 | 9,624 | 27 | .. | 7,032 | 22,520 |
| Sash, doors and blinds | 1 | 300 | 625 | 4 | .. | 900 | 2,000 |
| Tin, copper and sheet iron | 10 | 16,416 | 8,780 | 21 | .. | 4,122 | 15,939 |
| Tobacco—manufactured | 64 | 689,100 | 613,479 | 1,207 | 224 | 205,368 | 1,002,572 |
| Woolen goods | 9 | 93,550 | 125,432 | 74 | 44 | 22,764 | 203,205 |
| Watch repairing and Silversmithing, | 1 | 1,600 | 1,550 | 2 | .. | 1,720 | 2,875 |
| Wool carding | 10 | 6,750 | 13,220 | 11 | 1 | 1,242 | 17,820 |
| Wagons, carts, &c | 20 | 15,960 | 6,365 | 37 | .. | 12,552 | 22,781 |
| TOTALS | 688 | $2,091,452 | $2,761,759 | 2,674 | 321 | $545,538 | $4,010,422 |

These enumerated industries were distributed among the Piedmont counties as follows, viz: Cigars, pottery, and sash, doors and blinds, only in Loudoun; gold and copper mining, watch repairing, dentistry, brick making and liquor distilling, only in Fauquier; bar iron only in Franklin; cotton goods and mattresses only in Albemarle; printing in Nelson and Bedford; iron casting in Fauquier, Bedford and Henry; pig iron in Loudoun, Franklin and Patrick; carpentry in Fauquier and Amherst; hats and caps in Loudoun, Fauquier and Bedford; flour and meal in all the counties but Culpeper and Patrick; leather in all but Culpeper, Nelson and Patrick; sawed lumber in all but Madison and Patrick; furniture in Loudoun, Fauquier, Amherst, Bedford and Franklin; cooperage in Loudoun and Albemarle; boots and shoes in all but Culpeper, Franklin and Patrick; carriages in Loudoun, Fauquier, Madison and Bedford; blacksmithing in all but Culpeper, Albemarle, Nelson, Henry and Patrick; agricultural implements in Loudoun, Madison, Greene, Orange, Albemarle, Bedford and Franklin; wool carding in Fauquier, Greene, Amherst, Bedford and Franklin; woolen goods in Loudoun, Fauquier, Culpeper and

Albemarle; men's clothing in Fauquier, Greene and Franklin; tobacco manufactured in Albemarle, Bedford, Franklin, Henry and Patrick; plaster ground in Loudoun, Fauquier, Rappahannock, Albemarle, Nelson and Bedford; saddlery and harness in all but Culpeper, Madison, Albemarle, Nelson, Amherst and Henry; and tin, copper and sheet iron ware in Loudoun, Fauquier, Madison, Greene, Bedford and Patrick.

The Blue Ridge counties in 1860 furnished the following manufacturing returns:

| COUNTIES. | Number of Establishments. | Capital Invested. | Cost of Raw Materials. | Number of Hands Employed. Male. | Female. | Annual Cost of Labor. | Annual Value of Products. |
|---|---|---|---|---|---|---|---|
| Carroll | 42 | $ 121,400 | $ 53,377 | 136 | .... | $ 29,382 | $ 105,007 |
| Floyd | 10 | 13,515 | 14,894 | 18 | .... | 4,326 | 23,210 |
| Grayson | 10 | 22,600 | 56,470 | 16 | .... | 3,936 | 70,240 |
| Totals | 62 | $157,515 | $124,741 | 170 | .... | $37,644 | $198,457 |

Comparing these totals with those of the State, this section shows about 1–70th of the establishments, 1–163d of the invested capital, 1–160th of the cost of raw material, 1–154th of the males employed, 1–178th of the cost of labor, and 1–210th of the annual value of products.

The following were the Details of Manufacturing in the Blue Ridge Section in 1860:

| INDUSTRIES. | Number of Establishments. | Capital Invested. | Cost of Raw Materials. | Number of Hands Employed. Male. | Female. | Annual Cost of Labor. | Annual Value of Products. |
|---|---|---|---|---|---|---|---|
| Boots and shoes | 1 | $ 215 | $ 305 | 1 | .... | $ 360 | $ 1,100 |
| Fire-arms | 1 | 1,500 | 472 | 3 | .... | 360 | 1,100 |
| Flour and meal | 30 | 40,150 | 93,656 | 36 | .... | 7,334 | 117,528 |
| Cabinet furniture | 2 | 1,600 | 482 | 4 | .... | 1,620 | 2,280 |
| Leather | 8 | 6,350 | 8,885 | 15 | .... | 2,940 | 14,860 |
| Distilled liquors | 1 | 500 | 405 | 1 | .... | 336 | 700 |
| Saddlery and harness | 2 | 1,300 | 1,040 | 4 | .... | 1,050 | 2,780 |
| Wool carding | 3 | 4,400 | 5,170 | 3 | .... | 340 | 6,384 |
| Copper ore | 4 | 70,000 | 5,700 | 78 | .... | 17,520 | 31,633 |
| Copper smelting | 1 | 25,000 | 2,100 | 12 | .... | 2,880 | 5,880 |
| Iron castings | 1 | 500 | 500 | 2 | .... | 600 | 2,000 |
| Lumber—sawed | 5 | 2,800 | 4,036 | 6 | .... | 1,200 | 8,122 |
| Linseed oil | 1 | 500 | 360 | 1 | .... | 120 | 810 |
| Tin, copper and sheet iron ware | 2 | 2,700 | 1,630 | 4 | .... | 984 | 3,300 |
| Totals | 62 | $157,515 | $124,741 | 170 | .... | $37,644 | $198,457 |

These enumerated industries were distributed among the counties as follows: Boots and shoes, fire-arms and distilled liquors were only made in Floyd; copper mining and smelting, iron casting and linseed oil making were confined to Carroll; flour and meal and leather were made in all the counties; cabinet furniture, saddlery and harness and wool carding were industries of Floyd and Carroll; lumber sawing and tin, &c., ware making, were conducted in Carroll and Grayson.

Carroll, as a consequence of its greater amount of water-power, leads in manufacturing.

THE VALLEY counties in 1860 had the following returns of their MANUFACTURING RESULTS:

| COUNTIES. | Number of Establishments. | Capital Invested. | Cost of Raw Materials. | Number of Hands Employed. | | Annual Cost of Labor. | Annual Value of Products. |
|---|---|---|---|---|---|---|---|
| | | | | Male. | Female. | | |
| Augusta | 197 | $ 630,010 | $ 615,546 | 471 | 31 | $ 129,114 | $ 915,713 |
| Botetourt | 65 | 198,200 | 226,591 | 241 | 6 | 55,458 | 357,955 |
| Clarke | 16 | 63,700 | 121,102 | 42 | .... | 14,310 | 176,075 |
| Frederick | 127 | 276,280 | 499,961 | 373 | 53 | 98,576 | 729,051 |
| Montgomery | 45 | 61,880 | 76,700 | 136 | 3 | 39,920 | 155,235 |
| Page | 60 | 137,175 | 163,197 | 108 | .... | 19,560 | 206,136 |
| Pulaski | 30 | 51,200 | 32,880 | 84 | .... | 22,212 | 72,295 |
| Rockbridge | 220 | 550,716 | 552,116 | 637 | 1 | 159,203 | 958,743 |
| Roanoke | 22 | 157,300 | 205,406 | 124 | .... | 18,288 | 274,012 |
| Rockingham | 122 | 384,550 | 274,556 | 321 | 11 | 74,908 | 422,588 |
| Shenandoah | 48 | 257,805 | 86,755 | 200 | 5 | 40,372 | 169,338 |
| Smyth | 9 | 61,000 | 36,640 | 97 | .... | 23,892 | 89,200 |
| Warren | 36 | 100,360 | 169,459 | 88 | .... | 19,821 | 251,250 |
| Washington | 199 | 173,215 | 193,786 | 338 | 4 | 92,736 | 360,066 |
| Wythe | 24 | 447,800 | 61,760 | 330 | 6 | 59,814 | 165,550 |
| TOTALS | 1,220 | $3,560,191 | $3,316,550 | 3,590 | 120 | $868,214 | $5,303,216 |

A comparison of these Valley aggregates with those for the State, shows that the Valley had *about* 1-3½th of the establishments, 1-5th of the capital invested, paid 1-6th of the cost of material, employed 1-7th of the male and 2-26th of the female hands, paid 1-8th of the cost of labor, and received 1-8th of the value of products.

The following table gives the DETAILS, by INDUSTRIES, in THE VALLEY:

| INDUSTRIES. | Number of Establishments. | Capital Invested. | Cost of Raw Material. | Number of Hands Employed. | | Annual Cost of Labor. | Annual Value of Products. |
|---|---|---|---|---|---|---|---|
| | | | | Male. | Female. | | |
| Agricultural implements | 9 | $ 18,900 | $ 16,097 | 62 | .... | $ 17,844 | $ 45,875 |
| Boots and shoes | 65 | 53,971 | 55,757 | 183 | 19 | 50,712 | 139,609 |
| Blacksmithing | 130 | 47,835 | 37,451 | 263 | .... | 60,768 | 130,543 |
| Buckskin dressing | 1 | 150 | 2,200 | 3 | .... | 450 | 3,190 |
| Bituminous coal | 1 | 20,000 | 775 | 12 | .... | 4,152 | 11,200 |
| Carpentering | 19 | 20,050 | 24,794 | 108 | .... | 29,868 | 83,685 |
| Carriages | 28 | 65,225 | 34,448 | 106 | 1 | 55,776 | 129,775 |
| Cigars | 7 | 9,300 | 15,250 | 41 | .... | 11,460 | 37,380 |
| Clothing—men's | 15 | 11,440 | 20,925 | 30 | 15 | 9,728 | 37,441 |
| Clothing—ladies' | 1 | 150 | 2,000 | .... | 4 | 1,200 | 6,000 |

## TABLE OF INDUSTRIES CONTINUED.

| INDUSTRIES. | Number of Establishments. | Capital Invested. | Cost of Raw Material. | Number of Hands Employed. Male. | Female. | Annual Cost of Labor. | Annual Value of Products. |
|---|---|---|---|---|---|---|---|
| Cooperage | 18 | $ 5,290 | $ 5,536 | 39 | .... | $ 6,396 | $ 15,595 |
| Confectionery | 1 | 6,800 | 4,420 | 9 | .... | 2,088 | 8,250 |
| Cement | 1 | 75,000 | 42,100 | 150 | .... | 42,000 | 180,000 |
| Coffins | 2 | 650 | 610 | 3 | .... | 1,260 | 2,300 |
| Crackers, bread, &c | 1 | 400 | 1,200 | 2 | .... | 360 | 1,900 |
| Dentistry | 2 | 950 | 950 | 2 | .... | 960 | 2,900 |
| Fertilizers | 1 | 400 | 750 | 2 | .... | 300 | 1,200 |
| Flour and meal | 309 | 1,190,030 | 2,132,017 | 407 | .... | 88,294 | 2,446,870 |
| Furniture—cabinet | 33 | 33,900 | 15,478 | 93 | .... | 24,769 | 57,355 |
| Fire-arms | 2 | 250 | 250 | 2 | .... | 480 | 1,100 |
| Gas | 1 | 17,600 | 2,400 | 4 | .... | 1,440 | 5,000 |
| Gloves and mittens | 4 | 3,000 | 6,485 | 12 | 24 | 4,692 | 12,420 |
| Hats and caps | 4 | 12,400 | 3,400 | 6 | 2 | 1,902 | 8,200 |
| Iron castings | 11 | 48,200 | 21,910 | 55 | .... | 15,344 | 64,450 |
| Iron—bar, sheet and railroad | 12 | 156,725 | 50,815 | 127 | .... | 26,868 | 97,710 |
| Iron—blooms | 1 | 27,000 | 25,825 | 14 | .... | 5,040 | 32,000 |
| Iron—pig | 11 | 457,405 | 91,157 | 385 | .... | 78,792 | 220,273 |
| Lead ore | 1 | 5,000 | 1,460 | 40 | .... | 3,600 | 9,000 |
| Lead and shot | 1 | 300,000 | 18,670 | 125 | .... | 21,600 | 52,000 |
| Leather | 73 | 220,050 | 151,542 | 188 | .... | 44,202 | 258,061 |
| Lumber—sawed | 198 | 198,677 | 119,557 | 289 | .... | 60,936 | 254,364 |
| Liquors—malt | 1 | 2,000 | 1,010 | 1 | .... | 180 | 1,676 |
| Liquors—distilled | 54 | 130,813 | 113,948 | 66 | .... | 20,820 | 288,313 |
| Lime | 1 | 1,300 | 1,100 | 6 | .... | 1,872 | 7,500 |
| Manganese | 1 | 2,000 | 500 | 10 | .... | 3,600 | 5,250 |
| Marble and stone work | 4 | 5,075 | 3,800 | 12 | .... | 1,686 | 7,400 |
| Millinery | 3 | 700 | 7,500 | .... | 9 | 1,080 | 12,050 |
| Machinery, steam engines, &c | 1 | 8,000 | 5,950 | 10 | .... | 2,400 | 14,000 |
| Millwrighting | 3 | 300 | 300 | 5 | .... | 1,500 | 2,800 |
| Oil—linseed | 1 | 500 | 508 | 1 | .... | 156 | 1,000 |
| Paper—printing | 1 | 22,500 | 10,000 | 7 | 4 | 3,000 | 18,000 |
| Painting | 2 | 965 | 5,065 | 12 | .... | 3,660 | 11,000 |
| Pottery | 5 | 2,400 | 640 | 11 | .... | 3,468 | 7,300 |
| Photographs | 3 | 3,800 | 1,285 | 3 | .... | 1,440 | 4,100 |
| Printing | 11 | 46,200 | 8,999 | 46 | 7 | 9,996 | 38,305 |
| Plaster—ground | 15 | 14,500 | 19,480 | 16 | .... | 1,710 | 23,852 |
| Plaster—quarried | 2 | 17,000 | 4,000 | 30 | .... | 6,600 | 16,600 |
| Salt | 2 | 43,000 | 23,600 | 55 | .... | 17,400 | 72,000 |
| Saddlery and harness | 34 | 31,900 | 23,901 | 77 | .... | 21,285 | 60,648 |
| Silver-plating | 1 | 150 | 79 | 1 | .... | 240 | 550 |

## TABLE OF INDUSTRIES CONCLUDED.

| INDUSTRIES. | Number of Establishments. | Capital Invested. | Cost of Raw Material. | Number of Hands Employed. | | Annual Cost of Labor. | Annual Value of Products. |
|---|---|---|---|---|---|---|---|
| | | | | Male. | Female. | | |
| Soap and candles.................... | 1 | $ 1,200 | $ 4,500 | 2 | .... | $ 360 | $ 5,100 |
| Spokes, hubs and felloes............ | 1 | 1,800 | 606 | 4 | .... | 480 | 1,200 |
| Staves, shooks and heading......... | 1 | 1,100 | 5,630 | 8 | .... | 2,520 | 12,650 |
| Tin, copper and sheet iron ware..... | 25 | 28,750 | 38,648 | 63 | .... | 16,504 | 64,955 |
| Tobacco—manufactured............ | 5 | 25,100 | 24,831 | 87 | .... | 9,416 | 58,060 |
| Wagons, carts, &c................ | 42 | 23,015 | 14,757 | 108 | .... | 25,143 | 57,492 |
| Wool carding....................... | 15 | 3,300 | 17,720 | 15 | .... | 1,374 | 24,145 |
| Woolen goods....................... | 13 | 124,550 | 75,747 | 90 | 37 | 25,834 | 138,160 |
| Watch repairing and silver smithing, | 4 | 3,025 | 1,098 | 5 | .... | 2,460 | 4,400 |
| TOTALS....................... | 1,220 | $3,560,191 | $3,316,550 | 3,590 | 120 | $568,214 | $5,303,216 |

Agricultural implements were made in Frederick, Augusta, Rockbridge, Pulaski and Washington; boots and shoes in all the counties but Smyth; blacksmithing is credited to all but Frederick, Warren, Page, Roanoke and Smyth, in all of which there were fully as many shops as in the others in proportion to population; Frederick alone had buck-skin dressing, fertilizer, soap and candle and malt liquor making, silver plating; Washington alone made ladies' clothing, and had mill-wrighting; Page alone made iron blooms; Wythe monopolized mining lead ore and making lead and shot and linseed oil; Rockbridge alone made spokes, hubs and folloes, staves, shooks and heading, and cement; Montgomery, only, mined bituminous coal; Warren made the lime; Augusta had the dentistry, bread and cracker making, the gas works, manganese mining and millinery; Smyth the plaster quarrying, and Wythe the making of machinery and steam engines; carpentry was carried on in Frederick, Rockingham, Rockbridge, Montgomery and Washington; carriages were made in all the counties except Page, Roanoke and Smyth; cigars were manufactured in Frederick, Augusta and Rockbridge; gloves and mittens in Frederick and Shenandoah; hats and caps in Frederick, Augusta, Rockbridge and Wythe; coffins in Rockbridge and Washington; fire-arms in Shenandoah and Washington; wagons and carts in all but Roanoke and Smyth; saddlery and harness in all but Clarke, Montgomery and Washington; tin, copper and sheet iron ware in all but Clarke, Warren, Roanoke, Pulaski and Smyth; distilled liquors in all save Frederick, Clarke, Shenandoah, Roanoke, Wythe and Smyth; woolen goods in Frederick, Rockingham, Augusta, Rockbridge, Botetourt and Roanoke; men's clothing in Frederick, Rockingham, Augusta, Rockbridge, Montgomery and Washington; flour and meal in all but Shenandoah and Wythe (which no doubt were among the largest grinders of the group); cabinet furniture in all except Clarke, Warren, Roanoke and Smyth; cooperage in Frederick, Warren, Shenandoah, Rockingham, Augusta, Rockbridge and Montgomery; iron castings in Frederick, Warren, Shenandoah, Rockingham, Augusta, Rockbridge, Botetourt, Roanoke and Pulaski; bar iron in Warren, Page, Shenandoah, Augusta, Rockbridge, Pulaski, Wythe and Smyth; pig iron in Page, Shenandoah, Rockingham, Augusta, Rockbridge, Botetourt and Wythe; salt in Smyth and Washington; leather in all but Clarke and Warren; lumber sawed in all but Clarke and Wythe; plaster ground in Frederick, Page, Augusta and Rockbridge; tobacco manufactured in Frederick, Roanoke and Washington; pottery in Shenandoah, Augusta and Washington; confectionery in Augusta and Rockbridge; watch repairing, &c., in Frederick, Montgomery and Washington; wool carding was done in Augusta, Rockbridge, Pulaski and Washington; printing in Frederick, Warren, Shenandoah, Rockingham, Botetourt, Montgomery and Wythe; painting in Rockbridge and Montgomery; marble and stone work in Augusta, Rockbridge and Montgomery; photographs in Augusta, Rockbridge and Montgomery, and printing paper was made only in Augusta.

The APPALACHIAN counties gave these MANUFACTURING RETURNS in 1860:

| COUNTIES. | Number of Establishments. | Capital Invested. | Cost of Raw Material. | Number of Hands Employed. | | Annual Cost of Labor. | Annual Value of Products. |
|---|---|---|---|---|---|---|---|
| | | | | Male. | Female. | | |
| Alleghany | 27 | $ 49,635 | $ 93,556 | 74 | .... | $ 24,684 | $ 132,851 |
| Bath | 22 | 41,200 | 43,385 | 87 | .... | 6,924 | 59,280 |
| Bland | .... | ........ | ........ | .... | .... | ........ | ........ |
| Buchanan | .... | ........ | ........ | .. | .... | ........ | .. ..... |
| Craig | 5 | 11,400 | 10,930 | 9 | .... | 2,988 | 15,838 |
| Giles | 10 | 44,660 | 48,890 | 12 | .... | 2,656 | 61,736 |
| Highland | 12 | 16,200 | 15,935 | 16 | .... | 3,330 | 24,060 |
| Lee | 1 | 7,000 | 140 | 3 | .... | 270 | 600 |
| Russell | 27 | 41,781 | 68,500 | 36 | .... | 9,348 | 105,096 |
| Scott | 2 | 2,300 | 2,656 | 5 | .... | 864 | 4,885 |
| Tazewell | 15 | 15,587 | 8,511 | 21 | .... | 4,296 | 16,020 |
| Wise | 1 | 300 | 300 | 2 | .... | 360 | 725 |
| TOTALS | 122 | $230,063 | $292,803 | 215 | .... | $55,720 | $421,091 |

Appalachia, compared with the whole State in manufacturing, had *about* 1–13th of the establishments, 1–98th of the invested capital, paid 1–34th of the cost of raw material, employed 1–133rd of the labor, paid 1–110th of the cost of labor, and received 1–104th of the value of products.

In 1860 but little of Appalachia was reached by internal improvements, and nearly all the manufacturing done was for home consumption. No portion of the State has larger resources for manufacturing.

The DETAILS of MANUFACTURING in APPALACHIA for 1860 were:

| INDUSTRIES. | Number of Establishments. | Capital Invested. | Cost of Raw Material. | Number of Hands Employed. | | Annual Cost of Labor. | Annual Value of Products. |
|---|---|---|---|---|---|---|---|
| | | | | Male. | Female. | | |
| Agricultural implements | 1 | $ 800 | $ 141 | 1 | .... | $ 240 | $ 900 |
| Blacksmithing | 8 | 7,135 | 2,505 | 15 | .... | 3,252 | 8,100 |
| Boots and shoes | 7 | 2,200 | 3,335 | 12 | .... | 3,960 | 9,132 |
| Brick | 1 | 600 | 250 | 2 | .... | 240 | 1,200 |
| Cement | 1 | 10,000 | 16,620 | 30 | .... | 10,800 | 30,000 |
| Flour and meal | 38 | 121,400 | 209,333 | 41 | .... | 10,440 | 249,347 |
| Furniture—cabinet | 5 | 1,005 | 740 | 5 | .... | 1,380 | 4,025 |
| Iron—bar | 3 | 16,000 | 4,817 | 12 | .... | 2,670 | 9,300 |
| Iron—castings | 1 | 3,500 | 685 | 3 | .... | 1,260 | 2,690 |
| Leather | 23 | 42,337 | 26,547 | 39 | .... | 8,200 | 57,206 |
| Lumber—sawed | 12 | 10,500 | 7,945 | 18 | .... | 5,040 | 16,414 |
| Liquor—distilled | 5 | 6,292 | 6,494 | 8 | .... | 1,920 | 6,679 |
| Saddlery and harness | 11 | 5,419 | 5,787 | 22 | .... | 4,938 | 15,651 |
| Wagons, carts, &c | 3 | 975 | 400 | 4 | .... | 1,080 | 1,949 |
| Wool carding | 3 | 1,900 | 7,200 | 3 | .... | 300 | 8,600 |
| TOTALS | 122 | $230,063 | $292,803 | 215 | .... | $55,720 | $421,091 |

The agricultural implements were made in Highland, the brick in Bath, the iron castings in Craig, and the cement in Alleghany; boots and shoes were made in Alleghany, Russell and Wise; cabinet furniture in Alleghany, Tazewell and Russell; bar iron in Alleghany and Lee; distilled liquors in Craig and Scott; sawed lumber in Bath, Alleghany and Russell; wagons and carts in Highland, Bath and Russell; leather in all the counties but Giles, Lee, Buchanan and Wise; flour and meal in Highland, Bath, Alleghany, Craig and Russell; saddles and harness in Highland, Bath, Alleghany, Tazewell and Russell; wool carding was carried on in Bath and Russell, and blacksmithing in Highland, Bath, Giles and Russell.

## SECTION II.—FACILITIES FOR MANUFACTURING IN VIRGINIA.

The facilities Virginia presents for the successful prosecution of many kinds of manufactures may be summed up as—

1st. A great variety and abundance of RAW MATERIALS, so distributed that they can be obtained at a moderate cost at numerous points.

2d. Ample supplies of WATER POWER, the cheapest of motors, in almost every portion of the State; large areas favorably disposed for using the force of WIND as a moving power; and CHEAP FUEL, as WOOD from the ever-growing forests, or COAL, the concentrated fuel, the most efficient aid in the production of power and in many of the processes of manufacture.

3d. A CLIMATE healthy and every way favorable for industrial pursuits, being generally free from the extremes that hinder the successful and profitable employment of labor the whole year.

4th. CONVENIENCE of access TO MARKETS, both domestic and foreign, by ocean highways, navigable rivers, canals, railways, &c., that furnish numerous channels of communication and cheap conveyance.

5th. A good SUPPLY OF human and animal LABOR, at hand or easily attainable, that can be had for fair and moderate wages.

6th. A large SURPLUS of the best of FOOD for man or beast, furnishing a cheap market.

7th. HOMES, the fee-simple of which can be BOUGHT by the savings of common industry, or which can be cheaply RENTED.

8th. A desire on the part of the State and people to have all kinds of manufacturing, for which facilities are here found, introduced and encouraged.

These are the essentials for securing the location of the world's workshops. That Virginia possesses these advantages, as much as almost any known country, is generally conceded, and the results from the few large manufacturing enterprises that have been carried on in the State demonstrate that these facilities have not been over estimated.

It is easy to explain why comparatively little use has been made of the manufacturing resources of Virginia. An extensive domain, a prolific soil and genial climate, have invited her population to the more pleasant pursuit of agriculture, and satisfied with the abundance that flowed from a not laborious cultivation of the gifts of Providence of one kind, they have been content to hold in reserve, almost untouched, the larger and in some respects more valuable legacy embodied in the raw materials for manufactures and the forces for their exploitation entailed upon them by the same unstinted bounty. The chaos that has come of war incites, by its wide-spread disasters, to a cosmos calling for a larger and more general development; and Virginia, epitomizing in herself, like England, the varied resources that have given strength and wealth to nations, now resolutely determines to cultivate all the arts born of industry and vindicate a claim to pre-eminence in these, as she has in other pursuits, by the fruits furnished in due time.

The chapters in this volume on the Mineral, Animal and Vegetable Resources of the State, and the accompanying physical maps, show: that *iron, copper, lead, gold, salt, coal, limestone, manganese, clays*, and other minerals are abundant and widely distributed; that many varieties of *timber* abound in all sections, while other products of the vegetable kingdom, materials to work up, are exceedingly plentiful; and that large supplies of animal products, to be converted into more valuable forms by labor, are presently available, and that the quantity can be increased so as to equal almost any demand.

The facts given warrant the statement that the *raw materials, developed and undeveloped, in Virginia, are sufficient in quantity and quality, in nearly every portion of the State, to supply the elements for almost every known form of manufacturing industry, even when conducted on the most extensive scale.*

A perusal of the chapter descriptive of Virginia, and a study of the accompanying maps and sections, must convince any one that a State so permeated by rivers, having their sources in elevated mountain ranges where the deposition of moisture is almost constant, and that descend through not only hundreds, but thousands of feet in their long way to the sea, crossing successive steps or "benches" of country, and having their general course at right angles to the highly inclined rock formations of every section of the State above Tidewater, must furnish an almost unlimited quantity of water-power, while in Tidewater the regular flow of the tides, the fall of the smaller streams and the steady movements of the air, furnish an abundance of natural motive power. The supply of wood and coal for fuel may be stated as inexhaustible, as the forests here renew themselves without man's aid, and the 59,000 square miles of the Appalachian Coal Basin confront her whole western boundary. A large area of this, as well as of the Triassic Coal Basins, lies within the State. No part of the State has any lack of means for producing power to propel machinery.

As an example of the water-power in Virginia, the James river may be instanced. In the ten miles from the head of tide to Bosher's dam, this river falls 130 feet and has, by estimation, a constant average of 44,800 horse-power. Less than 2,000 of this power is now used for the extensive manufacturing establishments of Richmond and Manchester. It is well to repeat that this great surplus power is in the midst of a fertile and healthy region, where the climate is favorable for work the year round, where timber, coal and other raw materials are near at hand, and where sea-going vessels drawing fourteen feet of water can come to the very doors of the manufacturing establishments, and where a canal that penetrates for 200 miles a region rich in agricultural and mineral resources has its tidewater terminus. Following up this broad and deep river, by the line of the completed James River and Kanawha Canal, there is found a fall of 513 feet, including the 130 above mentioned, in the 145 miles between Richmond and Lynchburg,* distributed among the fifty-one locks of the canal, located along the river, between the points named, furnishing a very large amount of water-power, already under control by the dams constructed for the canal, and that can be had for manufacturing purposes at a nominal rent. In the thirty miles between Lynchburg and the western base of the Blue Ridge the fall is 193 feet, also locked and dammed, and in the twenty-one miles more to Buchanan, in the Valley, the present terminus of the canal, 196 miles from Richmond, the fall is over 130 feet. At Clifton Forge, 227 miles from Richmond, the place to which the canal will probably be soon completed to a junction with the Chesapeake and Ohio Railroad, this river is 1,036 feet above mean tide. At Covington, also on the Chesapeake and Ohio Railroad, 243 miles from Richmond by the river, the water is 1,246 feet above tide, and the river is still a very considerable stream, affording fine water-power. In the sixty miles from Covington to the head of Jackson's river, the true James, there is fully a thousand feet more of available fall. No mention has been made of the numerous large and small affluents of the James, shown on the maps, all descending from high levels and contributing to that stream from all directions. It will hardly be considered an exaggeration, in view of the known facts, to say that more than 100,000 available horse-power is now running to waste in the waters of the James alone.

* At Lynchburg the James is six hundred feet wide, and has an average depth of four feet.

The rivers that originate in Middle Virginia have from 200 to 500 feet of available fall; those in Piedmont from 300 to 800; those in the Blue Ridge, in the southwest, many hundred; the streams of the Valley have from 500 to 1,500 feet of descent that can be utilized; and those of Appalachia fully 1,000 feet. The waters of the Potomac, including the Shenandoah, those of the Rappahannock, the Pamunkey, the Appomattox, Roanoke, the Kanawha or New, and the branches of the Tennessee, may be especially mentioned in connection with those of the James as having large amounts of good water-power. Excellent mill-seats may be found in all portions of the State.

The chapter on Climate presents the facts which show that Virginia has a medium climate, especially fitted for manufacturing pursuits. It is rarely that the streams are frozen, and many operations can here be carried on in the open air that elsewhere must have not only shelter, but artificial heat provided for their successful prosecution. The maps of the United States Statistical Atlas, Plate XLI., show that no portion of the United States north of latitude 35° is more free from consumption than Virginia, while most of the State is in the favored belt. From malarial diseases the deaths, by the same authority, Plate XLII., are less than 100 in 10,000 in almost the entire State; most of Tidewater is in the belt of 250 to 550 in 10,000. No portion of the State is depicted as having the worst malarial districts, and nearly all of it is in the most *highly favored* areas in the United States. Plate XLV. brings to similar conclusions in regard to intestinal diseases, most of the State being in the area of 250 deaths in 10,000 from this class of diseases. By Plate XLVI. no part of the Union suffers less from enteric, cerebro-spinal and typhus fevers, a large portion of the State having less than 250 deaths in 10,000, and more than half of it from 250 to 550 from this class of diseases. These carefully compiled maps, published by authority of the General Government, settle the character of Virginia as that of an extremely healthy country.

An inspection of the maps and a perusal of the chapters on Commerce and Internal Improvements will show that Virginia is admirably situated with reference to all the great markets of the country, being midway on the Atlantic coast, penetrated by broad arms of the sea that bring ships farther inland than those of any other Atlantic State, and everywhere intersected by lines of railway having connections with every part of the country. It may be safely asserted that the ways to and from the sea (always the ways of industrial activity) through Virginia territory are, naturally, more numerous and command a larger area than those of any other State. When a few short intervals in lines of communication are filled up, every part of the State will have excellent facilities for traffic.

The desire is general to promote manufacturing industries, that the stores of raw materials may be utilized and a market at home be secured for the products of the soil. Such being the almost unanimous wish of the people, the Legislature is disposed to foster manufacturing enterprises to the extent of its constitutional ability.

The chapter on Population shows that Virginia has, in proportion to her population, a very large number of able-bodied males of the active age, and the experience of those that have used the labor here so abundant, under sensible management and vigilant oversight, essentials to success everywhere, proves that it is of the best kind.

especially for the heavier and coarser sorts of manufactures. There are no more successfully conducted manufactures than those of tobacco, iron, &c., in Virginia. Laborers of the better class are also numerous, and Virginia is but a few hours from the great centres of population in the United States, and but a few days' sail from Europe. The number of laboring animals (see Chapter IV.) is here very large, and the conditions are very favorable for a cheap and continuous supply.

The large agricultural resources of the State, and the numbers engaged in farming, grazing, &c., and its commercial location, making it an outlet for the products of the West, insure to this region an abundance of cheap food. The materials for building are so plentiful and such is the character of the climate, that cheap and comfortable houses can be readily had. The prices current show that Virginia can furnish *food, fuel, clothing, and a home,* as cheaply as any portion of the United States; and ample provision has been made for educational and religious instruction. (See chapters on Education and Religion).

For the MANUFACTURE OF IRON Virginia has especial advantages—the varieties of ore are numerous, the quantity great and the quality good; fuel, wood for charcoal, soft bituminous coal for coke, and splint or block coal to use raw, is plentiful and very accessible, and therefore cheap.

The following estimate of the cost of making pig iron (1875) was made by a Pennsylvania company for a site in Amherst county, in Piedmont, on the James River and Kanawha Canal:

| | |
|---|---|
| Two tons ore @ $1, delivered | $ 2 00 |
| One and a half tons Anthracite coal @ $6.50 per ton | 9 75 |
| Limestone | 25 |
| Labor | 3 25 |
| Interest, &c., per ton of iron made | 1 00 |
| Cost at furnace | $16 50 |
| Freight, canal, &c., to Philadelphia | 2 50 |
| Total cost in Philadelphia | $19 00 |

A report prepared in reference to iron manufacturing in Staunton, in The Valley, in 1875, gives the following estimates for materials delivered: Iron ores yielding from 35 to 58 per cent. metallic iron, requiring $2\frac{1}{4}$ tons of crude ore per ton of iron of 2,240 pounds, $1.25 to $2.50; limestone per ton, 50 cents; New River coke (containing 91.7 to 93.8 per cent. pure carbon and but $\frac{3}{10}$ of 1 per cent. of sulphur), requiring from $1\frac{1}{4}$ to $1\frac{3}{10}$ tons per ton of iron per long ton, $5. The estimated cost of a long ton of pig, made at Staunton, was $17.25. That was the *actual* cost, including everything, at Quinnimont, West Virginia, on the Chesapeake and Ohio Railroad, it was stated by the manufacturers.

The American Iron and Steel Association in a late report says, speaking of Virginia and adjacent States, they are "rich in iron ore, much of it of the best quality; * * possess vast deposits of bituminous coal. Labor is abundant and cheap; access to iron markets is not difficult—so that, with sufficient capital, enterprise and skill, the manufacture of pig iron and bar iron may be pursued successfully and profitably."

In 1874, Mr. Harriss-Gastrell, of the British Embassy at Washington, made a voluminous and able report to his government on the Iron and Steel Industries of the United States, in which frequent reference is made to Virginia. On page 176 he states that he had been informed that ores can be mined and put on the cars at from 50 cents to $1 per ton. On page 178 the following statement is made as to the cost of a ton of Bessemer steel ore from fifty miles west of Richmond:

| | |
|---|---|
| Cost of mining, &c | $1 00 |
| Royalty | 50 |
| Freight to Richmond | 1 00 |
| Hauling to station, through Richmond | 1 00 |
| Freight to Philadelphia | 1 50 |
| Incidentals | 1 00 |
| Total | $6 00 |

"The above computation would, at the recent prices of such ores in the Anthracite districts of Pennsylvania, have left a large margin for interest, sinking fund and profit."

On page 200 he says "the cost of labor per ton of ore appears to be, for the United States, about $2: Michigan shows $1.83 per ton; New York shows $2.05; New Jersey nearly $3; and Pennsylvania about $1.87 per ton. In Virginia the cost of labor per ton is only 77 cents; in Wisconsin, Iron Ridge ores mainly, only 92 cents; and in Missouri nearly $1.40; while North Carolina runs it up to $3.60." On page 201 it is stated that materials per ton cost, for the United States, about 37 cents: for Michigan, 50 cents; for New York, 44 cents; for New Jersey, 47 cents; for Pennsylvania, 35 cents; and for Ohio, 31 cents. "In Virginia the cost of material appears to be less than 15 cents." The value of the ore per ton is given as $1.92 in Virginia; $4 in New York; $3.60 in Pennsylvania; $2.20 in Missouri, &c. On page 212, in estimating the cost of production at exporting points of ores, this "blue book" makes the cost in the Lake Superior and Missouri regions, in 1873, about $4 per ton; in the Lake Champlain, from $3.50 to $4; in Pennsylvania, $2.50; and in the South, $2. On page 270 a table of weekly wages of furnace hands is given, with the following result for the "Richmond district, in Virginia," viz: keeper, $15; gutter-men, $12; fillers, ore-breakers and wheelers, $10 each; foreman, $30; engineer, $16; hours of labor per week, 84. For the Pittsburg, Pennsylvania, district the figures are: keeper, $26; helper, $19.50; fillers, $15.75; ore-breakers and wheelers, $9.60; coal-rackers or common laborers, $7.20; foreman, $30; engineer, $31.50; hours of labor, 84. The cost of making a ton of iron in Pittsburg is given on page 273 as $30.73, from ordinary ores. On page 278 a statement is made as to cost of material and labor in Virginia, confirming previous ones. On page 282, in conclusions on iron manufacture in the South, the report says: "The fact seems to be that coke pig iron can be made for from $15 to $18, and on an average for $16, including interest on original outlay, and a fair profit on ores and fuel." On pages 292 and 302 statements given show how cheaply charcoal iron can be produced in Virginia. On page 606 the cost of materials for a ton of nails is given as $58.75, in Virginia, or less than in any other State; in Pennsylvania it was $76.55; in Missouri, $79.08.

## Additions to Section I—Results of Manufactures.

The following tables and remarks are from an article by George Baughman, Esq., in Hunt's Merchants Magazine of New York, for January, 1859, Volume XL. They were compiled with great care, from data collected at the establishments, and present a much better exhibit of the manufacturing and mechanical industries of Richmond in 1858 than the census returns of 1860, before given, do for the year 1859:

*Manufacturing and Mechanical Statistics of Richmond for the year* 1858.

| | Number of Establishments. | No. of Hands Employed. | Value of Tools and Machinery. | Value of Real Estate Occupied. | Amount of Sales |
|---|---|---|---|---|---|
| Tobacco—Chewing | 53 | 4,052 | $ 515,000 | $ 636,000 | $ 6,228,496 |
| Smoking | ...... | 300 | 20,000 | 12,000 | 22,000 |
| Stemmeries | 6 | 600 | 3,000 | 30,000 | 187,500 |
| Cigars | 8 | 21 | ........ | 16,000 | 22,932 |
| Flour | 7 | 375 | 400,000 | 656,000 | 4,643,637 |
| Corn meal | 8 | 38 | 8,000 | 53,000 | 221,000 |
| Iron rolling mills | 2 | 410 | 158,000 | 192,000 | 481,500 |
| Iron and steel mill | 1 | | | | |
| Foundries and machine shops | 7 | 650 | 191,000 | 212,000 | 795,000 |
| Architectural foundry | 1 | 14 | 5,000 | 7,500 | 15,000 |
| Stove foundry | 1 | 16 | 8,200 | 10,000 | 15,000 |
| General foundry | 1 | 12 | 3,500 | 3,000 | 12,000 |
| Railroad machine shops | 4 | 159 | 34,750 | 66,000 | 78,173 |
| Shapening mills | 2 | 16 | 4,375 | 3,250 | 17,500 |
| Iron railings | 6 | 42 | 7,500 | 22,000 | 40,000 |
| Nails | 1 | 175 | ........ | *150,000 | 237,500 |
| Blacksmiths | 42 | 126 | 12,600 | 82,000 | 126,000 |
| Bell and brass founders | 1 | 6 | 2,000 | 1,500 | 5,000 |
| Coppersmith | 1 | 14 | 6,000 | 7,500 | 14,000 |
| Saw maker | 1 | 10 | 2,000 | 8,000 | 15,000 |
| File maker | 1 | 4 | 1,000 | 3,000 | 4,000 |
| Tin ware, stoves, plumbing and lightning rods | 12 | 91 | 10,000 | 87,500 | 250,000 |
| Silver plater | 1 | 4 | 400 | 1,500 | 4,000 |
| Agricultural implements and foundries | 6 | 105 | 10,000 | 50,000 | 200,000 |
| Book binders | 6 | 36 | 3,900 | 20,000 | 53,502 |
| Bakeries | 30 | 126 | 5,000 | 131,000 | 300,000 |
| Boot and shoe makers | ...... | 398 | 7,075 | 75,000 | 253,000 |
| Brush makers | 2 | 3 | 200 | 2,000 | 2,000 |
| Boxes—merchandise packing | 2 | 7 | 500 | 4,000 | 5,211 |
| Boxes and cases—tobacco | ...... | 90 | 1,000 | 50,000 | 250,852 |

* Capital.

*Manufacturing and Mechanical Statistics Continued.*

| | Number of Establishments. | No. of Hands Employed. | Value of Tools and Machinery. | Value of Real Estate Occupied. | Amount of Sales |
|---|---|---|---|---|---|
| Bottling—soda, ale and beer | 6 | 36 | $ 4,500 | $ 12,500 | $ 40,310 |
| Butchers | 48 | 96 | ........ | 120,000 | 557,151 |
| Building—Brick making | 7 | 210 | 5,000 | 69,000 | 143,500 |
| Brick laying | 13 | 225 | 23,000 | 19,000 | 300,000 |
| Carpenters | 37 | 295 | 20,450 | 143,000 | 330,000 |
| Plasterers | 12 | 70 | 700 | 2,000 | 70,000 |
| Painters | 23 | 106 | 1,900 | 17,250 | 76,500 |
| Sash, blind and door makers | 5 | 35 | 1,200 | 9,800 | 24,500 |
| Mouldings | ...... | 6 | 1,000 | 3,000 | 6,000 |
| Planing mills | 2 | 30 | 10,000 | 30,000 | 60,000 |
| Slater | 1 | 10 | 300 | 2,000 | 10,000 |
| Saw mill | 1 | 16 | 3,500 | 5,700 | 29,400 |
| Architectural plaster ornaments | 1 | 3 | 500 | 2,000 | 3,000 |
| Architects | 5 | 11 | 2,500 | 10,000 | 10,000 |
| Stone cutters | 3 | 24 | 600 | 36,000 | 12,000 |
| Marble cutters | 3 | 40 | 2,100 | 36,500 | 60,000 |
| Cabinet makers | 13 | 105 | 2,000 | 52,500 | 346,000 |
| Carriage makers | 11 | 165 | 5,000 | 78,000 | 239,000 |
| Clothing | 60 | 420 | 2,000 | ........ | 459,000 |
| Coopers | 11 | 805 | 25,000 | 42,000 | 220,000 |
| Confectioners | 26 | 48 | 3,000 | 42,000 | 83,333 |
| Carver—wood | 1 | 1 | ........ | 420 | 750 |
| Cotton factories | 2 | 460 | 122,500 | 169,000 | 435,000 |
| Cedar and willow ware | 2 | 6 | ........ | 5,000 | 3,000 |
| Curriers | 3 | 13 | 1,000 | 17,000 | 205,000 |
| Dyeing | 3 | 14 | 3,000 | 12,500 | 14,000 |
| Distillery | 1 | 75 | 40,000 | 20,000 | 260,000 |
| Gas works | 1 | 60 | ........ | 283,000 | 107,085 |
| Gunsmiths | ...... | 20 | 5,000 | 20,000 | 30,000 |
| Glass works | 1 | 55 | 2,000 | 15,000 | 40,000 |
| Hatters | ...... | 21 | 1,000 | 4,000 | 65,000 |
| Jewelry makers and repairers | ...... | 50 | 2,500 | 10,000 | 60,000 |
| Ivory cutters and carvers | 2 | 4 | 500 | 2,000 | 4,000 |
| Lime burners—shell | 2 | 6 | 1,000 | ........ | 20,900 |
| Lock maker | 1 | 5 } | 1,100 | 4,500 | 8,900 |
| Lock repairers | 3 | 4 } | | | |
| Looking glass and frame | 2 | 5 | 300 | 9,000 | 4,000 |
| Lard refinery | 1 | 4 | 2,000 | 10,000 | 5,000 |
| Leather belting and hose | 1 | 2 | 1,000 | 2,500 | 10,000 |

*Manufacturing and Mechanical Statistics Continued.*

| | Number of Establishments. | No. of Hands Employed. | Value of Tools and Machinery. | Value of Real Estate Occupied. | Amount of Sales |
|---|---|---|---|---|---|
| Millwright | ...... | 25 | $ 2,500 | ........ | $ 26,000 |
| Milliners and mantua makers | 60 | 400 | ........ | 40,000 | 117,000 |
| Paper mill | 1 | 40 | 25,000 | 30,000 | 60,000 |
| Plaster mills | 2 | 14 | 5,700 | 8,000 | 28,000 |
| Paper hanging and upholsterers | 3 | 29 | ........ | 28,000 | 111,500 |
| Phosphate of lime | 1 | 8 | 500 | 2,000 | 12,000 |
| Piano makers | 2 | 12 | 1,000 | 8,000 | 9,500 |
| Plumbers | 2 | 4 | ........ | 4,000 | 3,000 |
| Penitentiary—sundries | 1 | ...... | 10,043 | ........ | 81,389 |
| Stoneware | 1 | 12 | 500 | 10,000 | 10,000 |
| Saddle and harness makers | 8 | 78 | ........ | 48,000 | 120,000 |
| Soap and candle makers | 5 | 40 | 15,000 | 24,500 | 115,000 |
| Sail maker | 1 | 11 | ........ | 2,000 | 12,000 |
| Tannery | 1 | 4 | 2,500 | 3,500 | 6,000 |
| Turners | 4 | 12 | 1,200 | 6,000 | 10,000 |
| Umbrellas | ...... | 5 | 100 | 3,000 | 2,500 |
| Wheelwrights | 15 | 45 | 1,500 | 15,000 | 20,000 |
| Water works | 1 | ...... | ........ | 350,000 | 32,278 |
| Printing—book and job | 9 | 207 | 136,500 | 125,350 | 272,500 |
| Printing—newspaper and periodical | 16 | | | | |
| Total | .......... | 11,811 | $1,819,193 | $4,609,270 | $19,878,896 |

Deduct value of manufactures included in the above, not the products of Richmond, viz:

| | | |
|---|---|---|
| Agricultural implements | $ 15,000 | |
| Furniture | 120,000 | |
| Carriages | 60,000 | |
| Leather | 130,000 | |
| Guns, &c. | 15,000 | |
| Paper Hangings | 40,000 | |
| | | $390,000 |
| Total product of Richmond | | $19,488,896 |

RECAPITULATION.

| | |
|---|---|
| Different kinds of manufacturing and mechanical establishments | 91 |
| Number of persons employed—*i. e.*, principals, clerks and operatives | 11,811 |
| Amount of capital invested in necessary tools and machinery | $1,819,193 |
| Amount of capital invested in real estate occupied by establishments | 4,609,270 |
| Total amount of products in twelve months | 19,488,896 |

No estimate was made of the capital invested in raw materials.

*Artistic.*

| | Number of Establishments. | No. of Hands. | Value of Tools and Machinery. | Value of Real Estate. | Amount of Sales |
|---|---|---|---|---|---|
| Ambrotypes and photographs | 7 | 17 | $ 3,000 | $ 32,000 | $ 28,000 |
| Portrait and landscape painters | ...... | 3 | ...... | ........ | ...... |
| Artistic founders | ...... | 1 | ...... | ........ | 4,000 |
| Total | 7 | 21 | $3,000 | $32,000 | $32,000 |

*Comparison of Richmond with other American Cities.*

| | Products of Manufactures. | | | | Comparison of Population, Property, &c. | | | |
|---|---|---|---|---|---|---|---|---|
| | Year. | Value of Manufactures per capita of Population. | No. of Hands Employed. | Amount to each Hand Employed. | Year. | Population. | Real and Personal Property. | Per Head. |
| Philadelphia | 1850 | $148 | 66,474 | $ 910 | 1854 | 480,000 | ............ | ...... |
| New York | 1850 | 204 | 83,620 | 1,258 | 1855 | 625,000 | $487,060,838 | $ 779 |
| Boston | 1855 | 319 | Not stated. | ...... | 1855 | 162,629 | 241,932,200 | 1,420 |
| Buffalo | 1855 | 137 | 6,320 | 1,491 | 1855 | 74,214 | 33,037,711 | 445 |
| Chicago | 1857 | 119 | 10,573 | 1,467 | 1857 | 130,000 | 36,256,249 | 279 |
| Richmond | 1858 | 433 | 11,811 | 1,650 | 1858 | { 30,000 white<br>15,000 black | 47,802,719 | 1,593 |
| Detroit | .... | .... | ...... | ...... | 1854 | 40,373 | 12,524,095 | 310 |

"By a comparison of the list of our manufactures with any of the above cities, the difference in the average to each hand will be seen chiefly to be in our milling business, in which 375 hands turn out over four and a half million dollars; and this illustrates another great advantage we enjoy in our great water power, and still another in being at the outlet of an interior which produces the only wheat, the flour from which has always been shipped to extreme southern latitudes without spoiling. The advantages of Richmond over the cities named above, as a manufacturing locality, is without question. She has them in her immense water power, in her immediate vicinity to an almost illimitable field of the best coal, and in her great convenience to the very best iron ore, leaf tobacco, wheat, cotton, and almost every other kind of raw material."

*General Recapitulation of Business, &c., of Richmond for* 1858.

| | Number of Hands. | Value of Tools and Machinery. | Value of Real Estate Occupied. | Value of Products. |
|---|---|---|---|---|
| Manufacturing and mechanical | 11,611 | $ 1,819,193 | $ 4,609,270 | $ 19,488,896 |
| Artistic | 21 | 3,000 | 32,000 | 32,000 |
| Merchandising | 2,384 | ............ | 3,962,800 | 37,142,826 |
| | | | | $56,663,722 |
| Auction sales of real and personal property | 61 | ............ | 68,000 | 7,665,180 |
| Live stock | 54 | ............ | 20,000 | 290,837 |
| Industrial | 740 | 312,580 | 152,500 | 509,101 |
| Miscellaneous | 495 | ............ | 392,000 | 839,025 |
| Professional | 287 | 139,900 | 310,000 | 394,450 |
| Inspectors, &c | 426 | ............ | ............ | 270,807 |
| Total | 10,279 | $2,274,673 | $9,566,570 | $66,723,115 |

"No place in the State, and but few, if any, in the whole country, possess greater natural advantages for productive industry. With a mild and equable climate and healthful locality, with complete railroads and canal of nearly 1,000 miles, radiating from Richmond, penetrating forests, mines, grazing and agricultural districts, abounding in every variety of raw material for the loom, anvil, buhr, screw, saw, &c., and by their connections, giving quick and cheap access to the products of the South and Southwest generally, and with an unobstructed outlet by the river to the ocean for coastwise and foreign export, and with an almost-unlimited demand for every article of merchandise and manufacture, we really believe that Richmond has scarcely a parallel for combined manufacturing and commercial advantages."

A recent* British "Blue Book" gives these returns of IRON AND STEEL MANUFACTURES IN VIRGINIA for 1869–'70:

In *making and repairing railroad cars*, there were employed 7 establishments, using 7 steam engines with 250 horse-powers, 1 water wheel with 70 horse-power, 469 men, and having $1,205,600 invested capital, paying $258,578 for wages, and $330,458 for materials, the products being worth $613,036. The products of forged iron were valued at $42,750. In *making machinery*, 28 establishments were at work, using 15 steam engines with 223 horse-powers, 3 water wheels with 124 horse-powers, working 501 men and 22 boys, having $714,527 capital invested, paying $214,723 in wages, and $238,963 for materials, producing 13 boilers, 14 stationary engines, 160 tobacco presses and machines, 2 water wheels, doing $480,182 worth of miscellaneous and repair work, producing in all $591,182. In *iron casting*, 54 establishments were engaged, 15 using 245 horse-powers of steam engines, and 19 using 388 horse-powers of water wheels; 57 cupola furnaces were used, having a daily capacity of 127 tons of melted metal; 541 men and 12 boys were employed; the capital invested was $554,235, and $199,275 were paid for wages, using 5,547

* Report of Mr. Harriss-Gastrell, of British Legation, on Iron and Steel Industries in the United States, 1874.

tons of pig iron, valued at $199,788, and 2,995 tons of scrap iron, worth $79,141, with 6,242 tons of coal, costing $42,521, and other materials $2,312—a total for materials of $323,762—producing 5,300 car wheels, 700 feet of railing, $4,835 worth of hollow-ware, 1,890 stoves, 1,059 tons of agricultural castings, and 5,344 tons of miscellaneous castings, all valued at $762,274. In the *manufacture of nails*, Virginia had one establishment using 2 water wheels having 100 horse-power, working 160 men, with $125,000 invested capital, paying $722,460 for wages, using 4,000 tons of plate iron and 50 tons of coal, the materials all costing $224,200, producing 3,950 tons of nails valued at $350,000, the materials for a ton costing $58.75, the labor $21.55, and the value was $88.90; the materials cost less than in any other State. In *manufacturing iron, and articles from it*, Virginia had 89 establishments, using 25 steam engines with 735 horse-powers, 58 water wheels with 1,986 horse-powers, employing 2,338 men, 4 women and 72 youths, with $2,318,635 invested capital, paying $833,660 for wages and $2,027,590 for materials, producing to the value of $3,605 940.

# CHAPTER VI.

# THE COMMERCE OF VIRGINIA.

## Section I.—Commercial Results.

In 1870 only about 1–20th (4.89 per cent.) of the people of Virginia were employed in trade and transportation, while the average proportion for the United States was 9.52 per cent. This may be assumed to have been the usual proportion. Therefore, notwithstanding the great advantages the State possesses in resources and location, the commercial results she can present are comparatively meagre, although other communities have grown rich from the traffic drawn from her borders.

In 1870 the population of Tidewater Virginia was 346,305, and of these only 3,387 were reported as engaged in trade and transportation, of which number only 2,805 were natives of the State.

The Foreign Commerce of Virginia has been generally confined to the exportation of raw materials. Most of the imports consumed in the State have reached it through Baltimore, Philadelphia and New York.

Mr. Jefferson, in his "Notes on Virginia," gives the following exhibit of the *Average Export Trade* of the State (taking one year with another) *previous* to the Revolution of 1776:

No. 1.

| ARTICLES. | QUANTITY. | PRICE. | AMOUNT. |
|---|---|---|---|
| Tobacco | 55,000 hhds. of 1,000 lbs. | $ 30 per hhd. | $ 1,650,000 |
| Wheat | 800,000 bushels. | $5-6 per bush. | 666,666⅔ |
| Indian corn | 600,000 bushels. | $ ⅓ per bush. | 200,000 |
| Shipping | ........ | ........ | 100,000 |
| Masts, planks, scantling, shingles and staves | ........ | ........ | 66,666⅔ |
| Tar, pitch and turpentine | 30,000 barrels. | $1⅓ per barrel. | 40,000 |
| Peltry, viz: skins of deer, beavers, otters, musk-rats, raccoons and foxes | 180 hhds. of 600 lbs. | $5-12 per lb. | 42,000 |
| Pork | 4,000 barrels. | $10 per barrel. | 40,000 |
| Flax seed, hemp and cotton | ........ | ........ | 8,000 |
| Pit coal, pig iron | ........ | ........ | 6,666⅔ |
| Peas | 5,000 bushels. | $ ⅔ per bush. | 3,333⅓ |
| Beef | 1,000 barrels. | $3⅓ per barrel. | 3,333⅓ |
| Sturgeon, white shad, herring | ........ | ........ | 3,333⅓ |
| Brandy from peaches and apples, and whiskey | ........ | ........ | 1,666⅔ |
| Horses | ........ | ........ | 1,666⅔ |
| (This sum is equal to £850,000 Virginia money—607,142 guineas). | | Total........ | $2,833,333⅓ |

16

Previous to the war of 1812 Norfolk monopolized most of the trade of the British West Indies, and derived much profit from it. This trade subsequently revived, but has not as yet assumed its former proportions. Doubtless, now that interior communications have been generally established, it will again seek its best distributing points for its largest customers through Virginia ports.

During the fiscal year ending September 30th, 1831, the domestic* exports of Virginia were valued at $4,149,986, and the imports at $488,552.

In 1840 the domestic† exports of the State amounted to $4,778,220, and the imports to $545,685, and 31 commercial and 64 commission houses, with a capital of $4,299,500, were engaged in foreign trade.

The official reports of the Bureau of Statistics, in the Department of the Treasury of the United States, on Commerce and Navigation, have furnished the commercial information here given, unless otherwise stated.

## No. 2.

*Statement Showing the* NUMBER *of* AMERICAN *and* FOREIGN VESSELS, *with their* TONNAGE *and* CREWS, *that* ENTERED *Virginia Ports from Foreign Countries during the Fiscal Years* 1858 *to* 1860, *and* 1866 *to* 1874.

| YEAR. | AMERICAN VESSELS. | | | FOREIGN VESSELS. | | | AGGREGATE. | | | Proportion to Whole Tonnage Entering U. S. (in round numbers). |
|---|---|---|---|---|---|---|---|---|---|---|
| | Number. | Tons. | Crews. | Number. | Tons. | Crews. | Number. | Tons. | Crews. | |
| 1858 | 165 | 73,422 | 2,337 | 94 | 18,910 | 733 | 259 | 102,332 | 3,070 | 1- 66th. |
| 1859 | 139 | 62,781 | ...... | 97 | 26,556 | ...... | 236 | 89,337 | ...... | 1- 89th. |
| 1860 | 185 | 80,977 | ...... | 88 | 16,785 | ...... | 273 | 97,762 | ...... | 1- 84th. |
| 1866 | 15 | 3,101 | 38 | 38 | 15,923 | ...... | 53 | 19,024 | ...... | 1-432nd |
| 1867 | 36 | 15,845 | ...... | 31 | 10,530 | ...... | 67 | 26,375 | ...... | 1-288th. |
| 1868 | 20 | 6,840 | 212 | 43 | 13,686 | 483 | 63 | 20,526 | 695 | 1-374th. |
| 1869 | 19 | 3,273 | 119 | 33 | 9,790 | 318 | 52 | 13,063 | 437 | |
| 1870 | 42 | 7,495 | 268 | 26 | 7,778 | 263 | 68 | 15,273 | 531 | 1-611th. |
| 1971 | 32 | 7,083 | 231 | 21 | 10,104 | 370 | 53 | 17,187 | 601 | 1-625th. |
| 1872 | 16 | 5,324 | 140 | 74 | 51,140 | 2,236 | 90 | 56,464 | 2,376 | 1-192nd |
| 1873 | 21 | 5,440 | 165 | 80 | 55,568 | 2,650 | 101 | 61,008 | 2,815 | 1-195th. |
| 1874 | 65 | 16,993 | 472 | 45 | 27,670 | 1,060 | 110 | 44,663 | 1,532 | 1-291th. |

The items for 1858 show the condition of the trade of the State previous to the late war (1861–'65), during which the commerce and shipping of the State were completely destroyed. The other years show a gradual return of prosperity, when compared with the whole country.

In 1874 more details were given, and the reports state that the entries, *with cargoes*, were of American vessels 63, with 15,971 tons and 439 in crews, and of foreign vessels 33, with 21,704 tons and 884 in crews. The entries *in ballast* were 2 American vessels, with 1,022 tons and 33 in crews, and 12 foreign vessels, with 5,966 tons and 140 in crews.

* Martin's Gazetteer, 1835. † Howe's Historical Collections of Virginia, 1845.

## No. 3.

*Statement Showing the* NUMBER *of* AMERICAN *and* FOREIGN VESSELS, *with their* TONNAGE *and* CREWS, *that* CLEARED *from Virginia Ports for Foreign Countries during the Fiscal Years* 1858 *to* 1860, *and* 1866 *to* 1874.

| YEAR. | AMERICAN VESSELS. | | | FOREIGN VESSELS. | | | AGGREGATE. | | | Proportion to Whole Tonnage Cleared from U. S. (in round numbers). |
|---|---|---|---|---|---|---|---|---|---|---|
| | Number. | Tons. | Crews. | Number. | Tons. | Crews. | Number. | Tons. | Crews. | |
| 1858 | 217 | 66,766 | 2,095 | 100 | 21,878 | 897 | 317 | 88,644 | 2,992 | 1- 79th. |
| 1859 | 205 | 65,377 | ...... | 95 | 19,371 | ...... | 300 | 84,748 | ...... | 1- 94th. |
| 1860 | 180 | 59,611 | ...... | 88 | 20,770 | ...... | 268 | 80,381 | ...... | 1-110th. |
| 1866 | 13 | 5,949 | ...... | 49 | 20,095 | ...... | 62 | 26,044 | ...... | 1-326th. |
| 1867 | 32 | 6,800 | ...... | 40 | 19,564 | ...... | 72 | 26,364 | ...... | 1-328th. |
| 1868 | 53 | 15,479 | 499 | 57 | 19,370 | 699 | 110 | 34,849 | 1,198 | 1-259th. |
| 1869 | 58 | 18,370 | 592 | 67 | 19,641 | 657 | 125 | 38,011 | 657 | |
| 1870 | 41 | 9,906 | 321 | 66 | 22,239 | 746 | 107 | 32,145 | 1,067 | 1-286th. |
| 1871 | 43 | 10,192 | 319 | 49 | 13,435 | 446 | 92 | 23,627 | 765 | 1-412th. |
| 1872 | 76 | 19,270 | 624 | 64 | 22,886 | 718 | 140 | 42,156 | 1,342 | 1-256th. |
| 1873 | 71 | 20,050 | 571 | 69 | 26,661 | 891 | 140 | 46,711 | 1,462 | 1-246th. |
| 1874 | 80 | 25,517 | 680 | 78 | 39,466 | 1,102 | 158 | 64,983 | 1,782 | 1-206th. |

Of the vessels that cleared in 1874 *with cargoes,* 80 were American, having 25,517 tons and 680 in crews, and 77 were foreign, having 39,019 tons and 1,091 in crews. The departures *in ballast* were 1 foreign vessel of 447 tons, with 11 in its crew.

## No. 4.

*Statement Showing the* NUMBER OF AMERICAN AND FOREIGN OCEAN STEAM VESSELS, *with their* TONNAGE AND CREWS, *that* CLEARED *from Virginia Ports for Foreign Countries, and that* ENTERED *from Foreign Countries, during the Fiscal Years* 1870, 1871, 1872, 1873, 1874.

| Year. | CLEARED. | | | | | | | | | ENTERED. | | | | | | | | | Proportion to Whole Entering U. S. |
|---|---|---|---|---|---|---|---|---|---|---|---|---|---|---|---|---|---|---|---|
| | AMERICAN. | | | FOREIGN. | | | TOTAL. | | | AMERICAN. | | | FOREIGN. | | | TOTAL. | | | |
| | Number. | Tons. | Crews. | Number. | Tons. | Crews. | Number. | Tons. | Crews. | Number. | Tons. | Crews. | Number. | Tons. | Crews. | Number. | Tons. | Crews. | |
| 1870 | .. | .... | .. | 1 | 1,442 | 46 | 1 | 1,442 | 46 | .. | .... | .. | .. | ........ | ...... | .. | ........ | ...... | |
| 1871 | .. | .... | .. | .. | ...... | .... | .. | ...... | .... | .. | .... | .. | 3 | 4,423 | 195 | 3 | 4,423 | 195 | 1-666th. |
| 1872 | 2 | 331 | 12 | 2 | 3,275 | 96 | 4 | 3,606 | 108 | 2 | 269 | 17 | 17 | 26,807 | 1,505 | 19 | 27,076 | 1,522 | 1-118th. |
| 1873 | .. | .... | .. | 8 | 10,488 | 317 | 8 | 10,488 | 317 | .. | .... | .. | 25 | 38,488 | 2,075 | 25 | 38,488 | 2,075 | 1-107th. |
| 1874 | 1 | 212 | 20 | 7 | 11,866 | 306 | 8 | 12,078 | 326 | 1 | 213 | 18 | 7 | 13,170 | 664 | 8 | 13,383 | 692 | 1-360th. |

All these clearances and entrances were through the port of Norfolk, which has every advantage that can be desired for the arrival and departure of the *largest* ocean steamships. The water at the wharves of Norfolk is always deep enough to permit the largest vessels to come alongside.

# No. 5.

*Statement of the* VALUE OF IMPORTS *from, and* DOMESTIC EXPORTS *to, Foreign Countries through Virginia Ports, Specifying the Country, during the fiscal years named.*

| COUNTRY FROM AND TO WHICH. | 1869. | | 1870. | | 1871. | | 1872. | | 1873. | | 1874. | |
|---|---|---|---|---|---|---|---|---|---|---|---|---|
| | Imports. | Exports. | Imports. | Exports. | Imports. | Exports. | Imports. | Exports. | Imports. | Exports. | Imports. | Exports. |
| Nova Scotia, N. Br. and Pr. Ed. Is. | | | | | | | | | 5,488 | 11,087 | 19,269 | 20,935 |
| Quebec | | | | | | | | | 702 | | | |
| Dominion of Canada | 8,543 | 47,205 | 11,967 | 14,526 | 10,556 | | 4,761 | | | | | |
| Other British North American Possessions | 1,085 | | | | | | | | | | | |
| Mexico | | | | | | | 25,000 | | | | | |
| Central American States | | | | | | | | 1,450 | | | | |
| Cuba | 10,551 | 30,838 | 25,212 | 26,745 | 7,995 | 28,506 | | 46,294 | | 26,688 | | 37,045 |
| British West Indies | 5,591 | 326,124 | | 169,220 | 380 | 198,937 | 515 | 275,043 | 1,670 | 174,325 | 46,881 | 140,202 |
| Danish West Indies and Aa. Possessions | | 18,600 | | | 31,218 | | | 19,222 | | 10,865 | | 5,963 |
| French West Indies and French Poss. in Aa. | | 17,997 | | 16,060 | | | | 5,460 | | 94,032 | | 2,295 |
| United States of Colombia | | | | | | | | | | 5,370 | | |
| British Guiana | | | | | | | | | | 50,929 | | 80,955 |
| Brazil | | 370,138 | | 621,023 | | 548,167 | | 958,791 | 44,030 | 1,119,658 | 63,609 | 1,423,801 |
| Uruguay | | 1,206 | | | | | | 204,904 | | | | |
| Argentine Republic | 6,538 | | | 38,393 | | | | | | | | |
| England | 179,309 | 1,386,719 | 103,708 | 1,647,875 | 158,631 | 447,100 | 597,672 | 590,376 | 856,940 | 1,108,146 | 181,979 | 1,108,406 |
| Scotland | 45,370 | | | | | | | | 13,494 | 43,552 | 4,340 | 123,347 |
| Ireland | | | | 24,750 | | 101,637 | | 142,357 | | 14,010 | | 198,808 |
| Holland | | | | | | | | 3,110 | | | | |
| Netherlands | | | | | | | | | | | | 418,329 |
| Bremen | | 69,784 | | | | | | | | | | |
| Germany | | | | | | | | 84,565 | | * 131,983 | | |
| Austria | | 114,700 | | 279,400 | | 169,400 | | 314,600 | | 495,800 | | 530,000 |
| France | | 418,328 | | 130,000 | | 452,460 | | 602,141 | | | | 516,097 |
| Italy | | 436,340 | | 15,251 | | 69,885 | | 261,765 | | 134,290 | | 257,058 |
| Spain | | 35,591 | 66 | | | | | 16,309 | | 59,599 | | 34,214 |
| Portugal | | | | | | | | | | | 46 | |
| Azores, Madeira, &c. | | | | | | | | | | | 449 | 3,600 |
| Total | $259,749 | $3,307,450 | $141,313 | $2,983,258 | $177,562 | $2,046,310 | $627,948 | $3,518,387 | $923,651 | $3,478,607 | $336,566 | $5,299,670 |

* 20,000 a re-export.

These summarized returns of the Bureau of Statistics give only the values of imports and exports, not the articles. To find out what the State trades in with other countries, other sources of information must be sought. The facts* of the trade of Richmond are the only ones accessible, but from those for one or two years, compared with Statements 5 and 6, a very good idea of the general trade may be formed. The cotton statement, hereafter given, will also help to show the courses of Virginia trade.

ARTICLES* AND VALUES *of* DIRECT TRADE *of* RICHMOND *during the Fiscal Year* 1872.

| IMPORTS. | | | |
|---|---|---|---|
| *From Nova Scotia:* | | | |
| 227 | boxes smoked herrings..... | $25 | |
| 980 | tons lump plaster........... | 861 | |
| | | | $886 |
| *From England:* | | | |
| 7,558⅛ | tons iron rails (old)......... | 239,613 | |
| 3,052 | tons iron rails (new)........ | 19,801 | |
| 193,036 | lbs. bar iron................ | 3,289 | |
| 57,617 | sacks salt.................. | 47,327 | |
| 3,446 | gals. ale and porter......... | 3,643 | |
| 145 | gals. brandy................ | 279 | |
| 441 | gals. gin................... | 254 | |
| 512⅛ | gals. whiskey............... | 463 | |
| 452½ | gals. sherry................ | 571 | |
| 692½ | gals. claret............... .. | 701 | |
| 8 | cases champagne........... | 44 | |
| 12,100 | lbs. licorice................ | (?) 1,005 | |
| 16¾ | tons coal................... | 40 | |
| 6 | hounds..................... | 25 | |
| | Furniture ........... ..... | 629 | |
| | China and earthenware..... | 11,472 | |
| | | | $329,155 |
| | Total imports........ | | $330,041 |

*The Direct Imports of Richmond in 1874 were:*

| | |
|---|---|
| Coffee from Brazil........................ | $ 223,909 |
| Coffee from Venezuela.................... | 40 |
| Lump gypsum from Nova Scotia.......... | 7,314 |
| Guano from Nevassa Islands.............. | 5,830 |
| Salt from England......................... | 57,599 |
| Stout from England....................... | 1,122 |
| Bass mats................................. | 298 |
| Oil paintings.............................. | 24 |
| Total imports................ | $296,036 |

| EXPORTS. | | |
|---|---|---|
| *To France:* | | |
| 2,033 hhds. leaf tobacco.......... | $318,153 | |
| 1,010 bags oak bark.............. | 1,000 | |
| 790 bags quercitron............. | 1,155 | |
| 6,000 staves ...................... | 420 | |
| | | $320,728 |
| *To Austria:* | | |
| 2,214 hhds. leaf tobacco.......... | | $487,450 |
| *To Brazil:* | | |
| 67,089 bbls. flour .................. | 786,022 | |
| 832 bbls. rosin.................. | 2,725 | |
| 30 bbls. pitch.................. | 149 | |
| 500 kegs lard.................... | 2,513 | |
| 84 bundles of window frames.. | 475 | |
| Hams, boards, books, hardware and clothing........ | 298 | |
| | | $792,178 |
| *To Holland:* | | |
| 60 hhds. tobacco stems........ | | $3,110 |
| *To Bremen:* | | |
| 481 hhds. leaf tobacco.......... | 75,750 | |
| 157 hhds. tobacco stems........ | 7,900 | |
| 14 boxes manufact'd tobacco.. | 315 | |
| 622 bags quercitron............. | 600 | |
| | | $84,565 |
| *To Scotland:* | | |
| 290 hhds. tobocco strips........ | | $43,552 |
| *To Ireland:* | | |
| 9,720 bbls. flour.................. | | $68,285 |
| *To England:* | | |
| 278 hhds. leaf tobacco.......... | 43,111 | |
| 1,167 hhds. tobacco strips........ | 162,398 | |
| 15,000 staves...................... | 1,000 | |
| | | $206,609 |
| *To Italy:* | | |
| 256 hhds. leaf tobacco.......... | 43,132 | |
| 6 boxes manufact'd tobacco.. | 80 | |
| | | $43,212 |
| Total exports....... | | $2,049,686 |

The Richmond trade with European countries is chiefly the exportation of tobacco, tan bark and staves, and the importation of salt, manufactured iron and malt liquors, the import trade being heretofore with England. The trade with Nova Scotia is the exchange of tobacco for lump plaster mined there. Brazil exchanges coffee for the flour of Richmond, that keeps so well in warm climates. naval stores and provisions. The enlargement of the course of direct trade that is taking place, resulting from the exportation of flour, tobacco, cotton, naval stores and other forest products, &c., in large quantities, will soon lead to an increase of imports to supply the sections from which the exports are drawn.

*Report of Richmond Chamber of Commerce, 1874.
Richmond Dispatch, January 1st, 1875.

No.

*Summary Statement of* DOMESTIC EXPORTS (*the Growth, Produce and Manufacture of the*

| ARTICLES. | 1858. | | 1868. | | 1869. |
|---|---|---|---|---|---|
| | Quantity. | Value. | Quantity. | Value. | Quantity. |
| Bark for tanning | ........... | $ 3,709 | ........... | ........... | ........... |
| Books | ........... | 185 | ........... | ........... | ........... |
| *Bread and Breadstuffs:* | | | | | |
| Bread and biscuits { Bbls / Box's | 3,052 / 400 | 11,672 | bbls. 810 | 627 | lbs. 24,758 |
| Indian corn ....Bush. | 165,249 | 114,034 | 125,152 | 152,101 | 81,600 |
| Indian corn meal ....Bbls. | 768 | 3,146 | 1,695 | 10,638 | 1,769 |
| Wheat ....Bush. | 92,139 | 119,422 | ........... | ........... | ........... |
| Wheat flour ....Bbls. | 334,302 | 2,459,004 | 29,312 | 355,480 | 36,514 |
| Other small grain and pulse | ........... | 9,168 | ........... | 141 | ........... |
| Maizena, &c | ........... | ........... | ........... | ........... | ........... |
| Bricks | ........... | ........... | ........... | 280 | ........... |
| Brooms, brushes, &c | ........... | ........... | ........... | 356 | ........... |
| Candles—adamantine ....Lbs. | 16,444 | 4,063 | ........... | ........... | ........... |
| Candles—sperm ....Lbs. | 900 | 400 | ........... | ........... | ........... |
| Candles—tallow ....Lbs. | ........... | ........... | 1,000 | 100 | ........... |
| Carriages, carts, &c | ........... | ........... | ........... | ........... | ........... |
| Cars—railroad, &c | ........... | (?) 2,200 | ........... | ........... | ........... |
| Coal—bituminous ....Tons | 1,146 | 5,131 | ........... | ........... | 201 |
| Coal—other | ........... | ........... | ........... | ........... | ........... |
| *Cotton and Manufactures of:* | | | | | |
| Sea Island | ........... | ........... | ........... | ........... | ........... |
| Other unmanufactured ....Lbs. | *213,351 | 28,976 | 4,108,510 | 956,228 | 2,643,851 |
| Colored manufactured | ........... | 1,855 | ........... | ........... | ........... |
| Uncolored manufactured | ........... | 11,000 | ........... | ........... | ........... |
| All manufactures of, not specified | ........... | 5,373 | ........... | ........... | ........... |
| Drugs, chemicals, &c., not specified | ........... | 185 | ........... | 2,957 | ........... |
| Fancy articles, not specified | ........... | ........... | ........... | ........... | ........... |
| *Fruits:* | | | | | |
| Not specified | ........... | ........... | ........... | 644 | ........... |
| Apples—dried ....Lbs. | ........... | ........... | ........... | ........... | ........... |
| Preserved | ........... | ........... | ........... | ........... | ........... |
| Glass and glassware | ........... | 129 | ........... | ........... | ........... |
| Jewelry | ........... | 420 | ........... | ........... | ........... |
| Hay ....Tons. | ........... | ........... | ........... | ........... | ........... |
| Hemp—manufactures of | ........... | ........... | ........... | ........... | ........... |
| Hoop skirts | ........... | ........... | ........... | ........... | ........... |
| India rubber goods | ........... | 200 | ........... | ........... | ........... |
| *Iron and Manufactures of:* | | | | | |
| Castings ....Cwt. | 113 | 782 | ........... | ........... | ........... |

*495 bales.

6.

*United States) from Virginia Ports to Foreign Countries, during the fiscal years named*

| 1869. | 1870. | | 1871. | | 1872. | | 1873. | | 1874. | |
|---|---|---|---|---|---|---|---|---|---|---|
| Value. | Quantity. | Value. | Quantity. | Value. | Quantity. | Value. | Quantity. | Value. | Quantity. | Value. |
| ......... | ......... | $ 575 | ......... | $ 360 | ......... | $ 3,595 | ......... | $4,863 | ......... | $86? |
| ......... | ......... | ......... | ......... | ......... | ......... | ......... | ......... | 100 | ......... | ......... |
| 1,576 | ......... | ......... | ......... | ......... | lbs. 207 | 21 | ......... | ......... | ......... | ......... |
| 72,490 | ......... | ......... | 40,554 | 37,545 | 91,723 | 64,396 | 62,653 | 42,983 | 12,212 | 10,627 |
| 8,053 | 1,220 | 3,790 | 586 | 2,520 | 6 | 24 | ......... | ......... | ......... | ......... |
| ......... | 54,377 | 81,765 | 9,171 | 11,380 | 28,639 | 48,686 | ......... | ......... | ......... | ......... |
| 407,520 | 89,549 | 691,464 | 83,225 | 630,855 | 150,353 | 1,226,734 | 117,809 | 1,126,468 | 174,412 | 1,526,887 |
| ......... | ......... | 614 | ......... | 1,920 | ......... | 2,029 | ......... | 1,223 | ......... | ......... |
| ......... | ......... | ......... | ......... | ......... | ......... | 196 | ......... | ......... | ......... | ......... |
| ......... | ......... | ......... | ......... | ......... | ......... | ......... | ......... | ......... | ......... | ......... |
| ......... | ......... | ......... | ......... | ......... | ......... | ......... | ......... | ......... | ......... | ......... |
| ......... | ......... | ......... | ......... | ......... | ......... | ......... | ......... | ......... | ......... | ......... |
| ......... | ......... | ......... | ......... | ......... | ......... | ......... | ......... | ......... | ......... | ......... |
| ......... | ......... | ......... | ......... | ......... | 240 | 37 | ......... | ......... | ......... | ......... |
| ......... | ......... | ......... | ......... | ......... | ......... | ......... | ......... | ......... | ......... | ......... |
| ......... | 60 | 24,237 | 30 | 26,196 | ......... | ......... | ......... | ......... | ......... | ......... |
| 1,005 | ......... | ......... | ......... | ......... | 132 | 2,419 | 2,189 | 9,843 | 1,563 | 7,708 |
| ......... | ......... | ......... | ......... | ......... | ......... | ......... | ......... | ......... | ......... | ......... |
| ......... | ......... | ......... | ......... | ......... | ......... | ......... | ......... | ......... | ......... | ......... |
| 713,076 | †4,289,611 | 1,038,304 | ‡2,414,300 | 327,109 | §1,750,416 | 372,470 | ‖3,509,099 | 676,583 | ¶9,253,710 | 1,434,203 |
| ......... | ......... | ......... | ......... | ......... | ......... | ......... | ......... | ......... | ......... | ......... |
| ......... | ......... | ......... | ......... | ......... | ......... | ......... | ......... | ......... | ......... | ......... |
| 414 | ......... | ......... | ......... | ......... | ......... | ......... | ......... | ......... | ......... | ......... |
| 450 | ......... | 42 | ......... | ......... | ......... | ......... | ......... | ......... | ......... | ......... |
| ......... | ......... | ......... | ......... | ......... | ......... | 17 | ......... | ......... | ......... | ......... |
| 119 | ......... | ......... | ......... | ......... | ......... | ......... | ......... | ......... | ......... | ......... |
| ......... | ......... | ......... | 80 | 5 | ......... | ......... | ......... | ......... | ......... | ......... |
| ......... | ......... | 25 | ......... | 60 | ......... | ......... | ......... | ......... | ......... | ......... |
| ......... | ......... | 25 | ......... | ......... | ......... | ......... | ......... | ......... | ......... | ......... |
| ......... | ......... | ......... | ......... | ......... | ......... | ......... | ......... | ......... | ......... | ......... |
| ......... | ......... | ......... | ......... | ......... | 7 | 175 | ......... | ......... | ......... | ......... |
| ......... | ......... | ......... | ......... | ......... | ......... | ......... | ......... | 1,043 | ......... | ......... |
| ......... | ......... | ......... | ......... | ......... | ......... | 14 | ......... | ......... | ......... | ......... |
| ......... | ......... | ......... | ......... | ......... | ......... | ......... | ......... | ......... | ......... | ......... |
| ......... | ......... | ......... | ......... | ......... | ......... | ......... | ......... | ......... | ......... | ......... |

† 9,652 bales. ‡ 5,254 bales. § 3,854 bales. ‖ 7,791 bales. ¶ 20,524 bales.

No. 6—

| ARTICLES. | 1858. | | 1868. | | 1869. |
|---|---|---|---|---|---|
| | Quantity. | Value. | Quantity. | Value. | Quantity. |
| *Iron and Manufactures of:* | | | | | |
| Boilers for steam engines | ... | ... | ... | ... | ... |
| Machinery, not specified | ... | ... | ... | ... | ... |
| Nails and spikes ... Lbs. | 10,000 | 4,000 | ... | ... | ... |
| All other manufactures of iron | ... | 6,948 | ... | ... | ... |
| *Steel and Manufactures of:* | | | | | |
| Cutlery | ... | ... | ... | ... | ... |
| Edge tools | ... | ... | ... | ... | ... |
| Fire-arms | ... | ... | ... | ... | ... |
| *Leather and Manufactures of:* | | | | | |
| Leather ... Lbs. | 1,138 | 301 | ... | ... | ... |
| Saddlery and harness | ... | ... | ... | ... | ... |
| Boots and shoes ... Pairs. | ... | ... | ... | ... | ... |
| Lime and cement | ... | ... | ... | ... | ... |
| Matches | ... | ... | ... | ... | ... |
| Musical instruments | ... | ... | ... | ... | ... |
| *Naval Stores:* | | | | | |
| Rosin and turpentine ... Bbls. | 6,167 | 9,090 | 12,283 | 42,577 | 13,887 |
| Tar and pitch ... Bbls. | 2,001 | 3,256 | 120 | 323 | 1,210 |
| *Oils:* | | | | | |
| Mineral, crude ... Gals. | ... | ... | ... | ... | ... |
| Do. refined ... Gals. | ... | ... | ... | ... | 630 |
| Animal, lard ... Gals. | ... | ... | ... | ... | ... |
| Do. whale ... Gals. | ... | ... | 80 | 85 | ... |
| Vegetable, essential | ... | ... | ... | ... | ... |
| Paints and varnish | ... | 22 | ... | ... | ... |
| Paper and stationery | ... | 775 | ... | ... | ... |
| *Provisions:* | | | | | |
| Bacon and hams ... Lbs. | 4,498 | 671 | 350 | 73 | ... |
| Beef ... Bbls. | 177 | 3,418 | ... | ... | ... |
| Butter ... Lbs. | 7,637 | 1,199 | 625 | 225 | 90 |
| Cheese ... Lbs. | 4,440 | 536 | 1,617 | 185 | ... |
| Condensed milk | ... | ... | ... | ... | ... |
| Fish—pickled ... Bbls. | ... | ... | 87 | 185 | ... |
| Fish—otherwise cured | ... | ... | ... | ... | ... |
| Lard ... Lbs. | 45,753 | 6,040 | 2,500 | 475 | 100 |
| Meats—preserved | ... | ... | ... | 75 | ... |
| Oysters | ... | ... | ... | 1,000 | ... |
| Pickles | ... | ... | ... | ... | ... |
| Pork ... Bbls. | 822 | 14,586 | ... | ... | ... |

CONTINUED.

| 1869. | 1870. | | 1871. | | 1872. | | 1873. | | 1874. | |
|---|---|---|---|---|---|---|---|---|---|---|
| Value. | Quantity. | Value. | Quantity. | Value. | Quantity. | Value. | Quantity. | Value. | Quantity. | Value. |
| ........ | ........ | ........ | ........ | ........ | ........ | 1,050 | ........ | ........ | ........ | ........ |
| 53,394 | ........ | ........ | ........ | ........ | ........ | ........ | ........ | ........ | ........ | 200 |
| ........ | ........ | ........ | ........ | ........ | 100 | 6 | ........ | ........ | ........ | ........ |
| ........ | ........ | ........ | ........ | ........ | ........ | 901 | ........ | ........ | ........ | ........ |
| | | | | | | | | | | 5 |
| ........ | ........ | ........ | ........ | ........ | ........ | 230 | ........ | 12 | ........ | ........ |
| ........ | ........ | 125 | ........ | ........ | ........ | ........ | ........ | ........ | ........ | ........ |
| ........ | ........ | ........ | ........ | ........ | ........ | 50 | ........ | ........ | ........ | ........ |
| ........ | ........ | ........ | ........ | ........ | ........ | ........ | ........ | ........ | ........ | ........ |
| ........ | ........ | ........ | ........ | ........ | ........ | 25 | ........ | ........ | ........ | ........ |
| ........ | ........ | ........ | ........ | ........ | 250 | 408 | ........ | ........ | ........ | ........ |
| ........ | ........ | ........ | ........ | ........ | ........ | ........ | ........ | ........ | ........ | ........ |
| ........ | ........ | ........ | ........ | ........ | ........ | 13 | ........ | ........ | ........ | ........ |
| ........ | ........ | ........ | ........ | 75 | ........ | ........ | ........ | ........ | ........ | ........ |
| 43,960 | 4,347 | 10,090 | 1,007 | 2,816 | 705 | 3,061 | 3,617 | 13,442 | 427 | 1,691 |
| 2,934 | 608 | 1,617 | 106 | 332 | 159 | 498 | 520 | 1,257 | 20 | 50 |
| ........ | ........ | ........ | ........ | ........ | 1,000 | 250 | ........ | ........ | ........ | ........ |
| 305 | 100 | 50 | ........ | ........ | 2,430 | 920 | ........ | ........ | 20,000 | 5,000 |
| ........ | 215 | 320 | ........ | ........ | ........ | ........ | ........ | ........ | ........ | ........ |
| ........ | ........ | ........ | ........ | ........ | ........ | ........ | ........ | ........ | ........ | ........ |
| ........ | ........ | ........ | ........ | 80 | ........ | ........ | ........ | 450 | ........ | ........ |
| ........ | ........ | ........ | ........ | ........ | ........ | 70 | ........ | ........ | ........ | ........ |
| ........ | ........ | ........ | ........ | ........ | ........ | ........ | ........ | ........ | ........ | ........ |
| ........ | ........ | ........ | ........ | ........ | 4,588 | 428 | 125 | 20 | ........ | ........ |
| ........ | lbs. 1,000 | 55 | ........ | ........ | lbs. 1,684 | 136 | lbs. 1,000 | 80 | ........ | ........ |
| 30 | ........ | ........ | ........ | ........ | ........ | ........ | ........ | ........ | ........ | ........ |
| ........ | ........ | ........ | 856 | 97 | ........ | ........ | ........ | ........ | ........ | ........ |
| ........ | ........ | ........ | ........ | ........ | ........ | 13 | ........ | ........ | ........ | ........ |
| ........ | ........ | ........ | 50 | 200 | ........ | ........ | ........ | ........ | ........ | ........ |
| 20 | ........ | ........ | ........ | 20 | ........ | ........ | ........ | ........ | ........ | ........ |
| 15 | 3,750 | 825 | 150 | 30 | 30,596 | 3,671 | 33,926 | 4,054 | 26,094 | 2,650 |
| ........ | ........ | ........ | ........ | 10 | ........ | ........ | ........ | ........ | ........ | ........ |
| ........ | ........ | ........ | ........ | 94 | ........ | ........ | ........ | 3,276 | ........ | ........ |
| ........ | ........ | ........ | ........ | ........ | ........ | ........ | ........ | ........ | ........ | ........ |
| ........ | ........ | ........ | lbs. 10,250 | 1,025 | ........ | ........ | ........ | ........ | ........ | ........ |

No. 6—

| ARTICLES. | 1858. | | 1868. | | 1869. |
|---|---|---|---|---|---|
| | Quantity. | Value. | Quantity. | Value. | Quantity. |
| *Provisions:* | | | | | |
| Potatoes.......Bush. | 75 | 73 | ........ | ........ | ........ |
| Vegetables....... | ........ | ........ | ........ | ........ | ........ |
| *Rags:* | | | | | |
| Cotton.......Lbs. | ........ | ........ | 1,616 | 100 | ........ |
| Rice.......Trs. | 10 | 269 | ........ | ........ | ........ |
| *Seeds:* | | | | | |
| Clover.......Bush. | ........ | ........ | ........ | ........ | ........ |
| Flax.......Bush. | ........ | ........ | 2 | 7 | ........ |
| Garden....... | ........ | ........ | ........ | ........ | ........ |
| Soap.......Lbs. | ........ | ........ | ........ | ........ | ........ |
| Spirits from grain.......Gals. | 1,062 | 526 | ........ | ........ | ........ |
| Spirits of turpentine.......Gals. | 2,453 | 1,239 | 112 | 84 | bbls. 1,001 |
| Starch.......Lbs. | ........ | ........ | 1,200 | 64 | ........ |
| Sugar—refined.......Lbs. | 3,400 | 507 | ........ | ........ | ........ |
| Confectionery.......Lbs. | ........ | ........ | ........ | ........ | ........ |
| Tallow....... | ........ | ........ | ........ | ........ | ........ |
| *Tobacco and Manufactures of:* | | | | | |
| Leaf.......Hhds. | 25,999 | 4,094,008 | lbs. 16,302,780 | 2,421,175 | lbs. 11,311,564 |
| Manufactured.......Lbs. | 57,127 | 15,205 | 59,203 | 81,250 | ........ |
| Vinegar.......Gals. | ........ | ........ | ........ | ........ | ........ |
| Wax.......Lbs. | 13,035 | 3,907 | 1,280 | 470 | ........ |
| Wearing apparel....... | ........ | 100 | ........ | ........ | ........ |
| *Wood and Manufactures of:* | | | | | |
| Boards, &c.......M ft. | 72 | 1,203 | 114 | 2,835 | 200 |
| Shingles.......M. | 7,747 | 39,738 | 1,067 | 6,932 | 1,839 |
| Box shooks....... | ........ | ........ | ........ | ........ | ........ |
| Other shooks, staves and headings.......M. | 6,457 | 220,719 | 4,562 | 242,943 | ........ |
| Hoop and other poles.......M. | ........ | ........ | 10 | 450 | ........ |
| Fire-wood.......Cords | ........ | ........ | ........ | ........ | 10 |
| Logs, masts, &c....... | ........ | ........ | ........ | ........ | ........ |
| Lumber, sawed and hewn.......Tons | 260 | 3,755 | ........ | ........ | 418 |
| All other timber....... | ........ | 3,561 | ........ | ........ | ........ |
| Household furniture....... | ........ | 2,860 | ........ | ........ | ........ |
| Manufactures of wood, not specified....... | ........ | 41,524 | ........ | 428 | ........ |
| *All articles, not enumerated:* | | | | | |
| Unmanufactured....... | ........ | 1,232 | ........ | 12,510 | ........ |
| Manufactured....... | ........ | 2,939 | ........ | 254 | ........ |
| Total....... | ........ | $7,262,765 | ........ | $4,244,551 | ........ |

CONTINUED.

| 1869. | 1870. | | 1871. | | 1872. | | 1873. | | 1874. | |
|---|---|---|---|---|---|---|---|---|---|---|
| Value. | Quantity. | Value. | Quantity. | Value. | Quantity. | Value. | Quantity. | Value. | Quantity. | Value. |
| ......... | ......... | ......... | ......... | ......... | ......... | ......... | 12 | 16 | ......... | ......... |
| 3,788 | ......... | ......... | ......... | ......... | ......... | ......... | ......... | ......... | ......... | ......... |
| ......... | ......... | ......... | ......... | ......... | ......... | ......... | ......... | ......... | ......... | ......... |
| ......... | ......... | ......... | ......... | ......... | ......... | ......... | ......... | ......... | ......... | ......... |
| ......... | ......... | ......... | ......... | ......... | ......... | ......... | ......... | 80 | ......... | ......... |
| ......... | ......... | ......... | ......... | ......... | ......... | ......... | ......... | ......... | ......... | ......... |
| ......... | ......... | ......... | ......... | 1,875 | ......... | ......... | ......... | ......... | ......... | ......... |
| ......... | ......... | ......... | ......... | ......... | 552 | 33 | ......... | ......... | ......... | ......... |
| ......... | ......... | ......... | ......... | ......... | ......... | ......... | ......... | ......... | ......... | ......... |
| 660 | gals. 80 | 45 | ......... | ......... | ......... | ......... | ......... | ......... | ......... | ......... |
| ......... | ......... | ......... | ......... | ......... | ......... | ......... | ......... | ......... | ......... | ......... |
| ......... | ......... | ......... | ......... | ......... | ......... | ......... | ......... | ......... | ......... | ......... |
| ......... | ......... | ......... | ......... | ......... | ......... | 9 | ......... | ......... | ......... | ......... |
| ......... | 700 | 90 | ......... | ......... | 60 | 11 | 21,401 | 1,544 | ......... | ......... |
| 1,552,961 | lbs. 6,246,119 | 862,855 | lbs. 6,124,079 | 752,542 | lbs. 11,646,717 | 1,327,160 | lbs. 7,493,036 | 900,501 | lbs. 18,365,515 | 1,928,659 |
| 45,073 | ......... | 18,070 | ......... | ......... | 635 | 17,315 | ......... | 223,278 | ......... | 13,380 |
| ......... | 200 | 80 | ......... | ......... | ......... | ......... | ......... | ......... | ......... | ......... |
| ......... | ......... | ......... | ......... | ......... | ......... | ......... | ......... | ......... | ......... | ......... |
| ......... | ......... | ......... | ......... | ......... | ......... | ......... | ......... | 100 | ......... | 200 |
| 10,183 | 43 | 1,475 | 10 | 260 | 126 | 3,013 | ......... | ......... | 31 | 474 |
| 12,722 | 989 | 6,589 | 795 | 6,490 | 2,219 | 16,189 | 1,445 | 10,935 | 912 | 6,587 |
| 133 | ......... | ......... | ......... | ......... | ......... | ......... | ......... | ......... | ......... | ......... |
| 353,721 | ......... | 184,274 | ......... | 240,306 | ......... | 416,824 | ......... | 413,710 | ......... | 310,242 |
| ......... | ......... | ......... | ......... | ......... | 800 | 11 | ......... | ......... | ......... | ......... |
| 60 | ......... | ......... | 2 | 8 | ......... | ......... | ......... | ......... | ......... | ......... |
| ......... | ......... | ......... | ......... | ......... | ......... | ......... | ......... | 111 | ......... | ......... |
| 23,590 | cubic ft. 26,844 | 6,500 | ......... | ......... | cubic ft. 160 | 120 | cubic ft. 22,635 | 9,527 | cubic ft. 7,046 | 4,069 |
| ......... | ......... | 7,125 | ......... | ......... | ......... | 2,610 | ......... | 11,317 | ......... | 2,794 |
| ......... | ......... | ......... | ......... | ......... | ......... | ......... | ......... | 3,050 | ......... | ......... |
| 50 | ......... | 576 | ......... | ......... | ......... | 1,455 | ......... | 595 | ......... | ......... |
| | | 4,875 | | | | 150 | | | | 158 |
| 17,369 | ......... | ......... | ......... | ......... | ......... | ......... | ......... | ......... | ......... | ......... |
| 1,536 | ......... | 8,638 | ......... | 2,100 | ......... | ......... | ......... | ......... | ......... | ......... |
| $3,327,450 | ......... | $2,983,258 | ......... | $2,046,3[illegible] | ......... | $3,518,387 | ......... | $3,458,[illegible] | ......... | $5,290,670 |

# No. 7.

*Statement of the* DIRECT TRADE (*Imports and Domestic Exports*) OF VIRGINIA PORTS *during the fiscal years named.*

| YEARS. | CUSTOMS DISTRICTS. | IMPORTS. | DOMESTIC EXPORTS. | IMPORTS. | | EXPORTS. | |
|---|---|---|---|---|---|---|---|
| | | | | In American Vessels. | In Foreign Vessels. | In American Vessels. | In Foreign Vessels. |
| 1858 | Richmond | $ 665,906 | $6,346,399 | ........ | ........ | ........ | ........ |
| | Norfolk and Portsmouth | 174,997 | 561,185 | ........ | ........ | ........ | ........ |
| | Alexandria | 113,265 | 325,057 | ........ | ........ | ........ | ........ |
| | Petersburg | 122,165 | 5,992 | ........ | ........ | ........ | ........ |
| | Tappahannock | 2,723 | 24,132 | ........ | ........ | ........ | ........ |
| | Total | $1,079,056 | $7,262,765 | $785,217 | $293,839 | $5,890,324 | $1,372,441 |
| 1868 | Richmond | $ 29,260 | $2,525,457 | ........ | ........ | ........ | ........ |
| | Norfolk and Portsmouth | 15,740 | 1,719,094 | ........ | ........ | ........ | ........ |
| | Alexandria | 6,686 | ........ | ........ | ........ | ........ | ........ |
| | Petersburg | 4,943 | ........ | ........ | ........ | ........ | ........ |
| | Total | $56,579 | $4,244,551 | ........ | ........ | ........ | ........ |
| 1869 | Richmond | $ 41,214 | $1,836,428 | ........ | ........ | ........ | ........ |
| | Norfolk and Portsmouth | 205,591 | 1,371,796 | ........ | ........ | ........ | ........ |
| | Alexandria | 8,532 | 34,334 | ........ | ........ | ........ | ........ |
| | Petersburg | 4,402 | 34,892 | ........ | ........ | ........ | ........ |
| | Total | $259,739 | $3,327,450 | ........ | ........ | ........ | ........ |
| 1870 | Richmond | $ 91,777 | $1,636,770 | $23,924 | $67,853 | $355,069 | $1,281,701 |
| | Norfolk and Portsmouth | 14,451 | 1,307,440 | 66 | 14,385 | 150,633 | 1,156,807 |
| | Alexandria | 33,822 | 39,048 | 2,953 | 30,869 | 8,440 | 30,608 |
| | Petersburg | 1,263 | ........ | ........ | 1,263 | ........ | ........ |
| | Total | $141,313 | $2,983,258 | $26,943 | $114,370 | $514,142 | $2,469,116 |
| 1871 | Richmond | $ 68,563 | $1,418,262 | $11,419 | $ 57,144 | $656,744 | $ 761,518 |
| | Norfolk and Portsmouth | 94,091 | 628,048 | 28,618 | 65,473 | 158,079 | 469,969 |
| | Alexandria | 14,908 | ........ | 12,410 | 2,498 | ........ | ........ |
| | Total | $177,562 | $2,046,310 | $52,447 | $125,115 | $814,823 | $1,231,487 |
| 1872 | Richmond | $ 227,263 | $2,574,060 | $ 1,406 | $225,857 | $1,593,530 | $ 980,530 |
| | Norfolk and Portsmouth | 290,128 | 888,037 | 98,523 | 191,605 | 379,667 | 508,370 |
| | Alexandria | 15,310 | 56,290 | 3,015 | 12,295 | 2,317 | 53,973 |
| | Petersburg | 95,247 | ........ | ........ | 95,247 | ........ | 95,247 |
| | Total | $627,948 | $3,518,387 | $102,944 | $525,004 | $1,975,514 | $1,638,120 |

No. 7—Continued

| Years. | Customs Districts. | Imports. | Domestic Exports. | Imports. In American Vessels. | Imports. In Foreign Vessels. | Exports. In American Vessels. | Exports. In Foreign Vessels. |
|---|---|---|---|---|---|---|---|
| 1873 | Richmond | $286,599 | $2,179,523 | $ 727 | $285,872 | $1,102,329 | $1,077,194 |
| | Norfolk and Portsmouth | 146,367 | 1,235,068 | 2,400 | 143,967 | 297,136 | 937,932 |
| | Alexandria | 13,424 | 26,125 | 5,264 | 8,160 | 26,125 | ........... |
| | Petersburg | 476,661 | 17,750 | 41,558 | 435,103 | ........... | 17,750 |
| | Total | $923,051 | $3,458,466 | $49,949 | $873,102 | $1,425,590 | $2,032,876 |
| 1874 | Richmond | $156,260 | $3,463,626 | $ 3,421 | $152,839 | $1,703,965 | $1,759,661 |
| | Norfolk and Portsmouth | 80,381 | 1,831,036 | 1,432 | 78,949 | 555,812 | 1,275,224 |
| | Alexandria | 27,606 | 5,008 | 14,686 | 12,920 | 5,008 | ........... |
| | Petersburg | 72,319 | ........... | 45 249 | 27,070 | ........... | ........... |
| | Total | $336,566 | $5,299,670 | $64,788 | $271,778 | $2,264,785 | $3,034,885 |

The *direct* Importations of Virginia do not embrace a great variety of articles when compared with those of the chief importing centres of the country, but an inspection of the following tables of the different *articles*, and their *quantity* and *value*, that have been imported since 1868, will show a marked increase both in kinds and quantities, allowing for the exceptional state of trade since 1873. The importations of each of the four Virginia cities engaged in the foreign trade are presented separately. Each one should do much more of this business.

The Direct* Trade of Richmond for the calendar year 1875 was as follows:

| Imports. | | Exports. | |
|---|---|---|---|
| Coffee from Brazil | $520,407 | Flour | $1,073,409 |
| Cave earth from West Indies | 7,035 | Lard | 10,762 |
| Gypsum from Nova Scotia | 3,349 | Cotton goods | 2,360 |
| Salt from England | 34,733 | Rosin | 1,740 |
| Bags and bass mats from England | 372 | Box cars and car trucks | 3,120 |
| Bottled beer from England | 2,103 | Dressed hoops | 16,652 |
| Medical stores from England | 759 | Staves | 17,609 |
| Other articles | 219 | Lumber and timber | 34,698 |
| Total direct | $568,962 | Locust tree nails | 1,012 |
| Brought "in bond" from other districts | 17,440 | Bituminous coal | 4,498 |
| Total imports | $586,402 | Iron tanks, boilers, &c | 4,270 |
| | | Tobacco (leaf) | 1,007,589 |
| | | Tobacco (strips) | 76,427 |
| | | Quercitron | 460 |
| | | Baskets, banisters and hogsheads | 273 |
| | | Miscellaneous | 284 |
| | | Total exports | $2,243,716 |

* From Richmond Dispatch January 1st, 1876.

## No. 8.

Imports *of* Richmond *direct from Foreign Countries during the fiscal years named.*

| ARTICLES. | 1868. | | 1869. | | 1870. | | 1871. | | 1872. | | 1873. | | 1874. | |
|---|---|---|---|---|---|---|---|---|---|---|---|---|---|---|
| | Quantity. | Value. | Quantity. | Value. | Quantity. | Value. | Quantity. | Value. | Quantity. | Value. | Quantity. | Value. | Quantity. | Value. |
| Coffee ........ Lbs. | | | | | | | | | | | 328,450 | $44,030 | 414,403 | $83,602 |
| Salt ........ Lbs. | 6,653,043 | $26,574 | 5,955,873 | $25,507 | 10,829,980 | $39,937 | 10,433,008 | $36,766 | 13,026,949 | $46,077 | 14,817,209 | 69,397 | 12,786,302 | 62,156 |
| Sugar—brown ........ Lbs. | | | 460 | 33 | 393 | 36 | | | | | | | | |
| Molasses ........ Gals. | | | 33,974 | 6,047 | 33 | 12 | | | | | | | | |
| Crackers, &c. ........ Lbs. | | | | | | | | | | | 6,274 | 1,013 | | |
| Potatoes ........ Bus. | | | | | | | | | | | | | 20 | 9 |
| Fruits and nuts ........ | | | | | | | | 173 | | | | | | |
| Spices ........ Lbs. | | | | | | | | | | | | | 5,700 | 1,261 |
| Oil—salad ........ Gals. | | | | | | | | | | | | | 76 | 148 |
| Oil—fish ........ Gals. | | | 101 | 153 | 128 | 195 | | | | | | | | |
| Fish—cured ........ | | | | 800 | | | | | | 25 | | | | |
| Soda—bicarbonate ........ Lbs. | 23,226 | 824 | | | | | | | | | | | | |
| Gum Arabic ........ | 5,042 | 584 | | | | | | | | | | | | |
| Spirits in casks ........ Gals. | 352 | 529 | | | 229 | 323 | | | | | 3,048 | 2,643 | 193 | 190 |
| Spirits in bottles ........ Doz. | | | 108 | 697 | | | | | 204 | 302 | | | | |
| Wine in casks ........ Gals. | | | 62 | 98 | 31 | 44 | | | | | 1,344 | 1,272 | | |
| Wine in bottles ........ Doz. | | | | | | | | | | | 8 | 44 | | |
| Cigars ........ Lbs. | | | | | 44 | 85 | | | | | | | | |
| Malt liquors, beer, &c. ........ Gals. | | | | | | | | | 3,368 | 3,466 | 900 | 1,004 | 2,744 | 3,673 |
| Paintings ........ | | | | | | | | | | | | | | 14 |
| Coal—bituminous ........ Tons. | | | | | | | 32 | 74 | 17 | 40 | | | | |
| Earthen and stoneware, china, &c. ........ | | | | | | | | 3,812 | | 9,780 | | 1,658 | | 10 |
| Gypsum ........ Tons. | 715 | 749 | 3,013 | 3,408 | 5,338 | 4,965 | 4,225 | 3,667 | 1,600 | 1,391 | 765 | 727 | 3,835 | 3,927 |

| | | | | | | | | | | | | | | |
|---|---|---|---|---|---|---|---|---|---|---|---|---|---|---|
| Chemicals, not specified | | | | | | 6,181 | | 8,470 | | | | 2,006 | | |
| Iron—bar.........Lbs. | | | | | | | 142,069 | 2,377 | 1,553,401 | 23,090 | | | | |
| Iron—scrap.........Tons. | | | 232 | 4,449 | 1,256 | 33,811 | 422 | 11,724 | 4,356 | 142,448 | 5,112 | 163,606 | | |
| Cabinet ware | | | | | | | | | | 129 | | | | |
| Personal property—household, &c. | | | | | | | | | | 500 | | | | |
| Flax—manufactures of | | | | | | | | | | | | | | 46 |
| All other articles, not specified | | | | | | 137 | | 1,500 | | 25 | | | | 1,224 |
| Total values | | $29,260 | | $41,214 | | $91,777 | | $68,563 | | $227,263 | | $286,599 | | $156,260 |
| Brought in American vessels | | | | $1,308 | | | | | | | | | | $3,421 |
| Brought in Foreign vessels | | | | $39,906 | | | | | | | | | | $152,839 |
| Imports free of duty | | $ 749 | | $ 3,408 | | $8,394 | | | | $1,906 | | $44,757 | | $87,529 |
| Imports paying duty | | $28,511 | | $37,806 | | $83,383 | | | | $225,357 | | $241,842 | | $68,731 |

Richmond has many advantages as a point for the importation, storage and distribution of coffee. The flour there made, owing to climatic causes, both in perfecting the grain and the flour, commands a superior price in the coffee-producing regions, so the ships that carry the flour to its best market bring a return cargo to where the climate is dry enough to keep coffee safely in store, and where means of transit are good to the chief-consuming localities. In former years Richmond was a leading coffee mart. The above table shows a resumption of this trade in 1873, when it imported 1-978th of the quantity brought into the United States, which was nearly *three hundred million pounds*, valued at over *forty-four million dollars*—New York importing over 161 and Baltimore over 61 million pounds. In 1874 Richmond imported 1-713th of the coffee brought to the United States, and was the 12th port in rank.

# No. 9.

## Imports *of* Norfolk and Portsmouth *direct from Foreign Countries during the Fiscal Years named.*

| ARTICLES. | 1868. | | 1869. | | 1870. | | 1871. | | 1872. | | 1873. | | 1874. | |
|---|---|---|---|---|---|---|---|---|---|---|---|---|---|---|
| | Quantity. | Value. | Quantity. | Value. | Quantity. | Value. | Quantity. | Value. | Quantity. | Value. | Quantity. | Value. | Quantity. | Value. |
| Animals—living | | | | | | | | | | | | $ 11 | | |
| Coffee ........ Lbs. | 1,486 | $ 231 | | | | | | | | | | | | |
| Salt ........ Lbs. | 3,946,648 | 7,437 | 80,290 | $ 106 | 4,145,211 | $ 11,002 | 3,067,287 | 7,227 | 3,321,936 | $10,834 | 6,247,415 | 20,404 | 3,276,249 | $9,580 |
| Sugar ........ Lbs. | 2,767 | 76 | | | | | | | | | | | | |
| Molasses ........ Gals. | 5,868 | 1,174 | 19,065 | 5,485 | | | | | | | | | | |
| Tea ........ Lbs. | | | | | | | | | 138 | 75 | 368 | 247 | 369 | 176 |
| Biscuits, crackers, &c. ........ Lbs. | | | | | | | | | 312 | 54 | | | | |
| Provisions—meats | | | | | | | | | | 91 | | | | |
| Seeds, not specified | | | | | | | | | | 1,209 | | 2,141 | | 585 |
| Wheat ........ Bus. | | | | | | | | | | | 7 | 15 | 15 | 26 |
| Oats ........ Bus. | | | | | | | | | | | 20 | 10 | | |
| Rye ........ Bus. | | | | | | | | | | | 3 | 5 | | |
| Potatoes ........ Bus. | | | | | | | | | | | 5 | 4 | | |
| Peas ........ Bus. | | | | | | | | | | | 3 | 4 | | |
| Meal | | | | | | | | | | | | 10 | | 8 |
| Mustard ........ Lbs. | 36 | 8 | | | | | | | | | | | | |
| Mackerel—pickled ........ Bbls. | | | | | | | | | 1 | 10 | 1 | 2 | 100 | 645 |
| Fish | | | | 1,495 | | | | | | | | 12 | | |
| Herring ........ Bbls. | | | | | | | | | | | 773 | 914 | | |
| Spirits in casks ........ Gals. | 625 | 1,235 | | | 78 | 125 | | | 1,060 | 1,729 | 792 | 1,460 | 409 | 624 |
| Spirits in bottles ........ Doz. | | | | | | | | | 5 | 34 | 1 | 10 | 13 | 76 |
| Wine in casks ........ Gals. | | | | | | | 1,513 | 530 | | | | | 215 | 393 |
| Wine in bottles ........ Doz. | | | | | | | | | 2 | 2 | 31 | 216 | 5 | 16 |

| | | | | | | | | | | | | | | |
|---|---|---|---|---|---|---|---|---|---|---|---|---|---|---|
| Fruits and nuts | | | | | | 66 | | | | 2 | | 5 | | |
| Malt liquors—beer, &c. Gals. | | | | | | | | | 495 | 497 | 769 | 410 | | |
| Soda—bicarbonate Lbs. | | | | | | | | | | | | | 10 | 2 |
| Soda—caustic Lbs. | | | | | 6,783 | 266 | | | | | | | | |
| Coal—bituminous Tons. | 407 | 675 | | | 313 | 739 | | | | | | | 107 | 823 |
| Perfumery | | | | | | | | | | | | 6 | | |
| Drugs, chemicals, &c. | | 383 | | | | | | | | 1 | | 23 | | |
| Gums Lbs. | | | | | | | | | 8,269 | 578 | 4,393 | 597 | 4,587 | 605 |
| Oils—essential Lbs. | 10 | 45 | | | | | | | | | | | | |
| Copper—manufactures of | | 41 | | | | | | | | 101 | | 439 | | 625 |
| Brass—manufactures of | | | | | | | | | | | | 55 | | |
| Glass—manufactures of | | 6 | | | | | | | | 10 | | 108 | | 6 |
| Earthenware, &c. | | | | 1 | | 220 | | | | 1,218 | | 9,080 | | 2,406 |
| India Rubber—manufactures of | | | | | | | | | | | | 168 | | 6 |
| Paper—manufactures of | | | | | | | | | | 5 | | 46 | | |
| Iron, chains, anchors, &c. Lbs. | 2,600 | 101 | | | | | | | 2,599 | 123 | 38,260 | 2,448 | 33,549 | 2,073 |
| Iron—scrap Tons. | 62 | 2,952 | 21 | 944 | | | 83 | 799 | | | 29 | 886 | 22 | 676 |
| Iron—railroad Lbs. | | | 10,592,403 | 187,941 | | | 3,630,432 | 56,906 | 13,306,236 | 207,436 | | | | |
| Iron—bar Lbs. | | | | | | | | | | | 338,547 | 9,498 | | |
| Iron—pig Lbs. | | | | | | | | | | | | | 290,817 | 3,517 |
| Iron and steel—manufactures of—not specified | | 178 | | 2 | | 151 | | 7 | | 6,359 | | 19,648 | | 30,328 |
| Guns, muskets, &c. No. | 24 | 260 | | | | | | | | 424 | | 373 | | 819 |
| Hardware and cutlery | | | | | | 256 | | | | 2,240 | | 8,478 | | 4,381 |
| Machinery | | | | | | 311 | | | | 5,010 | | 16,057 | | 1,126 |
| Tin—manufactures of | | | | | | | | | | | | 10 | | |
| Lead—manufactures of | | | | | | | | | | | | 12 | | |
| Jewelry | | | | | | | | | | 273 | | 94 | | |
| Metals—composition | | | | | | | | | | 321 | | | | |
| Gypsum Tons. | 252 | 441 | 57 | 88 | | | | | 200 | 328 | | | | |
| Guano Tons. | | | | | 18 | 992 | 450 | 24,667 | | | | | 100 | 513 |

## No. 9—Continued.

| ARTICLES | 1868. | | 1869. | | 1870. | | 1871. | | 1872. | | 1873. | | 1874. | |
|---|---|---|---|---|---|---|---|---|---|---|---|---|---|---|
| | Quantity | Value. | Quantity | Value. | Quantity. | Value. | Quantity. | Value. | Quantity. | Value. | Quantity. | Value. | Quantity. | Value. |
| Hair—manufactures of | | | | | | | | | | | | $ 34 | | |
| Leather manufactures—not specified | | | | | | | | | | $120 | | 446 | | $809 |
| Soap—toilet ... Lbs | 8 | $ 12 | | | | | | | | | | | | |
| Silk—dress-goods ... Yds | 36 | 69 | | | | | | | | 382 | | | | |
| Silk—manufactures of | | | | $ 9 | | | | $ 4 | | 6 | | 143 | | 163 |
| Paintings | | | | | | | | | | | | | | 25 |
| Books | | | | | | | | | | | | 53 | | 5 |
| Fancy Goods | | | | 6 | | | | | | | | 359 | | |
| Straw Goods | | | | | | | | | | | | 23 | | |
| Gloves ... Doz | | | | | | | | | | | 1 | 6 | | 1 |
| Flax—manufactures of | | | | 1 | | | | 50 | | 89 | | 1,810 | | 25 |
| Hemp—manufactures of | | | | | | | | 990 | | 201 | | 643 | | 623 |
| Cassimeres, shawls, &c | | | | | | | | | | | | 152 | | |
| Carpets ... sq yds | 6 | 26 | | | | | | | | | 408 | 477 | 36 | 50 |
| Woolen dress goods ... sq yds | | | | | | | | | | | 3,062 | 717 | 1,895 | 526 |
| Blankets | | | | | | | | | | 30 | | 6 | | 41 |
| Woolen manufactures—not specified | | | | | | | | | | 111 | | 224 | | 19 |
| Clothing—made | | | | | | | | | | 1,240 | | 1,304 | | |
| Clothing—not specified | | | | | | | | | | 2,201 | | 2,706 | | 1,174 |
| Cotton manufactures—not specified | | 77 | | 1 | | $ 34 | | | | 477 | | 3,097 | | |
| Cotton Cloth ... sq yds | | | | | | | | | | | 110 | 16 | 59 | 22 |
| Cotton, jeans, &c ... sq yds | | | | | | | | | | | 118 | 19 | | |
| Cotton hosiery, &c | | | | | | | | | | 1,183 | | 28 | | 22 |
| Cotton—printed ... sq yds | | | | | | | | | | | | | 300 | 162 |

| | | | | | | | | | | | | | | |
|---|---|---|---|---|---|---|---|---|---|---|---|---|---|---|
| Cabinetware | | | | | | | | | | 1 | | 475 | | 40 |
| Wood—manufactures of | | | | 200 | | 62 | | | | | | | | |
| Lumber, unmanufactured wood, &c. | | | | | | | | 353 | | 25,000 | | | | |
| Personal property | | | | | | 194 | | 1,300 | | 19,860 | | 39,309 | | 16,511 |
| All other articles | | 35 | | 9,301 | | 33 | | 335 | | 231 | | 1,057 | | 78 |
| Total | | $15,740 | | $205,591 | | $14,451 | | $94,091 | | $290,128 | | $146,367 | | $80,381 |
| Brought in American vessels | | | | $ 3,057 | | | | | | | | | | $ 1,431 |
| Brought in foreign vessels | | | | $202,534 | | | | | | | | | | $78,949 |
| Imports free of duty | | $ 441 | | $ 5,453 | | $ 1,186 | | | | $ 45,766 | | $ 40,153 | | $18,450 |
| Imports paying duty | | $15,299 | | $200,138 | | $13,265 | | | | $244,362 | | $106,214 | | $61,931 |

In 1873 Norfolk and Portsmouth imported 1-129th, and in 1874 1-232nd of the salt brought to the Union.

Norfolk and Portsmouth have unrivaled advantages for doing a large portion of the immense *grocery trade* of the country, so favorably are they situated in reference to the ocean highways that lead to and from the lands where sugar, molasses, spices, coffee, tropical fruits, &c., &c., are the staple products, and so much nearer are they to the centre of population, and therefore of consumption, in the United States than any other seaport that can lay claim to being in the "offing" for this trade. The table suggests more than it presents, and the same is true of those for the other cities.

# No. 10.

IMPORTS *of* PETERSBURG *direct from Foreign Countries during the fiscal years named.*

| ARTICLES. | 1868. | | 1869. | | 1870. | | 1871. | | 1872. | | 1873. | | 1874. | |
|---|---|---|---|---|---|---|---|---|---|---|---|---|---|---|
| | Quantity. | Value. | Quantity. | Value. | Quantity. | Value. | Quantity. | Value. | Quantity. | Value. | Quantity. | Value. | Quantity. | Value. |
| Iron—railroad........Lbs. | | | | | | | | | 8,955,022 | $79,915 | 19,326,186 | $379,671 | | |
| Iron—hoop........Lbs. | 9,907 | 63 | | | | | | | | | | | | |
| Iron—manufactures of........ | | | | | | | | | | | | 27,935 | | |
| Steel—railroad bars, &c........Lbs. | | | | | | | | | | | 2,249,559 | 67,655 | | |
| Iron and steel manufactures—not specified........ | | | | | | $ 1,263 | | | | 10,785 | | | | $39,380 |
| Cabinetware........ | | | | | | | | | | | | 900 | | |
| Personal property........ | | | | | | 7,465 | | | | | | 500 | | |
| Guano........Tons. | | | | | | | | | | | | | 4,190 | $42,898 |
| Cordage, rope, &c........Lbs. | | | | | | | | | | | | | 1,383 | 41 |
| Beer........Gals. | | | | | | | | | 40 | 49 | | | | |
| Brass—manufactures of........ | | | | | | | | | | 20 | | | | |
| Glass—cylinder........Lbs. | | | | | | | | | 2,097 | 129 | | | | |
| Castings—iron, &c........Lbs. | | | | | | | | | 3,350 | 150 | | | | |
| Machinery........ | | | | | | | | | | 114 | | | | |
| Salt........Lbs. | 792,300 | 3,349 | 1,230,668 | $4,402 | | | | | 1,140,160 | 3,249 | | | | |
| Tea........Lbs. | | | | | | | | | 95 | 56 | | | | |
| Spirits in casks........Gals. | | | | | | | | | 43 | 146 | | | | |
| Wine in casks........Gals. | | | | | | | | | 33 | 103 | | | | |
| Wine in bottles........Doz. | | | | | | | | | 51 | 461 | | | | |
| Rags for paper........Lbs. | | | | | 52,099 | 1,597 | | | | | | | | |
| Cotton—manufactures of........ | | 120 | | | | | | | | | | | | |
| Total value........ | | $4,943 | | $4,402 | | $10,325 | | | | $95,247 | | $476,661 | | $72,319 |
| Brought in American vessels........ | | | | | | | | | | | | | | $45,249 |
| Brought in Foreign vessels........ | | | | $4,402 | | | | | | | | | | $27,070 |
| Imports free of duty........ | | | | | | $9,062 | | | | | | $ 500 | | $42,898 |
| Imports paying duty........ | | $4,913 | | $4,402 | | $1.263 | | | | $95,247 | | $476,161 | | $29.421 |

Petersburg, with its deeper port of City Point, has facilities for foreign commerce that should give her a larger and steadier import trade than is indicated above, and a large and productive area of country is naturally tributary to her wharves for sending to and receiving from abroad. The table leaves the impression that her trade has been spasmodic.

## No. 11.

IMPORTS *of* ALEXANDRIA *direct from Foreign Countries during the fiscal years named.*

| ARTICLES. | 1868. | | 1869. | | 1870. | | 1871. | | 1872. | | 1873. | | 1874. | |
|---|---|---|---|---|---|---|---|---|---|---|---|---|---|---|
| | Quantity. | Value. | Quantity. | Value. | Quantity. | Value. | Quantity. | Value. | Quantity. | Value. | Quantity. | Value. | Quantity. | Value. |
| Gypsum........................Tons. | 1,195 | $1,142 | 2,940 | $2,647 | 3,180 | $ 2,953 | 6,300 | $5,669 | 3,350 | $ 3,015 | 5,854 | $ 5,264 | 15,485 | $13,910 |
| Salt..............................Lbs. | 2,422,198 | 5,476 | 2,424,091 | 5,495 | 4,955,577 | 30,102 | 1,659,339 | 8,997 | 6,209,527 | 10,532 | 2,952,841 | 7,517 | 3,770,388 | 12,918 |
| Hemp—manufactures of............ | ............ | ....... | ............ | 390 | ............ | ....... | ............ | 242 | ............ | 1,763 | ............ | 643 | ............ | ....... |
| Potatoes..........................Bus. | ............ | ....... | ............ | ....... | ............ | ....... | ............ | ....... | ............ | ....... | ............ | ....... | 1,946 | 778 |
| Coal—bituminous..............Tons. | ............ | ....... | ............ | ....... | 10 | 48 | ............ | ....... | ............ | ....... | ............ | ....... | ............ | ....... |
| Fruits and nuts...................... | ............ | ....... | ............ | ....... | ............ | 719 | ............ | ....... | ............ | ....... | ............ | ....... | ............ | ....... |
| Total value of imports.. | ............ | $6,636 | ............ | $8,532 | ............ | $33,822 | ............ | $14,908 | ............ | $15,310 | ............ | $13,424 | ............ | $27,606 |
| Brought in American vessels........ | ............ | ....... | ............ | $2,647 | ............ | $ 2,953 | ............ | ....... | ............ | ....... | ............ | ....... | ............ | $14,686 |
| Brought in Foreign vessels.......... | ............ | ....... | ............ | $5,885 | ............ | $30,869 | ............ | ....... | ............ | ....... | ............ | ....... | ............ | $12,920 |
| Imports free of duty.................... | ............ | $1,142 | ............ | $2,647 | ............ | $30,869 | ............ | ....... | ............ | $ 3,015 | ............ | $5,264 | ............ | $13,910 |
| Imports paying duty.................... | ............ | $5,494 | ............ | $5,885 | ............ | $2,953 | ............ | ....... | ............ | $12,295 | ............ | $8,160 | ............ | $13,696 |

In 1873 Alexandria imported 1-258th of the salt of the Union, and there was brought into Virginia 1-3rd of the whole importation. In 1874 Alexandria imported 1-8th of the gypsum and 1-232nd of the salt.

Alexandria confines her importations, it would seem, to the gypsum of Nova Scotia and the salt of England. Her advantages for commerce are excellent, and the completion of works of internal improvement that are in progress will doubtless restore to her the foreign trade she formerly enjoyed.

There can be no question but that many of the imports that are consumed in the West, Southwest and South could reach consumers more cheaply, expeditiously and in better condition by way of the Virginia ports than by any other, and present indications lead to the conclusion that the import tables of the future will be filled with fewer empty spaces and more figures above the thousands than those above presented.

The COASTWISE TRADE of Virginia is very large in proportion to the number of her commercial population.

The following tables present all the facts contained in the United States Reports on Commerce and Navigation. Only the three years given have any coastwise trade report:

## No. 1.

ENTRANCES *into Virginia Customs Districts, in the Coastwise Trade, during the fiscal year* 1871.

| CUSTOMS DISTRICTS. | STEAMERS. | | | SAILING VESSELS. | | | TOTAL ENTRANCES. | | |
|---|---|---|---|---|---|---|---|---|---|
| | No. | Tons. | Crews. | No. | Tons. | Crews. | No. | Tons. | Crews. |
| Richmond | 519 | 382,837 | 13,231 | 114 | 21,956 | 798 | 633 | 404,793 | 14,029 |
| Petersburg | 429 | 349,059 | 10,255 | 36 | 5.387 | 202 | 465 | 354,446 | 10,457 |
| Norfolk and Portsmouth | 1,213 | 1,080,292 | 32,109 | 133 | 15,130 | 730 | 1,346 | 1,095,422 | 32,839 |
| Alexandria | 138 | 66,233 | 2,153 | 64 | 8,501 | 304 | 202 | 74,734 | 2,457 |
| Cherrystone | ........ | ......... | .......... | 5 | 198 | 21 | 5 | 198 | 21 |
| Tappahannock | 88 | 66,286 | 1,185 | 1 | 45 | 3 | 89 | 66,331 | 1,188 |
| Yorktown | 263 | 240,234 | 7,028 | 19 | 1,356 | 75 | 282 | 241,590 | 7,103 |
| Aggregate | 2,650 | 2,184,941 | 65,961 | 372 | 52,573 | 2,133 | 3,022 | 2,237,514 | 68,094 |

The seven Virginia customs districts entered about 1-25th of the vessels and 1-15th of the tonnage of all from the 98 districts then in the United States. The number of *entrances* was nearly the same as those of New York city, and the tonnage was 452,655 tons *more*—facts that prove the great value of the home trade of the State.

## No. 2.

CLEARANCES *from Virginia Customs Districts, in the Coastwise Trade, during the fiscal year* 1871.

| CUSTOMS DISTRICTS. | STEAMERS. | | | SAILING VESSELS. | | | TOTAL CLEARANCES. | | |
|---|---|---|---|---|---|---|---|---|---|
| | No. | Tons. | Crews. | No. | Tons. | Crews. | No. | Tons. | Crews. |
| Richmond | 518 | 380,670 | 13,183 | 14 | 1,866 | 61 | 532 | 382,536 | 13,244 |
| Petersburg | 421 | 346,614 | 10,167 | 8 | 494 | 30 | 429 | 347,108 | 10,197 |
| Norfolk and Portsmouth | 765 | 691,748 | 21,076 | 55 | 5,088 | 245 | 820 | 696,836 | 21,321 |
| Alexandria | 138 | 67,115 | 2,179 | 44 | 7,763 | 225 | 182 | 74,878 | 2,404 |
| Tappahannock | 83 | 63,654 | 1,129 | 1 | 45 | 3 | 84 | 63,699 | 1,132 |
| Yorktown | 265 | 242,012 | 7,080 | 4 | 211 | 16 | 269 | 242,223 | 7,096 |
| Aggregate | 2,190 | 1,791,813 | 54,814 | 126 | 15,467 | 580 | 2,316 | 1,807,280 | 55,394 |

The *clearances* from Virginia ports embraced about 1-39th of the vessels, 1-16th of the tonnage and 1-17th of the crews of all the coastwise trade of the United States for the year. The tonnage cleared was greater than that of any district in the United States, excepting New York, Chicago and Milwaukee.

## No. 3.

ENTRANCES *into Virginia Customs Districts, in the Coastwise Trade, during the fiscal year* 1872.

| CUSTOMS DISTRICTS. | STEAMERS. | | | SAILING VESSELS. | | | TOTAL ENTRANCES. | | |
|---|---|---|---|---|---|---|---|---|---|
| | No. | Tons. | Crews. | No. | Tons. | Crews. | No. | Tons. | Crews. |
| Cherrystone | 1 | 872 | 25 | 8 | 192 | 21 | 9 | 1,064 | 46 |
| Richmond | 603 | 463,916 | 14,354 | 156 | 26,903 | 885 | 759 | 490,819 | 15,239 |
| Petersburg | 481 | 420,622 | 11,672 | 28 | 3,202 | 131 | 509 | 423,824 | 11,803 |
| Norfolk and Portsmouth | 1,258 | 1,137,280 | 31,451 | 186 | 22,052 | 933 | 1,444 | 1,159,332 | 32,384 |
| Alexandria | 162 | 82,894 | 2,476 | 34 | 8,663 | 231 | 196 | 91,557 | 2,707 |
| Tappahannock | 82 | 60,959 | 1,927 | 2 | 95 | 7 | 84 | 61,054 | 1,934 |
| Yorktown | 135 | 125,459 | 3,617 | 7 | 776 | 34 | 142 | 126,235 | 3,651 |
| Aggregate | 2,722 | 2,292,002 | 65,522 | 421 | 61,883 | 2,242 | 3,143 | 2,353,885 | 67,764 |

The *entrances* of 1872 were about 1-23rd of the vessels and 1-14th of the tonnage of the whole coastwise and fishing trade of the Union. The tonnage that entered Virginia was greater than that of any district of the country with the single exception of Milwaukee, Wisconsin. There were 153 more vessels entered than to New York city in this trade. The increase over the previous year is quite respectable.

## No. 4.

CLEARANCES *from Virginia Customs Districts, in the Coastwise Trade, during the fiscal year* 1872.

| CUSTOMS DISTRICTS. | STEAMERS. | | | SAILING VESSELS. | | | TOTAL CLEARANCES. | | |
|---|---|---|---|---|---|---|---|---|---|
| | No. | Tons. | Crews. | No. | Tons. | Crews. | No. | Tons. | Crews. |
| Cherrystone | ...... | ...... | ...... | ...... | ...... | ...... | ...... | ...... | ...... |
| Richmond | 603 | 463,709 | 14,345 | 34 | 4,796 | 170 | 637 | 468,505 | 14,515 |
| Petersburg | 466 | 409,505 | 11,358 | 11 | 2,017 | 74 | 477 | 411,522 | 11,432 |
| Norfolk and Portsmouth | 984 | 909,845 | 26,042 | 90 | 11,596 | 445 | 1,074 | 921,441 | 26,487 |
| Alexandria | 161 | 82,177 | 2,455 | 32 | 7,832 | 209 | 193 | 90,009 | 2,664 |
| Tappahannock | 80 | 59,382 | 1,880 | 1 | 45 | 3 | 81 | 59,427 | 1,883 |
| Yorktown | 135 | 125,459 | 3,617 | ...... | ...... | ...... | 135 | 125,459 | 3,617 |
| Aggregate | 2,429 | 2,050,077 | 59,697 | 168 | 26,286 | 901 | 2,597 | 2,076,363 | 60,598 |

The *clearances* of 1872 were 1–23d, with 1–14th of the tonnage of all that occurred in the Union for the year. The increase over 1871 was more than 12 per cent. in the number of vessels and nearly 15 per cent. in tonnage. The increase of tonnage from Richmond, Petersburg, Norfolk and Alexandria is noteworthy.

## No. 5.

ENTRANCES *into Virginia Customs Districts, in the Coastwise Trade, during the fiscal year* 1873.

| CUSTOMS DISTRICTS. | STEAMERS. | | | SAILING VESSELS. | | | TOTAL ENTRANCES. | | |
|---|---|---|---|---|---|---|---|---|---|
| | No. | Tons. | Crews. | No. | Tons. | Crews. | No. | Tons. | Crews. |
| Cherrystone | ........ | .......... | .......... | 3 | 111 | 10 | 3 | 111 | 10 |
| Richmond | 526 | 463,869 | 12,577 | 182 | 30,092 | 1,025 | 708 | 493,961 | 13,602 |
| Petersburg | 364 | 389,347 | 9,047 | 3 | 219 | 12 | 367 | 389,566 | 9,659 |
| Norfolk and Portsmouth | 1,170 | 1,138,069 | 31,501 | 117 | 17,338 | 653 | 1,287 | 1,155,407 | 32,154 |
| Alexandria | 189 | 97,208 | 2,766 | 24 | 6,917 | 176 | 213 | 104,125 | 2,942 |
| Tappahannock | 88 | 66,620 | 2,015 | ........ | .......... | ........ | 88 | 66,620 | 2,015 |
| Yorktown | 130 | 134,792 | 3,505 | 2 | 122 | 8 | 132 | 134,914 | 3,513 |
| Aggregate | 2,467 | 2,289,905 | 62,011 | 331 | 54,799 | 1,884 | 2,798 | 2,344,704 | 63,895 |

Eighteen hundred and seventy-three gave, in the entrances to Virginia ports, about 1-27th of the vessels and 1-15th of the tonnage of the coasting trade of the Federal Union. The tonnage entrances of Chicago and Milwaukee alone were greater. The diminished aggregates show the effects of the great panic of 1873, that prostrated the trade of the whole country. The tonnage that entered Norfolk was greater than that which entered Baltimore or Boston.

## No. 6.

CLEARANCES *from Virginia Customs Districts, in the Coastwise Trade, during the fiscal year* 1873.

| CUSTOMS DISTRICTS. | STEAMERS. | | | SAILING VESSELS. | | | TOTAL CLEARANCES. | | |
|---|---|---|---|---|---|---|---|---|---|
| | No. | Tons. | Crews. | No. | Tons. | Crews. | No. | Tons. | Crews. |
| Cherrystone | ........ | .......... | .......... | ........ | .......... | ........ | ........ | .......... | ........ |
| Richmond | 509 | 450,997 | 11,743 | 34 | 5,762 | 211 | 543 | 456,759 | 11,954 |
| Petersburg | 335 | 363,323 | 9,013 | 5 | 1,083 | 26 | 340 | 364,406 | 9,039 |
| Norfolk and Portsmouth | 866 | 918,948 | 25,057 | 48 | 4,724 | 209 | 914 | 923,672 | 25,266 |
| Alexandria | 190 | 97,208 | 2,766 | 23 | 6,375 | 161 | 213 | 103,583 | 2,927 |
| Tappahannock | 68 | 67,468 | 2,010 | ........ | .......... | ........ | 88 | 67,468 | 2,010 |
| Yorktown | 129 | 133,731 | 3,477 | 2 | 122 | 8 | 131 | 133,853 | 3,485 |
| Aggregate | 2,117 | 2,031,675 | 54,066 | 112 | 18,066 | 615 | 2,229 | 2,049,741 | 54,681 |

The customs districts of Virginia in 1873 *cleared* about 1-38th of the vessels and 1-14th of the tonnage that was engaged in the coastwise and fishing trade of the United States. The clearances, of course, were diminished by the stoppage of trade consequent to the panic.

Immigration to Virginia, *direct* from foreign countries, began in 1871, through the port of Norfolk, which has monopolized this business.

The following tables, compiled from the United States official returns, embrace all the information that is collected.

Not a single death on-ship-board is reported among the immigrants to Virginia during the years for which statistics are given.

The harbors of Virginia possess unsurpassed advantages as landing places for immigrants seeking homes in almost any portion of the United States. (See maps Nos. 3 and 4.)

## No. 1.

| YEARS. | SEX. | ARRIVALS. | | | | | | | DEPARTURES. | | | |
|---|---|---|---|---|---|---|---|---|---|---|---|---|
| | | Immigrants. | | | | Foreigners—not Immigrants. | Occupied. | | | | | |
| | | | Ages. | | | | | | | | | |
| | | Whole number. | Under 15. | 15 and under 40 | 40 and upwards | | Cabin. | Other parts of ship. | Whole number. | Adults. | Children. | In sailing vessel—steerage. |
| 1871 | Males...... | 51 | 10 | 33 | 6 | 2 | 9 | 42 | 96 | 34 | 62 | 96 |
| | Females.... | 28 | 6 | 12 | 4 | 6 | 8 | 20 | 96 | 37 | 59 | 96 |
| | Total.. | 79 | 16 | 45 | 10 | 8 | 17 | 62 | 192 | 71 | 121 | 192 |
| 1872 | Males...... | 438 | 68 | 337 | 33 | ...... | 26 | 412 | 128 | 60 | 68 | 128 |
| | Females.... | 226 | 84 | 122 | 20 | ...... | 22 | 204 | 115 | 57 | 58 | 115 |
| | Total.. | 664 | 152 | 459 | 53 | ...... | 48 | 616 | 243 | 117 | 126 | 243 |
| 1873 | Males...... | 780 | 190 | 454 | 86 | ...... | ...... | ...... | ...... | ...... | ...... | ...... |
| | Females.... | 460 | 179 | 232 | 49 | ...... | ...... | ...... | ...... | ...... | ...... | ...... |
| | Total.. | 1,190 | 369 | 686 | 135 | ...... | 153 | 1,037 | ...... | ...... | ...... | ...... |
| 1874 | Males...... | 296 | 63 | 191 | 21 | *1 | ...... | ...... | ...... | ...... | ...... | ...... |
| | Females.... | 212 | 72 | 126 | 14 | ...... | ...... | ...... | ...... | ...... | ...... | ...... |
| | Total.. | 508 | 155 | 317 | 35 | 1 | 129 | 379 | ...... | ...... | ...... | ...... |

The immigration in 1871 was 1-2,080th, in 1872 1-309th, in 1873 1-39th, and 1874 1-226th of the whole of the intending settlers that came to the United States. These comparative figures show that a fair and growing business has been done in turning a portion of the tide of immigration into Virginia ports. There is no reason why steady progress should not be made and the State be thereby materiallly enriched.

* Citizen of the United States.

## No. 2.

*Table of the* Number *and* Nationality *of* Immigrants *that Arrived in Virginia during the years named.*

| From | 1871. | 1872. | 1873. | 1874. |
|---|---|---|---|---|
| England | 71 | 643 | 1,075 | 431 |
| Ireland | ........ | ........ | 13 | 8 |
| Scotland | ........ | 5 | 8 | 6 |
| Germany | ........ | 4 | 84 | 15 |
| France | ........ | 8 | 4 | 18 |
| Denmark | ........ | ........ | 6 | ........ |
| Sweden | ........ | ........ | ........ | 29 |
| Belgravia | ........ | 1 | ........ | ........ |
| Nova Scotia | ........ | 3 | ........ | ........ |
| Total immigrants | 71 | 664 | 1,190 | 507 |

It appears that England has furnished the largest number of immigrants, Germany the next, and Sweden comes third, corresponding thus in the element of nationality with the influx into the United States. Fully 9,000,000 immigrants have come into the Union since 1790, and over half of these have been of British and one-third of German origin; lately many Swedes and other Scandinavians have arrived. The United States Commissioner* of Immigration says of these people the British "speak our language and a large part are acquainted with our laws and institutions, and are soon assimilated with and absorbed into our body-politic;" the Germans, "being at once an industrious and an intelligent people, a large proportion settling in rural districts and developing the agricultural resources of the West and South, while the remainder, consisting largely of artisans and skilled workmen, find profitable employment in the cities and manufacturing towns;" the Scandinavians are "industrious, economical and temperate—their advent should be especially welcomed."

Fr. Kapp, one of the New York Commissioners of Emigration, in a work published in 1870, after a careful investigation, estimates the value of each male emigrant at $1,500, and of each female $750, making an average of $1,125, considered merely as laborers, as it will cost the country that much to rear them.

Special Report on Immigration by Edward Young, Chief of Bureau of Statistics, Washington, D. C.—to be had on application.

## No. 3.

*Table of* OCCUPATIONS *of* IMMIGRANTS *that Arrived in Virginia from* 1871 *to* 1874.

| OCCUPATION. | 1871. | 1872. | 1873. | 1874. |
|---|---|---|---|---|
| Architects | ........ | 1 | ........ | ........ |
| Blacksmiths | ........ | ........ | 6 | 3 |
| Butchers | ........ | 1 | ........ | 1 |
| Clergymen | ........ | 2 | 9 | ........ |
| Clerks | 3 | 6 | 8 | 7 |
| Carpenters | ........ | 40 | 20 | 1 |
| Engineers | ........ | 1 | ........ | ........ |
| Engine-makers | ........ | ........ | 8 | ........ |
| Farmers | 32 | 155 | 142 | 113 |
| Grocers | ........ | ........ | ........ | 5 |
| Iron workers | ........ | ........ | 9 | ........ |
| Joiners | ........ | 24 | ........ | ........ |
| Laborers | 4 | 39 | 92 | 17 |
| Mariners | ........ | 1 | ........ | ........ |
| Masons | ........ | 3 | 18 | 1 |
| Mechanics, not specified | ........ | 36 | ........ | 3 |
| Miners | ........ | 6 | 3 | ........ |
| Merchants | ........ | 18 | 63 | ........ |
| Machinists | ........ | ........ | 4 | 4 |
| Spinners | ........ | 5 | ........ | ........ |
| Shoemakers | ........ | ........ | 15 | 1 |
| Shipwrights | ........ | ........ | 2 | ........ |
| Seamstresses | ........ | ........ | 2 | ........ |
| Tailors | ........ | 14 | 10 | ........ |
| Tinners | ........ | ........ | 1 | ........ |
| Wheelwrights | ........ | ........ | 1 | ........ |
| Occupation not stated | 28 | ........ | ........ | ........ |
| Without occupation* | 4 | 312 | 777 | 351 |
| Total | 71 | 664 | 1,190 | 507 |

The large percentage of "skilled labor" represented among these tabulated occupations is worthy of note. It is difficult to estimate the value of such labor, coming as it does from old countries where *skill* has been accumulating for centuries, when introduced into a comparatively new and sparsely peopled country.

*Those classed as having "no occupation" are mostly women and children.

The Navigation Statistics that follow are compiled from the annual reports of the Register of the Treasury of the United States. They show the exact condition of the shipping of the State in each of a series of years, and present, in a concise form, the history of the changes that have taken place.

## No. 1.

General Statement *showing the* Number *and* Tonnage *of* Registered, Enrolled *and* Licensed Vessels *in Virginia at the close (June 30th) of each of the fiscal years named.*

| Years. | Registered. | | | | | | Enrolled. | | | | | | Licensed under 20 Tons. | | Aggregate. | |
|---|---|---|---|---|---|---|---|---|---|---|---|---|---|---|---|---|
| | Permanent. | | Temporary. | | Total. | | Permanent. | | Temporary. | | Total. | | | | | |
| | No. | Tons. | No. | Tons. | No. | Tons. | No. | Tons. | No. | Tons. | No. | Tons. | No. | Tons. | No. | Tons. |
| 1858* | ...... | †4,785.14 | ...... | 24,772.49 | ...... | 29,557.63 | ...... | 45,862.68 | ...... | ........... | ...... | 45,862.68 | ...... | 3,915.81 | ...... | 68,335.57 |
| 1868 | 1 | 186.40 | 75 | 14,365.15 | 76 | 14,551.51 | 340 | 14,890.24 | 12 | 1,439.27 | 352 | 16,329.51 | 482 | 4,691.25 | 910 | 35,572.31 |
| 1869 | 1 | 186.40 | 55 | 6,821.77 | 56 | 7,008.17 | 330 | 15,223.04 | 13 | 1,936.84 | 343 | 17,159.88 | 512 | 5,265.69 | 911 | 29,433.74 |
| 1870 | 1 | 186.40 | 28 | 7,427.84 | 29 | 7,614.24 | 305 | 14,700.51 | 12 | 1,960.54 | 317 | 16,661.05 | 511 | 4,996.36 | 857 | 29,271.65 |
| 1871 | 1 | 186.40 | 16 | 1,341.23 | 17 | 1,527.63 | 472 | 22,951.48 | 11 | 2,314.20 | 483 | 25,265.68 | 525 | 5,304.47 | 1,025 | 32,097.78 |
| 1872 | 1 | 212.67 | 23 | 3,648.74 | 24 | 3,861.41 | 537 | 26,942.13 | 1 | 849.66 | 537 | 26,942.13 | 595 | 5,925.02 | 1,157 | 37,078.23 |
| 1873 | ...... | ........... | 20 | 3,850.97 | 20 | 3,850.97 | 463 | 22,613.01 | 11 | 1,595.60 | 474 | 24,208.61 | 615 | 5,896.31 | 1,109 | 33,955.89 |
| 1874 | ...... | ........... | 15 | 2,910.76 | 15 | 2,910.76 | 360 | 16,719.53 | 10 | 2,464.27 | 370 | 19,183.80 | 632 | 6,319.35 | 1,017 | 28,413.91 |

* The number of vessels is not given in the report for 1858. † The fractions of a ton in 1858 were reported 95ths.

In 1874 Virginia had about 1-32nd of the vessels of the United States, under the above classification, and 1-171th of the tonnage. Many of the vessels belonging to the State are engaged in the oyster trade, which does not require vessels of a large size, and besides the extensive tidal waters of this State are so protected that smaller vessels can be more advantageously employed than where rougher waters are to be encountered.

## No. 2.

*Statement showing the Number and Tonnage of Enrolled and Licensed Iron Vessels in Virginia at the close of the fiscal years named.*

| YEARS. | ENROLLED. Permanent. | | LICENSED UNDER 20 TONS. | | TOTAL. | |
|---|---|---|---|---|---|---|
| | No. | Tons. | No. | Tons. | No. | Tons. |
| 1873 | 7 | 728.03 | 1 | 16.48 | 8 | 744.51 |
| 1874 | 9 | 884.19 | 1 | 16.48 | 10 | 900.67 |

The above are all *included* in the General Statement of Registered, Enrolled, &c., Vessels—Table No. 1.

There are no returns of iron vessels in Virginia previous to 1873. Only 205 iron vessels belonged to the entire United States in 1874, and Virginia about 1-20th of all.

## No. 3.

*Statement of the* STEAM TONNAGE *of Virginia at the close (June 30th) of each of the fiscal years named.*

| YEARS. | REGISTERED. | | ENROLLED. | | LICENSED UNDER 20 TONS. | | TOTAL. | |
|---|---|---|---|---|---|---|---|---|
| | No. | Tons. | No. | Tons. | No. | Tons. | No. | Tons. |
| 1858* | ...... | ......... | ....... | 4,691.63 | ....... | ......... | ..... | 4,691.63 |
| 1868 | 5 | 1,076.87 | 45 | 4,215.73 | 7 | 116.47 | 58 | 5,409.07 |
| 1869 | 4 | 1,279.27 | 46 | 4,474.75 | 10 | 157.16 | 60 | 5,911.18 |
| 1870 | 5 | 1,255.58 | 50 | 4,645.54 | 9 | 143.00 | 64 | 6,044.12 |
| 1871 | 2 | 299.42 | 50 | 4,814.84 | 9 | 139.16 | 61 | 5,253.42 |
| 1872 | 3 | 528.95 | 55 | 5,363.66 | 10 | 153.13 | 68 | 6,045.74 |
| 1873 | 4 | 306.35 | 54 | 5,092.25 | 15 | 222.44 | 73 | 5,621.07 |
| 1874 | 2 | 219.93 | 59 | 5,204.83 | 13 | 180.29 | 74 | 5,605,05 |

The above are all *included* in the General Statement of Registered, &c., Vessels.

*Only tonnage is given in the report for 1858, and the fractions of tons for that year are 95ths.

## No. 4.

*General Statement showing the Number and Tonnage of Sailing and Steam Vessels, Barges and Canal Boats in Virginia Customs Districts at the close of the years named.*

| YEARS. | SAILING VESSELS. | | STEAM VESSELS. | | CANAL BOATS. | | BARGES. | | TOTAL. | |
|---|---|---|---|---|---|---|---|---|---|---|
| | No. | Tons. | No. | Tons. | No. | Tons. | No. | Tons. | No. | Tons. |
| 1868.................. | 814 | 26,840.41 | 58 | 5,409.07 | 23 | 2,051.36 | 15 | 1,271.47 | 910 | 35,572.31 |
| 1869.................. | 798 | 18,467.18 | 60 | 5,911.18 | 23 | 1,727.73 | 30 | 3,327.65 | 911 | 29,433.74 |
| 1870.................. | 756 | 20,343.84 | 64 | 6,044.12 | 26 | 1,934.55 | 11 | 949.14 | 857 | 29,271.65 |
| 1871.................. | 830 | 18,428.67 | 61 | 5,253.42 | 119 | 7,156.88 | 15 | 1,258.81 | 1,025 | 32,097.78 |
| 1872.................. | 927 | 20,702.10 | 68 | 6,045.74 | 143 | 8,795.31 | 19 | 1,535.07 | 1,157 | 37,078.22 |
| 1873.................. | 923 | 20,875.36 | 73 | 5,621.07 | 92 | 5,910.95 | 21 | 1,548.51 | 1,109 | 33,955.89 |
| 1874.................. | 917 | 20,796.46 | 74 | 5,605.05 | 4 | 140.43 | 22 | 1,871.97 | 1,017 | 28,413.91 |

## No. 5.

*Statement showing the Class, Number and Tonnage of Iron Vessels in Virginia at the close of the fiscal years named.*

| YEARS. | STEAM VESSELS. | | BARGES. | | TOTAL. | |
|---|---|---|---|---|---|---|
| | No. | Tons. | No. | Tons. | No. | Tons. |
| 1873 .................................... | 8 | 744.51 | ......... | ............... | 8 | 744.51 |
| 1874 .................................... | 8 | 744.51 | 2 | 156.16 | 10 | 900.67 |

The above are all *included* in the General Statement—Table 1—of Number, &c., of Sailing Vessels, &c., in Virginia.

The MERCHANT MARINE of Virginia—that is, the number and amount of tonnage of merchant vessels *belonging to* the several customs districts and ports of the State—has been increasing in a satisfactory manner, as appears from the following table showing its condition at the close of each of the fiscal years named:

## No. 6.

| YEARS. | SAILING VESSELS. | | STEAM VESSELS. | | UNRIGG'D VESSELS | | TOTAL. | |
|---|---|---|---|---|---|---|---|---|
| | No. | Tons. | No. | Tons. | No. | Tons. | No. | Tons. |
| 1870*.................................. | 791 | 14,778.07 | 57 | 4,055.23 | 29 | 2,213.56 | 877 | 21,046.86 |
| 1871.................................... | 832 | 16,343.86 | 61 | 5,094.05 | 135 | 8,378.95 | 1,028 | 29,816.86 |
| 1872.................................... | 900 | 17,538.57 | 67 | 5,811.71 | 159 | 9,950.62 | 1,126 | 33,300.90 |
| 1873.................................... | 926 | 17,311.54 | 67 | 4,966.53 | 123 | 8,987.98 | 1,116 | 31,266.05 |
| 1874.................................... | 791 | 15,487.41 | 73 | 5,209.01 | 28 | 1,927.12 | 892 | 22,623.54 |

* The reports in this form began to be made in 1870.

The depression in trade incident to the panic of 1873 accounts for the decrease of tonnage in 1873 and 1874, in which Virginia suffered in common with the other States. Only six of the twenty Atlantic and Gulf-coast States had any increase in tonnage, and the leading commercial State, New York, had a larger proportional decrease than Virginia.

The following table shows how the Merchant Marine of Virginia was distributed among the Customs Districts of the State June 30th, 1874:

No. 7.

| CUSTOMS DISTRICTS. | SAILING VESSELS | | STEAM VESSELS. | | UNRIGG'D VESSELS | | TOTAL. | |
|---|---|---|---|---|---|---|---|---|
| | No. | Tons. | No. | Tons. | No. | Tons. | No. | Tons. |
| Alexandria | 81 | 2,096.70 | 14 | 497.50 | ...... | ............ | 95 | 2,594.20 |
| Cherrystone | 211 | 4,410.26 | 1 | 21.45 | ...... | ............ | 212 | 4,431.71 |
| Norfolk and Portsmouth* | 304 | 4,556.11 | 48 | 4,371.47 | 15 | 1,012.32 | 367 | 9,339.90 |
| Petersburg | 4 | 37.00 | 3 | 34.00 | ...... | ............ | 7 | 71.00 |
| Richmond | 6 | 248.20 | 6 | 268.11 | 13 | 914.80 | 25 | 1,431.11 |
| Tappahannock | 84 | 2,077.38 | ...... | ............ | ...... | ............ | 84 | 2,077.38 |
| Yorktown | 101 | 2,061.76 | 1 | 16.48 | ...... | ............ | 102 | 2,078.24 |
| Aggregate | 791 | 15,487.41 | 73 | 5,209.01 | 28 | 1,927.12 | 892 | 22,623.54 |

Virginia had in 1874 about 1-24th of the merchant vessels held on the Atlantic and Gulf coasts, and 1-32nd of all belonging to the Union; her tonnage was about 1-148th of that of the Atlantic and Gulf coasts, and 1-213th of all held in the United States; her rank was 7th in number of vessels and 11th in tonnage, outranking the other Southern States, excepting Maryland, in the number of vessels, and that State and Louisiana in tonnage. The merchant marine of Norfolk and Portsmouth alone surpassed that of either of the States of North Carolina, South Carolina, Georgia, Florida, Alabama or Mississippi; in fact few places in the country have a larger number of sailing vessels than either Norfolk or Cherrystone.

SHIP BUILDING ought to be a leading industry in this State, because of the abundance of all the materials required both for iron and wooden vessels, and of the best quality, at hand, and therefore cheap, while her climate is favorable for *active work the year round.* The following statement shows a steady progress in this important industry, allowing for the anomalous condition of affairs in part of 1873 and in 1874.

*The Norfolk Landmark of January 16th, 1876, reports that at the commencement of 1876 that that port had 384 vessels, with a tonnage of 15,803.51, registered, enrolled and licensed, and had licensed in the coasting trade 114 vessels, with a tonnage of 8,285.77. The entrances from foreign ports in 1875 were 25 vessels, with a tonnage of 14,968, and the clearances to foreign ports were 121 vessels, with a tonnage of 53,683—showing a decided increase over the returns of 1874.

# No. 8.

*Statement of the Number and Tonnage of* VESSELS *of all kinds* BUILT *in Virginia during the fiscal years named.*

| YEARS. | STEAM VESSELS. | | | | RIVER STEAMERS. | | | | SAILING VESSELS. | | | | | | BARGES. | | CANAL BOATS. | | AGGREGATE. | |
|---|---|---|---|---|---|---|---|---|---|---|---|---|---|---|---|---|---|---|---|---|
| | Side-wheel. | | Stern-wheel. | | Propellers. | | Total. | | Schooners. | | Sloops. | | Total. | | | | | | | |
| | No. | Tons. | No. | Tons. | No. | Tons. | No. | Tons. | No. | Tons. | No. | Tons. | No. | Tons. | No. | Tons. | No. | Tons. | No. | Tons. |
| 1858 | .... | .......... | .... | .......... | .... | .......... | 1 | .......... | 10 | .......... | 2 | .......... | 14 | .......... | .... | .......... | .... | .......... | 15 | *1,397.23 |
| 1868 | 1 | 49.94 | 4 | 134.35 | 4 | 326.76 | 9 | 511.25 | 5 | 131.15 | 7 | 82.68 | 12 | 214.23 | 1 | 41.23 | .... | .......... | 22 | 766.71 |
| 1869 | .... | .......... | .... | .......... | 1 | 19.98 | 1 | 19.98 | 13 | 361.39 | 15 | 173.83 | 28 | 535.22 | 8 | 483.82 | .... | .......... | 37 | 1,039.02 |
| 1870 | .... | .......... | .... | .......... | 4 | 555.51 | 4 | 555.51 | 9 | 209.96 | 28 | 203.29 | 37 | 413.25 | 1 | 107.15 | 1 | 53.69 | 43 | 1,129.60 |
| 1871 | .... | .......... | 5 | 350.51 | .... | .......... | 5 | 350.51 | 16 | 426.28 | 16 | 135.07 | 32 | 561.35 | .... | .......... | .... | .......... | 37 | 911.86 |
| 1872 | 2 | 464.72 | 2 | 50.84 | 1 | 14.61 | 5 | 530.17 | 17 | 340.74 | 26 | 237.84 | 43 | 578.58 | 7 | 258.03 | 23 | 1,526.07 | 78 | 2,922.85 |
| 1873 | 1 | 10.85 | .... | .......... | 9 | 631.23 | 10 | 642.08 | 36 | 504.18 | 24 | 173.70 | 50 | 677.88 | 3 | 192.26 | 15 | 944.05 | 78 | 2,456.27 |
| 1874 | 1 | 51.33 | 1 | 27.65 | 7 | 466.02 | 9 | 545.00 | 16 | 383.59 | 19 | 206.89 | 35 | 590.48 | 6 | 503.10 | .... | .......... | 50 | 1,638.58 |

In 1873 there was built at Norfolk *one iron steam vessel* of 116.44 tons.

In 1873 there were built in Virginia 1-16th of all the sailing vessels constructed in the country, having 1-23rd of the tonnage. She furnished 1-28th of all the vessels of all kinds built, and 1-224th of the tonnage.

In 1874 Virginia built 1-43rd of all the vessels made in the United States that year, having 1-270th of the tonnage. Her rank was the 9th in the number of vessels and the 19th in tonnage. She built 1-27th of the sailing vessels with 1-360th of the tonnage, and 1-45th of the steam vessels, having a prominent place in constructing these. Virginia is not credited with the building of any canal boats in 1874, an omission difficult to account for when one considers the number of miles of canal in operation in the State.

* The fractions of a ton in 1858 were reported 95ths.

## Section II.—The Commercial Advantages of Virginia.

Few States are as well provided by the beneficent Creator with the natural highways for coast and foreign commerce as Tidewater Virginia, for the reason that nowhere have tidal waters a richer development into navigable bays, roads, harbors, inlets, creeks and rivers that, like the members of a highly organized body, penetrate and permeate every portion of the country, so that there is at least a linear mile of tide-washed shore to every six square miles of its land surface.

Captain John Smith, of famous memory, whom intercourse with the world had made familiar with the business of the merchant, and who spoke from the deck of a large experience, was the first enlightened explorer of the wealth of water-ways pertaining to Virginia. He says in his history, "There is but one entrance by Sea into this Country, and that is at the mouth of a very goodly bay 18 or 20 myles broad. * * Within is a country that may have the prerogative over the most pleasant places knowne for large and pleasant navigable Rivers; heaven and earth never agreed better to frame a place for man's habitation."

Chesapeake Bay is the most striking feature, from the commercial standpoint, not only on the map of Virginia, but also on that of the United States.

It should be noted that this is the *only great land-locked arm* of the Atlantic, the ocean of commerce, in the United States; that it *is crossed by the central parallel* of population*, and is therefore nearer to more of the ends of traffic, the consumers, than any other commodious bay on the Eastern seaboard, where "nearness to Europe, the abundance of its water-power, the variety and value of its forests, its inexhaustible resources in coal and iron, and the excellence of its harbors,"† have fixed the commercial and manufacturing centres of the country.

Ranging through nearly three degrees of latitude, or some 200 miles of northing and southing in its length, and varying in width from 3 to 30 miles, expanding in all directions, and with deep and ever-fluid waters everywhere, this bay lacks no requisite as a magnificent *continental harbor*.

It may be remarked that the *drainage basin of the Ohio river alone*, considered in reference to Chesapeake Bay as a commerciating medium, would warrant the application of the term *continental* to the advantages for traffic offered by this bay. For example, the area of that basin is 207,111 square miles, four times that of England,‡ its population in 1870 was 7,806,453, it produced in that census-year 146,714,000 pounds of tobacco, 67,513,000 bushels of wheat, 231,917,000 bushels of Indian corn, 110,000 bales of cotton, and employed in manufacturing 311,000 horse-powers of steam and 132,000 of water.§ All this region and its resources is nearer to the ports of Chesapeake bay, by more than a day's run of expensive land carriage, than to any other Atlantic harbors.

In proof that advantages claimed for the Chesapeake waters as the emporia for

---

*See article by Prof. J. E. Hilgard, Scribner's Magazine, 1872.

†Statistical Atlas of the U. S. 1874.

‡See Table II, page 7.

§A. von Steinwehr in U. S. Statistical Atlas.

the commerce of the country concentric to it may be realized, the growth of the trade of Baltimore, situated almost at its northern extremity and 180 miles from the sea, may be cited, as shown in the following official table of the Exports and Imports of that city:

| YEARS. | Domestic Exports. | Imports. |
|---|---|---|
| 1851* | $ 5,635,786 | $ 6,650,645 |
| 1858 | 9,878,386 | 8,930,157 |
| 1868 | 13,857,391 | 12,930,733 |
| 1870 | 14,330,248 | 19,512,468 |
| 1871 | 15,037,855 | 24,672,871 |
| 1872 | 18,325,321 | 28,836,305 |
| 1873 | 19,344,177 | 29,287,603 |
| 1874 | 27,513,111 | 29,302,138 |

This unexampled growth, in spite of the great commercial depression of 1873-'4, shows the advantages of location when utilized by the enterprise and opulence of great corporations and princely merchants that have opened ways of communication between the surplus products of such fertile regions as the valleys of the Ohio, the Mississippi, the Missouri and the Arkansas, and the wharves from which they may be carried, at all seasons of the year, to the lands where they are always in demand.

Seventy miles of the length of Chesapeake bay, where its width is from 14 to 30 miles, lies wholly within the territory of Virginia; it is not subject to violent storms, there are commodious harbors all along its shores, its waters are deep and generally free from obstructions. A vessel bound up it, when once fairly within the "Virginia Capes," and following the "sailing directions," runs on an air line of N. ½° E. for over 50 miles. The exit and entrance can always be easily made, and without any delay, through a deep and clear channel, into this broad-armed bay, that drains more than 50,000 square miles of country.

Commodore Maury,† the noted Geographer of the Sea, remarks: "Naturally, and both in a geographical and military point of view, Norfolk with Hampton Roads at the mouth of the Chesapeake Bay as its lower harbor, and San Francisco inside of the Golden Gate in California, occupy—one on the Pacific, the other on the Atlantic—the most important maritime positions that lie within the domains of the United States. Each holds the commanding point on its sea front; each has the finest harbor on its coast; and each with the most convenient ingress and egress for ships—is as safe from wind and wave as shelter can make them. Nor is access to either ever interrupted by the frosts of winter. In the harbors of each there is

* Returns for the whole State of Maryland.

† Physical Survey of Virginia, page 4 (1868).

room to berth not only all the ships of commerce, but the navies of the world also."

The following table, from the United States Coast Survey Report for 1857, shows the character of the channels into Chesapeake bay, and from it to some of the harbors and anchorages of Virginia:

| VIRGINIA HARBORS AND ANCHORAGES. | Least Water in Channel-way in feet. | | | |
|---|---|---|---|---|
| | Mean tides. | | Spring tides. | |
| | Low water. | High water. | Low water. | High water. |
| Between the Capes at entrance to Hampton Roads | 30.0 | 32.5 | 29.8 | 32.8 |
| Anchorage in Hampton Roads | 59.0 | 61.5 | 58.8 | 61.8 |
| From Hampton Roads to Sewall's Point | 25.0 | 27.5 | 24.8 | 27.8 |
| South of Sewall's Point 1½ miles | 21.0 | 23.5 | 20.8 | 23.8 |
| Up to Norfolk | 23.0 | 25.5 | 22.8 | 25.8 |
| From Hampton Roads to James River, entering *north* of Newport-News Middle ground | 22.0 | 24.5 | 21.7 | 24.8 |
| Same to *south* of do | 27.0 | 29.5 | 26.7 | 29.8 |
| York river from abreast the tail of York Spit up to Yorktown | 33.0 | 35.5 | 32.7 | 35.8 |
| Elizabeth river between Norfolk and the Navy-yard | 25.5 | 28.0 | 25.3 | 28.3 |

The broad estuary of the Chesapeake receives from Virginia many navigable rivers, the tides of which can carry large ships far into the interior, to the great advantage of the country.

THE POTOMAC, a wide and deep river, the northeastern boundary of Virginia, is navigable for 110 miles from where it enters the bay, some 65 miles from the ocean.

*Alexandria*, a flourishing commercial city of Virginia, is on this river, some eight miles from the head of navigation at Georgetown and Washington. It is an important centre of lines of transportation,* and many advantages for commerce, especially the coastwise trade, as its canal and railway communications are with the coal, timber, iron, &c., of the interior, that are required at other points on the Atlantic seaboard. Alexandria is a port of entry.

There are many landings on the Potomac, and lines of steamers and sailing vessels connect them with all portions of the country, giving great facilities for cheap transportation to a very extensive and valuable portion of the Northern Neck.

THE RAPPAHANNOCK is navigable to *Fredericksburg*, ninety-two miles from its mouth at the bay, some forty miles from the ocean, for steamers and sailing vessels, to which point the channel has *eight feet*† *at low water*, which it is proposed to in-

*See Chapter on Transportation. †Report of the Chief of the U. S. Engineers, 1874.

crease to ten. This river is crossed at Fredericksburg by the great North and South Line of railroad from Washington to Richmond, and a partially completed line extends westward towards Gordonsville and the Chesapeake and Ohio and Midland Railroads. The opening of this traffic route to the interior will doubtless restore to this city the commerce it formerly had, and the development of the mineral wealth not far from it will lead to an appreciation of its commercial advantages. Fredericksburg is in the customs-district of Tappahannock.

*Port Royal*, twenty-two miles below Fredericksburg, is accessible to vessels of a larger capacity.

*Tappahannock*, the port of entry for the river and the one that receives credit for all its commerce, is sixty miles below Fredericksburg, and to it vessels drawing eleven and a half feet can ascend.

*Urbanna* is a port some twenty-six miles below Tappahannock and seventeen miles from the bay.

Lines of steamers run on the Rappahannock, and touch not only at the ports named, but at many landings along the whole length of the river.

THE PIANKETANK is navigable for some fourteen miles, and MOBJACK BAY and its rivers furnish deep entrances to the Gloucester Peninsula.

THE YORK is a wide, deep, and almost straight *belt* of water, reaching over forty miles from the bay to the junction of the PAMUNKEY and the MATTAPONY, the rivers that form it, and that are themselves navigable for many miles for light draught vessels. Ships drawing twenty-seven feet can go to within a short distance of West Point, at the head of the York, and those requiring *thirteen feet to its wharves at low water.

*Yorktown* is about sixteen statute miles from the bay and thirty from the ocean. The Coast Survey Report for 1857 says of the approach to this "port of entry": "No one can look at the chart of the lower part of York river, from the entrance up to Yorktown, without pronouncing it a harbor of the first class. There is no bar at the mouth of this river, and the least water to be passed over in entering it is thirty-three feet at low tide, near the tail of York Spit, in Chesapeake bay. After passing this the water deepens to six, seven and eight fathoms, increasing in passing up the channel to eleven and twelve fathoms abreast of Yorktown, where the shore is very bold, and wharves carried out a distance of fifty feet would strike four and a half and five fathoms of water. The channel of the river is more than a mile in width, and with a few buoys and beacons judiciously placed, the heaviest line-of-battle ships could beat up and down the river without the least difficulty. Yorktown is situated about thirteen† nautical miles from the entrance of the river into Chesapeake bay. The location is elevated, and it could be easily fortified at moderate expense against attack either by land or water. It affords a harbor sufficient for the largest navy and commercial marine, and next to Newport, Rhode Island, it is, in my judgment, the safest and the most commodious harbor in the United States." Newport harbor is in an island; therefore, in the opinion of Coast Survey authority, Yorktown is the "safest and most commodious harbor" in the main land of the United States.

---

*U. S. Coast Survey Maps, 1866. †A misprint in the Report makes it 30.

It is proposed to make Yorktown one of the deep water termini of the Chesapeake and Ohio Railway. In that event it is difficult to realize the future of such a harbor so situated in reference to the sea and to the interior that the completion of that railway will place it in commercial relations with.

*West Point*, at the head of the York, is connected with Richmond by railroad, and with Baltimore by a daily line of steamers that call at Yorktown and the other landings on the river. A line of steamers plies between Yorktown and Norfolk by way of *Mathews Courthouse and Cherrystone*, the port of entry of the Eastern Shore.

THE MATTAPONY is navigable to *Aylett's*, a place some thirty miles above West Point, and the PAMUNKEY to *Oyster Shell Landing*, some thirty-five miles above West Point.

THE JAMES is navigable to *Richmond*, a port of entry with a custom-house, one hundred and ten miles, for vessels drawing fourteen feet of water, and to *City Point*, at the mouth of the Appomattox, some sixty miles below Richmond, for those drawing fifteen feet. It has, as before stated, thirty feet of depth, at low water, at its entrance at *Hampton Roads*.

*Richmond* occupies a commanding position as a commercial and manufacturing city, with superior advantages for transportation in all directions by the many lines of railways, canal, steamers, vessels, &c., that have found there a natural centre for the accumulation and distribution of the articles of trade. Some of the advantages of its location are emphasized by the following *table, showing comparative distances between Atlantic ports and principal western railroad centres by all-rail travel, by Chesapeake and Ohio Railroad and its projected connections, and by more northerly routes.

| MILES FROM PORT OF | To Cincinnati. | To Louisville. | To St. Louis. | To Memphis. | To Nashville. | To Columbus, O. | To Indianapolis. | To Chicago. | To New Orleans. |
|---|---|---|---|---|---|---|---|---|---|
| Richmond, via Chesapeake and Ohio | 573 | †640 | †890 | 1,017 | 825 | 564 | 688 | 832 | ...... |
| Baltimore, via Baltimore and Ohio | 591 | 699 | 931 | 1,076 | 884 | 517 | 705 | 828 | ...... |
| Philadelphia, via Pennsylvania Railroad | 668 | 775 | 992 | 1,152 | 960 | 548 | 736 | 823 | ...... |
| New York, via Erie Railway | 861 | 997 | 1,201 | 1,354 | 1,182 | 755 | 935 | 983 | ...... |
| New York, via New York Central | 883 | 940 | 1,144 | 1,354 | 1,176 | 761 | 830 | 980 | ...... |
| Boston, via New York Central | 941 | 998 | 1,202 | 1,426 | 1,234 | 829 | 888 | 1,039 | ...... |
| Washington, via Chesapeake and Ohio Railroad | 593 | 660 | 910 | 1,037 | 845 | ...... | ...... | 852 | ...... |
| Washington, via Baltimore and Ohio Railroad | 613 | 720 | 953 | 1,097 | 905 | ...... | ...... | 852 | ...... |
| Washington, via Pennsylvania Central Railroad | 646 | 753 | 989 | 1,130 | 938 | ...... | ...... | 842 | ...... |
| New York, via Washington and Ches. and Ohio Railroad | ...... | 888 | 1,138 | 1,265 | ...... | ...... | ...... | ...... | 1,394 |
| New York, via Erie and A. and G. W. | ...... | 997 | 1,201 | 1,354 | ...... | ...... | ...... | ...... | 1,751 |
| New York, via New York Central and L. S. and M. S. | ...... | 940 | 1,260 | 1,354 | ...... | ...... | ...... | ...... | 1,694 |

There are many landings on the James and the numerous lines of steamers and sailing vessels that run regularly between Richmond and Norfolk, Baltimore,

* Compiled from pamphlet issued by Fisk & Hatch, Bankers, New York, 1873.

† Will be shortened thirteen miles by improvements now in progress.

Philadelphia, New York and other places make the trade of this noble river an active one, and furnish the best of facilities for reaching markets to all products that come to its shores.

Several of the branches of the James are navigable rivers—the APPOMATTOX, 12 miles to *Petersburg*, a port of entry and a thriving city; the CHICKAHOMINY to a considerable distance for steamers and vessels of a light draught; PAGAN CREEK is a fine stream to *Smithfield;* the NANSEMOND is navigable some fifteen miles to the flourishing town of *Suffolk*, at the intersection of the Atlantic, Mississippi and Ohio and the Seaboard and Roanoke Railways; the lower reaches of this river are broad and deep.

The ELIZABETH is a broad arm of the Hampton Roads estuary of the James, extending for twelve miles, the last four of which are expanded as the superb harbor between the cities of *Norfolk and Portsmouth*, and the Navy Yard of the United States—its most important one—at Gosport. Beyond this harbor, navigation is extended by ship canals to the navigable sounds and rivers of North Carolina. The entrance to the Elizabeth has always a depth of twenty-one feet, which at spring tides reaches 23.8, while the harbor of Norfolk and Portsmouth has from 25.5 to 28.3 feet of water.

A recent publication,* speaking of Norfolk, says: "The grand current of the Elizabeth (opposite Fort Norfolk) is so broad and deep that the largest ship that floats can swing around there. * * The trains of the Atlantic, Mississippi and Ohio Railroad discharge their freights ot cotton and grain directly upon wharves at the steamers' sides, and the unusual facilities are yearly increased and improved. * The importance of Norfolk as a port for the future is certainly indisputable; and it is not at all improbable that in a few years it will have direct communication with European ports by means of ocean steamers owned and controlled in this country. * The Elizabeth river is not so lively now as when at the beginning of this century the river could not be seen, so thick was the shipping between the Norfolk and Portsmouth shores. In the financial crash which came at that time sixty Norfolk firms interested in maritime commerce failed. * * The eastern and southern branches of the Elizabeth are superior in depth to the Thames at London, or the Mersey at Liverpool. The depth of water in the harbor at Norfolk is twenty-eight feet, or nearly twice that regularly maintained at New Orleans, and the harbor is spacious enough to admit the commercial marine of the whole country. It has been estimated that thirty miles of excellent water-front for wharfage can readily be afforded. * Norfolk lies within thirty-two miles of the Atlantic. Northward stretch the Chesapeake and its tributaries, navigable nearly a thousand miles; westward is the James, giving communication with Richmond, and five hundred miles of water way; southward run the canals to Currituck, Albemarle and Pamplico, communicating with two thousand miles of river channel. She affords naturally the best seaport for most of North Carolina and Tennessee, besides large sections of Northern Georgia, Alabama, Mississippi and the Southwest. A thorough system of internal improvements in Virginia, giving lines leading from tide-water in that State to the Northwest, would enable Norfolk almost to usurp the commercial pre-emi-

*The Great South. By Edward King, 1875.

nence of New York. Pittsburg and Wheeling and Toledo are geographically nearer to the Capes of Virginia than to Sandy Hook; and it is almost certain that in the future many of the highways to the sea from the West will run through Virginia, and the ports furnishing outlets to the Western cities will be along the beautiful and capacious Chesapeake bay."*

Lines of railways, canals, steamships and vessels of all kinds connect this port with all portions of the country. Its commercial advantages—the results of its position—can hardly be overestimated, and the growth of its cotton-trade, already described, shows that it may aspire to the first rank not only in this, but in all the export and import trade of the country.

HAMPTON ROADS, on account of its nearness to the sea, its accessibility, the depth and expansion of its waters, the thoroughly land-locked character of its situation, the condition of the surrounding land and its ample security in troublous times, may justly be called *The Harbor* of the Mid-Atlantic coast of the United States. When the storm signals are up all the shipping at sea along the Middle coast of the Union flies to Hampton Roads for refuge, and it is no uncommon sight to see hundreds of vessels of every class riding here at ease without a strain upon their anchor chains, while in sight, without the Capes, a furious storm is raging. Again, ships freighted with the precious cargoes of the tropics, but cleared for other ports where the climate is damp and uncongenial to their sensitive lading, come here to await orders and a favorable season. The London, England, Public Ledger (the merchants' journal of that world's mart), of the 13th of January, 1875, had the following statement:

*Brazil Coffee in United States Ports December 30th*, 1874.

| | | | | | |
|---|---|---|---|---|---|
| New York | 8,891 | Bags. | Savannah | 4,000 | Bags. |
| Baltimore | 15,786 | " | Mobile | 1,000 | " |
| *Hampton Roads* | 9,612 | " | New Orleans | 4,733 | " |
| Richmond | 2,500 | " | Galveston | 2,000 | " |
| Charleston | 2,500 | " | | | |
| Total | | | | 51,022 | " |
| 1873 | | | | 66,372 | " |

The uninformed reader would have inferred that the place reported as *second* in the possession of the stock of coffee on hand, and that held nearly *one-fifth* of the whole of this commodity—which in 1873 was imported into the United States to the value of 44 million dollars, or 1–15th of the whole import trade of the country, and in 1874 to the value of 55 million dollars, or 1–18th of the importations for the year—must be one of the most active commercial cities in the Union, and he would be surprised to learn that it is the magnificent world's-harbor, named from what is now the mere village of *Hampton*. But this leads to the inevitable conclusion that from the shores of this broad anchorage—where the Great Eastern had but to run out its gang plank to make a landing on the natural shore—this and similar products, as sugar, molasses, spices, fruits, &c., the growth of the Bahamas, the West

*These extended extracts from the Great South are given because the articles from which the book was made originally appeared in Scribner's Magazine, a leading New York monthly, and the writer is an Englishman by birth and a New Yorker by location.

Indies and the northern portions of South America, where they naturally come, in transit* to the chief markets of consumption, they should be sent inland to those points of consumption by routes shorter and cheaper than any other.

†"Commodore Maury, of Virginia, better known to science as Lieut. Maury, from his researches on the laws of currents and deep sea lore, speaking of the relative merits of Norfolk and New York as commercial harbors, says of the road-stead in the vicinity of which the deep water terminus of the Chesapeake and Ohio Railroad will be located, and which is common to vessels seeking the wharves at Norfolk, Yorktown or Newport's News, thus describes it: 'Geographically considered, the harbors of Norfolk or Hampton Roads and New York occupy the most important and commanding positions on the Atlantic coast of the United States. They are more convenient to the ocean than Baltimore, Philadelphia and Boston are, because they are not so far from the sea.

"'Depth of water that can be carried out, and distance of the sea from

| | | | | |
|---|---|---|---|---|
| Hampton Roads, distant | ...................... 15 miles—depth | | | 28 feet. |
| New York, | " ...................... 30 " | $3\frac{3}{4}$ fathoms, | | 23 " |
| Boston, | " ...................... 100 " | $3\frac{1}{2}$ | " | 21 " |
| Philadelphia, | " ...................... 100 " | $3\frac{3}{4}$ | " | 23 " |
| Baltimore, | " ...................... 160 " | $2\frac{3}{4}$ | " | 16 " |

"'Between the three last and the sea there is a tedious bay navigation, but each of the first two is situated upon a well sheltered harbor, that opens right out upon the sea with beautiful offings, those of Hampton Roads surpassing the others in all the requirements of navigation, both as to facility of ingress and egress, certainty of land fall, depth of water, and holding ground.'

"He also shows, that to reach the Chesapeake, vessels cross the Gulf Stream at its narrower part, and take advantage of the eddies on its southeastern edge; going in the opposite direction to Europe, by following the Gulf Stream for a longer distance, will be helped along their course 50 to 100 miles per day."

The *ship channel* from Hampton Roads to the ocean is an *air-line* of sixteen nautical miles.

The following comparative tables of distances by available routes, from the "Report of a Select Committee of the United States Senate on Transportation Routes to the Seaboard, 1874," show the advantages of the situation of Hampton Roads (*and, consequently, of all commercial points in Virginia on the James, the York, the Elizabeth, &c.*), in reference to Western trade, whether export or import, coastwise or foreign:

| | MILES. |
|---|---|
| Hampton Roads to New York, via ocean | 293 |
| Hampton Roads to New York, via inland‡ route | 343 |
| Hampton Roads to Philadelphia, via ocean and Delaware Bay | 300 |
| Hampton Roads to Philadelphia, via inland‖ route | 223 |
| Hampton Roads to Baltimore, via Chesapeake Bay | 200 |
| Hampton Roads to Washington, via Chesapeake Bay and Potomac River | 182 |

* See maps 3 and 4.

† From a pamphlet issued by Fisk & Hatch, Bankers, New York, on the Chesapeake and Ohio Railroad, 1873.

‡ Viz: via Chesapeake Bay, Chesapeake and Delaware Canal and Delaware and Raritan Canal.

‖ Viz: via Chesapeake Bay and Chesapeake and Delaware Canal.

The next table was prepared to show the advantages that would accrue to Western trade by completing the James River and Kanawha Canal (a work sure to be done at no distant day) and give an outlet to the sea by cheap water transportation through a route that is but little interrupted by ice.

| DISTANCES FROM | To the Capes of Virginia. | To New York. |
|---|---|---|
| Cairo, mouth of Ohio, by rivers and James River and Kanawha Canal | 1,301 | ........... |
| Cairo, via nearest rivers and canals | ........... | 1,522 |
| Cairo, via river, gulf and ocean | ........... | 3,052 |
| Louisville, Ky., by rivers and James River and Kanawha Canal | 932 | ........... |
| Louisville, Ky., by nearest rivers, lake and canals | ........... | 1,153 |
| Louisville, Ky., by rivers, gulf and ocean | ........... | 3,421 |
| Louisville, Ky., by rail | ........... | 887 |
| Cincinnati, by rivers and James River and Kanawha Canal | 800 | ........... |
| Cincinnati, by nearest canals, lake and river | ........... | 1,004 |
| Cincinnati, by rivers, gulf and ocean | ........... | 3,553 |
| Cincinnati, by rail | ........... | 777 |
| Point Pleasant, West Virginia, by James River and Kanawha Canal and rivers | 597 | ........... |
| Point Pleasant, West Virginia, by rivers, gulf and ocean | ........... | 3,756 |
| Wheeling, by James River and Kanawha Canal and rivers | 770 | ........... |
| Wheeling, by rivers, gulf and ocean | ........... | 3,929 |
| Pittsburg, by rivers and James River and Kanawha Canal | 860 | ........... |
| Pittsburg, by rivers, gulf and ocean | ........... | 4,019 |
| Pittsburg, by rail | ........... | 444 |
| Memphis, by rivers and James River and Kanawha Canal | 1,540 | ........... |
| Memphis, by river, gulf and ocean | ........... | 2,613 |
| Memphis, by rail | ........... | 1,123 |
| Memphis, by rail to Norfolk | 921 | ........... |
| Memphis, by rail to Norfolk and ocean | ........... | 1,214 |
| Saint Louis, by rivers and James River and Kanawha Canal | 1,479 | ........... |
| Saint Louis, by river, gulf and ocean | ........... | 3,230 |
| Saint Louis, by rivers, canals and lake | ........... | 1,962 |
| Saint Louis, by rail | ........... | 1,110 |

Norfolk and Portsmouth as a Cotton-Port have advantages for the collection and distribution of the larger portion of the immense cotton crop of the United States that may fairly be claimed as superior to those of any other, and that, against powerful competition, raised it from comparative insignificance a few years ago to the fifth rank* in 1872, and the third in 1874, among American ports in the net annual receipts of cotton.

*See following tables of cotton receipts.

The *cotton-belt** *of the United States* extends from the Valley of the James, in Virginia, on the north, to that of the Rio Grande, in Texas, on the south, conforming in the line of its extension to the general trend of the Gulf and Atlantic coasts and the Appalachian mountains, but bounded on all its northwestern border by the isotherm of sixty Fahrenheit that follows the flanks of this mountain system from Virginia through the Carolinas and Georgia into Alabama, and then follows them northward through Tennessee and Kentucky into the southeastern angle of Missouri.

The largest *production of cotton** is in the middle zone of the cotton-belt—that in the Atlantic cotton States lies midway between the mountains and the sea, or in the Midland country; and the same is true of Alabama and Tennessee. while in Mississippi, Arkansas and Louisiana it is in the Valleys of the Mississippi, Yazoo, Arkansas and Red rivers, and again in Texas through the Middle country. Of the cotton crop† of 1870 (some 3,660,000 bales) 575,000, or about 6-36ths, were produced on the waters that flow directly into the Atlantic from the States of Virginia, North and South Carolina, Georgia and Florida; 864,000, or about 9-36ths, on the waters that flow into the Gulf, east of the Mississippi, from the States of Georgia, Florida, Alabama, Mississippi and a small portion of Louisiana; 110,000, or about 1-36th, on the waters that flow into the Ohio from Tennessee and Kentucky; 1,134,000, or about 13-36ths in the comparatively narrow Valley of the Mississippi and on the small rivers that run into it from the mere western borders of the States of Tennessee and Mississippi, and the eastern ones of Missouri and Arkansas, and a strip of Louisiana on each side of the river, the area of the whole being but 65,646 square miles; 112,000, or about 1-36th, on the waters of the Arkansas, in the State of the same name and in Missouri; 340,000, or about 3-36ths, on the waters of Red river, in Arkansas, Louisiana and Texas, and 325,000, or about 3-36ths, on the other waters of Texas. Memphis, on the Mississippi, in Tennessee, was nearer than any other interior city to fully half of the cotton product above enumerated.

The port of Norfolk and Portsmouth is *situated*‡ in the northeastern corner of this cotton-belt, where, if that belt were extended, it would pass into the Atlantic, so that geographically in this, with its Hampton Roads, most commodious harbor of the American Atlantic, is naturally the pier-head of the cotton-zone, hither the bales naturally tend, and hence they as naturally take the steam and sails of commerce to bear them on in the same direction they have hitherto pursued, swiftly and cheaply, either coastwise, by inland tidal ways and ship canals, or along the safe coast to the domestic ports of the great cotton manufacturing centres§ of the United States, or to foreign ports, the world's cotton markets, by way of the ever-flowing Gulf stream that inclines from its course towards the Capes of Virginia, as if to invite and speed them whither the wants of trade require.

Two extensive systems of railways, that by their connections reach nearly every portion of the cotton-growing country, have their termini on the wharves of Norfolk and Portsmouth, and furnish ample facilities for the *collection* at this market of a

*See Cotton Maps of U. S. Statistical Atlas and of Census of 1870.

†See Map of River Systems of U. S., by Gen. von Steinwehr, in U. S. Statistical Atlas.

‡See Map No. 4.

§See Report of U. S. Senate on Transportation Routes to the Sea, page 242 (1874).

large share of the annual cotton crop. The Atlantic, Mississippi and Ohio, the representative of one of these systems, is part of a great trunk line from this port to Memphis, passing through some three hundred miles of the cotton-belt in Tennessee, Alabama and Mississippi, and terminating, as before stated, at the inland depot of half the cotton product; this road and its feeders, therefore, reaches all of the western and southwestern cotton fields. The Seaboard and Roanoke, the representative of the other system, is a portion of the Atlantic coast lines of railway that penetrate every portion of the Atlantic and Gulf cotton States, and reach, as before stated, fully 15-36ths of the yearly cotton crop. Two ship canals join the waters of this port with those of the sounds of North Carolina, that branch into a productive cotton region. These lines of internal improvements furnish communication by the shortest and cheapest routes of inland transit between the gin-houses of the planters and the warehouses and wharves of the factors and shippers, at a port where full provision is made for storing, compressing, shipping or selling cotton. The rates* of transit for cotton to this port from the interior must continue to be cheaper than to others, because the distances are shorter and the lines of transportation diverging as they do cannot combine to raise rates, at the same time the facilities for traffic are ample.

The requirements for the *reception* and *distribution* of cotton at this port are fully provided. The railway cars run out upon the wharves, where the largest of merchant vessels may lay alongside and receive the bales directly into their holds, saving thereby the large expense and waste incident to ports where several handlings and drayage and lighterage have to be undergone previous to shipment by sea. Powerful hydraulic presses are at hand to compress the bales so that ships can carry much more than their registered tonnage. Warehouses are provided where, safely stored, the bales can await the pleasure of their owners.

The large cotton-consuming centres of the United States are in the Middle and New England sections, where in 1870 three-fourths of all the cotton goods made in the country were manufactured; therefore, the *domestic cotton trade* is mostly to the ports of those States that are in the vicinity of the cotton mills. Norfolk and Portsmouth have the advantage of regular lines of steamers and sailing vessels to Baltimore, Philadelphia, New York, Providence and Boston—the ports of these manufacturing centres—by which the spinners may receive the raw material directly from the quays of the Virginia port, brought *without loss of direction* a considerable portion of the way between them and the producer *by cheap water carriage*, and burdened by a minimum of way charges. It is evident that this arrangement, that enables the consumer and the producer of cotton to meet half way with the least intervention of expense, delay or middlemen, must be highly advantageous to both, and must ultimately lead them to seek the market so located. The statements of the coastwise trade that follow show that the advantages of this port for carrying on the home cotton trade have not been exaggerated.

That the enormous *foreign cotton exportation* of the country can be best conducted through this port hardly admits of question in the light of the statements that follow. It is of the first importance to a foreign consumer, like England, that

---

*See Report of U. S. Senate on Transportation Routes to the Sea, page 242 (1874).

manufactures nine-tenths of the world's cotton goods and imports all of its raw cotton, to obtain the raw material as cheaply as possible. To do that, it must employ the largest vessels; load them to their utmost capacity, and have them make the speediest of voyages, after they have obtained their cargoes where the producer will furnish them for the least money. It is clear that these demands of the foreign cotton-trade can be more fully met here than elsewhere. This port has deeper water at its wharves, and is more easily reached by large vessels than any other* American port. Its climate† is mild at all times, and there is neither ice nor snow to delay in the winter and spring months, when most of the cotton is shipped. The facilities for the rapid delivery of cargo on shipboard, and in the best condition for stowage, have been noted. And then the highways of the sea are but a few hours distant, and there is always unobstructed exit to as well as entrance from them. What has been done is but an earnest of what will be done hereafter, and now that the advantages of this port for the foreign cotton-trade have become known, it will doubtless speedily attain to the position of pre-eminence to which, in all respects, in this trade, it is justly entitled.

The tabular statements that follow have been compiled from the most reliable sources of information to confirm by facts the foregoing generalizations.

*Previous to the war of* 1861–5, Norfolk and Portsmouth were hardly known as a cotton-port, simply because there were no lines of continuous railways that penetrated the cotton-zone to bring the crop to that market. The following statement‡ shows the condition of this trade at that time, when it was a mere neighborhood business:

No. 1.

MOVEMENT OF COTTON *at* NORFOLK AND PORTSMOUTH, 1858 *to* 1861.

| YEARS. | RECEIPTS (Bales). | EXPORTS. | |
|---|---|---|---|
| | | Coastwise. | Foreign. |
| 1858–'9 | 6,174 | 6,174 | § |
| 1859–'60 | 17,777 | 17,488 | 289 |
| 1860–'1 | 33,193 | 32,941 | 252 |
| | 57,144 | 56,603 | 541 |

*Since the war* the consolidation of existing lines of railways, the opening of new ones, the extension of ship canals, the establishment of direct trade with Europe, increased facilities for coastwise trade, the erection of powerful cotton presses, and, above all, the knowledge of the fact that the trade can be more cheaply carried on here than elsewhere, have given an impetus to the movement of cotton from this port, and raised it from the eighth to the third rank.

* See description of the harbor of Norfolk in this volume.

† See chapter on Climate.

‡ Report of Grandy & Sons, Cotton Factors, Norfolk.

§ In 1858 Richmond exported 213,351 pounds (495 bales), valued at $28,976, and this was the only cotton exported from Virginia.

## No. 2.

*Statement** *of the* Direct Exportation *of* Cotton *from* Norfolk and Portsmouth, 1868 *to* 1875.

| YEARS. | BALES. | POUNDS. | VALUE. |
|---|---|---|---|
| 1868 | ........ | 4,038,525 | $936,358 |
| 1869 | ........ | 2,643,851 | 713,076 |
| 1870 | 9,652 | 4,289,611 | 1,038,304 |
| 1871 | 5,354 | 2,414,300 | 327,109 |
| 1872 | 3,854 | 1,750,416 | 372,470 |
| 1873 | 7,569 | 3,414,918 | 658,833 |
| 1874 | 20,524 | 9,253,710 | 1,434,203 |
| 1875 † | 67,212 | ........ | 4,578,638 |

The Virginia cotton trade during this period was confined to this port, with the following exceptions: Richmond exported 69,985 pounds in 1868, valued at $19,870, and in 1873 Petersburg exported 94,781 pounds (222 bales), valued at $17,550.

## No. 3.

*The* Cotton-Trade *(in Bales) of* Norfolk and Portsmouth *for the Cotton-years (ending August 31st) named.*

| COTTON-YEARS. | TOTAL NET ‡ RECEIPTS. | EXPORTATION. | | | | TAKEN ON * LOCAL ACCOUNT. |
|---|---|---|---|---|---|---|
| | | Coastwise. | Direct. | On through bills, via other ports. | Total foreign export. | |
| 1858–'9 | 6,174 | 6,174 | ........ | ........ | ........ | ........ |
| 1859–'60 | 17,777 | 17,488 | 289 | ........ | ........ | ........ |
| 1860–'1 | 33,193 | 39,941 | 252 | ........ | ........ | ........ |
| 1865–'6 | 59,096 | ........ | 733 | ........ | ........ | ........ |
| 1866–'7 | 126,297 | ........ | 14,168 | ........ | ........ | ........ |
| 1867–'8 | 155,591 | ........ | 8,279 | ........ | ........ | ........ |
| 1868–'9 | 164,789 | ........ | 7,527 | ........ | ........ | ........ |
| 1869–'70 | 178,352 | ........ | 4,745 | ........ | ........ | ........ |
| 1870–'1 | 302,930 | ........ | 5,142 | ........ | ........ | ........ |
| 1871–'2 | 258,730 | 254,043 | 4,687 | ........ | ........ | 55,000 |
| 1872–'3 | 405,412 | 397,130 | 8,282§ | ........ | ........ | 75,000 |
| 1873–'4 | 472,446‖ | 418,328 | 20,346 | 28,897 | 49,243 | 95,000 |
| 1874–'5¶ | 392,235 | 309,636 | 67,312 | 16,645 | 83,457 | ........ |

* From the Reports of the U. S. Bureau of Statistics.
† Furnished by Mr. Miller, of the Collector's office, through Col. W. H. Taylor.
‡ 1865 to 1874—report of Messrs. Grandy. 1858 to 1861—Merchants and Mechanics Exchange Report.
§ Messrs. Grandy point out an error in the Report of the U. S. Bureau of Statistics.
‖ The Norfolk Landmark makes this 467,571.
¶ Furnished by A. Tredwell, Secretary and Superintendent Norfolk and Portsmouth Cotton Exchange, through Col. W. H. Taylor.

No. 4.—The receipts for 1871–'2 reached this port—

| | | |
|---|---|---|
| By Atlantic, Mississippi and Ohio Railroad | 125,598 | bales. |
| By Seaboard and Roanoke Railroad | 108,746 | " |
| By Albemarle and Chesapeake and Dismal Swamp Canals | 28,386 | " |
| Total receipts | 258,730 | " |

No. 5.—*The exportation* of Cotton during the cotton-year* 1874–'5, from Norfolk and Portsmouth, was as follows:

| | | | | |
|---|---|---|---|---|
| To Great Britain | Direct | 63,629 | | |
| | Via New York | 3,000 | | |
| | Via Baltimore | 1,363 | | |
| | Via Boston | 11,463 | | |
| | Via Philadelphia | 500 | | |
| | | | 89,955 | bales. |
| To Havre, via Philadelphia | | | 119 | " |
| To Antwerp, via Philadelphia | | | 200 | " |
| To Amsterdam, direct | | | 2,180 | " |
| To Bremen, direct | | | 1,403 | " |
| To New York, direct | | | 127,549 | " |
| To Boston and Providence, direct | | | 112,435 | " |
| To Baltimore, direct | | | 48,466 | " |
| To Philadelphia, direct | | | 21,186 | " |
| Total export | | | 393,493 | " |
| On hand September 1st, 1875 | | | 179 | " |

This port has lines of steamers running to Boston, Providence, New York, Philadelphia, Baltimore, &c., that aggregated a tonnage of 32,082 in 1874, furnishing facilities for the large trade indicated above.

*The trade of the cotton-year* 1875–'6, for three months (September 1st to December 3d, 1875,) for this port is reported* as follows;

| | | |
|---|---|---|
| No. 6.—Stock on hand August 31st, 1875 | 179 | bales. |
| Transit receipts for the quarter | 145,310 | " |
| Local receipts for the quarter | 64,278 | " |
| Total | 209,767 | " |

*Exports.*

| | | | |
|---|---|---|---|
| To Great Britain, direct | 31,908 | | |
| To the Continent, direct | 1,817 | | |
| To New York, direct | 88,661 | | |
| To Philadelphia, direct | 10,027 | | |
| To Baltimore, direct | 19,744 | | |
| To Boston, direct | 25,093 | | |
| To Providence, direct | 14,972 | | |
| | | 192,222 | bales. |
| On hand and shipboard Dec. 3d, 1875 | | 17,545 | " |

*Furnished by A. Tredwell, Esq., Secretary and Superintendent Norfolk and Portsmouth Cotton Exchange, through Col. W. H. Taylor.

The United States cotton crop* for the year ending September 1, 1875, was 3,827,845 bales, of which 2,674,448 were exported to foreign countries and 1,200,473 were taken by home spinners, of which 129,613 were consumed in the South. The average weight of the crop was 408 pounds per bale.

The Norfolk Virginian, of December 3d, 1875, furnishes the following facts: On the second of December, the ship H. S. Gregory, drawing 21 7-12ths feet, was cleared by Messrs. Reynolds Brothers from this port for Liverpool, England, with a cargo consisting of 7,176 bales of cotton, weighing 3,221,971 pounds; 10,000 tree-nails and 3,000 staves. This was the largest cargo of cotton that ever left Norfolk, and is thought to be the largest that ever left any United States port. The tonnage of the ship was 2,207 tons, and it had not the slightest difficulty in clearing its moorings.

The same day the brig R. B. Grove was cleared by Messrs. Ricks & Milhado, for Havre, with a cargo of 1,817 bales of cotton, weighing 830,898 pounds. The tonnage of this vessel is only 463, and its cargo was the largest, compared with tonnage, that ever left the port. On a voyage from New Orleans, two years ago, this brig carried 1,545 bales (707,316 pounds), so it carried from Norfolk 272 bales (23,572 pounds) more than it did from New Orleans. This was the first cargo of cotton ever shipped direct from Norfolk to Havre.

The three powerful hydraulic cotton presses that have recently been erected here have contributed largely to the above results; one of them, belonging to the Messrs. Reynolds, can compress† 800 bales a day.

The following quarterly statement is from the same—Virginian:

## No. 7.

*Cotton-Trade of 1874–'5 and 1875–'6 compared.*

| | Comparison of Exports. | | | | | |
|---|---|---|---|---|---|---|
| | 1st Quarter of Cotton Year 1875–'6. | | | 1st Quarter of Cotton Year 1874–'5. | | |
| | Bales. | Pounds. | Value. | Bales. | Pounds. | Value. |
| September | ............ | ............ | ............ | 93 | 40,808 | 6,325 |
| October | 4,440 | 1,975,802 | 276,612 | 1,462 | 667,044 | 100,056 |
| November | 18,463 | 8,498,150 | 1,133,351 | 11,546 | 5,227,862 | 784,147 |
| Total | 22,903 | 10,473,952 | $1,409,963 | 13,101 | 5,935,714 | $890,528 |
| Excess of 1875–'6 | 9,802 | 4,538,238 | $519,435 | ............ | ............ | ............ |

The above does not include the shipment of December 2d, before given.

The export trade in cotton to foreign countries from American ports has undergone many changes, as is shown by the following, but the tendency appears to be to ship from the Atlantic ports.

*Richmond Enquirer January 19, 1876.

† Cotton pamphlet of Southern Fertilizing Company, of Richmond, through Col. John Ott, Secretary.

## No. 8.

*Bales of* Cotton Exported *from United States Ports to Foreign Countries,* 1870 *to* 1873.

| FROM | 1870. | 1871. | 1872. | 1873. |
|---|---|---|---|---|
| New Orleans | 1,005,530 | 1,302,535 | 888,976 | 1,177,058 |
| Mobile | 200,838 | 287,074 | 137,977 | 132,130 |
| South Carolina | 97,109 | 175,650 | 111,388 | 160,169 |
| Georgia | 265,631 | 464,369 | 295,798 | 375,895 |
| Texas | 152,559 | 221,242 | 116,597 | 210,438 |
| North Carolina | 50 | 70 | .............. | 1,632 |
| Virginia | 9,660 | 5,417 | 3,807 | 7,722 |
| New York | 413,701 | 667,958 | 373,071 | 573,498 |
| Boston | 1,677 | 3,005 | 18,128 | 11,128 |
| Philadelphia | .............. | 1,380 | 2,108 | 6,792 |
| Baltimore | 32,162 | 37,567 | 14,311 | 20,948 |
| Portland, Maine | .............. | 475 | 143 | 2,257 |
| San Francisco | .............. | .............. | 12 | 324 |
| Total United States | 2,173,917 | 3,166,742 | 1,957,314 | 2,679,986 |

## No. 9.

Cotton* Exported *from the United States, and to what Foreign Ports, year ending August 31st,* 1873.

| EXPORTED TO | Bales. | EXPORTED TO | Bales. |
|---|---|---|---|
| Liverpool | 1,842,117 | Santander | 1,280 |
| London | 336 | Malaga | 7,753 |
| Glasgow | 701 | San Sebastian, &c | 2,543 |
| Queenstown, Cork, &c | 50,487 | Genoa | 36,470 |
| Cowes, Falmouth, &c | 11,455 | Trieste | 2,947 |
| Havre | 251,172 | Salerno | 844 |
| Rouen | 1,731 | Narva | 5,903 |
| Amsterdam | 32,404 | Cronstadt | 56,227 |
| Bremen | 191,586 | Revel | 51,426 |
| Hamburg | 24,691 | Helsingfors | 1,060 |
| Antwerp | 25,387 | Mexico | 997 |
| Rotterdam | 15,706 | Other ports | 783 |
| Gottenburg and Stockholm | 10,136 | | |
| Uddevella | 1,650 | Total Export | 2,679,986 |
| Barcelona | 52,194 | | |

* United States Bureau of Statistics—Cotton pamphlet of Southern Fertilizing Company, Richmond.

## No. 10.

*Export of Cotton, Foreign and Coastwise, from Southern Ports, for Cotton-Year* 1873.

| Shipping Ports. | Bales. | |
|---|---|---|
| | To Foreign Ports. | To Coastwise Ports. |
| Charleston, South Carolina | 160,169 | 225,016 |
| Fernandina, St. Marks, &c., Florida | ........................ | 14,068 |
| Galveston, Texas | 210,438 | 133,304 |
| Mobile, Alabama | 132,130 | 197,131 |
| New Orleans | 1,177,058 | 228,968 |
| North Carolina ports | 1,632 | 59,898 |
| Savannah, Georgia | 375,895 | 248,752 |
| Virginia ports | 7,722 | 724,791 |
| | 2,065,044 | 1,831,928 |

## No. 11.

*The* Cotton Crops* *of* 1873–'4 *and* 1874–'5 *and* Receipts *at the several Ports.*

| States where grown. | Actual. (Bales.) Year ending Sept. 1, 1874. | Estimated. (Bales.) Year ending Sept. 1, 1875. | Ports where marketed, &c. | Actual. (Bales.) Year ending Sept. 1, 1874. | Estimated. (Bales.) Year ending Sept. 1, 1875. |
|---|---|---|---|---|---|
| Texas | 500,000 | 550,000 | Galveston, &c | 389,045 | 400,000 |
| Louisiana | 420,000 | 480,000 | New Orleans | 1,221,698 | 1,230,000 |
| Mississippi | 675,000 | 610,000 | Mobile | 299,578 | 375,000 |
| Alabama | 575,000 | 650,000 | Florida | 14,185 | 25,000 |
| Florida | 75,000 | 100,000 | Savannah | 625,857 | 675,000 |
| Georgia | 600,000 | 665,000 | Charleston | 438,194 | 475,000 |
| South Carolina | 400,000 | 400,000 | North Carolina | 57,895 | 90,000 |
| North Carolina | 225,000 | 275,000 | Virginia† | 505,876 | 450,000 |
| Arkansas | 400,000 | 360,000 | New York, Boston & Baltimore | 251,962 | 250,000 |
| Tennessee | 300,000 | 210,000 | Overland | 237,572 | 200,000 |
| | | | Southern consumption | 128,526 | 130,000 |
| Total crop | 4,170,000 | 4,300,000 | Total crop | 4,170,388 | 4,300,000 |

The above statement shows that in 1874 Norfolk was the *third* market in the United States.

*Financial Chronicle, New York, in Cotton pamphlet of Southern Fertilizing Company.

† Norfolk received 472,446 bales of the 505,876.

No. 12.—The excellent and suggestive Cotton-port Map of the Norfolk Landmark gives the following as the *net* receipts of cotton at the United States ports in 1874. By *net* receipts it means cotton sent *direct* to a port and that has not been counted at any other port.

| | | |
|---|---|---|
| 1. New Orleans | 1,186,032 | bales. |
| 2. Savannah | 634,083 | " |
| 3. Norfolk and Portsmouth | 467,571 | " |
| 4. Charleston | 428,352 | " |
| 5. Galveston | 367,053 | " |
| 6. Mobile | 296,731 | " |
| 7. New York | 210,820 | " |
| 8. Philadelphia | 43,203 | " |
| 9. Boston | 40,465 | bales. |
| 10. Wilmington (N. C.) | 20,729 | " |
| 11. Baltimore | 16,272 | " |
| 12. Port Royal (S. C.) | 9,643 | " |
| 13. Providence | 6,038 | " |
| Total | 3,726,997 | bales. |

The following table* gives the Production, Home Consumption, Exports, &c., of the Cotton of the United States during the period embracing the returns given for Virginia:

No. 13.

| Years ending August 31. | Production. Bales. | Home Consumption. Bales. | Exports. Bales. | Average net weight per bale. Lbs. | Middling Upland. Average price per lb. in New York in cents and 100ths. | Middling Upland. Average price per lb. in Liverpool, in pence and 100ths. |
|---|---|---|---|---|---|---|
| 1858-'9 | 4,018,914 | 927,651 | 3,021,403 | 447 | 12.08 | 6.63 |
| 1859-'60 | 4,861,292 | 978,043 | 3,774,173 | 461 | 11.00 | 5.97 |
| 1860-'1 | 3,849,469 | 843,740 | 3,127,568 | 477 | 13.01 | 8.50 |
| 1861-'2 | No trustworthy statistics for these years. | ......... | ......... | ......... | 31.29 | 18.37 |
| 1862-'3 | | ......... | ......... | ......... | 67.91 | 22.46 |
| 1863-'4 | | ......... | ......... | ......... | 101.50 | 27.17 |
| 1864-'5 | | ......... | ......... | ......... | 83.38 | 19.11 |
| 1865-'6 | 2,269,316 | 666,100 | 1,554,664 | 441 | 43.20 | 15.30 |
| 1866-'7 | 2,097,254 | 770,030 | 1,557,054 | 444 | 31.59 | 10.98 |
| 1867-'8 | 2,519,554 | 906,636 | 1,655,816 | 445 | 24.85 | 10.52 |
| 1868-'9 | 2,366,467 | 926,374 | 1,465,880 | 444 | 29.01 | 12.12 |
| 1869-'70 | 3,122,551 | 865,160 | 2,206,480 | 440 | 23.98 | 9.89 |
| 1870-'1 | 4,362,317 | 1,110,196 | 3,166,742 | 442 | 16.95 | 8.55 |
| 1871-'2 | 3,014,351 | 1,237,330 | 1,957,314 | 443 | 20.48 | 10.78 |
| 1872-'3 | 3,930,508 | 1,201,127 | 2,679,986 | 464 | 18.15 | 9.65 |

*Great Britain is the Cotton Market of the World*, because she manufactures 9-10ths of the cotton goods that are made; therefore, in considering the cotton trade of any point, it is a matter of interest to know the facts of demand in the country that regulates the trade in this great staple.

* By B. F. Nourse, of Boston—From Cotton pamphlet of Southern Fertilizing Company, Richmond, 1875.

## No. 14.

### RAW* COTTON IMPORTED *into* GREAT BRITAIN, *and from what Countries*, 1858 *to* 1872.

| YEARS. | United States | Mexico. | British West India Islands and British Guiana. | Colombia and Venezuela. | Brazil. | The Mediterranean, exclusive of Egypt. | Egypt. | British Possessions in the East Indies. | China. | Other Countries. | TOTAL IMPORTED. |
|---|---|---|---|---|---|---|---|---|---|---|---|
| | Lbs. | Lbs. | Lbs. | Lbs. | Lbs. | Lbs. | Lbs. | Lbs. | Lbs. | Lbs. | Lbs. |
| 1858 | 833,237,776 | ............ | 367,808 | 74,114 | 18,617,672 | 15,792 | 38,232,320 | 132,722,576 | ............ | 11,073,888 | 1,034,342,176 |
| 1859 | 961,707,264 | ............ | 692,256 | 6,496 | 22,478,960 | 439,040 | 37,667,056 | 192,330,880 | ............ | 10,767,120 | 1,225,989,072 |
| 1860 | 1,115,890,608 | ............ | 1,050,784 | 225,120 | 17,286,864 | 82,544 | 43,954,064 | 204,141,168 | 8,020 | 8,303,680 | 1,390,938,752 |
| 1861 | 819,500,528 | ............ | 485,304 | 154,896 | 17,290,336 | 587,104 | 40,892,096 | 369,040,448 | ............ | 9,033,024 | 1,256,984,736 |
| 1862 | 13,524,224 | 3,131,520 | 5,563,376 | 1,170,736 | 23,339,008 | 6,225,856 | 59,012,464 | 392,654,528 | 1,766,016 | 17,585,344 | 523,973,296 |
| 1863 | 6,394,080 | 19,278,112 | 25,181,856 | 2,623,600 | 22,603,168 | 13,806,576 | 93,552,368 | 434,420,784 | 30,656,336 | 20,655,824 | 670,084,128 |
| 1864 | 14,198,688 | 25,539,024 | 26,738,992 | 5,500,368 | 38,017,504 | 21,755,216 | 125,493,648 | 506,527,392 | 86,157,008 | 38,770,240 | 894,102,384 |
| 1865 | 135,832,480 | 36,664,880 | 16,536,912 | 14,699,328 | 55,403,152 | 27,239,072 | 176,838,144 | 445,947,600 | 35,855,792 | 30,501,744 | 978,502,000 |
| 1866 | 520,061,136 | 352,240 | 3,600,352 | 11,599,392 | 68,524,400 | 11,510,688 | 118,260,800 | 615,302,240 | 5,837,440 | 22,419,376 | 1,377,514,096 |
| 1867 | 528,166,800 | 2,464 | 4,810,288 | 9,713,872 | 70,430,080 | 6,780,480 | 126,285,264 | 498,317,008 | 627,184 | 17,852,464 | 1,262,885,904 |
| 1868 | 574,478,016 | ............ | 2,725,856 | 4,808,160 | 98,796,768 | 6,702,304 | 129,182,928 | 493,706,640 | ............ | 16,339,440 | 1,328,761,616 |
| 1869 | 457,358,944 | 40,544 | 1,695,868 | 8,085,728 | 79,417,968 | 13,506,640 | 160,450,280 | 481,440,170 | 448 | 19,574,936 | 1,221,571,232 |
| 1870 | 716,248,848 | 2,016 | 2,314,256 | 4,767,056 | 64,234,688 | 11,510,912 | 143,710,438 | 341,536,608 | 10,528 | 55,031,760 | 1,339,367,120 |
| 1871 | 1,038,677,920 | ............ | 2,671,536 | 6,582,240 | 86,158,800 | 3,777,424 | 176,166,480 | 431,209,744 | 102,144 | 32,793,488 | 1,778,139,776 |
| 1872 | 625,600,080 | 31,136 | 1,460,960 | 7,960,624 | 112,509,824 | 8,031,744 | 177,581,712 | 443,234,736 | 252,112 | 82,184,544 | 1,408,837,472 |

* Ellison & Co., of Liverpool—From Cotton pamphlet of Southern Fertilizing Company, Richmond, 1875.

*The European Consumption of Cotton*, and the *Sources of Supply for* 1872–'73, *bales*, are summed up by M. Ott-Truempler,* of Zurich, an eminent statistician, follows:

No. 15.

| Sources of Supply. | English Consumption. | Continental Consumption. | Total European. |
|---|---|---|---|
| American | 1,654,000 | 669,000 | 2,323,000 |
| Indian | 737,000 | 795,000 | 1,532,000 |
| Brazil | 509,000 | 144,000 | 653,000 |
| Egypt | 306,000 | 87,000 | 393,000 |
| Sundry | 129,000 | 189,000 | 318,000 |
| Total | 3,335,000 | 1,884,000 | 5,219,000 |

* Appleton's American Cyclopedia, 1874.

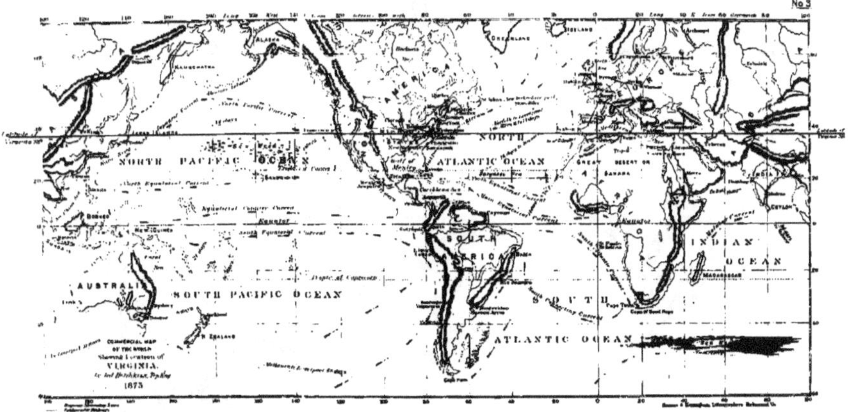
No 3
NORTH PACIFIC OCEAN
SOUTH PACIFIC OCEAN
NORTH
ATLANTIC OCEAN
SOUTH
ATLANTIC OCEAN
INDIAN
OCEAN
SOUTH
AMERICA
AFRICA
AUSTRALIA
GREAT DESERT OR SAHARA
COMMERCIAL MAP
VIRGINIA.

*bale*

foll

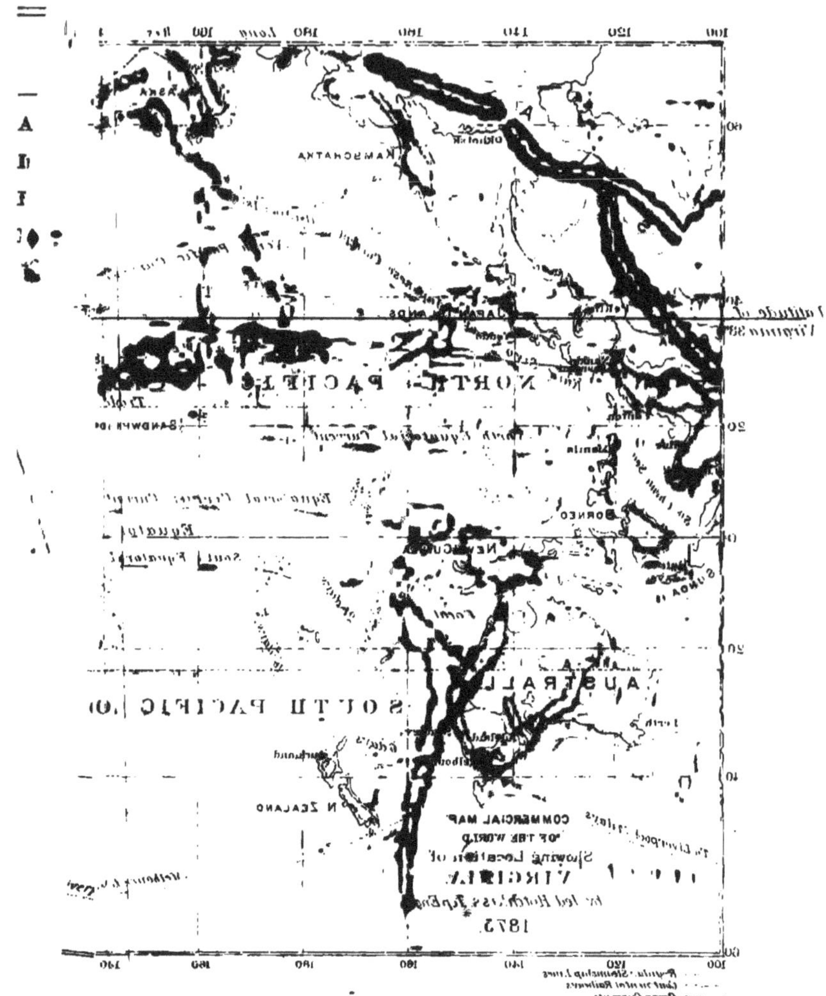

# VIRGINIA.

---

## *PART II—POLITICAL SUMMARY.*

---

CHAPTER VII—The Population of the State.

CHAPTER VIII—Religious Advantages.

CHAPTER IX—Educational Advantages.

CHAPTER X—Internal Improvements.

CHAPTER XI—Government.

# CHAPTER VII.

## THE POPULATION OF VIRGINIA.

The statistics of the population of Virginia, compiled from the official Reports of the Censuses of the United States for 1860 and 1870, are here presented for each of the great Natural Divisions of the State as described in this summary. The results of two decades are given for comparative purposes, but it should be borne in mind that the census of 1870 followed a long and exhausting war, in which Virginia suffered a great loss of human life and destruction of the means of subsistence, as well as a dismemberment, by which she was deprived of 23,000 square miles of territory and 442,014 of population.

On the 1st of June, 1860* and 1870, the POPULATION of the SECTIONS of VIRGINIA, *by* NUMBERS *and* RACE, were as follows:

Table I.

| | AGGREGATE. | | WHITES. | | BLACKS. | |
|---|---|---|---|---|---|---|
| | 1860. | 1870. | 1860. | 1870. | 1860. | 1870. |
| Tidewater | (a) 344,782 | (b) 346,297 | 167,129 | 168,650 | 177,570 | 177,475 |
| Middle | (c) 371,035 | (d) 363,932 | 164,800 | 161,996 | 206,235 | 201,905 |
| Piedmont | 209,132 | (e) 207,204 | 115,236 | 121,107 | 93,896 | 86,085 |
| Blue Ridge | 24,500 | 28,550 | 23,117 | 26,479 | 1,383 | 2,079 |
| Valley | (f) 194,290 | (g) 197,967 | 153,517 | 159,927 | 40,773 | 38,027 |
| Appalachia | (h) 76,901 | (i) 81.197 | 67,974 | 73,922 | 7,817 | 7,270 |
| Virginia | (j) 1,219,630 | (k) 1,225,163 | 691,773 | 712,089 | 527,763 | 512,841 |

Including—(a) 83 Indians; (b) 170 Indians and 2 Chinese; (c) 2 Chinese; (d) 29 Indians; (e) 12 Indians; (f) 13 Indians; (g) 1 Indian; (h) 10 Indians; (i) 5 Indians; (j) 106 Indians and 2 Chinese; (k) 229 Indians and 4 Chinese.

The *gain*† of the entire population from 1860 to 1870‡ was .045 per cent.; the *gain* of the whites was .029 per cent.; the *loss* of the blacks was .009 per cent.

* The population is given for the territory of Virginia as it now (1874) is and as it was in 1870.

† In 1863 the State of West Virginia was created, and 50 counties of Virginia were assigned to it, but the returns here given are for Virginia as it now is.

‡ This embraces the four years of war.

The Statistical Atlas of the United States (1874) gives the following as the population of the *present* (1870) territory of Virginia, at each census—it may be considered a good approximation:

| | Persons. | Persons to a Square Mile. |
|---|---|---|
| 1790 | 691,737 | 18.05 |
| 1800 | 801,608 | 20.92 |
| 1810 | 869,131 | 22.69 |
| 1820 | 928,558 | 24.24 |
| 1830 | 1,034,481 | 27.00 |
| 1840 | 1,015,260 | 26.50 |
| 1850 | 1,119,348 | 29.11 |
| 1860 | 1,219,630 | 31.80 |
| 1870 | 1,225,163 | 31.95 |

The population of the United States was 31,443,381 in 1860, and 38,558,371 in 1870, in which year Virginia was the 10th State in the number of people.

The next table gives the Area of each section and of the State and the Population to the square mile.

Table II.

| | Square Miles. | 1,000ths of State. | Population to Square Mile. |
|---|---|---|---|
| Tidewater | 11,350 | .252 | 30.5 |
| Middle | 12,470 | .277 | 29.2 |
| Piedmont | 6,680 | .149 | 32.5 |
| Blue Ridge | 1,230 | .027 | 23.2 |
| Valley | 7,550 | .168 | 26.2 |
| Appalachia | 5,720 | .127 | 14.2 |
| Virginia | 45,000 | 1.000 | 27.2 |

The census of 1870 gives 38,348 square miles as the area of Virginia (this, as stated elsewhere, is incorrect), and on that basis gives it a population of 31.95 to the square mile. The number in 1870, in the United States, omitting the territories, was 19.21, and, including them, 10.70 to the square mile. The centre of population in the United States, according to the Statistical Atlas, was in 1820 sixteen miles north of Woodstock, in Virginia; in 1830 it had passed to nineteen miles west southwest of Moorefield; in 1840 to sixteen miles south of Clarksburg; in 1850 to twenty-three miles southeast of Parkersburg, and in 1870 to forty-eight miles east by north of Cincinnati. The land-surface area of the United States, omitting territories, was, in 1870, 1,984,467 square miles, and including them 3,603,884. The area of land and water is about 4,000,000. So Virginia had about one forty-fourth of the area of the States and one-eightieth of the whole country.

## Table III.

| | NATIVE. | | FOREIGN BORN. | | Having one or both parents foreign. | Having foreign father. | Having foreign mother. | Having foreign father and mother |
|---|---|---|---|---|---|---|---|---|
| | 1860. | 1870. | 1860. | 1870. | 1870. | 1870. | 1870. | 1870. |
| Tidewater........... | 335,640 | 339,440 | 9,232 | 6,817 | 14,526 | 14,109 | 12,560 | 12,143 |
| Middle............... | 367,492 | 350,983 | 4,543 | 3,977 | 9,092 | 6,698 | 7,140 | 6,756 |
| Piedmont............ | 208,124 | 206,140 | 1,008 | 1,084 | 2,241 | 2,172 | 1,707 | 1,629 |
| Blue Ridge.......... | 24,454 | 28,512 | 46 | 46 | 148 | 143 | 83 | 78 |
| Valley............... | 192,194 | 193,397 | 2,096 | 1,590 | 3,990 | 3,800 | 2,758 | 2,568 |
| Appalachia.......... | 75,213 | 80,937 | 1,588 | 260 | 797 | 755 | 503 | 461 |
| Virginia............. | 1,201,117 | 1,211,409 | 18,513 | 13,754 | 30,794 | 29,077 | 24,751 | 23,634 |

By this table (III) it appears that in 1870 over 988 out of every 1,000 of the population of Virginia were born in the United States, or that less than 12 in each thousand were foreign born. The table also shows that the foreign fathers were more numerous than the mothers—as it should, because more males come to the country than females, and marry here. The foreign population is most numerous in the sections near the sea.

Table IV is Selected Nativities of the Native Population of Virginia in 1870, showing *where* most of the people were born.

## Table IV.

| | NATIVES—WHERE BORN. | | | | | | |
|---|---|---|---|---|---|---|---|
| | Whole Number. | Virginia or West Va. | North Carolina. | Maryland. | New York. | Ten'essee | Pen'sylva'a |
| Tidewater...................... | 339,500 | 302,620 | 7,202 | 2,956 | 2,130 | 77 | 1,257 |
| Middle.......................... | 359,964 | 347,539 | 3,222 | 2,628 | 1,845 | 124 | 1,114 |
| Piedmont....................... | 198,460 | 198,065 | 638 | 726 | 402 | 83 | 1,418 |
| Blue Ridge..................... | 28,512 | 26,194 | 2,105 | 7 | 2 | 71 | 35 |
| Valley.......................... | 196,397 | 189,755 | 1,425 | 952 | 243 | 1,195 | 1,179 |
| Appalachia..................... | 80,947 | 74,401 | 2,251 | 64 | 26 | 2,578 | 74 |
| Virginia........................ | 1,203,760 | 1,137,574 | 16,843 | 7,328 | 4,648 | 4,138 | 4,070 |

Table IV reveals the fact that nine hundred and forty-five in every thousand of the population (1870) were born in Virginia or West Virginia—the latter State having so recently been taken from Virginia—and that thirty of the remaining fifty-five of the one thousand were born either in North Carolina, Maryland, New York, Tennessee or Pennsylvania—states, three of which now border on Virginia, and Pennsylvania did before West Virginia was separated. Trade with the great commercial city of New York has promoted intercourse and interchange of residence with the state in which it is situated. North Carolina touches the State a long distance, bordering most of the sections, and her children are found in all. The same is true of Maryland, save that she is remote from Blue Ridge and Appalachia. Tennessee has sent her people to the Valley and Appalachia, which adjoin her.

Table V gives the Selected NATIVITIES of the FOREIGN-BORN Population of the Sections of Virginia in 1870.

Table V.

| | Whole Number. | British America. | England and Wales. | Ireland. | Scotland. | Great Britain (not stated). | Germany. | France. | Sweden and Norway. | Holland. | Italy. | Switzerland. | Austria. |
|---|---|---|---|---|---|---|---|---|---|---|---|---|---|
| Tidewater........ | 6,815 | 111 | 737 | 3,258 | 349 | 3 | 2,505 | 253 | 26 | 40 | 121 | 67 | 55 |
| Middle........... | 3,999 | 120 | 850 | 1,535 | 215 | ........ | 869 | 50 | 17 | 183 | 18 | 41 | 10 |
| Piedmont........ | 1,036 | 34 | 198 | 385 | 62 | 1 | 239 | 11 | 2 | 6 | 10 | 18 | ...... |
| Blue Ridge....... | 46 | ........ | 16 | 18 | ...... | ........ | 11 | ...... | ........ | ...... | 1 | ...... | ...... |
| Valley........... | 1,550 | 51 | 198 | 714 | 50 | 1 | 419 | 44 | 1 | 2 | 11 | 21 | 11 |
| Appalachia ...... | 280 | 8 | 41 | 173 | 14 | ........ | 10 | 6 | ........ | ...... | 1 | 1 | ...... |
| Virginia....... | 13,726 | 324 | 2,040 | 6,080 | 710 | 5 | 4,053 | 364 | 46 | 231 | 162 | 148 | 76 |

Of the foreign population, Ireland furnished nearly one-half, Germany one-third, England one-sixth and Scotland one-twentieth. The foreign population has been gathered from more than fifty different foreign States, representing all the leading nationalties of the world. Forty-nine of the foreigners are blacks from Africa, Europe, West Indies and Canada, and there are four Chinese from China. The native population is gathered from forty-one States and Territories, so that more than ninety different States are here represented.

Over 49 per cent. of the foreign-born population were found in Tidewater, where they are located in the seaport cities. Over 29 per cent. lived in the Middle country, and nearly 8 per cent. in Piedmont, while the Valley had over 11 per cent.

Of the population born in the Virginias, 659,230 were whites and 503,368 blacks, so 9,424 blacks were born in other States, of which Maryland furnished 1,679, North Carolina 6,373, South Carolina 223, and Tennessee 287; they are gathered from thirty States of the Union.

Table VI shows the condition of the Population of Virginia in 1870 in respect to SEX, RACE and NATIVITY.

## Table VI.

| | TOTALS. | | | NATIVE. | | | FOREIGN. | | |
|---|---|---|---|---|---|---|---|---|---|
| | Whole No. | Males. | Females. | Whole No. | Males. | Females. | Whole No. | Males. | Females. |
| Whites | 712,089 | 348,720 | 363,369 | 698,388 | 340,736 | 357,652 | 13,701 | 7,984 | 5,717 |
| Blacks | 440,593 | 214,758 | 225,835 | 440,553 | 214,731 | 225,822 | 40 | 27 | 13 |
| Mulattoes | 72,248 | 33,470 | 38,778 | 72,239 | 33,465 | 38,774 | 9 | 5 | 4 |
| Total Negro | 512,841 | 248,228 | 264,613 | 512,792 | 248,196 | 264,596 | 49 | 32 | 17 |
| Indians | 229 | 106 | 123 | 229 | 106 | 123 | ......... | ......... | ......... |
| Chinese | 4 | 4 | ......... | ......... | ......... | ......... | 4 | 4 | ......... |
| Total of all Races | 1,225,163 | 597,058 | 628,105 | 1,211,409 | 559,038 | 622,371 | 13,754 | 8,020 | 5,734 |

This table shows that 419 out of each 1,000 of the population belong to the colored races, and 581 to the white races—in other words, seven-twelfths of the people are white and five-twelfths colored; 58 per cent. of the population being white and 42 per cent. colored.

Of the negroes, 14 per cent. are mulattoes, or mixed, and 86 per cent. blacks, or unmixed. The mulattoes generally intermarry, expressing a decided preference for the mixed over the pure negro, consequently the tendency is to increase the mixed race.

The females in all cases, except in that of foreigners, are considerably in excess of the males. Of the whites nearly 49 per cent., of the negroes a little over 48 per cent., and of the mulattoes 46 per cent., are males.

The Indians are the remnant of the once powerful Pamunkey tribe, living on a reservation.

The next tabular statement (VII) gives the statistics of what the census calls the SCHOOL, the MILITARY and the CITIZEN OR VOTING Population.

## Table VII.

| | School Population—5 to 18. | | | Military Population, 18 to 45. | Citizen Population, 21 and over. | Total Male Population. |
|---|---|---|---|---|---|---|
| | Male. | Female. | Total. | Male. | Male. | |
| Whites | 114,561 | 111,026 | 225,587 | 123,124 | 161,500 | ......... |
| Negroes | 85,510 | 85,644 | 171,154 | 83,488 | 107,691 | ......... |
| Indians | 32 | 39 | 71 | 42 | 47 | ......... |
| Chinese | ......... | ......... | ......... | 4 | 4 | ......... |
| Natives | 199,665 | 196,269 | 395,934 | 202,072 | 261,948 | ......... |
| Foreign | 438 | 440 | 878 | 4,586 | 7,294 | ......... |
| All classes | 200,103 | 196,709 | 396,812 | 206,658 | 269,242 | 597,058 |

The School Population of the State, by Report of the Superintendent of Public Instruction, for 1872–'3, was—

Table VIII.

| | Males. | Females. | Total. | Aggregate. |
|---|---|---|---|---|
| White…………………………………………… | 128,967 | 124,444 | 253,411 | 424,107 |
| Black…………………………………………… | 87,399 | 83,297 | 170,696 | |

The average percentage of these in attendance at public schools in 1872–'3 was, of whites, .255 per cent.; of blacks, .154 per cent.; or .215 for all—so that over one-fifth of the Virginia School Population, which includes *all between* 5 *and* 21 *years of age* (not 5 and 18 as in the census), actually attended the *public* schools—so that if all that attended are considered, over one-fourth of this class were receiving instruction. According to Table VII, the males of this vigorous class—the hope of the Commonwealth, those between 5 and 18*—formed 16⅓ per cent. of the whole population, that is, nearly *one-sixth of all* the people, while the females were 16 1-12th per cent. Nearly *one-third* of all the people in the State were between 5 and 18, a most striking fact, illustrating the vigor of the population, the healthfulness of the State, &c.

The arms-bearing population—the vigorous and active men, the bread-winners—those between 18 and 45, constituted *over one-sixth* of the population, and that, too, after this class had been more than twice decimated by war during the decade. The *white* males were nearly 60 per cent. of this class.

The voting population of Virginia includes all males over 21, except idiots and lunatics, persons convicted of bribery in any election, of embezzlement of public funds, treason or felony, and officers, soldiers, seamen or marines of the United States army or navy merely *stationed* in the State. *The citizens*, those that have the right to vote, are *all males over* 21 *who are citizens of the United States, who have resided in Virginia one year and in the election district three months before the election at which they may desire to vote*, excepting as above. This brings the number of voters to 266,680, or .217 per cent. of the population—over one-fifth. At the State election of 1869 the vote cast was 220,739, so that about .83 per cent. of the voters exercised their electoral privileges.

The total male population of Virginia (1870) was 597,058; that of all the United States was 19,493,565; so Virginia had over .03 per cent. of the whole, while of the natural militia (18 to 45), she had over 27 in each 1,000 of all, ranking as the 12th State, while she ranks as the 9th in the militia of *native* population.

Of the citizenship population of the United States—8,425,941—Virginia had .03⅓ per cent., holding the 10th rank.

The school population of the United States (5 to 18) was 12,055,443 (males, 6,086,872; females, 5,968,571); so Virginia had one-thirtieth of this class.

* The census states that of the school and military ages the *first* years are *inclusive*, the *last exclusive*.

The following table (IX) gives the Ages of the population, in 1870, for the State:

Table IX.

| | In 100,000. | Total. | Male. | Female. |
|---|---|---|---|---|
| Population of Virginia | .............. | 1,225,163 | 597,058 | 628,105 |
| *Under one* year old | 2,922 | 35,802 | 18,071 | 17,731 |
| *One* year old | 2,960 | 36,261 | 18,480 | 17,781 |
| *Under two* years | 5,882 | 72,063 | 36,551 | 35,512 |
| *Two* years old | 3,159 | 38,700 | 19,790 | 18,910 |
| Under *three* years | 9,041 | 110,763 | 56,311 | 54,422 |
| *Three* years old | 3,026 | 37,081 | 18,436 | 18,645 |
| *Under four years* | 12,067 | 147,844 | 74,777 | 73,067 |
| *Four years old* | 2,908 | 35,625 | 18,089 | 17,536 |
| *Under five years* | 14,975 | 183,469 | 92,866 | 90,603 |
| *Five* to *nine* | 12,377 | 151,638 | 76,737 | 74,901 |
| Under ten years | 27,352 | 335,107 | 169,603 | 165,504 |
| Ten to fourteen | 13,258 | 162,436 | 82,976 | 79,460 |
| Under fifteen | 40,610 | 497,543 | 252,579 | 244,964 |
| Fifteen to seventeen | 6,754 | 82,738 | 40,390 | 42,348 |
| Under eighteen | 47,364 | 580,281 | 292,969 | 287,312 |
| Eighteen to nineteen | 4,163 | 51,006 | 23,946 | 27,060 |
| Under twenty | 51,527 | 631,287 | 316,915 | 314,372 |
| Twenty | 2,214 | 27,122 | 10,901 | 16,221 |
| Under twenty-one | 53,741 | 658,409 | 327,816 | 330,593 |
| Twenty-one to twenty-four | 7,476 | 91,596 | 42,892 | 48,704 |
| Under twenty-five | 61,217 | 750,005 | 370,708 | 379,297 |
| Twenty-five to twenty-nine | 7,190 | 88,090 | 38,803 | 49,287 |
| Under thirty | 68,407 | 838,095 | 409,511 | 428,584 |
| Thirty to thirty-four | 5,808 | 71,162 | 31,880 | 39,282 |
| Under thirty-five | 74,215 | 909,257 | 441,391 | 467,866 |
| Thirty-five to thirty-nine | 5,509 | 67,488 | 31,723 | 35,765 |
| Under forty | 79,724 | 976,745 | 473,114 | 503,631 |
| Forty to forty-four | 4,624 | 56,652 | 26,513 | 30,139 |
| Under forty-five | 84,348 | 1,033,397 | 499,627 | 533,770 |

Table IX—*Continued.*

| | In 100,000. | Total. | Male. | Female. |
|---|---|---|---|---|
| Forty-five to forty-nine | 4,025 | 49,313 | 24,987 | 24,326 |
| Under fifty | 88,373 | 1,082,710 | 524,614 | 558,096 |
| Fifty to fifty-four | 3,580 | 43,860 | 22,250 | 21,610 |
| Under fifty-five | 91,953 | 1,126,570 | 546,864 | 579,706 |
| Fifty-five to fifty-nine | 2,249 | 27,566 | 14,440 | 13,126 |
| Under sixty | 94,202 | 1,154,136 | 561,304 | 592,832 |
| Sixty to sixty-four | 2,305 | 28,221 | 14,652 | 13,569 |
| Under sixty-five | 96,507 | 1,182,357 | 575,956 | 606,401 |
| Sixty-five to sixty-nine | 1,380 | 16,916 | 8,806 | 8,110 |
| Under seventy | 97,887 | 1,199,273 | 584,762 | 614,511 |
| Seventy to seventy-four | 1,053 | 12,904 | 6,315 | 6,589 |
| Under seventy-five | 98,940 | 1,212,177 | 591,077 | 621,100 |
| Seventy-five to seventy-nine | 525 | 6,433 | 3,120 | 3,313 |
| Under eighty | 99,465 | 1,218,610 | 594,197 | 624,413 |
| Eighty to eighty-nine | 435 | 5,325 | 2,410 | 2,915 |
| Under ninety | 99,900 | 1,223,935 | 596,607 | 627,328 |
| Ninety to ninety-nine | 81 | 998 | 386 | 612 |
| Under one hundred | 99,981 | 1,224,933 | 596,993 | 627,940 |
| One hundred, &c | 19 | 230 | 65 | 165 |

There were 890,056 ten years and over in age, and of these 412,665, over 46 per cent., had occupation of some kind. Of the 96,439 males between 10 and 15, over 35 per cent., or 33,954, were employed; and of the 93,576 females of the same class, 14,392, or about 15 per cent., had occupation. Of the 295,262 males between 16 and 59, 275,501, or over 93 per cent., were actively employed, and of the 333,752 females of same age, 58,026, or over 17 per cent., had occupation. Of the 35,754 males that were 60 and over, 28,009, or about 80 per cent., were still of the occupied class, while of the 35,273 females, only 2,783, or less than 8 per cent., were of the busy class. Of all that were 10 and over, 244,550, or more than 59 per cent. were engaged in agriculture; 98,521, over 23 per cent., were in professional and personal service; 20,181, about 5 per cent., in trade and transportation; and 49,413, about 12 per cent., in manufactures and mining.

## Table X.

*Population of Virginia by Ages and Sexes.*

| AGES. | IN 100,000. | TOTAL. | MALE. | FEMALE. |
|---|---|---|---|---|
| Under 1 | 2,922 | 35,802 | 18,071 | 17,731 |
| 1 | 2,960 | 36,261 | 18,480 | 17,781 |
| 2 | 3,159 | 38,700 | 19,790 | 18,910 |
| 3 | 3,026 | 37,081 | 18,436 | 18,645 |
| 4 | 2,908 | 35,625 | 18,089 | 17,536 |
| 5 to 9 | 12,377 | 151,638 | 76,737 | 74,901 |
| 10 to 14 | 13,258 | 162,436 | 82,976 | 79,460 |
| 15 to 17 | 6,754 | 82,738 | 40,390 | 42,348 |
| 18 to 19 | 4,163 | 51,006 | 23,946 | 27,060 |
| 20 | 2,214 | 27,122 | 10,901 | 16,221 |
| 21 to 24 | 7,476 | 91,596 | 42,892 | 48,704 |
| 25 to 29 | 7,190 | 88,090 | 38,803 | 49,287 |
| 30 to 34 | 5,808 | 71,162 | 31,880 | 39,282 |
| 35 to 39 | 5,509 | 67,488 | 31,723 | 35,765 |
| 40 to 44 | 4,624 | 56,652 | 26,513 | 30,139 |
| 45 to 49 | 4,025 | 49,313 | 24,987 | 24,326 |
| 50 to 54 | 3,588 | 43,860 | 22,250 | 21,610 |
| 55 to 59 | 2,249 | 27,566 | 14,444 | 13,126 |
| 60 to 64 | 2,305 | 28,221 | 14,652 | 13,569 |
| 65 to 69 | 1,380 | 16,916 | 8,806 | 8,810 |
| 70 to 74 | 1,053 | 12,904 | 6,315 | 6,589 |
| 75 to 79 | 525 | 6,433 | 3,120 | 3,313 |
| 80 to 89 | 435 | 5,325 | 2,410 | 2,915 |
| 90 to 99 | 81 | 998 | 386 | 612 |
| 100 and over | 19 | 230 | 65 | 165 |
| | 100,000 | 1,225,163 | 597,058 | 628,105 |

This table (X) is instructive, showing at a glance the number of people in the State at twenty-five different periods of human life, and the same for each of the sexes. It also shows the composition of any 100,000 of the inhabitants, from which the proportion or percentage those of any given age bear to the whole may be readily ascertained.

If space permitted, comparisons could be made with other states, which would show that the climate of Virginia must be exceedingly favorable to the duration of life, compared with other sections. A few examples, taken from the old settled states, must suffice. Selecting the period of 21 to 24 years of age, in 100,000, Virginia had 7,476; Maryland 7,202; New Hampshire 7,071; New York 7,059; Illinois 7,367; North Carolina 6,840; and the average for the United States was 7,475. Again, taking the period of 50 to 54 years of age, Virginia had, in the same ratio, 3,580, Illinois 3,228; Kentucky 3,089; and the United States 3,548. The average of the United States, from 75 to 79, was 455; the number in Virginia was 525; in Maryland 458; Kentucky 388; North Carolina 464; Tennessee 358; Texas 169, and Pennsylvania 15. Taking the age from 90 to 99, the United States average in 100,000 was 43; the number in Virginia was 81; in Pennsylvania 38; in Ohio 38; in New York 43; in Kentucky 45; in Connecticut 65; in Maryland 49, and in Missouri 17. Of those over 100 years old, Virginia had 19 in the 100,000; the average in the United States 9; Connecticut had 4; Massachusetts 3; Maryland 12; Pennsylvania 3, and New York 4.

The next table (XI) shows the population of the State in 1870, by *Ages and Colors.* The census does not give the numbers for each 100,000 in these cases. This table (XI) embraces the same persons as table X, only they are here separated so as to show the numbers of each race.

Table XI.

| | Whites. | | | Blacks. | | |
|---|---|---|---|---|---|---|
| | Total. | Males. | Females. | Total. | Males. | Females. |
| All ages | 712,089 | 348,720 | 363,369 | 512,841 | 248,228 | 264,613 |
| Under 1 | 20,043 | 10,227 | 9,816 | 15,755 | 7,842 | 7,913 |
| 1 | 19,952 | 10,280 | 9,672 | 16,302 | 8,195 | 8,107 |
| Under 2 | 39,995 | 20,507 | 19,488 | 32,057 | 16,037 | 16,020 |
| 2 | 21,424 | 11,114 | 10,310 | 17,271 | 8,674 | 8,597 |
| Under 3 | 61,419 | 31,621 | 29,798 | 49,328 | 24,711 | 24,617 |
| 3 | 20,233 | 10,088 | 10,145 | 16,842 | 8,344 | 8,498 |
| Under 4 | 81,652 | 41,709 | 39,943 | 66,170 | 33,055 | 33,115 |
| 4 | 19,304 | 9,939 | 9,365 | 16,313 | 8,146 | 8,167 |
| Under 5 | 100,956 | 51,648 | 49,308 | 82,483 | 41,201 | 41,282 |
| 5 to 9 | 83,701 | 42,750 | 40,951 | 67,908 | 33,975 | 33,933 |
| Under 10 | 184,657 | 94,398 | 90,259 | 150,391 | 75,176 | 75,215 |
| 10 to 14 | 93,060 | 47,652 | 45,408 | 69,352 | 35,314 | 34,038 |
| Under 15 | 277,717 | 142,050 | 135,667 | 219,743 | 110,490 | 109,253 |

TABLE XI—*Continued.*

| | Whites. | | | Blacks. | | |
|---|---|---|---|---|---|---|
| | Total. | Males. | Females. | Total. | Males. | Females. |
| 15 to 17 | 48,826 | 24,159 | 24,667 | 33,894 | 16,221 | 17,673 |
| Under 18 | 326,543 | 166,209 | 160,334 | 253,637 | 126,711 | 126,926 |
| 18 to 19 | 30,267 | 14,423 | 15,844 | 20,728 | 9,517 | 11,211 |
| Under 20 | 356,810 | 180,632 | 176,178 | 274,365 | 136,228 | 138,137 |
| 20 | 14,963 | 6,588 | 8,375 | 12,151 | 4,309 | 7,842 |
| Under 21 | 371,773 | 187,220 | 184,553 | 286,515 | 140,537 | 145,979 |
| 21 to 24 | 55,857 | 26,431 | 29,426 | 35,726 | 16,454 | 19,272 |
| Under 25 | 427,630 | 213,651 | 213,979 | 322,242 | 156,991 | 165,251 |
| 25 to 29 | 51,493 | 23,029 | 28,464 | 36,579 | 15,767 | 20,812 |
| Under 30 | 479,123 | 236,680 | 242,443 | 358,821 | 172,758 | 186,063 |
| 30 to 34 | 42,701 | 19,091 | 23,610 | 28,447 | 12,787 | 15,660 |
| Under 35 | 521,824 | 255,771 | 266,053 | 387,268 | 185,545 | 201,723 |
| 35 to 39 | 39,935 | 18,526 | 21,409 | 27,539 | 13,191 | 14,348 |
| Under 40 | 561,759 | 274,297 | 287,462 | 414,807 | 198,736 | 216,071 |
| 40 to 44 | 32,621 | 15,036 | 17,585 | 24,010 | 11,463 | 12,447 |
| Under 45 | 594,380 | 289,333 | 305,047 | 438,817 | 210,199 | 228,618 |
| 45 to 49 | 30,206 | 15,145 | 15,061 | 19,095 | 9,839 | 9,256 |
| Under 50 | 624,586 | 304,478 | 320,108 | 457,912 | 220,038 | 237,874 |
| 50 to 54 | 26,615 | 13,478 | 13,137 | 17,236 | 8,767 | 8,469 |
| Under 55 | 651,201 | 317,956 | 333,245 | 475,148 | 228,805 | 246,343 |
| 55 to 59 | 18,267 | 9,499 | 8,768 | 9,296 | 4,940 | 4,356 |
| Under 60 | 669,468 | 327,455 | 342,013 | 484,444 | 233,745 | 250,699 |
| 60 to 64 | 16,840 | 8,621 | 8,219 | 11,378 | 6,029 | 5,349 |
| Under 65 | 686,308 | 336,076 | 350,232 | 495,822 | 239,774 | 256,048 |
| 65 to 69 | 10,773 | 5,508 | 5,265 | 6,142 | 3,297 | 2,845 |
| Under 70 | 697,081 | 341,584 | 355,497 | 501,964 | 243,071 | 258,893 |
| 70 to 74 | 7,684 | 3,739 | 3,945 | 5,215 | 2,573 | 2,642 |
| Under 75 | 704,765 | 345,323 | 359,442 | 507,179 | 245,644 | 261,535 |
| 75 to 79 | 3,943 | 1,887 | 2,056 | 2,490 | 1,233 | 1,257 |
| Under 80 | 708,708 | 347,210 | 361,498 | 509,669 | 246,877 | 262,792 |

TABLE XI—*Concluded.*

| | WHITES. | | | BLACKS. | | |
|---|---|---|---|---|---|---|
| | Total. | Males. | Females. | Total. | Males. | Females. |
| 80 to 89 | 2,955 | 1,345 | 1,610 | 3,370 | 1,065 | 1,305 |
| Under 90 | 711,663 | 348,555 | 363,108 | 512,039 | 247,942 | 264,097 |
| 90 to 99 | 398 | 156 | 242 | 600 | 230 | 370 |
| Under 100 | 712,061 | 348,711 | 363,350 | 512,639 | 248,172 | 264,467 |
| 100, &c. | 28 | 9 | 19 | 202 | 56 | 146 |

By this table (XI) among the whites the males exceeded the females for all ages up to 15, except in the class of 3-year olds; from 15 to 45 the females were in excess; from 45 to 70 the males exceeded, and from 70 on the females. Among the blacks the females were in excess under 1; the males from 1 to 3; the females at 3 and 4; the males from 5 to 18; the females from 18 to 45; the males from 45 to 70, and the females from 70 on. These returns are by no means as reliable for the ages of the blacks as for those of the whites.

The white males between 15 and 17 exceeded the black 7,938; the white males under 21 exceeded the black 46,683, and under 45 the excess was 79,134. Of the whole male population the whites were in a majority of 100,492. Among the whites the males were 48.9 per cent. of all, and among the blacks they were 48.4 per cent.

In this connection it may be well to note the deaths in Virginia, by ages, during the census year 1870, as stated in the United States mortality tables of that year.

| AGE. | Males. | Females. | AGE. | Males. | Females. |
|---|---|---|---|---|---|
| Unknown | 6 | 3 | 35 to 40 | 230 | 309 |
| Under 1 | 1,798 | 1,575 | 40 to 45 | 229 | 263 |
| 1 | 680 | 624 | 45 to 50 | 257 | 202 |
| 2 | 397 | 406 | 50 to 55 | 290 | 244 |
| 3 | 225 | 199 | 55 to 60 | 224 | 162 |
| 4 | 124 | 143 | 60 to 65 | 301 | 278 |
| Total under 5 | 3,224 | 2,947 | 65 to 70 | 255 | 230 |
| 5 to 10 | 365 | 328 | 70 to 75 | 277 | 266 |
| 10 to 15 | 239 | 291 | 75 to 80 | 188 | 183 |
| 15 to 20 | 306 | 385 | 80 to 85 | 196 | 188 |
| 20 to 25 | 362 | 471 | 85 to 90 | 80 | 87 |
| 25 to 30 | 241 | 365 | 90 to 95 | 41 | 44 |
| 30 to 35 | 207 | 330 | 95 and over | 34 | 55 |
| | | | Total | 7,552 | 7,631 |
| | | | Aggregate | ......... | 15,183 |

Over 42 per cent. of the males that died were under 5, while of the females of this class but 38 per cent. died. In Missouri over 48 per cent. of the male and 47 per cent. of the female deaths were of those under 5, and in Illinois over 50 per cent. of the deaths, both of males and females, were of those under 5.

The following table (XII) gives the number of people in Virginia over 80 years of age, by sexes:

Table XII.

| All Ages. | Total. | Male. | Female. |
|---|---|---|---|
| 80 and over | 6,553 | 2,861 | 3,692 |
| 80 | 2,319 | 973 | 1,316 |
| 81 | 388 | 207 | 181 |
| 82 | 437 | 207 | 230 |
| 83 | 390 | 200 | 190 |
| 84 | 443 | 217 | 226 |
| 85 | 573 | 246 | 327 |
| 86 | 244 | 111 | 133 |
| 87 | 240 | 113 | 127 |
| 88 | 172 | 79 | 98 |
| 89 | 114 | 57 | 57 |
| 90 | 461 | 188 | 273 |
| 91 | 88 | 35 | 53 |
| 92 | 75 | 24 | 51 |
| 93 | 56 | 22 | 34 |
| 94 | 63 | 29 | 34 |
| 95 | 111 | 31 | 80 |
| 96 | 45 | 20 | 25 |
| 97 | 29 | 15 | 14 |
| 98 | 49 | 16 | 33 |
| 99 | 21 | 6 | 15 |
| 100 and over | 230 | 65 | 165 |

The males were in excess of the females at 81, 83 and 85, and of equal number at 89. The whole number of this class in the United States was 149,252 (68,250 males, 81,002 females); so Virginia had .044 per cent. of all. Of the population of the United States, .003 per cent. belonged to this class of persons over 80, while Virginia had over .005 per cent. of her population in it.

The Blind Population of Virginia was, in 1870, as follows:

| | | | |
|---|---|---|---|
| Males | 455 | Black males | 175 |
| Females | 440 | Black females | 192 |
| White males | 272 | Mulatto males | 8 |
| White females | 214 | Mulatto females | 34 |
| Total whites | 486. | Total negroes | 409 |
| | | Aggregate | 895 |

These were all natives of the United States but 18 males and 2 females, white, who were born in Great Britain and Ireland (14 of them in Ireland, 13 males); all the rest were born in Virginia and West Virginia, except 7 whites and 2 negroes in Maryland, 1 white in Massachusetts, 2 in New York, 1 in Ohio, 5 in Pennsylvania, 3 in Tennessee, 1 in Vermont, 3 in the District of Columbia, and 9 whites and 4 blacks in North Carolina.

The proportion of this unfortunate class to the whole population was .0007 per cent.; in the whole United States it was .0005. The number in Virginia over the average is readily explained. Her excellent Institution—a State charity—for this class brings them to the State to be educated. (See Education).

Forty blind attended that Institution in 1872–'3. The ages of the blind of all classes were: 1 under 1 year; 12 from 1 to 5; 29 from 5 to 10; 55 from 10 to 15; 46 from 15 to 20; 89 from 20 to 30; 73 from 30 to 40; 100 from 40 to 50; 91 from 50 to 60; 119 from 60 to 70; 148 from 70 to 80; 85 from 80 to 90; 35 from 90 to 100, and 11 over 100. The State has made most liberal provision for the education of all the young blind, whether rich or poor, belonging to it.

The Deaf-Mute Population of Virginia in 1870 was—

| | | | |
|---|---|---|---|
| Aggregate | 534 | Black males | 65 |
| | — | Black females | 52 |
| Males | 298 | Mulatto males | 10 |
| Females | 236 | Mulatto females | 6 |
| White males | 223 | Total negroes | 133 |
| White females | 178 | | —— |
| Total whites | 401 | Total in United States | 16,205 |

These were all natives of the United States, except one male and one female born in Ireland, and all born in Virginia or West Virginia, except 1 white in Alabama, 1 in Louisiana, 4 in Maryland, 1 in Mississippi, 2 in North Carolina, 1 in Pennsylvania, 1 in Tennessee, and 1 mulatto in Maryland. Provision is also made for the education and training of this class of unfortunates by Virginia. (See Education). The ages of the deaf and dumb were: 14 from 1 to 5 years; 41 from 5 to 10; 106 from 10 to 15; 75 from 15 to 20; 116 from 20 to 30; 73 from 30 to 40; 51 from 40 to 50; 24 from 50 to 60; 21 from 60 to 70; 12 from 70 to 80; and 1 between 90 and 100. Eighty deaf-mutes attended the State Institution in 1872–'3.

The Idiotic Population of Virginia in 1870 was—

| | | | |
|---|---|---|---|
| Males | 691 | Black males | 212 |
| Females | 439 | Black females | 131 |
| White males | 428 | Mulatto males | 51 |
| White females | 280 | Mulatto females | 28 |
| Total white | 708 | Negroes—total | 422 |
| | | Aggregate | 1,130 |

These were all born in the United States but 1 white male from Australia, and the rest in the State and West Virginia, except 2 from Kentucky, 2 white and 3 black from Maryland, 1 from Missouri, 1 from New Jersey, 2 from New York, 14 white and 2 black from North Carolina, 5 from Tennessee, 1 from Texas and 1 from the District of Columbia.

No provision has been made for this class in Virginia, but there are private institutions for training them in the United States.

The Insane in Virginia in 1870 were—

| | | | |
|---|---|---|---|
| Aggregate | 1,125 | Black males | 99 |
| | —— | Black females | 117 |
| Males | 595 | Mulatto males | 20 |
| Females | 530 | Mulatto females | 20 |
| White males | 475 | Total negroes | 256 |
| White females | 393 | Indian males | 1 |
| Total white | 868 | Insane in United States | 37,432 |

Of these, 17 white males and 1 female were born in foreign countries (6 males and 5 females in Germany, and 11 males and 1 female in Great Britain and Ireland). Of the natives 2 were born in Alabama, 1 in Indiana, 4 whites and 1 black in Maryland, 1 each in Missouri, New York, Pennsylvania and South Carolina, 4 in North Carolina, 7 in Tennessee; all others were born in Virginia and West Virginia. Two of the insane were under 5 years old; 1 from 5 to 10; 24 from 10 to 15; 46 from 15 to 20; 216 from 20 to 30; 230 from 30 to 40; 246 from 40 to 50; 174 from 50 to 60; 108 from 60 to 70; 53 from 70 to 80; 21 from 80 to 90; 3 from 90 to 100, and 1 over 100.

The Commonwealth of Virginia has made liberal provision for this class of her people.

The *Eastern Lunatic Asylum* of Virginia, at Williamsburg, in Tidewater, the oldest institution of the kind in America, has been in existence over 100 years. This asylum treated 311 patients in 1873. Of the 62 admitted that year for the first time, 17 died and 21 were discharged recovered. The report of the superintendent for the year ending September 30th, 1875, states that at that time there were 305 patients in this asylum (140 males and 164 females). Eight of these paid in full and five in part for their support, while 292 were cared for by the State. Of the 33 discharged, over 71 per cent. were cured. The deaths among those under treatment were 5.1 per cent. This asylum has a farm, garden and work shops attached.

The *Western Lunatic Asylum* at Staunton, in the Valley, has been in operation 45 years. This asylum treated 449 patients in 1872 and '3. There were admitted in the 2 years 107; discharged recovered 68, and 38 died. From the opening of this asylum in 1828, to September 30th, 1875, it had treated 2,614 (1,549 males and 1,065 females), of which 1,125 were discharged as cured of insanity, 240 as improved, 155 as not improved, while 738 died and 356 remained. The percentage of recoveries to admissions was 43.03 (41.58 of males and 45.16 of females). The deaths in 1875 were but 4 per cent. of the patients.

The *Central Lunatic Asylum*, at Richmond, is the first one established in America *for the colored people exclusively*. In 1872–'3 there were treated there 250 patients; 35 were discharged and 21 died.

All these great charities are well conducted and compare favorably with the best.

The census of 1870 gives the number of persons born in each month of that census year and surviving at the end of the year, with the following results for Virginia:

| When Born. | Number Born. | | | |
|---|---|---|---|---|
| 1869—June | 423 | | | |
| July | 1,101 | 3,479 | | |
| August | 1,955 | | 11,713 | |
| September | 2,576 | | | |
| October | 2,805 | 8,234 | | |
| November | 2,853 | | | 35,802 for the year. |
| December | 3,955 | | | |
| 1870—January | 3,611 | 11,388 | | |
| February | 3,822 | | 24,089 | |
| March | 4,152 | | | |
| April | 4,254 | 12,701 | | |
| May | 4,295 | | | |

It appears from this tabulation that of the vigorous children begotten in Virginia the month of May produced the most, nearly 12 per cent. of all, and June the least, or about 1.1 per cent. Considering the production by seasons, spring had over 35 per cent. of the year's product, while summer had but about 9. More than half the births of the "surviving" infants occurred in winter and spring. It seems that in Connecticut and Massachusetts May is *the* birth-month, as in Virginia, while in Maine, Ohio and Missouri it is in March.

In the last 9 months 32,324 were born; the number in 1860, for the year, was 35,244. The number of living persons in the State to each one of these that survived was 34.22 in 1870 and 34.61 in 1860.

By table IX there were 2,922 in the 100,000 of the population of Virginia in 1870 that were under 1 year old. The proportion for the United States was 2,854; for England and Wales in 1861 it was 2,959; for France (1861), 2,169; for Italy (1861), 3,319; for Norway, 3,042. The *observed* number for the United States is given; but the adjusted number is 3,212, in which proportion the Virginia number would be 3,288—a most favorable showing for the State. The same comparison could be made for other ages.

**Population of the Cities and Towns of Virginia** *containing over* 1,000 *inhabitants in* 1870.

The cities in the following table (XIII) are assigned to Tidewater, because they are mostly commercial ones, although some of them belong to Middle Virginia counties and have most of their territory in that section.

Table XIII.

| | CITY. | COUNTY. | AGGREGATE. | | WHITE. | | NEGRO. | | NATIVE. | FOR'GN. |
|---|---|---|---|---|---|---|---|---|---|---|
| | | | 1860. | 1870. | 1860. | 1870. | 1860. | 1870. | 1870. | 1870. |
| Middle and Tidewater. | Richmond...... | Henrico..... | 37,907 | 51,038 | 23,632 | 27,928 | 14,275 | 23,110 | 47,260 | 3,778 |
| | Petersburg..... | Dinwiddie... | 18,266 | 18,505 | 9,342 | 8,744 | 8,924 | 10,185 | 18,505 | 445 |
| | Alexandria .... | Alexandria.. | 12,652 | 13,570 | 9,851 | 8,269 | 2,801 | 5,300 | 12,763 | 807 |
| | Fredericksburg | Spotsylvania | 5,022 | 4,046 | 3,309 | 2,715 | 1,713 | 1,331 | 3,867 | 179 |
| | Manchester.... | Chesterfield. | 2,793 | 2,599 | 1,828 | 1,517 | 965 | 1,082 | 2,559 | 40 |
| Tidewater. | Norfolk........ | Norfolk...... | 14,620 | 19,229 | 10,290 | 10,462 | 4,330 | 8,766 | 18,490 | 739 |
| | Portsmouth.... | Norfolk...... | 9,488 | 10,492 | 8,011 | 6,874 | 1,477 | 3,617 | 10,016 | 476 |
| | Hampton....... | Elizabeth C'y | 1,848 | 2,300 | 993 | 460 | 855 | 1,840 | 2,282 | 18 |
| | Williamsburg.. | James City.. | 2,732 | 1,392 | 974 | 893 | 137 | 499 | 1,340 | 52 |

The first group, located at the head of tide, at the lower falls of the rivers, and in two sections, are *manufacturing* as well as *commercial* cities. They *all* have a great supply of water power to turn machinery, and at the same time the advantage of the tides that float shipping to the very doors of the manufactories and open the way for commerce. No places can be more favorably situated for these purposes, having communications inland to the sources of supply of raw material and being in a climate where frost rarely clogs the wheels of machinery or closes the water-ways of navigation. Richmond and Manchester are really but one city, separated by the James river, which is spanned by several bridges.

The second group includes the purely commercial cities of the State. Norfolk and Portsmouth are in reality but one—they have the same harbor; they are most favorably located for commerce, having a harbor that is deep, commodious, land-locked, always accessible, at the sea, and yet so far inland that they have 10 hours advantage over most others in nearness to the Great West.

A study of the tables will give the character of the population; it is rarely that cities have so few foreigners. Richmond and Petersburg are largely engaged in the manufacture of tobacco, and as most of the labor employed in that important and valuable industry is negro, so those cities have a large number of that class in their population.

In Middle Virginia proper the towns of any size are few—it is a planting region; but, as before stated, it has a claim to all the first group just given; it also has an interest in Lynchburg on its Piedmont border.

## Table XIV.

*Cities and Towns of Middle Virginia.*

| TOWN. | COUNTY. | AGGREGATE. | | WHITES. | | BLACKS. | | NATIVES. | FOREIGN. |
|---|---|---|---|---|---|---|---|---|---|
| | | 1860. | 1870. | 1860. | 1870. | 1860. | 1870. | 1870. | 1870. |
| Danville........ | Pittsylvania... | ......... | 3,463 | ........ | 1,398 | ......... | 2,065 | 3,433 | 30 |
| Farmville...... | Prince Edward | 1,536 | 1,543 | 683 | 598 | 853 | 945 | 1,518 | 25 |

Danville is an important tobacco manufacturing city.

The Piedmont cities and towns are subjoined in Table XV of Population:

| CITY, &c. | COUNTY. | AGGREGATE. | | WHITE. | | NEGRO. | | NATIVE. | FOREIGN. |
|---|---|---|---|---|---|---|---|---|---|
| | | 1860. | 1870. | 1860. | 1870. | 1860. | 1870. | 1870. | 1870. |
| Lynchburg..... | Campbell...... | 6,853 | 6,825 | 3,802 | 3,472 | 3,051 | 3,353 | 6,554 | 271 |
| Charlottesville. | Albemarle..... | * | 2,838 | * | 1,365 | * | 1,473 | 2,748 | 90 |
| Culpeper....... | Culpeper...... | 1,056 | 1,800 | 519 | 1,000 | 537 | 800 | 1,740 | 60 |
| Warrenton .... | Fauquier...... | 604 | 1,256 | 564 | 704 | 40 | 552 | 1,214 | 42 |
| Liberty ........ | Bedford....... | 722 | 1,208 | 399 | 519 | 323 | 689 | 1,202 | 6 |
| Leesburg ...... | Loudoun...... | † | 1,144 | 1,083 | 791 | † | 353 | 1,134 | 10 |

As before stated, Lynchburg belongs to both Middle and Piedmont; it is largely engaged in tobacco manufacture, and therefore employs a large negro population. Charlottesville is the seat of the University of Virginia.

The next table (XVI) presents the *Cities and Towns of the Valley:*

| CITY, &c. | COUNTY. | AGGREGATE. | | WHITES. | | NEGROES. | | NATIVE. | FOREIGN. |
|---|---|---|---|---|---|---|---|---|---|
| | | 1860. | 1870. | 1860. | 1870. | 1860. | 1870. | 1870. | 1870. |
| Staunton ...... | Augusta....... | 3,875 | 5,120 | 2,865 | 3,585 | 1,010 | 1,535 | 4,895 | 225 |
| Winchester.... | Frederick..... | 4,392 | 4,477 | 3,004 | 3,100 | 1,388 | 1,377 | 4,375 | 102 |
| Lexington...... | Rockbridge.... | 2,135 | 2,873 | 1,438 | 1,982 | 697 | 891 | 2,810 | 63 |
| Harrisonburg.. | Rockingham... | † | 2,036 | 1,023 | 1,409 | † | 627 | 1,978 | 58 |
| Wytheville..... | Wythe......... | 1,111 | †1,671 | 1,069 | 1,198 | 42 | 473 | 1,635 | 36 |
| Salem.......... | Roanoke ...... | 612 | 1,355 | §590 | 855 | §22 | 500 | 1,346 | 9 |

All these towns have of late increased in population. Staunton is reckoned a city in the State organizations; it owes much of its prosperity to the 3 female colleges and 2 State asylums there located.

Harrisonburg, Winchester, and Wytheville are county towns of large counties. Lexington is the seat of Washington and Lee University and the Virginia Military

* No census. † Blacks not separated. ‡ 3 Indians included. § Does not include all the blacks.

Institute, making it an important town. Salem is the seat of Roanoke College. In all these towns the white population exceeds the negro.

The Appalachian country and Blue Ridge are pastoral regions, having no towns of any size.

PAUPERISM *and* CRIME.

The census of 1870 gives the statistics of these two social evils, with the following figures, for Virginia:

| | | | |
|---|---|---|---|
| Population | 1,225,163 | Number supported by public charity in the year | 3,890 |
| Whites | 712,089 | Cost of supporting | $303,081 |
| Negroes | 512,841 | Cost of each (average) | $77.91 |
| Natives | 1,211,409 | Number receiving support June 1, 1870 | 3,280 |
| Foreigners | 13.754 | Natives (whites 3,254, negroes 1,912)... | 3,254 |
| | | Foreigners | 26 |

These statistics show that only some 317 in each 10,000 of the inhabitants were under the necessity of asking for public charity—a very small proportion when contrasted with other states, and proving how abundant are the means of livelihood and how small a burden is laid upon the tax payers for the support of paupers. Beggary is almost entirely unknown. The cost of pauperism is only 24 cents to each of the population.

The tables of crime show that there were only 1,090 convictions during the year, or less than 9 for each 10,000 of the population. On the 1st of June there were in all the prisons of the State 1,244 prisoners; of these 1,232 were natives (331 whites and 901 negroes); 12 were foreigners—so that only 10 in 10,000 were held in jails or prisons. Of course many of these were for minor offences and persons awaiting trial.

These facts indicate that in Virginia there is an exceptional freedom from these too great national curses, an elevated and healthy condition of public morals and a general independence in living.

The report of the Superintendent of the Virginia Penitentiary—*the only prison in the State*—for 1872-'3, shows that only 216 persons were committed to it during that year; 33 of these were whites and 181 were negroes. This is only about 1 in 5,000 of the population. Only 54 of these were committed for crimes against the person. The remaining 162 were for crimes against property; 10 for petit larceny, the second offence; 36 for house-breaking; 13 for house-breaking and larceny; 26 for burglary; 39 for grand larceny; 10 for felony; 10 for murder in the second degree (*none* in the first degree); 1 for unlawful voting; 3 for obtaining goods under false pretences; 15 for rape and attempt at rape.

The whole number confined in the Penitentiary for the same time was 759, of which 150 were whites and 609 negroes. Virginia punishes with imprisonment for a number of offences that in other states are accounted among minor delinquencies; her laws are very stringent for all offences against the person, even debarring from the rights of citizenship those that act as seconds in duels, as well as the principals, even when no fatal results follow.

These facts, taken in connection with the statement that the State has a territory of 45,000 square miles, one and a fourth million people, and a city with sixty thousand inhabitants, speak volumes for the moral condition of the body politic in Virginia. Taine says: "the aim of every society is that each one should be always his own constable, and end by not having any other." Virginia can claim as near an approach to this as any known country.

# CHAPTER VIII.

## RELIGIOUS ADVANTAGES.

In proportion to its population, there is no portion of the United States* better supplied with church organizations and churches than Virginia, and in none is there a more "generous provision for the ordinances of the gospel," a more able and zealous ministry, or a more conscientious observance of religious duties, including the consecration of the Sabbath.

The following table gives the census returns of all the denominations in the State:

Table I.

| | 1870. | | | | 1860. | | |
|---|---|---|---|---|---|---|---|
| | Organizations. | Edifices. | Sittings. | Property. | Churches. | Accommodations. | Property. |
| Methodists (Episcopal) | 1,011 | 901 | 270,617 | $1,449,565 | 1,403 | 438,244 | $1,619,010 |
| Baptists (Regular) | 795 | 749 | 240,075 | 1,279,648 | 787 | 298,029 | 1,243,505 |
| Baptists (other) | 54 | 44 | 16,755 | 66,000 | 41 | 19,475 | 38,925 |
| Presbyterians (Regular) | 204 | 200 | 70,065 | 837,450 | 290 | 117,304 | 901,020 |
| Presbyterians (other) | ...... | ....... | ......... | ........... | 10 | 3,100 | 20,075 |
| Episcopal (Protestant) | 185 | 177 | 60,105 | 843,210 | 188 | 68,493 | 873,120 |
| Christian | 100 | 68 | 29,225 | 92,170 | 73 | 24,085 | 72,500 |
| Lutheran | 80 | 73 | 25,350 | 160,800 | 69 | 24,675 | 156,000 |
| United Brethren in Christ | 42 | 30 | 7,700 | 23,300 | ....... | .......... | .......... |
| Reformed Church in U. S. (German) | 24 | 16 | 5,900 | 38,500 | 12 | 4,000 | 24,400 |
| Friends | 12 | 13 | 4,925 | 35,625 | 17 | 5,800 | 37,950 |
| Roman Catholic | 19 | 17 | 9,800 | 343,750 | 33 | 16,650 | 329,300 |
| Jewish | 8 | 7 | 1,890 | 35,300 | 3 | 700 | 10,500 |
| Reformed Church in America (Dutch) | 1 | 1 | 109 | 350 | ....... | .......... | .......... |
| Moravian (Unitas Fratrum) | 1 | 1 | 350 | 1,500 | 1 | 350 | 1,000 |
| New Jerusalem (Swedenborgian) | 3 | 3 | 550 | 2,200 | 1 | 100 | 500 |
| Universalists | ....... | ....... | ......... | ........... | 2 | 750 | 10,200 |
| Unknown (Local Missions) | 1 | 1 | 150 | 6,000 | ....... | .......... | .......... |
| Unknown (Union) | 42 | 64 | 21,570 | 62,600 | 175 | 46,080 | 121,000 |
| | 2,582 | 2,405 | 763,127 | $5,277,368 | 3,105 | 1,067,840 | $5,459,605 |

* See Plate XXXI of Statistical Atlas of the United States; also address of Dr. Hoge to Evangelical Alliance 1873.

In 1860 there were "accommodations" for over 87 per cent. of the entire population, and in 1870 for over 62 per cent. The average for the United States in 1860 was 69 per cent. There was in Virginia in 1860 a church to each 394 of the population, and in 1870 one for each 507. In New England in 1870 there was 1 church for 643 people. In the United States in 1860 there was a church to each 584. The sects in Virginia are not numerous when compared with other sections, and nearly all are included in 8 leading denominations. The most cordial relations exist between the different denominations, and they often unite their efforts in Christian labor. Sunday schools are diligently maintained by all for the religious instruction of the young, and the best talent in the churches is enlisted in their work. The clergy, with rare exceptions, confine themselves to the duties of their calling, or kindred work, the sentiment of the people being opposed to their taking part in politics, &c.

The census returns of 1860 and 1870 differ in their church statistics; the former give only the number of churches, making no distinction between organizations and churches; the latter give both, and show that nearly every organization in Virginia has a place for worship.

The leading denomination, it appears from these statistics, is the Methodist Episcopal, the American organization of the church of Wesley and his followers in England. This denomination has two colleges and numerous high schools in the State. The Baptists are second in number of sittings, and, like the Methodists, are widely and generally diffused throughout the State; they have a college and numerous high schools. The Presbyterians rank as the third; they claim descent from the Scotch church; one college, a Theological Seminary and many high schools are under their control. The fourth in order is the Protestant Episcopal, the American form of the Church of England, which was in Colonial times the established church in Virginia; a college, a Theological Seminary and numerous high schools pertain to this church. The table gives the details of the other religious bodies; only it should be stated that the Lutherans and Roman Catholics have each a college, and that nearly every denomination has excellent preparatory and high schools fostered by it.

The next table gives the distribution of the 8 leading denominations, all that are given by the census of 1870, in the grand divisions of the State.

## Table. II.

*Selected Statistics of Churches in Virginia in 1870.*

| | ALL DENOMINATIONS. | | | | Methodist Episcopal. | | Baptists. | | Presbyterian. | | Protestant Episcopal. | | Christian. | | Lutheran. | | United Brethren. | | German Reformed. | |
|---|---|---|---|---|---|---|---|---|---|---|---|---|---|---|---|---|---|---|---|---|
| | Organizations. | Edifices. | Sittings. | Property. | Organizations. | Sittings. | Organizations. | Sittings. | Organizations. | Sittings. | Organizations. | Sittings. | Organizations. | Sittings. | Organizations. | Sittings. | Organizations. | Sittings. | Organizations. | Sittings. |
| Tidewater.............. | 608 | 595 | 210,925 | $1,247,250 | 228 | 72,600 | 250 | 85,230 | 12 | 6,000 | 62 | 23,425 | 34 | 12,850 | 3 | 1,250 | ..... | ..... | ..... | ..... |
| Middle.................. | 627 | 617 | 193,860 | 1,447,443 | 223 | 64,830 | 228 | 74,080 | 77 | 24,750 | 55 | 16,150 | 22 | 6,675 | 1 | ..... | ..... | ..... | ..... | ..... |
| Piedmont.............. | 462 | 427 | 117,999 | 690,175 | 163 | 41,757 | 177 | 42,142 | 33 | 10,950 | 41 | 11,590 | 11 | 2,300 | 6 | 1,650 | ..... | ..... | 3 | 400 |
| Blue Ridge.............. | 77 | 60 | 17,618 | 24,200 | 39 | 6,650 | 33 | 9,118 | 2 | 800 | ..... | ..... | ..... | ..... | 2 | 700 | ..... | ..... | ..... | ..... |
| Valley.................. | 544 | 485 | 147,955 | 971,150 | 187 | 45,435 | 103 | 31,330 | 64 | 22,390 | 21 | 8,153 | 25 | 5,950 | 62 | 18,650 | 37 | 7,050 | 21 | 5,500 |
| Appalachia.............. | 264 | 221 | 68,770 | 152,150 | 168 | 39,345 | 58 | 14,950 | 16 | 5,175 | 3 | 800 | 8 | 1,450 | 6 | 3,100 | 1 | 400 | ..... | ..... |
| Total.......... | 2,582 | 2.405 | 757,127 | $4,532,368 | 1,010 | 270,270 | 849 | 256,850 | 204 | 69.265 | 85 | 60,105 | 100 | 29,225 | 80 | 25,350 | 38 | 7,450 | 24 | 5,500 |

The Methodists and Baptists are found in all parts of the State, the Methodists predominating in the Valley and Appalachia, and the Baptists in the Tidewater and Middle divisions. The Presbyterians have their greatest strength in Middle, Piedmont and Valley, especially in the central part of Middle and in most parts of the Valley, excepting the central portion of the Shenandoah Valley, where the population is of German origin and where the German Reformed, Lutheran and United Brethren churches are found. Much of the Valley was settled by Scotch, and there the Presbyterian churches are most numerous.

The *Protestant Episcopal* church has its greatest numbers in Tidewater, Middle and Piedmont, the portions of the State first settled by Englishmen, and many of its church edifices are those that were erected in colonial times for the established church. This denomination generally has churches in all the larger towns of the State; the same is true of the Presbyterians. The other leading denominations are also found in these centres of population, but they also occupy every other portion of the field of Christian effort more thoroughly than these. The *Christian* denomination is somewhat Baptist in its peculiarities, but it is a distinct church; it is quite influential in Tidewater, Middle and Valley Virginia. The *Lutherans* are numerous in portions of the Valley, where the original population was of German origin; the *German Reformed* church is found in the same localities, as is also the *United Brethren* (which, from resemblances, may be called the German Methodist church). The *Roman Catholic* churches are found in the large towns and cities, as a general rule.

The Friends have a number of churches, mostly in the northeast part of the State and in Richmond. Jewish synagogues are found in the large cities.

The Constitution* of the State—the *supreme* law, Article V, Section 14—provides that "No man shall be compelled to frequent or support any religious worship, place or ministry whatsoever, nor shall any man be enforced, restrained, molested or burthened in his body or goods, or otherwise suffer, on account of his religious opinions or belief; but all men shall be free to profess, and by argument to maintain their opinions in matters of religion, and the same shall in no wise affect, diminish or enlarge their civil capacities. And the General Assembly shall not prescribe any religious test whatever or confer any peculiar privileges or advantages on any sect or denomination, or pass any law requiring or authorizing any religious society or the people of any district within this Commonwealth to levy on themselves or others any tax for the erection or repair of any house of public worship, or for the support of any church or ministry, but it shall be left free to every person to select his religious instructor, and to make for his support such private contract as he shall please."

Article XI, Section [illegible], of the same constitution, secures to ecclesiastical bodies the right to all church property regularly conveyed to them.

Clause 18 of the Bill of Rights, a portion of the organic law, declares "That religion or the duty which we owe to our Creator, and the manner of discharging it, can be directed only by reason and conviction, not by force or violence; and, therefore, all men are equally entitled to the free exercise of religion according to the dictates of conscience; and that it is the mutual duty of all to practice Christian forbearance, love and charity towards each other."

Thus it will be seen that *the State has nothing whatever to do with religious matters, except to see that every man is left entirely free to follow the dictates of his own conscience and to secure to religious bodies their rights in such property as they have properly obtained* for church purposes.

---

*Code of 1873, page 82.

## CHAPTER IX.

### Provision for Education.

Through public and private liberality the most ample provision is made in Virginia for the education, both primary and advanced, of all the children of her people; and it may be stated, as an established fact, than an education, be it the simplest or the fullest, is within the reach of any one in the State that has the desire and the mental capacity to obtain it.

There are in Virginia, as in all countries where the benefits of a thorough education are understood, two systems of schools, *public* and *private;* the first supervised and provided for, wholly or in part, by the State; the second controlled and sustained by private enterprise, acting in individual or corporate capacity.

### Section I.

The Public School System of Virginia provides for instruction—

1st. *Primary*, in Public Free Schools.

2nd. *Intermediate*, in Graded and High Schools, which are also free.

3rd. *Advanced*, in the Military Institute, the Agricultural and Mechanical College and the Normal and Agricultural Institute.

4th. *Higher*, in the University of Virginia, with its literary, scientific, technical and professional schools.

In all these provision is made for the free, or comparatively free, instruction of the whole or of a portion of the youth of the Commonwealth.

### Primary and Intermediate Instruction.

The* Public Free School System of the State, that has for its object the primary and intermediate instrnction, *free* of direct charge, of all persons residing in the State between the ages of 5 and 21, completed the fifth year of its existence on the 1st of September, 1875, and it is conceded, by those most capable of judging, that it is one of the best managed and most efficient, all things considered, in this country of public free schools.

*Organization.*—The system is in charge of a Board of Education, composed of the Governor of the State, the Attorney General and the Superintendent of Public Instruction, the latter being the Executive officer of the System.

* In this educational summary free use is made of the able and exhaustive annual reports of Dr. Ruffner, the State Superintendent of Public Instruction.

The 99 counties of the State form 87* divisions, each having a county Superintendent of Schools, who has the general charge of the system for his county; there are also 6 cities that have Superintendents of Schools.

The counties of the State are subdivided into townships, some 454 in number, each of which constitutes a School District, and has a Board of three Trustees, charged with the local control of the system and its property, under the supervision of the County Superintendent.

It is evident that ample provision is here made for thorough supervision and at moderate expense, as only the Superintendents are salaried. The Trustees provide the place and name the teacher; the County Superintendent examines, and, if found capable, commissions the teacher, and then sees that his duties are properly discharged.

The only requisite for admission to the schools is the proper age and that the father, if alive and resident in the school district, and not a pauper, shall have paid the capitation tax, about one dollar, for the current year, this tax going to the school fund.

The *system is supported* by—1st, a capitation tax on every male citizen 21 years old and over, that may not exceed one dollar per capita; 2d, the annual interest of a fund belonging to the State, and known as the Literary Fund; 3d, an annual tax, on all the property in the State, that may not be less than 1-10th or more than ½ of one per cent.; and, 4th, any school district may levy an additional tax, but no tax to exceed ⅛ of one per cent. in a year.

*The Results of the Free School System.*

The following condensed table, showing the condition of the system for each of the five years that it has been in operation, gives a good idea of what is here done for primary and intermediate education:

| | 1871. | 1872. | 1873. | 1874. | 1875.* |
|---|---|---|---|---|---|
| Number of public schools | 3,047 | 3,695 | 3,696 | 3,902 | 4,185* |
| Number of graded schools | 0 | 107 | 123 | 155 | 155 |
| Number of pupils enrolled | 131,088 | 166,377 | 160,859 | 173,875 | 184,486 |
| Pupils in average daily attendance | 75,722 | 95,488 | 91,175 | 98,857 | 103,927 |
| Percentage of school population enrolled | 31.8 | 40.5 | 37.9 | 39.8 | 38.2 |
| Percentage of school population in average daily attendance | 18.8 | 23.2 | 21.5 | 22.6 | 21.5 |
| Number of teachers employed in public schools | 3,084 | 3,853 | 3,757 | 3,962 | 4,262 |
| Number of school-houses owned by districts | 190 | 504 | 764 | 1,031 | 1,256 |
| Value of public school property | $211.166 | $389,380 | $524,638 | $682,500 | $757,181 |
| Average number of months schools in session | 4.66 | 5.72 | 5.22 | 5.40 | 5.59 |
| Cost of tuition per month per enrolled pupil | $ 0.74 | $ 0.70 | $ 0.75 | $ 0.74 | $ 0.70 |
| Average monthly salary of teachers | $29.86 | $29.81 | $32 00 | $32.64 | $30.48 |
| Whole cost of public education for current expenses | $597,472 | $816,812 | $814,494 | $873,145 | $924.118 |

* Two counties in some cases having but one Superintendent.

*School Population.*—The school population embraces all persons between five and twenty-one years of age, and all these may attend the schools if they desire to. In 1872 the average age of those that actually attended was from 10 to 13.

School population of Virginia, 1873:

| | | | |
|---|---|---|---|
| White | Males 128,967 | Females 124,444 | 353,411 |
| Colored | Males 87,399 | Females 83,297 | 170,696 |
| Aggregate | | | 424,107 |

The table before given shows that 160,859 of these were enrolled for attendance—that is, indicated that they would attend, and did so, probably, with more or less regularity, they formed 37.9 per cent. of the school population; a large proportion when the ages it includes are regarded: 91,175 were in average attendance during the 5.22 months of the session for the year, or 21.5 per cent. of the school population; largely over one-fifth, showing that good use is made of the advantages so freely offered.

The school population of 1875* was:

| | | |
|---|---|---|
| White | 280,149 | 482,789. |
| Colored | 202,640 | |

The preceding table furnishes the details of enrollment, &c.

The public schools of Virginia have derived much advantage from asssistance rendered from the "Peabody Education Fund," through its able, efficient and sympathetic General Agent, Dr. Barnas Sears, who, in his annual report to the Trustees of that fund, in 1875, says, "The Public Schools of Virginia are constantly improving in character and increasing in number. The attendance is about ten thousand greater than it was last year. In a short time it may be expected that all the smaller and more remote country districts will feel their beneficent influence. The system of public instruction seems to be well grounded in the general sentiment of the people."

In 1875 there was contributed to Public Education in Virginia from the Peabody Education Fund $23,750, in aid of graded schools, teachers' institutes, and the Virginia Educational Journal.

---

*In 1875 there were in Virginia 99 counties, 6 cities of the first class and 4 of the second; 89 county and 8 city superintendents of schools, 458 school districts, 1,371 school trustees, and 444 school district boards. The white public schools were 3,121 in number, and the colored 1,064. In cities the schools were taught 9.69 and in the country 5.42 months, on an average, during the year. The enrolled pupils were 129,545 white and 54,941 colored. There were 74,056 white and 29,871 colored pupils in average daily attendance. Of the school population, 46.2 per cent. of the white and 27.1 per cent. of the colored were enrolled. The average cost of tuition was 70 cents, currency, a month to the enrolled pupil. The teachers were 3,723 white (2,360 males and 1,363 females), and 539 colored (351 males and 188 females).

The *private schools* of the State were attended by 23,285 pupils (19,466 white and 3,819 colored), taught by 1,229 white (454 males and 775 females), and 90 colored (33 males and 57 females) teachers.

There were in the colleges of the State 1,830 white students.

The entire school attendance in Virginia in 1875 was 207,771 pupils (149,011 white and 58,760 colored), or about 16 per cent. of the population.

The following table presents the statistics of the Public free schools for the year ending August 31st, 1872, for the grand divisions of the State:

| | Number of Counties & Cities. | School Population between 5 and 21 years old. | | | | | | | Schools. | | | | Teachers. | | | | | | | | | | |
|---|---|---|---|---|---|---|---|---|---|---|---|---|---|---|---|---|---|---|---|---|---|---|---|
| | | White. | | | Colored. | | | Total White and Colored. | | | | | White. | | | Colored. | | | Average white and colored. | Average Monthly Salaries.—(Dollars). From all sources. | | | |
| | | Male. | Female. | Total. | Male. | Female. | Total. | | White. | Colored. | Total. | Average months taught. | Male. | Female. | Total. | Male. | Female. | Total. | | Of males. | Of females. | Total. | Total from public funds. |
| Tidewater ............... | 33 | 28,644 | 17,062 | 49,815 | 27,823 | 37,035 | 55,865 | 109,497 | 487 | 260 | 747 | 6.00 | 422 | 223 | 664 | 71 | 52 | 123 | 787 | 32.13 | 23.33 | 29.45 | 29.07 |
| Middle .................... | 28 | 25,147 | 24,495 | 55,671 | 30,836 | 28,770 | 50,213 | 113,396 | 565 | 313 | 897 | 5.77 | 521 | 378 | 893 | 49 | 35 | 84 | 975 | 34.76 | 26.72 | 30.67 | 27.39 |
| Piedmont ................. | 14 | 21,460 | 19,868 | 41,364 | 14,174 | 13,631 | 28,599 | 61,199 | 470 | 158 | 638 | 5.51 | 436 | 172 | 608 | 35 | 14 | 49 | 657 | 30.52 | 26.76 | 29.13 | 28.08 |
| Blue Ridge ............... | 3 | 5,541 | 5,241 | 10,782 | 413 | 383 | 796 | 11,678 | 128 | 6 | 134 | 5.56 | 116 | 21 | 137 | 4 | .... | 4 | 141 | 22.57 | 20.77 | 22.41 | 19.81 |
| Valley ...................... | 15 | 29,248 | 27,555 | 54,764 | 5,368 | 6,323 | 13,094 | 69,868 | 833 | 91 | 818 | 5.27 | 607 | 210 | 816 | 52 | 33 | 83 | 873 | 32.97 | 32.24 | 31.78 | 26.80 |
| Appalachia ............... | 12 | 14,909 | 13,886 | 26,834 | 1,417 | 1,265 | 3,792 | 31,526 | 365 | 15 | 370 | 4.40 | 314 | 46 | 360 | 11 | 1 | 12 | 872 | 27.71 | 24.64 | 27.59 | 23.88 |
| | 105 | ........ | ........ | 247,002 | ........ | ........ | 164,019 | 411,021 | 2,788 | 907 | 3,695 | 5.72 | 2,946 | 1,147 | 3,493 | 224 | 136 | 360 | 3,853 | $30.58 | $28.25 | $29.81 | ...... |

*Totally distinct and separate* schools are provided for the white and for the colored children; the law requires that that they *shall not be mixed*.

*What is Taught.*—*In all* the primary schools are taught orthography, reading, writing, arithmetic, geography and English grammar; in some, other branches are also learned. In the *graded schools* provision is made for *intermediate* instruction, the pupil being advanced from grade to grade upon examinations; and in the higher grades are taught the sciences, languages, &c., &c., furnishing a preparation for college or university.

In 1872 there were 106 graded schools in operation, and in 1873 the number was 123, showing that the tendency is to improve the character of the schools.

The report for 1873 gives the following facts in regard to the *school houses* and *aids to instruction*, viz:

Of the 3,421 in use, 1,914 were built of logs (the usual comfortable pioneer building material in America); 1,329 were frame, 143 were brick, and 28 were of stone; 2,732 had grounds attached, 1,287 had good furniture, 167 were provided with wall maps, 85 with globes, 106 with reading charts, 95 with arithmetical charts, and 2,180 with black boards; 315 new school houses were built during the year. It is evident that the day is not distant when there will be in every neighborhood a well taught and well provided public free school. In fact the Constitution of the State provides that "a uniform system of public free schools" shall be fully introduced into all the counties of the State "by the year 1876 or as much earlier as practicable." It is proper to add that these schools are greatly assisted by donations from the "Peabody Education Fund," and also that they are patronized by all classes of citizens.

*Advanced Instruction.*

The VIRGINIA MILITARY INSTITUTE, located at Lexington, Rockbridge County, in the Great Valley, has completed the 34th year of its existence, and deservedly stands at the head of the State Institutions for *advanced* instruction. This is a

THE VIRGINIA MILITARY INSTITUTE, LEXINGTON, VA.

*military* and *scientific* school of a high grade, with the following Departments: (1) Mathematics; (2) Latin Language and English Literature; (3) Practical Engineering, Architecture and Drawing; (4) Animal and Vegetable Physiology, applied to Agriculture; (5) Infantry, Cavalry and Artillery Tactics, Military History and Strategy; (6) Natural and Experimental Philosophy; (7) Civil and Military Engineering and Applied Mechanics; (8) Practical Astronomy, Physics, Descriptive Geography and Geodesy; (9) Mineralogy, Geology and Metallurgy. These departments are in charge of 18 or more professors and assistants, with all needful appliances for illustration, &c. The organization is *strictly military*, the students are cadets, uniformed, divided into companies, officered, and drilled in the use of arms;

they perform all the duties of a soldier in camp, and are at all times subject to military laws and regulations; the professors are officers.

The Institute has proven itself a most valuable training school for army officers, and many of its graduates were distinguished during the late Confederate war; but it is as a *school of general and applied science* that it has a distinct place in the educational system of the State; it educates the civil and mining engineers, chemists, &c.—the skilled directors of practical industry.

Though a State institution, the Institute is open to all, and in 1872 the 139 students of Virginia met there 173 from other States, the very flower of their youth attracted by its reputation for discipline and training for active and professional life.

The Institute receives an annuity from the State, and in return furnishes *board and instruction, without charge*, annually to fifty young men, between the ages of 16 and 25, selected from every part of the Commonwealth. The State requires that these young men shall, after leaving the Institute, teach for not less than two years in the State: in this way it becomes an essential part of the public school system, giving advanced instruction and furnishing teachers of a high grade. The cost per year for a pay cadet is about $350.

THE VIRGINIA AGRICULTURAL AND MECHANICAL COLLEGE is located at Blacksburg, Montgomery county, in the southwest of the Great Valley. This is a new institution, opened for the first time in October, 1872, with five instructors and 132 students;* it is endowed by a donation of public lands from the General Government, and is designed as a school for the *advanced* training of the "industrial classes"—*for those that "handle tools."*

The course of instruction is as follows:

I. A *Literary Department*, in which are taught the English Language and Literature, the Ancient and the Modern Languages, and Moral Philosophy.

II. A *Scientific Department*, in which Mathematics, Natural Philosophy, Chemistry, Mineralogy, Geology, Botany and Zoology are taught.

III. A *Technical Department*, for Agriculture and Mechanics.

The study of Ancient Languages is not obligatory; French or German is; the Moral Philosophy course is a short one; in the other subjects named the instruction is intended to be thorough and adapted to the wants of the trained and skilled agriculturest and machinist. The degrees conferred, upon examinations, are Graduate in Agriculture, or in Mechanics.

A farm of 245 acres is attached to this college, and on it practical instruction is given in Agriculture, and students have an opportunity for engaging in remunerative manual labor. Provision is also made for practical mechanical training. Military drill is also required, and to promote efficiency in this the students dress in uniform.

This institution, as part of the school system of the State, educates without charge for tuition, use of rooms, laboratories, &c., a number of students equal to the number of the members of the House of Delegates (138 at this time), selected by the school trustees of counties, &c. (the districts of the Delegates), "with reference to the highest proficiency and good character," "from the white male students

* 197 the next year, and 222 the third.

of the free schools," or others if the trustees elect. The expenses of these "State students," including uniform, are from $100 to $150 for the school year, which (owing to the character of the school) embraces all the year, except two months from Christmas. The expenses of a "pay student" are $45 more for the session.

The course of study adopted is intended for three years, and during all that time farm and work-shop labor of a certain amount are required.

The HAMPTON NORMAL AND AGRICULTURAL INSTITUTE is located at Hampton, in Elizabeth City county, in the Tidewater country, and is designed, as its charter states, "For the instruction of youth in the various common school, academic and collegiate branches, the best methods of teaching the same, and the best mode of practical industry in its application to agriculture and the mechanic arts."

This Institute is for the exclusive benefit and use of the colored people of the State, and subserves a most important end in providing an advanced education and industrial training for this large class of the population of the State, which furnishes so much of its manual labor. One-third of the proceeds of the land donated to the State for agricultural colleges was given to this school, and in return it annually receives, free of charge for tuition, rooms, &c., 100 colored youths, selected for intelligence and character, from the free schools of the State.

A large farm is attached to this school, and it has shops of several kinds and a printing office, where the pupils are trained to labor, and at the same time they contribute largely to their own support.

This school is most ably and successfully managed, and is furnishing a large number of good teachers to the colored schools of the State.

It now has over 100 of the colored youth, of both sexes, of Virginia under its care. The system followed gives four days of school and two of labor in each week to the student.

The enrollment of students in 1874–'75 was 245—all between 14 and 25 years of age, one-third females; Virginia sent 144 that were educated free of charge for tuition and worked out half of their personal expenses. The total charge for every thing but books and clothing is $10 a month. The students earned in the session $6,750, at from 5 to 10 cents an hour, for work on the farm, in shops, &c. The expenses per scholar for the year averaged $105.

The UNIVERSITY OF VIRGINIA is the worthy head of the State system of public instruction and supplies, in the fullest and best manner, the means for obtaining the *Higher Education.*

This institution, now in the fiftieth year of its existence, holding a foremost place among the Universities of America, is located near Charlottesville, Albemarle county, in the lovely Piedmont section of the State.

The system of instruction is by *independent schools* for all the chief branches of human learning, leaving the student free to select and attend such as are suited to his tastes or adapted to his proposed pursuits in life. This *elective system*, inaugurated,* at the opening of this University, for the first time in America, has been so fruitful in results that all the leading institutions of the country are now adopting it. It seems superflous to dilate upon the wisdom of a plan of teaching that en-

*By Thomas Jefferson.

ables each one to perfect himself in that he is best fitted for, gives him credit and honors for his success, and does not clog his course with studies that "edify not."

The *independent schools* of the University now in operation are—

I. In the *Literary and Scientific Department:* (1) Latin; (2) Greek; (3) Modern Languages; (4) Moral Philosophy; (5) History, General Literature and Rhetoric; (6) Mathematics; (7) Natural Philosophy; (8) General and Applied Chemistry; (9) Applied Mathematics, Engineering and Architecture; (10) Analytical and Agricultural Chemistry; (11) Natural History, Experimental and Practical Agriculture. II. The *Medical Department:* with schools (1) of Medicine; (2) of Physiology and Surgery; (3) of Anatomy, &c. III. The *Law Department:* with schools (1) of International and Constitutional Law; (2) of Statute and Common Law. And, IV. The *Agricultural Department.* Each has the sub-division into such schools as are demanded by the nature and present development of the subject.

UNIVERSITY OF VIRGINIA,* CHARLOTTESVILLE, VA.

Each of these schools is in charge of an able professor, who, with his assistants, instructs by lectures, text-books and daily examinations.

The University confers no honorary degrees but to those that prove by examinations, generally in writing, that they understand not only the general principles, but also the details of the subjects taught in the *schools*, or in any school, and *to such only* are awarded its honors and certificates of scholarship—*attainments*, not time or a round of studies, are considered. It results from this high standard of requirements that the certificates of the University of Virginia are everywhere accepted as evidences of substantial acquirements, and their possession opens the way to position and influence for their possessor.

The academic degrees conferred at the University are: (1) *Proficient*, (2) *Grad-*

*Copied by permission from Scribner's Magazine, New York.

*uate in a school*, (3) *Bachelor of Letters*, (4) *Bachelor of Science*, (5) *Bachelor of Arts*, and (6) *Master of Arts;* the professional degrees are: *Bachelor of Law*, *Doctor of Medicine*, *Civil Engineer*, *Mining Engineer*, and *Civil and Mining Engineer*.

The session is a continuous one of nine months—from October to July—and the expenses for the session are:

| | |
|---|---|
| For Academic students from - - - - | $261 to $351 |
| For Law students from - - - - - | $266 to $356 |
| For Engineering students from - - - - | $276 to $366 |
| For Medical students from - - - - | $296 to $386 |

As part of the system of public instruction in Virginia, the University draws an annuity from the State, and in return it educates, *without payment of matriculation or tuition fees or rent*, forty "meritorious young men of limited means," one from each senatorial district, for two years, the State requiring that these young men shall teach in some public or private school in Virginia for two years after leaving the University, the emoluments of such service enuring to their own benefit. This "aid" is worth from $120 to $150, and reduces the cost of attending the University to that extent. The University has some thirteen scholarships, open to all by competitive examinations, and it extends a credit of three years after leaving to any worthy students not able to pay on entering; no tuition fees are charged to needy young men, of any religious denomination, preparing for the ministry. Thus it is seen that provision is made by which the benefits of this great University, with all its extensive appliances for educational purposes, are placed within the reach of the humblest.

As this is a State institution, where there is no State church, there is here no established form of worship, but, by common consent, each of the four leading denominations in the State—Methodists, Baptists, Presbyterians and Episcopalians—in rotation, sends a chaplain to the University for a term of two years, who daily conducts worship in the chapel, at set times, which the students are free to attend if they think proper—there are no requirements made. Results show that in no institution is there a higher standard of Christian morality or more church members among the students in proportion to numbers.

The number of students for the session of 1872-'3 was 342, of whom 157 were from Virginia and the others from 22 different states; the number of instructors was 21. The number for 1873-'4 was 353, and for 1874-'5, 373. The graduates of the Law School can practice in any of the courts of the State without further license.

The general control of the University is confided to a Board of nine Visitors, appointed by the Governor of the State, serving 4 years—3 from Piedmont, 2 from Tidewater, 2 from the Valley and 2 from Appalachia. The Board elects one of its number Rector.

This is but a meagre outline of the plan and work of this great and in all respects amply provided University—the worthy and cherished head of Virginia's Educational System, and (in the language of its Board of Visitors for 1873-'4) "the Normal School of the South—the Educator of Southern Educators."

By a recent (1876) act of the General Assembly the State has granted an annuity to the University, "on condition that the said institution during its continuance shall educate all students of the State of Virginia over the age of eighteen who shall be matriculated under rules and regulations prescribed by the Board of Visitors, without charge for tuition in the academic* department." * * "*Provided*, that no person shall be admitted as a student free of charge for tuition fees, under the provisions of this act, unless the faculty shall be satisfied, by actual examination of the applicant or by a certificate of some college or preparatory school, that he has made such proficiency in the branches of study which he proposes to pursue as will enable him to avail himself of the advantages afforded by the University." The effect of this is to open the doors of the University, without fee for tuition, to every young man in the State, because the free high schools furnish the requisite preparatory education.

A recent writer,† speaking of this institution, says: "Jefferson planned the University, and it still retains the characteristics which he gave it. In the departments of languages, literature, science, law, medicine, agriculture, and engineering, it has to-day 18 distinct schools. For more than half a century it has been preeminent among the higher institutions of learning in the country, and Northern colleges and universities have borrowed from it the feature of an elective system of study. It has laterally established excellent agricultural and scientific schools, has a fine laboratory, with an extensive collection of raw and manufactured materials, and an experimental farm inferior to none in the country. The institution bestows no honorary degrees, and makes the attainment of its 'Master of Arts' so difficult, that it will serve as a certificate of scholarship anywhere. Nearly one hundred and fifty of the graduates of the several schools are now professors in other colleges. The University is by no means aristocratic in its tendencies; a large proportion of the students pay their expenses with money earned by themselves, and, since the war, there have been many 'State students' who are provided with gratuitous instruction. The alumni form an army fourteen thousand strong."

The Virginia *Institution for the Deaf, the Dumb and the Blind* is located at Staunton, Augusta county, in the middle of the Valley, and makes ample provision for the education of these unfortunates of her population. This educational and industrial school has been in successful operation for 33 years and is second to none in the country in its efficiency.

The 47 boys and 42 girls in the Deaf-mute department in 1873 were taught the ordinary English Branches, with history, moral science, drawing and painting and the use of the "sign" language. The 26 boys and 10 girls of the blind department were taught the higher mathematics, natural sciences, French and vocal and instrumental music, in addition to the English Branches, history, &c. The boys are trained in shoe, cabinet, chair, mattress, broom and mat-making; in carpentry, tailoring, printing and book-binding. The girls are taught sewing, knitting, fancy work, &c., and make clothes, bind shoes, &c. The course of training occupies six years, and the entire charge a year, for everything but clothing, is $200 for those able to pay, but everything is free to the indigent mute and blind children of the State.

---

*This includes all the schools of the Literary and Scientific Department, except (9) and (10), as before enumerated.

†Edward King, of New York, in "The Great South."

The following table presents, in a condensed form, the Statistics in the State Institutions of Learning of Advanced and Higher
27 Grades for the year ending August 31st, 1872:

| NAME. | LOCATION. | No. of Instructors. | STUDENTS. | | | Tuition per session. | Board per month. | *State Students.* | Volumes in library. | When organized. | Session begins. | Months of session each year. |
|---|---|---|---|---|---|---|---|---|---|---|---|---|
| | | | From Virginia. | From other States. | Total. | | | | | | | |
| University of Virginia | Piedmont | 21 | 165 | 200 | 365 | $75 | $15 | †40 | 35,000 | 1825 | October. | 9 |
| Virginia Military Institute | Valley | 28 | 139 | 173 | 312 | 100 | 15 | 50 | 4,000 | 1839 | Septem'r | 10 |
| *Virginia Agricultural and Mechanical College | Valley | 6 | 132 | ........ | 132 | 40 | 10 | ‡133 | .......... | 1872 | August. | 10 |
| ¶ Hampton Normal and Agricultural Institute | Tidewater | 10 | (?)133 | ....... | 133 | ........ | 8 | 100 | 1,200 | 1868 | Septem'r | 9 |
| § Deaf, Dumb and Blind Institution | Valley | 11 | 118 | 7 | 125 | § | ........ | ........ | 1,500 | 1839 | Septem'r | 10 |
| ‖ Emory and Henry College | Valley | 5 | 36 | 147 | 183 | 60 | 13 | 16 | 4,550 | 1838 | Septem'r | 10 |
| Total | | 91 | 723 | 527 | 1,250 | | | 344 | 46,550 | | | |

It will be seen by the above that the State has 344 scholarships in its gift in these higher institutions of learning. The table itself is suggestive. Virginia is the centre of higher education for the Southern and Southwestern states of the Union especially, but it attracts students from all directions.

*For 1873—not organized in 1872. †As many as there are senatorial districts. ‡As many as there are members of House of Delegates. §$200 covers all expenses; to the indigent, free. ‖Given here, though not a State institution, because it teaches 16 for the State without charge.

¶ This institution is not properly classified: it does not claim the position here given it.

## SECTION II.—THE PRIVATE AND CORPORATE SCHOOL SYSTEM OF VIRGINIA.

Like the public school system just treated of, this has—

1st. *Primary*—private, church, and endowed schools;

2nd. *Intermediate*—private, church, and endowed high schools;

3rd. *Advanced*—private, church, and endowed colleges, &c.;

4th. *Higher*—in endowed University and Professional schools.

There were in operation in the State, for the educational year 1871–'72, some 647 *primary schools* of this kind, 610 for white and 37 for colored children, attended by 8,884 whites and 1,476 blacks—10,320 in all, having an average length of session of 6.75 months, at an average charge of $1.90 per month for tuition. The number of teachers engaged was 715. Some of these schools belong to the different churches, but most of them are private enterprises. The schools are well conducted. It is likely that as the public free school system becomes general the number of these will be reduced.

The schools of this State for *Intermediate Instruction* are of a very high order, many of them comparing favorably, in all respects, with institutions that elsewhere rank as colleges.

The number of high schools in the State (and they are found in every portion of it) in 1871–'2 was 181, with 574 teachers and 7,491 pupils; the average length of the sessions was 8.33 months, and the rate of tuition averaged $4.91 per month.

The high schools for boys, most of them the result of private enterprise (although there are some endowed academies), will compare, as preparatory schools for College and University, most favorably with those of any country in the character and number of their teachers, their courses of study and the efficiency of their training. Some of these are boarding schools, kept at the country homes of the principals; others are day schools, in the larger villages and towns.

Some of these schools deserve special mention; no doubt some omitted are equally as worthy.

In Albemarle county are the *Verulam* and *Brookland* schools and the *Charlottesville Institute;* in Alexandria, *St. John's* and *Alexandria and Potomac* academies; in Bedford, the *Bellevue High School;* in Culpeper, the *Virginia High School;* in Augusta, the *Staunton Academy;* in Fairfax, the *Episcopal High School;* in Fauquier, the *Clifton* school and *Piedmont* and *Bethel* academies; in Frederick, the *Shenandoah Valley Academy;* in Hanover, the *Hanover Academy;* in Loudoun, *Leesburg Academy;* in Louisa, *Aspen Hall Academy;* in Madison, *Locust Dale Academy;* in Nelson, *Norwood College* and *Elmington Classical and Military School;* the *Norfolk Academy*, at Norfolk; *University School*, at Petersburg; the *University School, Richmond Male Academy, Shockoe Hill Academy, German High School*, and a half dozen others known by the names of their principals, at Richmond; *Fancy Hill Academy* and *Lexington Academy*, in Rockbridge county; *Fredericksburg Academy*, in Fredericksburg; the *Goodson* and *Abingdon* academies, in Washington county. In every portion of the State are academies and high schools, taught by graduates of the Universities, Colleges or Military Institute, in which boys are prepared for college. Many boys from other states attend these schools.

*Female Collegiate* education has been most amply provided for in Virginia by private and denominational schools. The numerous female colleges in the State are not only organized on nearly the same plans as the universities and colleges for males, but they are as liberally patronized from other states.

Of denominational female high schools that, in their buildings, courses of study, number and character of teachers, &c., deserve to rank as colleges, the following may be named (1871–'2):

The Presbyterians have five: the *Augusta Female Seminary*, at Staunton; *Ann Smith Academy*, at Lexington; *Stonewall Jackson Institute*, at Abingdon; *Leavenworth Seminary*, at Petersburg, and *Southside Institute*, at Danville.

The Baptists have three: the *Hollins Institute*, in Roanoke county; *Richmond Female College*, at Richmond, and *Roanoke Female College*, at Danville.

The Episcopalians have four: the *Virginia Female Institute*, at Staunton; the *Southern Female Institute*, at Richmond; the *Piedmont Female Institute*, at Charlottesville, and *St. Paul's Church School*, at Petersburg.

The Lutherans have the *Staunton Female Seminary*, at Staunton.

The Roman Catholics have three: *Monte Maria Academy* and *St. Joseph's Asylum*, at Richmond, and *St. Mary's Academy*, at Alexandria.

The Christians have a *Collegiate Institute* at Suffolk.

The Methodist Episcopal Church South has four: the *Wesleyan Female Institute*, at Staunton; *Martha Washington College*, at Abingdon; *Mountain View Seminary*, at Bristol, and *Danville Female College*, at Danville.

These 21 large and flourishing schools, situated in all parts of the State, most of them with large buildings, apparatus, &c., and with numerous teachers, provide fully for higher female education. Besides these, there are hundreds of smaller and more private female schools in the numerous villages, towns and cities of the State, many of them conducted by ladies of refined taste and cultivation.

THE COLLEGES for *advanced instruction* are all excellent institutions, well provided with buildings, apparatus and able professors; many of them are well endowed, and all offer special advantages to those in need of aid in obtaining a collegiate education.

The Superintendent of Public Instruction says, in his Report for 1872: "The denominational character of several of our colleges is no objection whatever. It is a blessed fact that all our higher institutions are earnestly Christian without any of them being narrow in their spirit. High culture is liberalizing in religion as in everything else. It is both natural and proper that the Christian people of the several denominations should establish and maintain colleges where the special influence shall be in harmony with their own religious sentiments."

WILLIAM AND MARY COLLEGE, at Williamsburg, James City county, under Protestant Episcopal influence, is the oldest collegiate institution in Virginia, dating from the time of England's sovereigns, William and Mary, who contributed to its endowment, and were honored by having it named for them. This is especially the college of the Tidewater Region. It stands high as a training school; its roll of alumni includes many of the most noted Americans of the last 180 years.

WILLIAM AND MARY COLLEGE, WILLIAMSBURG, VA.*

HAMPDEN SIDNEY COLLEGE, in Prince Edward county, Middle Virginia, a Presbyterian seat of learning, next in age, enjoys a high reputation as a training school for professional studies and business life. Its system is that of a curriculum: it has a President, who is professor of Moral Science, and Professors of Natural Science, of Latin and German, of Greek and French, and of Mathematics. This college is situated in the country, away from any town.

EMORY AND HENRY COLLEGE, a Methodist Episcopal institution, in Washington county, in the southwestern part of the Great Valley, is one of the two very flourishing colleges belonging to that leading denomination. This institution adheres to the curriculum method of training, and has the usual number of chairs found in all well conducted colleges. This institution receives annually, selected from all portions of the State, sixteen young men (not able to incur the expenses of a collegiate course) without charge for tuition, board or lodging, in return for a grant made it by the State; these young men are required to teach the same as the State students of the University or Military Institute.

RANDOLPH MACON COLLEGE, at Ashland, Hanover county (not far from Richmond city), is the other college under the care of the Methodist Episcopal church. The course of study is *elective*, and it has schools of Latin, Greek, English, French, German, Pure Mathematics, Applied Mathematics, Natural Science, Chemistry, Physiology and Hygiene, Moral Philosophy and Metaphysics, Biblical Literature and Oriental Languages; it also has a preparatory or introductory course in charge of the professors. This is a very flourishing and popular institution.

RICHMOND COLLEGE, at Richmond city, belongs to the Baptists. By the zeal and liberality of its friends, this institution has been most liberally provided for and placed in the front rank among Virginia colleges. Its organization is into eight independent, academic schools and a Law school—making its system an *elective* one, modeled after that of the University of Virginia. Its *schools* are: Greek, Latin, Modern Languages, English, Mathematics, Mechanics, Chemistry, Philosophy and Law. The student can, upon examination, graduate in any school or obtain the usual degrees by graduating in a required number of schools.

---

*Copied by permission from Scribner's Magazine, New York.

Roanoke College is a Lutheran institution, located at Salem, Roanoke county, in one of the most attractive portions of the Valley. Though one of the youngest colleges, it is one of the most flourishing. Its system is the regular college curriculum, its students being divided into Freshman, Sophomore, Junior and Senior classes for a four years' course of study; it has also a Normal course for teachers of public schools—a select one for a mere business education, and a Preparatory Department for training boys for the college classes.

St. John's College, at Norfolk, is a lately established Roman Catholic college, with a full corps of Professors.

The Union Theological Seminary, near Hampden Sidney college, is the divinity school of the Presbyterians. It is a well endowed and ably conducted professional school.

The Protestant Episcopal Theological Seminary, near Alexandria, is the flourishing and well ordered divinity school for training the clergy of the Episcopal church.

Colver Institute, in Richmond, is a theological school belonging to the colored Baptists.

The Virginia Medical College, at Richmond, is an excellent school of medicine, with two courses of lectures each year, and the usual professors found in well conducted institutions of its kind. It has a hospital attached, where its students are familiarized with the diseases of the country.

The Polytechnic School, at New Market, in the noted Shenandoah Valley, is a recently organized high school, with an advanced scientific course, designed for training farmers, mechanics, &c. It is quite flourishing.

The Commercial College, the Old Dominion Business College, the School of Telegraphy, and the Normal School, at Richmond, offer facilities for special training for accountants, telegraph operators, &c.

There is also a *colored* Normal School at Richmond; for *in no educational arrangements of any kind whatsoever, in Virginia, are the two races mixed or even sent to the same institutions.* Unless mention has been made to the contrary, all the institutions that have been spoken of are for white persons *exclusively;* full provision is made for the colored people, but, *in all cases,* it is for them alone.

Washington and Lee University, located at Lexington, in Rockbridge county, in the heart of the Great Valley, stands at the head of the institutions for *Higher Culture* as fostered and developed by private and corporate liberality and enterprise. *It is not denominational or sectarian* in its character, but is controlled by a self-perpetuating Board of Trustees, composed of eminent and worthy citizens.

The plan of *independent schools* is followed, as at the University of Virginia—in fact, the organization, courses of study, &c., are much the same at these two great institutions of higher learning.

The schools are (1873): (1) Latin, with three classes; (2) Greek, with three classes; (3) Modern Languages, with two classes in both French and German; (4) English Language and Literature, with two classes; (5) Moral Philosophy, with two classes; (6) History and Political Economy, with two classes; (7) Mathematics, wlth three classes; (8) Applied Mathematics, with the division into Civil and Military Engineering and Astronomy, with three classes in Engineering and two in

Astronomy; (9) Natural Philosophy, with three sections and three courses; (10) Chemistry, Mineralogy and Geology; (11) Applied Chemistry, with two courses. The *Courses of Civil and Mining Engineering* extend over three years, and include a number of the *schools* just named; the *Course of Agriculture* extends over two years, and includes a number of the *classes* of the *schools*. The *Department of Law and Equity* includes (1) the School of Common and Statute Law, and (2) the School of Equity and Public Law, each with two classes.

WASHINGTON AND LEE UNIVERSITY, LEXINGTON, VA.*

There is also a *Business* school, and arrangements are being made for a distinct course of *Commerce* and one of *Mechanical Engineering*.

Students are graduated and degrees conferred as in the University of Virginia, as before stated.

The necessary expenses for the yearly session of nine months are from $230 to $300. This University offers a number of free scholarships, as prizes, to the most distinguished pupils of the high schools of Virginia; it aids young men by a credit of a number of years after completing their studies; it gives free tuition, when asked, to all young men studying for the Christian ministry; it grants special privileges to those intending to teach or to follow the profession of journalism; it offers a post-graduate course, with substantial emoluments, to its most distinguished graduates.

During the session of 1872–'3, Washington and Lee had 263 students—81 from Virginia and 182 from 20 other states. This University has large endowments, the benefactions of individuals and societies, and to these additions are being made every year. It has a high reputation as a school for higher culture and training—one that does its work thoroughly well.

The annexed table presents the statistics of the *advanced*, *technical* and *higher* schools—not state institutions—for the year 1872–'3.

* Copied by permission from Scribner's Magazine, New York.

| NAME. | LOCATION. | No. of Instructors. | STUDENTS. | | | Tuition per session. | Board per month. | When organized. | Volumes in library. | When session begins each year. | Months of session. | Denomination controlling. |
|---|---|---|---|---|---|---|---|---|---|---|---|---|
| | | | From Virginia | From other States. | Whole number of— | | | | | | | |
| Washington and Lee University | Valley | 21 | 81 | 219 | 300 | $70 | $15 | 1782 | 10,000 | September | 9 | None. |
| Emory and Henry College | Valley | 5 | 36 | 147 | 183 | 60 | 13 | 1838 | 4,850 | September | 9 | Methodists. |
| Roanoke College | Valley | 11 | 106 | 34 | 140 | 50 | 14 | 1853 | 8,000 | September | 9 | Lutherans. |
| Hampden Sidney College | Middle | 5 | 54 | 23 | 77 | 50 | 15 | 1776 | 3,500 | September | 9 | Presbyterians. |
| William and Mary College | Tidewater | 6 | 72 | 4 | 76 | 50 | 18 | 1693 | 5,000 | ........ | 9 | Episcopalians. |
| Richmond College | Tidewater | 11 | 150 | 8 | 158 | 70 | 10 | 1844 | ........ | October. | 9 | Baptists. |
| Randolph Macon College | Tidewater | 9 | 118 | 49 | 167 | 75 | 13 | 1831 | 15,000 | September | 9 | Methodists. |
| St. John's College | Tidewater | 9 | ...... | ........ | 35 | free. | free. | 1869 | ........ | ........ | ...... | R. Catholic. |
| | | 77 | 617 | 484 | 1,136 | ........ | ........ | ........ | ........ | ........ | ...... | ........ |
| Union Theological Seminary | Middle | 4 | ...... | ........ | 62 | free. | $15 | 1824 | 7,500 | ........ | ...... | Presbyterians. |
| Protestant Episcopal Seminary | Middle | 5 | ...... | ........ | 43 | free. | 20 | 1823 | 9,000 | September | 9 | Episcopalians. |
| | | 9 | ...... | ........ | 105 | ........ | ........ | ........ | ........ | ........ | ...... | ........ |
| Virginia Medical College | Tidewater | 13 | ...... | ........ | 39 | $135 | $20 | 1851 | 1,200 | October. | 5 | ........ |
| Commercial College | Tidewater | 5 | ...... | ........ | 75 | 40 | ........ | 1866 | ........ | ........ | ...... | ........ |
| Old Dominion Business College | Tidewater | 1 | ...... | ........ | 60 | 40 | ........ | 1868 | ........ | ........ | ...... | ........ |
| School of Telegraphy | Tidewater | 2 | ...... | ........ | 25 | 50 | ........ | 1871 | ........ | ........ | ...... | ........ |
| Normal School (white) | Tidewater | 3 | ...... | ........ | 40 | free. | ........ | 1867 | ........ | ........ | ...... | ........ |
| Polytechnic Institute | Valley | 3 | ...... | ........ | 71 | 50 | 12 | 1870 | ........ | ........ | ...... | ........ |
| | | 23 | ...... | ........ | 310 | ........ | ........ | ........ | ........ | ........ | ...... | ........ |
| Colver Institute (colored) | Tidewater | 4 | ...... | ........ | 70 | ........ | ........ | 1866 | 50 | ........ | ...... | Baptists. |
| Normal School (colored) | Tidewater | 5 | ...... | ........ | 110 | free. | ........ | 1867 | 500 | ........ | ...... | ........ |
| | | 9 | ...... | ........ | 180 | ........ | ........ | ........ | ........ | ........ | ...... | ........ |

The educational work done in Virginia in 1871-'2 is summed up by the Superintendent of Public Instruction in this way—

| | | |
|---|---|---|
| Number of Public SCHOOLS | | 3,695 |
| Number of Private Primary Schools | 647 | |
| Number of High Schools | 181 | |
| Number of Colleges | 10 | |
| Number of Technical Schools | 12 | |
| | —— | 850 |
| Whole number of Schools in State | | 4,545 |
| Number of TEACHERS in Public Schools | | 3,853 |
| Number of TEACHERS in Private Primary Schools | 715 | |
| Number of TEACHERS in High Schools | 574 | |
| Number of TEACHERS in Colleges | 124 | |
| Number of TEACHERS in Technical Schools | 66 | |
| | —— | 1,479 |
| Whole number of teachers in State | | 5,332 |
| Number of PUPILS in Public Schools | | 166,377 |
| Number of PUPILS in private Primary Schools | 10,320 | |
| Number of PUPILS in High Schools | 7,491 | |
| Number of PUPILS in Colleges | 1,813 | |
| Number of PUPILS in Technical Schools | 853 | |
| | —— | 20,477 |
| Whole number attending schools | | 186,854 |

| | |
|---|---|
| Average cost of TUITION per month in Public Schools, per enrolled pupil | $0.70 |
| Average cost of TUITION per month in Private Primary Schools | 1.90 |
| Average cost of TUITION per month in high Schools | 4.91 |
| Average cost of TUITION per month in Colleges and Technical Schools | 7.00 |
| Average cost of TUITION per month in all grades, per enrolled pupil | $3.62 |
| Average length of session of Public Schools, in months | 5.72 |
| Average length of session of Private Primary Schools, in months | 6.75 |
| Average length of session of High Schools, in months | 8.33 |
| Average length of session of Colleges and Technical Schools, in months | 9.00 |
| Average time for all grades, in months | 7.45 |

The school population—those between 5 and 21—was 411,021; so over 45 per cent. of the whole of this class attended schools of some kind during the year, showing that the ample facilities furnished were well made use of.

The Reports of the Superintendent of Public Instruction furnish the following facts in regard to collegiate education in Virginia:

The number of students attending her colleges has been as follows: in 1860 there were 1,738; in 1870 there were 1,936; in 1871, 1,930; in 1872, 1,799; in 1873, the numbers were 2,087, and in 1874, 2,168. The number of students from Virginia in 1872 was 909; in 1873 it was 1,235, and in 1874, 1,287.

The following table presents the statistics of college attendance in 1872 for the leading states:

| | Number attending in the State. | Number from the State in it. | Number from other States. | Number in other States. | Whole number from each State. | Number belonging to State. in proportion to Population attending College. | |
|---|---|---|---|---|---|---|---|
| | | | | | | To White Population. | To Whole Population. |
| New York | 2,213 | 1,668 | 545 | 774 | 2,442 | 1 in 1,773 | 1 in 1,790 |
| Virginia | 1,813 | 921 | 857 | 65 | 986 | 1 in 722 | 1 in 1,233 |
| Ohio | 1,639 | 1,301 | 338 | 409 | 1,710 | 1 in 1,521 | 1 in 1,557 |
| Pennsylvania | 1,622 | 1,145 | 427 | 474 | 1,669 | 1 in 2,011 | 1 in 2,110 |
| Massachusetts | 1,186 | 656 | 530 | 246 | 902 | 1 in 1,588 | 1 in 1,615 |
| Connecticut | 887 | 244 | 643 | 88 | 332 | 1 in 1,529 | 1 in 1,630 |

In Scotland the number at college is said to be 1 in 1,000, in Germany 1 in 2,500 and in England 1 in 5,800 of the population. In 1872–'3 there were, omitting Hampton, 1,937 students in the Virginia colleges—1,124 from the State and 813 from other states. These statistics show that Virginia stands in the *front rank, for the whole world*, in higher education.

## CHAPTER X.

### SECTION I.—INTERNAL IMPROVEMENTS AND TRANSPORTATION.

Virginia is well supplied with lines of railways and canals now in operation, and when those that are in progress or projected are completed, every portion of the State will be accessible by such improvements. Numerous turnpikes have been constructed by the State between important points in all sections, but more especially in the Blue Ridge, Valley and Appalachian ones; so there is no portion of the mountain region that has not been penetrated by well constructed highways.

The common roads of the State are very numerous, but the wear and neglect of a long war left most of them in a bad condition; they are, however, being improved under a "road law" that in due time will give to every part of the country good roads. In navigable waters the State is unrivaled, and lines of transportation, for both coastwise and foreign commerce, reach every portion of the large Tidewater country.

The RAILWAY SYSTEM of the State should first be regarded as a whole not only in reference to the State, but to the great through lines and general system of the United States, of which they form a part.

The ATLANTIC, MISSISSIPPI AND OHIO RAILROAD (A., M. & O.), is the longest line in the State. Commencing at the splendid harbor of Norfolk (which is but a few miles from the sea and accessible at all seasons to the largest vessels afloat, where it meets lines of steamers and sailing vessels plying in all directions, especially lines of steamers that run in connection with it to New York and to Baltimore, and with the Seaboard Railroad to the south) it runs northwest, west and southwest for 408 miles, across Tidewater, Middle, Piedmont, Blue Ridge and for 150 miles along the Great Valley to Bristol, on the Tennessee line, where it connects with the railways that extend south, southwest and west to Mobile, New Orleans, Memphis, &c., making it part of a grand trunk line from the ocean westward and southward; its *through* cars run to the Gulf of Mexico and to the Mississippi river.

The first division of the Atlantic, Mississippi and Ohio—the *Norfolk and Petersburg*—is the 81 miles across Tidewater between those cities, running southwest for 23 miles to Suffolk, a flourishing town at the head of navigation, on the Nansemond, near which it intersects the Seaboard and Roanoke Road to Weldon, in North Carolina, and south; then its course is northwest, nearly parallel to the James, through the middle of the Southside peninsula, by Windsor, Zuni, Ivor, Wakefield, Waverly and Disputanta stations, to Petersburg, at the head of tide on the Appomattox, a flourishing manufacturing and commercial city, where it meets the City Point branch of the Atlantic, Mississippi and Ohio, down the Appomattox to the James, the Richmond and Petersburg and the Petersburg and Weldon Railroads.

The *Southside Division* of the Atlantic, Mississippi and Ohio Road extends northwest from *Petersburg*, through the Middle Country, *to Lynchburg*, 123 miles, passing through Sutherland's Church Road, Ford's, Wilson's, Wellville, Blacks and Whites, Nottoway courthouse, Burk's (where it is crossed by the Piedmont Air-Line Road, formerly the Richmond and Danville, a through line from Richmond to the south and southwest), Rice's, High Bridge, Farmville (a flourishing place near Hampden Sidney College), Prospect, Pamplin's, Evergreen, Appomattox, Spout Spring, and Concord—giving railway facilities to a large and productive region, abounding in forest resources and mineral wealth.

The *Tennessee Division* of the Atlantic, Mississippi and Ohio extends from *Lynchburg to Bristol*, 204 miles, across Piedmont and along the Valley. At Lynchburg this railroad is crossed by the line of the Washington City, Virginia Midland and Great Southern Railroad—usually called the Virginia Midland—running from Washington City, where all the lines of the United States meet, southwest along the border of Piedmont and Middle Virginia to Danville, where it joins the Piedmont Air-Line, before mentioned. At Lynchburg this railroad also connects with the James River and Kanawha Canal, that follows the James River up from Richmond to this important and flourishing manufacturing city, and then continues on to Buchanan, in the Great Valley, beyond which it is projected to the Ohio River, and the General Government contemplates completing it. The stations beyond Lynchburg are Halsey's, Clay's, Forest, Goode's, Lowry's, Liberty (the county seat of the rich county of Bedford), Thaxton's, Lisbon and Buford's in Piedmont; the railway then crosses the Blue Ridge into the Valley, in which are Blue Ridge, Bonsack's, whence lines of stages run to Lexington; Gish's, Big Lick, whence a line of stages runs to Franklin; Salem (the flourishing county seat of Roanoke county and the location of Roanoke College, and where the Valley Railroad, now in course of construction, will meet the Atlantic, Mississippi and Ohio, giving a connection northeast through Lexington, Staunton, &c., to Baltimore); Dyerle's, Lafayette, Big Spring, Shawsville, Alleghany, whence stages run to Alleghany Springs; Big Tunnel, from which a tramway runs to the Montgomery White Sulphur Springs; Christiansburg, the county town of Montgomery county and the station for the Virginia Agricultural and Mechanical College, and for the Yellow Springs; Vicker's, Central, from which a railroad is projected down the Kanawha or New River 68 miles, to the Chesapeake and Ohio Railroad; New River, Dublin, the station for Newbern, the shire-town of Pulaski county; Martin's, Max Meadows, Wytheville, the fine county town of Wythe county; Rural Retreat, Atkins', Marion, the flourishing county seat of Smyth; Seven-Mile Ford, Glade Spring, from which a branch railway runs to Saltville and its great salt works and plaster banks; Emory, the seat of Emory and Henry College; Abingdon, the fine county town of Washington county, with its two female colleges—Martha Washington and Stonewall Jackson; and Goodson-Bristol, on the Tennessee line, a growing town, the seat of King's College and a flourishing female seminary.

This railway passes through as fine an agricultural region as any in the State, embracing lands of every variety and suited to every sort of culture: the "truck" or market garden lands of the Norfolk peninsula and the oyster beds and fishing grounds come first; then the sweet potato, peanut, corn, cotton and timber lands; then the fine corn and tobacco lands of the Middle country and the mineral lands of the gold belt; the rich grain lands and iron ore beds of Piedmont, the fruit lands of the Blue Ridge and its treasures of iron ore, the fertile grassy plains and hills of the Valley—the land of the stock raisers, of great corn and wheat fields, with metaliferous bands of lead, iron, zinc and copper and beds of salt, plaster and coal on either hand. It would require a volume to give the details of the unbroken stretch of 408 miles of east and west country, or more than 16,000 square miles, tributary to this great, well-built, well-equipped and well-managed railway.

By Report of 1874, the charges on this railway are: for through passengers, all classes, 3.07 cents a mile, and for way passengers 3.68. For through emigrant passengers the charge is two cents per mile; the average passenger rate is 3.54 cents. The average rate per ton per mile, on all classes of freight, is 2.41 cents.

Steamships from Liverpool connect with this line at Norfolk, and it conveys immigrants on to the west. This railway conveyed over 193,000 bales of cotton to Norfolk in 1874, or 42 per cent. of the 467,561 bales received by that city.

The Atlantic, Mississippi and Ohio is to be extended from Bristol, west, along the state line, 100 miles to Cumberland Gap, where it will meet a system of railways from Kentucky. This will be a very valuable extension, opening up a country rich in farming and grazing lands and in metallic wealth. It is also proposed to extend the line from Saltville across to Pound Gap, on the Kentucky line, to meet railways coming up from the Ohio river. This will bring the iron and coal of Appalachia into market. A charter has also been granted for a road from the Atlantic, Mississippi and Ohio down New River to the Chesapeake and Ohio, opening a way for the interchange of iron ore and coal with West Virginia, and developing a fine agricultural region. Lands of *every variety* and *price* are for sale along the whole length of this road—far cheaper than any of the wild lands of the West.

The second line in length in Virginia, the Washington City, Virginia Midland and Great Southern Railroad (W. C., V. M. & G. S.), or Virginia Midland (the consolidated Orange and Alexandria, Manassas Gap and Lynchburg and Danville Railroads), now runs from Alexandria southwest, along the line of the Middle and Piedmont and through the Piedmont and Middle country, 216.5 miles to Danville. The cars of this company run from Washington City, and they pass over a portion of the Chesapeake and Ohio Railroad; so this may, with propriety, be considered a line of 240 miles from Washington to Danville—*the real Piedmont Railway* of the State. It is now a part of the great mail line to the south and southwest. At Washington, the Capital of the United States, it meets lines of railways from all directions and ships and steamers near the head of tide on the Potomac. At Alexandria, 7 miles below, its next station, it meets the terminus of the Chesapeake and Ohio Canal, that has come down the Potomac from Cumberland; the Washington and Ohio Railway, that runs to Round Hill, in Piedmont, and is projected to the Ohio by way of Winchester, and crosses the railway from Washington to Richmond. Alexandria is a flourishing commercial city, from which steamers and vessels go up and down the Potomac. The stations, in order, are Springfield, Burke's, Fairfax, Clifton, Manassas (at which point the branch Manassas Gap Railroad leaves the main line and runs 61 miles across Piedmont and the Blue Ridge to the Valley Railroad at Strasburg), Bristoe, Nokesville, Catlett's, Warrenton Junction (from which a branch runs northwest 10 miles by Melrose to Warrenton, the county town of the fine county of Fauquier), Midland, Bealeton, Rappahannock, Brandy, Culpeper (the growing county seat of Culpeper county), Mitchell's, Rapid Anne, Orange Courthouse (the seat of justice for Orange county), Madison Run, Gordonsville, where it meets the Chesapeake and Ohio Railroad from Richmond, and runs over its line 21 miles past Lindsay's, Cobham, Keswick and Shadwell stations to Charlottesville, the county seat of Albemarle county, and near which is located the University of Virginia; it there leaves the line of the Chesapeake and Ohio, which crosses the Blue Ridge and the Valley, via Staunton, and Appalachia on to the Ohio river, &c. At Charlottesville the Midland Road is fairly *into* Piedmont, and thence it passes Red Hill, North Garden, Covesville, Faber's Mills, Rockfish, Elmington, Lovingston or Montreal (near the courthouse of Nelson county), Arrington, Tye River, New Glasgow, Amherst (the county town of Amherst county), McIvor's and Burford's to Lynchburg, where are the James River and Kanawha Canal and the Atlantic, Mississippi and Ohio Road, before described, giving connections East, West and South. From Lynchburg the stations are Lucado, Lawyer's Road, Covington, Otter River, Lynch's, Staunton River, Sycamore, Ward's Springs, Galveston, Whittles, Chatham (the county town of the large county of Pittsylvania), Dry Fork, and Fall Creek, to Danville,* a flourishing manufacturing town on the Piedmont Air-Line Road, from Richmond south and southwest.

The MANASSAS BRANCH of the Midland passes through the following stations from Manassas: Gainesville, Hay Market, Thoroughfare, Broad Run, The Plains, Salem, Rectortown, Piedmont and Markham in the Piedmont country; Linden on the Blue Ridge, and Happy Creek, Front Royal (county town of Warren county), Riverton (where the Shenandoah Valley Railroad crosses it), Buckton, Water Lick and Strasburg, to Strasburg Junction, in the Valley.

*The following statistics of the thriving town of Danville are compiled from a letter by J. T. Averett, Esq., in the Richmond Dispatch of January 6th, 1876:

*Danville, Pittsylvania County, Virginia.*

| Years. | Population. | Value of personal property. | Value of real estate. | TOBACCO TRADE. | | | |
|---|---|---|---|---|---|---|---|
| | | | | Pounds sold at warehouses. | Value of official sales. | Average per hundred. | Internal revenue receipts. |
| 1870 | 3,464 | $524,155 | $1,020,620 | 10,621,557 | $1,301,140 73 | $12 25 | ............... |
| 1871 | 3,990 | 527,691 | 1,141,030 | 13,191,406 | 1,582,969 72 | 12 00 | ............... |
| 1872 | 4,320 | 658,722 | 1,229,710 | 14,065,639 | 1,746,413 10 | 12 34 | ............... |
| 1873 | 5,130 | 921,906 | 1,337,375 | 14,181,890 | 1,694,524 96 | 11 94 | $ 948,377 49 |
| 1874 | 5,552 | 813,627 | 1,421,725 | 18,582,389 | 2,707,231 82 | 14 56 | 1,311,822 71 |
| 1875 | 6,183 | 919,844 | 1,506,735 | 15,018,640 | 2,761,154 35 | 18 38 | 1,041,591 76 |

(See table, continued, foot of next page.)

This very important railroad, operating 287½ miles and owning 337½ miles of line, and having over 10,000 square miles of country tributary to it, is becoming a most valuable auxiliary in the development of the State, as it not only passes through or near a fine farming, grazing or planting country for its whole length, branches included, but it runs for a long distance in one of the most attractive and promising iron producing regions in the State. As a *through* line it is the most direct from the National Capital for the whole of the great Piedmont country of Virginia, North Carolina, South Carolina and Georgia, on to the Gulf. As a State line it passes through the brown-stone quarries and good wheat lands of Manassas; has tributary to it all the Piedmont country, with its exceedingly rich and productive lands, among them the noted "red lands" of Amherst, Nelson, Albemarle, Orange, &c.; it has penetrated the fine timber lands of Campbell and Pittsylvania; it enters the Shenandoah Valley, crossing the Blue Ridge; it crosses the valleys of the Roanoke and the Dan, famed for their crops of tobacco, corn, &c. The abundant magnetic, hematite and specular iron ores of Culpeper, Orange, Albemarle, Nelson, Amherst, Campbell and Pittsylvania counties are along its line for nearly 200 miles, not to mention the lead, manganese and other ores here also found. This company has obtained, by grant or purchase by permission of the State, large tracts of land within five miles of its lines, which it will sell to intending settlers on long time and at reasonable rates. The rates of fare of this railway, per mile, are 4 cents for first class through and 4½ for first class way passengers, and 2½ and 3 cents for second class through and way respectively, averaging 4 cents a mile. The charges for freight average 4.44 cents a ton per mile, ranging from .94 of a cent to 7.55 cents.

The affairs of the company are well managed, and it has a future, as a great through line across the State, of great prosperity and usefulness before it.

THE CHESAPEAKE AND OHIO RAILROAD (C. & O.) has 222 miles of its 423 between Richmond and Huntington, on the Ohio, in Virginia. This is part of a great through line from some harbor of "The Peninsula," on or near Chesapeake bay, to the Mississippi at St. Louis, all completed but about 80 miles in Kentucky and the line down The Peninsula from Richmond. The road now in operation runs northwest from Richmond across the Middle, Piedmont, Blue Ridge, Valley and Appalachian country to West Virginia, and then across the Trans-Appalachian country in that State to the valley of the Ohio.

The *Eastern Division* of the Chesapeake and Ohio extends from Richmond to

These figures show more forcibly than words the prosperity of this city:

*Danville—Its December Tobacco Trade.*

| Years. | December Sales of Leaf Tobacco at Warehouses. | | | |
|---|---|---|---|---|
| | Pounds. | Value. | Average per hundred. | Internal revenue receipts. |
| 1872 | 507,343 | $ 40,028 62 | $ 8 89 | $45,293 30 |
| 1873 | 247,806 | 15,035 00 | 6 06 | 82,214 20 |
| 1874 | 951,689 | 196,798 43 | 20 67 | 58,265 10 |
| 1875 | 1,240,847 | 114,450 00 | 9 24 | 47,784 18 |

Staunton, in the Valley, 136 miles. It begins at new wharves belonging to the company, at the Harbor of Richmond, where ample arrangements have been made for shipping the immense quantities of coal, iron, timber, &c., that will pass over the road. It meets at Richmond the various lines that are named as terminating there. Vessels drawing 14 feet of water ascend the tides of the James to this point. The stations of this Division are Atlee's, Ashcake, Peake's, Hanover Courthouse, the county town of Hanover county; Wickham's, South Anna, Hanover Junction, where it crosses the line of the Richmond, Fredericksburg and Washington Railroad; Anderson's, Noel's, Hewlett's, Beaver Dam, Green Bay, Bumpass', Buckner's, Frederick's Hall, Tolersville, Louisa Courthouse, the county seat of Louisa county; Trevilian's, Green Springs, Melton's and Gordonsville, in the Middle country. At Gordonsville, as before stated, it meets the Midland Railroad from Washington City, and to the same point the Fredericksburg and Gordonsville Railroad is nearly completed; thence the road skirts Piedmont by Lindsay's, Cobham, Campbell's, Keswick and Shadwell, when it turns across Piedmont by Charlottesville—the seat of the University of Virginia and county town of the great county of Albemarle, where the Midland Railroad diverges to the southwest—Ivy and Mechum's River; then Greenwood and Afton on the Blue Ridge; and in the Valley, Waynesboro' and Fishersville to Staunton, the thriving county town of Augusta county and the seat of four female colleges, where the Valley Railroad from Baltimore crosses the Chesapeake and Ohio and runs to the Atlantic, Mississippi and Ohio at Salem. The *Middle Division* extends from Staunton to Hinton, West Virginia, 136 miles, and the *Western Division* from Hinton to Huntington, 148 miles. The station beyond Staunton, in the Valley, is Swoope's; then in Appalachia, Buffalo Gap, North Mountain, Variety Springs, Elizabeth Furnace, Pond Gap, Craigsville, Bell's Valley, Goshen—from which point lines of stages run to Lexington, the seat of Washington and Lee University and the Virginia Military Institute and to the Alum Springs of Rockbridge—Panther Gap, Millboro'—from which stages run to the Bath Alum, Warm, Hot and Healing springs—Mason's Tunnel, Crane's, Griffith's, Longdale, Peter's (whence a narrow gauge railway extends to the Lucy Selina Furnace, of the Longdale Iron Company), Clifton Forge—where it meets Jackson's river of the James and the line of the extension of the James River and Kanawha Canal, the Central water line, and where a branch line of the Chesapeake and Ohio is proposed down the James to Richmond, following the grade of the river; also a line some 30 odd miles long to the present terminus of the canal at Buchanan—Jackson's River, Lowmoor—from which a short branch runs to the Lowmoor iron mines—Covington, the county town of Alleghany county, from which stages run to the Healing, Hot and Warm Springs; Callaghan's and Alleghany (from which stages run to the Sweet Chalybeate and Sweet Springs), where the railroad passes into West Virginia. As a *through* line, with railway, steamboat and steamship connections east and west to all important points, with the lowest grades of any line in the United States across the Appalachian system of mountains, with its course in the mild latitude of Virginia, and with its shorter distances from the seaboard to all points in the West and Northwest, this is to become one of the most important trans-continental lines of the United States. This line was opened to the Ohio in 1873. As a *state* line this crosses the gold and iron belt of Middle Virginia, the magnetic, &c., iron belt of Piedmont, the specular and brown hematite iron belt of the Blue Ridge, the iron and limestone beds of the Valley, runs for 70 miles *with* the *brown* and *red* central iron ore belt of the Appalachian region; and for 86 miles literally runs *through*, by the cañon of New River and the Great Kanawha, in West Virginia, the beds of the Lower, Middle and Upper series of the great Appalachian Coal-field, where more than an aggregate of 80 feet of thickness in these three measures of cannel, splint, shop and other varieties of Bituminous Coal are exposed in nearly horizontal strata above the water level. The *mere mention* of these facts shows that this is to be one of the largest iron producing regions in the United States (see chapter on Geology), where raw coals and rich ores may be cast, as they are mined, into the furnace. The farming, planting and grazing lands along the whole line are among the best in the State, and the country adjacent thereto is rapidly developing. The trade over this railway, westward, from the oyster beds, fishing banks and market gardens of Tidewater must be large. The open character and unsurpassed excellence of the harbors at its eastern termini will bring to it the imports of all lands in and beyond the Atlantic. In fact, all the lines that terminate near the capes of Virginia must become the "*grocery* lines*" for the central belt of population of both continents. The Mediterranean products of Europe, the sweets and coffee of the West Indies and South America, will naturally come here for distribution to the interior of North America, and the products of the West for distribution along the Atlantic coasts of the Americas and Europe.

In the 8,000 square miles of country in Virginia that finds its outlet over this road there is an abundance of every variety of farming and of iron lands for sale at from one dollar and fifty cents to one hundred dollars per acre, depending on location, improvements, &c. The rates for first class passengers are 3 cents for *through* and 4 cents for *way* per mile; for second class, 2 cents *through* and 3 cents *way*—averaging 3 cents per mile. The rates for freight are from 1¼ to 4 cents a ton per mile, averaging 2 1-20 cents per ton a mile.

THE RICHMOND AND DANVILLE RAILROAD, a portion of the *Piedmont Air-Line* from Richmond to Atlanta, Georgia, extends from Richmond southwest to the state line just beyond Danville, 140½ miles, passing through the midst of the great Middle country, where it is noted as a tobacco producing region.

At the large and flourishing city of Richmond, the beginning of this line, this road meets the numerous lines of railways, canal, steamers, &c., that centre there; thence the stations are Manchester, the improving suburb of Richmond across the James, the county town of Chesterfield county, whence a branch extends to the harbor of Richmond at Rocketts; Belle Isle, Rockfield, Granite, Coalfield, the heart of the Richmond coal-basin; Tomahawk, Powhatan, Mattoax, Chula, Amelia Courthouse, the shire town of Amelia county; Jetersville, Jennings' Ordinary, Burkeville, where it crosses the line of the Atlantic, Mississippi and Ohio, giving connections east and west (see Atlantic, Mississippi and Ohio); Green Bay, Meherrin, Keysville, the junction with the proposed Roanoke Valley Railroad; Drake's Branch, Mossingford, Randolph, Roanoke, Clover, Scottsburg, Wolf Trap, Boston, New's Ferry, Barksdale Sutherlin, Ringgold and Danville, where it meets the Midland Railroad from Wash-

---

* **Colonel James McDonald, Secretary of the Commonwealth of Virginia.**

ington and Lynchburg and its own extension to Atlanta, Mobile and New Orleans.

As a through line, this connects with a line from Washington City to Richmond, and so becomes a very important line for trade and travel to the south and southwest; a line especially for bringing the products of the great southern Piedmont region to Virginia markets. As a local line the Richmond and Danville may claim the trade of over 8,000 square miles of territory—one of the most productive in the Middle country, and at the same time much of the trade of southwest Piedmont and Blue Ridge must also find its outlet by it. It passes through the Richmond coal-field and the fine granite quarries along the James; its line is near and on the combined gold and iron belt; copper, soapstone and other minerals await development in its vicinity. Fine bodies of magnetite are near the line of this railroad. A line of railway is in course of construction up the valley of the Roanoke from Clarksville to Keysville, on this railroad, which will bring to it the products of a very fertile country. There are many farms on this railway for sale at exceedingly low prices, and some thriving settlements have been made on or near it by English, Dutch and other settlers. The average rate per mile for through passengers is 3.39 cents, for 1st class way passengers 4 cents, and for 2nd class way 3½ cents—averaging 3 63-100 cents per mile. The average charge for freight is 4.08 cents a ton a mile.

The RICHMOND, FREDERICKSBURG AND POTOMAC (80 miles) and a portion of the BALTIMORE AND POTOMAC RAILROAD are run as one line from Richmond to Washington City and Baltimore, forming part of the great north and south railway that runs along the border between the Middle and Tidewater sections from New York city on through Virginia, by way of Washington, Alexandria, Fredericksburg, Richmond, Petersburg, Weldon, &c., to the south.

The Richmond, Fredericksburg and Potomac runs for 82 miles to Quantico, on the Potomac river, passing through Boulton, Hungary, Kilby's, Ashland, the seat of Randolph Macon College; Taylorsville, Hanover Junction, where it crosses the Chesapeake and Ohio Road; Chester, Penola, Milford, near Caroline Courthouse; Wordford, Guinea's, Fredericksburg, 61 miles from Richmond, and an important commercial and manufacturing city at the head of tide on the Rappahannock; Potomac Run, Brooke's, Richland, to Quantico, where it meets a line of steamers to Washington and joins the line of the Alexandria and Potomac (or Baltimore and Potomac Railroad), which continues its rail connection by Cherry Hill, Mount Pleasant, Wood Bridge, Long Branch, Franconia, and Alexandria city—where it crosses the Midland, Washington and Ohio, &c.—to Washington City. This has long been the favorite route for travel to the south, and is noted for its good management and most comfortable accommodations. Its *directness* will always make it a great trunk line. Locally, this passes through much exceedingly fine country, the valleys of the branches of the Pamunkey, the Mattapony, the Rappahannock and Potomac—all famed for their fertility, fine climate, pure water, &c., where many desirable homes and most valuable plantations are offered for sale at merely nominal prices—the result of the destruction incident to war.

The gold belt, with its valuable ores of iron, is not far away, on one side, and the marl beds of the Tertiary are near at hand on the other—both full of promise for future operations. The fine water-power of the Rappahannock, at the Falls near Fredericksburg, is partially utilized in manufacturing woolens, paper, &c., but it has an abundant supply for many operations on a large scale. The line of railway once completed to Gordonsville, crossing the gold and iron belt and connecting by the Chesapeake and Ohio with the coal-fields of Trans-Appalachia, this must become a manufacturing centre in the midst of large agricultural resources. The average charge for passengers on the Alexandria and Fredericksburg Road is 3 1-20 cents per mile, and for freight 3.1 cents. The average freight rate on the Richmond, Fredericksburg and Potomac was 4.17 cents per ton per mile. The speed of passenger trains is from 25 to 30 miles per hour.

The Richmond and Petersburg Railroad, 23 miles long, is a southern extension of the lines just described; it connects with them by a tunnel under a portion of Richmond, then crosses the James, through Manchester, Temple's, Drewry's Bluff, Halfway, Chester—near which it has a branch road into the Chesterfield part of the Richmond coal-basin and across its line to Osborne's, a landing on the James, where the coal is put into vessels—to Petersburg. This is an exceedingly well managed road, important as a link in the line of through trade and travel and as the outlet for the fine coal on its *Clover Hill Branch.* There is much land along it that needs inhabitants. At Petersburg it finds a flourishing city, the line of the Atlantic, Mississippi and Ohio Road, before spoken of, and the extension of the North and South line by the Petersburg and Weldon Railroad. The average fare is 3¼ cents a mile, and the average rate of freight 3 cents per ton. The speed is from 23 to 28 miles an hour.

The Petersburg and Weldon Railroad is another link in the North and South railway system, extending from Petersburg 63 miles, through Reams', Stony Creek, Jarratt's, Belfield, Hicksford, Gaston Junction, where the road branches, one branch going by Ryland's to Gaston and on to Raleigh, North Carolina—the other to Weldon, through Pleasant Hill and on to Goldsboro', North Carolina, and southward. At Weldon it meets the line of the Seaboard Railroad from Norfolk. This, like the Richmond and Petersburg, is important as part of the *through* line, the passenger cars running without change all the way from Washington to Weldon. It has a large scope of fertile country in the "cotton belt," the valleys of the Nottoway, Meherrin and Roanoke and their branches pertaining to it, in which there is much valuable land, some farms on the line of the railway being offered at $10* per acre.

The Seaboard and Roanoke Railroad extends from Portsmouth, opposite Norfolk and on its harbor, 80 miles southwest to Weldon, in North Carolina, making, by bay steamers from Baltimore, a daily line to the south by what is known as the "Atlantic Coast Line." At the splendid harbor of Norfolk this road connects with lines of steamers from all points and the Atlantic, Mississippi and Ohio Railroad; then it passes by Bower's Hill through Suffolk, the active county seat of Nansemond county, near which it passes under the Atlantic, Mississippi and Ohio; Buckhorn, Carrsville, Franklin, on the Blackwater, where it meets steamboats from the Chowan; Murfee's, Nottoway, Newsom's, Boykin's, Branchville, Margaretsville, Sea-

* Moore & Co.'s Circular for 1873-'4.

board and Gary's, to Weldon, where it joins the Petersburg and Weldon Railroad. This is an important line for trade from the cotton and naval stores region of North Carolina, and for cotton and travel from beyond; its traffic is very large by its line of steamers to the great cities. It runs through the heart of the best cotton producing part of Virginia, including the valleys of the Nansemond, Blackwater Nottoway, Meherrin, &c. In this region the noted sweet potato, truck and cotton lands are offered at from $8 and upwards* per acre.

The Richmond, York River and Chesapeake Railroad runs east from Richmond 38½ miles to the head of York river, the junction of the Mattapony and Pamunkey, at West Point, where it connects with a line of steamers for Baltimore by the way of Yorktown, Gloucester Point and other landings on the York, the length of the line to Baltimore being 220 miles. The stations from Richmond (where this road forms a close connection with the Richmond and Danville) are Fair Oaks, Dispatch, Summit, Tunstall's, White House, Fish Haul and Sweet Hall, to West Point. The time from Richmond to Baltimore is some 14 hours, giving a fine ride over the York and the Chesapeake—as noble a river and bay as can well be found. This is an important line for freight and travel, and its tributary country, the valleys of the Chickahominy, Pamunkey, Mattapony and York, are among the most fertile in Tidewater Virginia. Here, too, are lands and homes at nominal prices. The rate of fare is from 2½ to 5 cents a mile, averaging 4.36 cents. The average rate per ton for freight is 3.37 cents per mile.

The Washington and Ohio Railroad is a line that is intended to run from the harbors of Alexandria and Washington on the Potomac, by way of Leesburg, Winchester, in Virginia, and Capon Springs, Moorefield, &c., in West Virginia, and thence westward to Point Pleasant, at the mouth of the Great Kanawha on the Ohio, a distance of 325 miles, making the most direct line westward from the National Capital. Only 55 miles of this road are completed from Alexandria northwest across Middle and into Piedmont, passing through Carlin's Springs, Fall's Church, Vienna, Hunter's Mill, Thornton, Herndon, Guilford, Farmwell, Leesburg, the county seat of the splendid county of Loudoun; Clark's Gap, Hamilton, Purcellville, Round Hill, to Snickersville, where it connects with a line of stages across the Blue Ridge by Berryville to Winchester, in the Valley, on the line of the Valley branch of the Baltimore and Ohio.

This road, when completed, will be one of the most important routes in the country, and will open a region of unsurpassed mineral wealth. It now runs through and into one of the very finest and most productive sections of the State, rich in grain and pasture lands, and with deposits of iron, marble, limestone, &c., of great value. The lands here are higher in price than in other portions of the State, owing to their nearness to markets as well as their excellent character; but they are by no means as high as similar lands in other states. The valuable iron ores of the western slope of the Blue Ridge will be crossed by this road 62 miles from Alexandria. It soon penetrates the eastern part of the Appalachian coal-field in West Virginia. Average fare per mile, for passengers, four cents; average rate for a ton freight, per mile, seven cents, ranging from four to ten and two-thirds.

---

Moore & Co.'s Circular for 1873–'4.

The Valley Railroad, a branch of the great Baltimore and Ohio, that begins at Harper's Ferry, on the Baltimore and Ohio, at the mouth of the Shenandoah, and extends up the valley of that noted river by Winchester and Staunton to its head, and then across the valley of the James by Lexington, and the Roanoke to Salem, following the Great Valley for 213 miles, of which 193 are in the State of Virginia. The part in operation is from Harper's Ferry to Staunton; the rest is being constructed. This road is formed by a combination of the Winchester and Potomac, the Winchester and Strasburg, the Strasburg and Harrisonburg part of the Manassas Gap Railroad, and the Valley Railroad from Staunton to Salem.

The stations are Harper's Ferry, 81 miles from Baltimore and 41 miles from Washington City; and Charlestown, in West Virginia, where it crosses the partly made Shenandoah Valley Railroad; in Virginia—Wadesville, Stephenson's, Winchester, the flourishing county town of Frederick; Kernstown, Bartonsville, Newtown, Vaucluse, Middletown, Capon Road, Strasburg, where the Manassas branch of the Midland Railroad unites with this; Tom's Brook, Maurertown, Woodstock, the county town of Shenandoah county; Edinburg, a thriving village; Mt. Jackson, Forestville, New Market, an active business place, the seat of a Polytechnic Institute, and the point of departure of stages for Luray and across to Culpeper by Sperryville; Broadway, Cowan's, Linville, Harrisonburg, a large and flourishing town, the county seat of the rich and fertile county of Rockingham, from which point the Shenandoah Valley and Ohio Railroad is now being located via Franklin, Pendleton county, West Virginia, to some point on the Ohio; and the "Washington City and St. Louis Narrow Gauge Railroad" is being constructed by way of Bridgewater, Monterey, in Highland county, and on through West Virginia, aiming for St. Louis, Missouri; Mount Crawford, Rockland Mills, Mount Sidney, Verona to Staunton, the thriving county seat of the large and wealthy county of Augusta, where it forms a junction with the Chesapeake and Ohio, and to which point the Shenandoah Valley Railroad is being constructed. Beyond Staunton the Valley Railroad is under process of construction, and will pass through Mint Spring, Greenville, Midway, Fairfield, Lexington, the county town of the fine county of Rockbridge, the seat of Washington and Lee University and the Virginia Military Institute, and the terminus of the North River Branch of the James River and Kanawha Canal; Natural Bridge, Buchanan, where it crosses the main line of the James River and Kanawha Canal; Botetourt Springs, where Hollins' Institute, a female college, is located, to Salem, the seat of Roanoke College, where, as before stated, this railroad connects with the Atlantic, Mississippi and Ohio.

A glance at the map will show that this railway is an important part of several through lines. When completed to Salem, it will finish a connected line of railways from New York to New Orleans, running for nearly eight hundred miles along the Great Appalachian Valley (as the one between the Blue Ridge and the Kitatinny mountains is often called), by far one of the most beautiful and productive valleys in the United States, and abounding in mineral wealth. It also forms part of a through Western line by way of the Chesapeake and Ohio, and of a Southern one by that and the Midland. As part of the great system of roads owned or operated by the Baltimore and Ohio, this will have many advantages for shipment to and from all the noted centres of business activity. Locally this road passes for its whole length through a rich farming and grazing country, that always sends vast amounts of grain, farm products of all kinds and cattle to market. On each side of it are the great iron belts of the Blue Ridge and of Appalachia; and as it crosses at right angles the roads and canal from the coal-fields, it must become the great artery for the distribution of coal and iron ore. The population of the Valley is still small compared to its productive area, and so it has much fine land for sale at prices ranging from $10 to $150 per acre, according to improvements, location, &c., or at from one-fourth to one-half the value of such lands in the more thickly peopled parts of the same Great Valley in Pennsylvania and other states.

The Shenandoah Valley Railroad is in process of construction from Hagerstown, by Williamsport, in Maryland; Shepherdstown and Charlestown, West Virginia; and Berryville, the county seat of Clarke; Front Royal, of Warren, and Luray, of Page counties; up the valley of the South Fork of the Shenandoah, by Port Republic, New Hope, &c., to Staunton; from that point the road has not been definitely located, but it is expected that it will enter Appalachia and pass through Alleghany, Craig, Giles, Tazewell, Russell, Scott and Lee counties, and into East Tennessee to the system of railways there in operation. This will form part of the system of the Pennsylvania Railroad Company, connecting roads under its control, making a line of 449 miles from Hagerstown, Maryland, to Russellville, Tennessee.

The indication of the route is sufficient, coupled with what has been said of the country along it in the chapters of this summary, to show that this will become a most valuable highway for mineral and agricultural traffic, as well as for travel.

A charter has been obtained for extending the Railroad that now runs from Hagerstown, in Maryland, to *Martinsburg*, in West Virginia, on up the valley some 22 miles *to Winchester*, connecting important railways.

The Norfolk and Great Western Railroad has been located through the whole southern tier of counties of the state from Norfolk to Cumberland Gap, by most of the county towns of this range of counties, and by Danville, Bristol, &c. This would make a very direct line from Norfolk to the West, and would open a large and fertile portion of the state now distant from railways. A portion of the line would pass through the magnificent mineral deposits of Southwestern Virginia. Nothing is being done to this road now, but at no distant day the merits of the line will secure its construction. Among other *proposed* lines are: one from *Danville* by Rocky Mount *to Salem*, one from *Farmville to Charlottesville* and northeast through Piedmont; one from *Staunton* to Washington City by the most direct route; one down the Eastern Shore peninsula, &c. Others have been named in connection with the roads of which they will form a part. The Roanoke Valley Railroad is in course of construction from Clarksville to Keysville.

Horse railroads are in operation in Richmond, Norfolk and Alexandria.

*Table of Railroads in operation in Virginia January 1st, 1876.*

| NAME OF RAILROAD. | Length in Virginia. | TERMINAL STATIONS IN VIRGINIA. | TERMINUS IN OTHER STATES. | Whole length run. |
|---|---|---|---|---|
| | Miles. | | | |
| Atlantic, Mississippi & Ohio............. | 408 | Norfolk and Bristol-Goodson........... | .................. | |
| City Point Branch of A., M. & O....... | 9 | Petersburg and City Point............. | .................. | 427 |
| Saltville Branch of A., M. & O......... | 10 | Glade Spring and Saltville.............. | .................. | |
| Washington City, Va. Mid. & Gr. Southern | 243* | Washington and Danville.............. | Washington..... | |
| Manassas Branch...................... | 63 | Manassas and Strasburg Junction....... | .................. | 315 |
| Warrenton Branch..................... | 9 | W. Junction and Warrenton............ | .................. | |
| Chesapeake & Ohio...................... | 222 | Richmond and Alleghany................ | Hunt'gt'n, W.Va. | |
| Longdale (narrow-gauge) Branch...... | 8 | Longdale Junction and Furnace......... | .................. | 434 |
| Lowmoor Branch...................... | 2 | Lowmoor Junction and Lowmoor........ | .................. | |
| Richmond & Danville..................... | 141 | Richmond and Danville................. | Atlanta, Ga...... | 547 |
| Richmond, Fredericksburg & Potomac.. | 82 | Richmond and Quantico................. | .................. | |
| Coal Pits............................ | 4 | ........................................ | .................. | |
| Alexandria & Potomac.................. | 27 | Alexandria and Quantico............... | .................. | 123 |
| Alexandria & Washington.............. | 7 | Alexandria and Washington............ | Baltimore....... | |
| Richmond & Petersburg.................. | 23 | Richmond and Petersburg.............. | .................. | |
| Petersburg & Weldon.................... | 50 | Petersburg and North Carolina Line.... | Weldon, N. C.... | 106 |
| Gaston Branch....................... | 15 | ........................................ | Gaston, N. C.... | |
| Clover Hill............................... | 23 | Osborne's and Clover Hill............... | .................. | |
| Seaboard & Roanoke.................... | 60 | Portsmouth and North Carolina Line.... | Weldon, N. C.... | 80 |
| Richmond, York River & Chesapeake.... | 38 | Richmond and West Point............... | Baltimore....... | 38 |
| Washington & Ohio...................... | 52 | Alexandria and Round Hill.............. | .................. | 52 |
| Valley Railroad.......................... | 104 | Wadesville or W. Va. Line and Staunton | Baltimore ....... | 207 |
| Fredericksburg & Gordonsville†......... | 20 | Fredericksburg and Gordonsville........ | .................. | 20 |
| Miles of *completed* railroad *in* Virginia January 1st, 1876...................... | 1,617 | | | |

To summarize the railroad systems of the state in operation—

Tidewater has a north and south line *connecting the "head of tide"* of its navigable streams, and another system from the north coming down to the Eastern Shore.

*Four* lines run down its peninsulas *to deeper waters.*

Middle has north and south lines along each side of it, and one passing through half its length. The equivalent of six railways crosses the Middle Country.

Piedmont has a line along its border, and in it for four-fifths of its length, and is crossed or penetrated by five lines.

Three lines cross the Blue Ridge, and the lines along the valley are parallel to it.

The Valley has a line its whole length nearly completed, and another one-third of its length well under way: one road crosses it in the state, and another in West Virginia, near by.

One line runs for some distance with and across Appalachia.

* Including 7 miles of Alexandria and Washington Railroad, and 21 of Chesapeake and Ohio.

† But partially completed.

*Eight great through lines of trade and travel* either cross Virginia, to and from the centres of trade and population in other states, or start from such points in the state, and it has the advantage of being so situated as to compel the trade of a large portion of the South, Southwest and West of the United States to seek its borders.

To provide for TRANSPORTATION BY WATER, Virginia has spent large sums of money in improving the navigation of many of her rivers, not only in Tidewater, but in other portions of the state: the introduction of railways has done away with the use of most of those above tide for purposes of navigation, but the locks and dams furnish a large amount of fine water power in all portions of the state.

The navigable tidal rivers have been, and are being constantly improved, by the General Government and the cities of the state, by removing bars, opening channels, &c.

Several *canals* cross the Norfolk peninsula and connect the waters of Albemarle Sound and those of Chesapeake Bay, by way of Norfolk, making that city the entrepot for a vast system of *inland* steam and ship navigation, that will eventually embrace a large portion of the Atlantic and Gulf coasts of the United States. These canals are—

The ALBEMARLE AND CHESAPEAKE CANAL, with *two cuts*—first, the *Virginia*, eight miles long, connects the Southern Branch of Elizabeth river (the harbor of the United States Navy Yard, Gosport, a part of the harbor of Norfolk, deep enough for any vessel afloat) with the North Landing River that runs into Albemarle sound; and second, the *North Carolina Cut*, a *ship canal, open at all seasons*, from Norfolk to Albemarle sound, and all the tidal waters of North Carolina. The last is a great work, in complete order: it has but one lock, 220 feet long and 40 wide, and seven feet deep, through which vessels of 400 to 600 tons burden pass; it has a capacity for 30 millions tons a year. From 1860 to 1871, there passed through this canal 11,292 steamers, 6,832 schooners, 2,030 sloops, 5,812 lighters, 1,991 barges, 209 rafts, 6,002 boats, or 35,058 in all. Nearly 5,000 of these passages were in 1871. Steam is the motive power used. The freight brought to Norfolk by this canal embraced large quantities of cotton, salt fish, turpentine, lumber, shingles, staves, railroad ties, wood, juniper logs, bacon, peas and beans, wheat, fresh shad, watermelons, &c. The forest products of timber amounting to over 60 million feet of board measure.

The DISMAL SWAMP CANAL connects the same waters by another route, penetrating more of the swamp region of the Norfolk peninsula, but having the same kind of through trade. The receipts* by this canal for 1872 will not only give a good idea of the business of these ship canals, but also of the trade and products of the "*low country*": 1,365 bales of cotton, 8,606 barrels fish, 204,470 bushels of corn, 61,298 cubic feet of timber, 3,708,980 shingles, 179,975 staves, 166 bushels flaxseed, 13,128 bushels potatoes, 257,200 railroad ties, 5,111 cords of wood, 4,994 bushels of beans, 6,419 bushels of wheat, 7,108 cords of logs, 117,134 M. fresh shad, 127,120 plank, 14,058 posts, 113 cords of reeds for paper, 264,650 M. rails for fences, 604 cattle, 22,133 chickens, 53,523 dozen eggs.

By these canals there is a through route from North Carolina to Norfolk, then up Chesapeake bay to the Chesapeake and Delaware canal, eight feet deep and 14

*Report of President Rogers.

miles long, to Delaware bay; then by the Delaware and Raritan canal, seven feet deep and 43 miles long, to Raritan river, and by that to New York harbor.

It is hardly possible to overestimate the importance of the system of canals just described, and the effect the cheap transportation they can offer must have on the coastwise trade of nearly all the Atlantic States. An example of what may be done shows the probabilities of the near future. Barges on the James River and Kanawha canal may be loaded with iron or coal in Appalachia, and without break of bulk be delivered in Baltimore, Philadelphia, New York, Albany, many towns on the Great Lakes, &c.

The James River and Kanawha Canal, intended to continue water navigation to the sources of the James near the White Sulphur Springs, and then, after going through the Alleghany watershed, to descend the Greenbrier, New and Great Kanawha rivers to the Ohio, has been completed by the State, at great expense, from tidewater, at Richmond, across the Middle, Piedmont and Blue Ridge and far into the Valley Country, 198 miles, to Buchanan, where the Valley Railroad crosses the James. Much work has been done on the thirty-two miles between Buchanan and Clifton Forge, where the James River and Kanawha Canal reaches the line of the Chesapeake and Ohio Railroad. That portion will no doubt be completed at an early day, putting the canal in the line of the vast transportation of coal, iron, &c., that must come over the Chesapeake and Ohio. The State has offered to give this canal to the General Government, on condition that the work be extended to the Ohio and its capacity enlarged so that it may become a great *Central Water Line*, uniting the navigable waters of the Chesapeake and the Mississippi where the distance between those waters is the shortest and where Providence has cut away many of the obstacles that on other routes oppose the improvement. It is probable that the General Assembly, at its present session (1875–'6), will authorize the extension of this canal to the mouth of Craig's creek, 15 miles up the James beyond Buchanan, and the construction of a railway thence to the Clifton Forge station of the Chesapeake and Ohio Railroad, using the convict labor of the State in the work. This route would be obstructed but little by ice, and the heat would not be so great as to injure agricultural and other cargoes that suffer from a high temperature. The work has been pronounced practicable by competent authorities. This canal is now a valuable commercial line up the fertile valley of the James, with its large products of agriculture, to Lynchburg, a thriving commercial and manufacturing city, where it is brought into connections with the Atlantic, Mississippi and Ohio and the Midland railroads. Its continuation into the Valley by its main line to Buchanan and to Lexington by a branch up North River 19¾ miles long, gives it a large trade from those important points, and this will be largely increased when the Valley Railroad is completed to the same places. A branch of this canal extends up the Rivanna river for some distance. The fine granite, gneiss, limestone, sandstone, slate and other quarries; the large deposits of iron ores of several kinds, including magnetite and hematite; the copper and gold of the "gold belt;" the cement, manganese, &c., found all along the line of this canal, where it is in operation, add much to its importance, and when the mineral wealth of the tributary country is exploited, as it should and will be, its capacity will be taxed for transportation. The condition of the country it is yet to penetrate has been already given.

The fall* of this canal from Buchanan to mean tide level, at Richmond, is 812 feet; this gives a vast water power, utilized in some places, but offering great inducements for manufacturing enterprises. The fall at the tidewater connection is 84 feet in 1½ miles. The terminal dock and basin at Richmond are extensive works, and much used in the transfer of cargoes to and from warehouses and between canal boats and vessels of all kinds here brought side by side.

The following extracts from the annual report of 1875 of Colonel C. S. Carrington, President of the James River and Kanawha Canal Company, to the stockholders, furnish much valuable information in regard to this important canal and the country tributary to it:

"In regard to your property, there are facts now known which furnish reliable data for calculation, and give unusual certainty for estimates of its value when the connection with Clifton Forge is completed. The cost of the canal to Buchanan and the work done, and cost of the same, west of that point, and the capacity of the canal for transportation, whether in the amount of freight which it can now carry, or after its improvement, at the small cost reported, or in the character of this transportation in its adaptation to the products of agriculture and to the largest development of a great mineral region, and also the character of the rail line to Clifton Forge and its comparative capacity for transportation from the west to that point and beyond, are all known with reasonable certainty. The value of the coal and of the iron ores on this line of water and rail are also now well known. The information about these minerals is so full and precise as to permit an intelligent consideration and decision of the results of their cheap transportation on this line.

"After the completion of the canal to Clifton Forge this line of transportation will be rail from the valley of the Mississippi to Clifton Forge, and by water from Clifton Forge to tidewater, or in a narrow view, by rail from the great Kanawha coal-field to Clifton Forge (94 miles from its eastern boundary, and 130 miles from the centre of this field), with a grade from the west against the coal not exceeding 20 feet to the mile, except 12 miles of 30 feet, and with an annual capacity for transportation to Clifton Forge of 2,000,000 tons, and less than 1,000,000 tons with the same power, east of Clifton Forge to tidewater, because of higher grades. From Clifton Forge to tidewater the transportation will be by canal with an annual capacity of 3,000,000 tons, and with rates of transportation lower than on other canals of like dimensions, because, first, the season of navigation will be longer, averaging not less than eleven months in the year; and, second, this canal will have the advantage of back freights.

"This extension will be the completion of 'the last span of the bridge' which will give value to the whole. Many of the elements of a great tonnage appear from a glance at the line and its location. Its low railroad grades, and water, and genial climate, and terminal facilities secure the lowest rates of transportation across the Alleghany mountains to tidewater. In its central connection of the productive west with tidewater, it will pass for 230 miles through the valley of the James river, which has a capacity for agricultural production as great as any portion of this country east of the Alleghany mountains, and which, with the valley of the Kanawha, contains mineral wealth greater in quantity, variety and value than can be found on any other line of transportation in this country.

"Within range of the Kanawha river, the quantity of available coal is so very large, that, practically, for one thousand years to come, it may be regarded as unlimited, and it can be mined at a cheaper rate than coals are mined in Europe or America. (Testimony of Professor Ansted before committee United States Senate.) Major-General Gillmore, United States corps of engineers, in his report to the Board of Engineers, says that, with proper carrying facilities,

* Report of President Carrington, 1874.

at least 10,000,000 tons of coal per annum would be at once drawn from the Kanawha coal-field. The Kanawha coals are better, purer, and more available for all the requirements of trade and manufacture, than the coals of any other portion of the Alleghany coal-field. (Professor Daddow.) The value of these coals in making iron and its manufactures, and as steam and gas coals, and for household purposes, is not a matter of speculation. They are used daily for all of these purposes, with an ever increasing demand for them. The New river coke, in the eastern portion of this coal-field and nearest to the iron ores of Virginia, is shown, both by analysis and experiment, to be better for making iron and for use in iron manufacture than either the Connelville coke or anthracite coal. By like experiment the New river coal is proved to be at least the equal of the Cumberland coal; as a steam coal, and for gas and household purposes, the Kanawha coals are superseding other coals within the range of their economical transportation.

"The canal from Clifton Forge (including the North river branch) passes through not less than 175 miles of iron territory. This iron belt extends to within 75 miles of Richmond; but consider it as limited to 100 miles on the canal, 50 miles west of the Blue Ridge and 50 miles east of Lynchburg. West of the Blue Ridge, the iron ores are the fossil and red and brown hematite ores. There is no question as to the great quantity of these ores or of their value. They have been worked for many years past, and produced first class iron. Some of the furnaces of this region were once famous for the excellence of their iron for cannon and other purposes requiring iron of great strength.

"The iron ores east of Lynchburg are the magnetic, specular and limonite or brown hematite ores. General St. John and Professors Smith and Mallet, of the University of Virginia, referring in their recent report to the veins of these ores, say: 'They succeed each other so closely and in such number, and they attain at single localities such very large absolute dimensions, that it is safe to say, without calculating upon future developments, that there is ore already uncovered and in outcrop comparable as to mass with the more favored localities of iron production in the United States.' The amount of metallic iron in 16 analyses of these ores was 56, 58, 43, 38, 66, 57, 64, 53, 57, 66, 45, 31, 50, 58, 65 and 63 per cent. These magnetic ores are practically free from phosphorus and sulphur. Only a small portion of them are titaniferous. In favor of the above analyses, where the metallic iron was 65, 57, 65 and 66, the titanic acid was .15, .12, .10, and in the fourth only a trace. These ores are very accessible to the canal. They are generally comprised within a distance of a few miles from its banks, with descending grades to the canal landings, thus reducing within moderate limits the items of transportation by wagon and tramway, so often embarrassing in furnace operations. Among many other favorable conditions for making iron at low cost on the canal may be mentioned the abundance of limestone, yielding, west of the Blue Ridge, from 95 to 97 per cent. of lime, and east of Lynchburg, from 75 to 80 per cent. Good sites for furnaces, with ample grounds, a healthy and productive country, abundant supplies of cheap lumber from West Virginia and from the line of the Lynchburg and Danville railroad, water power at the dams across James river, and the free, convenient and cheap transportation by water for the delivery of supplies and stock and removal of product.

"The estimates of experts of the cost of making iron on the canal after its completion to Clifton Forge have been from $12.45 to $19 per ton of 2,240 pounds. There is almost a concurrence of opinion with these parties, that iron will be made on the canal and delivered at tidewater at as low cost, and probably lower cost than elsewhere in this country. The prices of iron indicate the necessity of its production in this country at cheaper rates. Capital largely interested elsewhere in making iron is now employed in this field. Such capital may come more slowly, but it is improbable that the capital of the country will long neglect the advantages of making first-class iron on this line. The substitution of steel for iron is rapidly increasing throughout the world. The Bessemer process, chiefly in vogue for making steel, requires pig iron free from phosphorus. Ores of this character are very scarce east of Lake Superior, and the demand for Bessemer pig iron is greater than the supply. The magnetic ores on the canal have now for several years been subjected to a thorough investigation by parties interested in making Bessemer pig iron. These investigations show that such iron can be made from these ores at a reduced cost. This fact, in connection with the position of these ores on the Atlantic seaboard, increases the probability of the rapid construction of furnaces on the line of the canal.

"There are now fifteen furnaces on the line of canal to Clifton Forge and in its vicinity. Those accessible to the Kanawha coals are in operation, and also some charcoal furnaces. All would be in blast if they could use the coals and cokes of Kanawha, and capital is reported as ready to build other furnaces as soon as it is assured of the extension of the canal to Clifton Forge.

"General St. John and Professors Smith and Mallet report 'that a single large blast furnace (of 65×16 feet) would, for the items of fuel, limestone, ore for admixture, product of pig iron and store supplies, demand an annual transportation of between 60,000 and 80,000 tons, and yet several of these furnaces are operated under single proprietorship in many of the old iron districts.' The annual product of such a furnace is 14,000 tons. The furnace at Quinnimont on New river, with an annual capacity of 10,000 to 12,000 tons, and situated at the coal bank, yields to the Chesapeake and Ohio Railroad a monthly revenue of some $10,000. The fifteen furnaces on the canal and in its vicinity are each probably capable of an annual production on average of 2,800 tons, or together 42,000 tons, an amount equal to the production of three of these large furnaces.

"The Lake Superior ores are transported in large quantities to furnaces in the east and in the valley of the Mississippi. Experts in the east, familiar with this demand and with these canal ores, make very large estimates of their shipments eastward as a substitute for Lake Superior ores. These magnetic ores are now used in combination with hematite ores, in a furnace near Richmond, to the extent of one-half the charge, and 'the iron thus made is well known among experts to rank among the strongest and best brands of American production.' (Report of General St. John and Professors Smith and Mallet.) They will be carried to the hematite ores on the canal west of the Blue Ridge. * * These ores will also be transported to the hematite ores on the line of the Chesapeake and Ohio Railroad and in the valley of the Ohio. If used in the same proportion as at the furnace near Richmond, every furnace of 14,000 tons will use 21,000 tons of these ores, and ten such furnaces, 210,000 tons, giving this amount of back freight to the canal, and an additional annual revenue of more than $70,000 at a toll rate of 3 mills per ton per mile.

"The granite, slate, cement and lime of the valley of James river are without practical limit in quantity, and of superior quality. The granite and slate have been sent to St. Louis, via New Orleans, by water and by rail, and their successful competition in that distant market was only prevented by their long transportation.

"The lime is made by one firm in Botetourt county to the extent of 50,000 barrels annually, and is being introduced into many of the Southern States, and the cement is used in Kentucky, and has been chosen for a lock to be constructed by the general government on the Kanawha river.

"The canal and railroad will be the line of transportation to and from the west for Lynchburg, 82 miles east of Clifton Forge. This city will be a distributing point for Kanawha coal to the railroads centreing there and to the country south and southwest penetrated by them. It is one of the largest and most prosperous tobacco markets of the State, and situated in the centre of the iron district on the canal, and with cheap coal from Kanawha, will become a great centre of iron manufacture."

The canal from Alexandria to Georgetown connects with the CHESAPEAKE AND OHIO CANAL, of Maryland, in which Virginia has an interest. This canal is valuable as an outlet to all portions of the State bordering on the Potomac above Alexandria. It brings to that city a large tonnage of coal from the celebrated Cumberland mines.

The Roanoke Navigation Company has improved the navigation of portions of the Roanoke river and of its branch, the Dan, giving water transit from Danville down through an important and highly productive country.

## Section II.—Transportation by Tidal Ways.

Few regions of equal size are as well provided by the beneficent Creator with natural highways for trade and transportation as Tidewater Virginia. Navigable bays, rivers, creeks, &c., penetrate and permeate every portion of it—so much so that there is *a mile of tidal shore* to every *six square miles* of territory.

Chesapeake Bay, lying within the domain of Virginia for over 70 miles of the 200 of its length, where its width is from 14 to 30 miles, is unsurpassed, as a great inland sea of diversified outline, for commercial purposes; it is not subject to violent storms; there are harbors all along its shores, none of which are rock bound or dangerous; its waters are deep and free from obstructions; a vessel bound up it, and following the "sailing directions," once fairly inside the "Capes of Virginia" runs on an air-line of north ¼° east for over 50 miles. Into this bay flow the waters of 50,000 square miles of productive country. It is rapidly becoming the "Mediterranean" for the outgoing and incoming commerce of the great Central Belt of American states, which here find an easy exit and entrance to and from the great ocean highways. This is the refuge for ships on all the middle coast from stress of weather.

The following table, from the United States Coast Survey Report for 1857, shows the character of the channels from the Bay to some of the harbors and anchorages of Virginia, and proves their advantages as ports for the largest class of vessels, especially as they are *never obstructed by ice:*

| | Least Water in Channel Way. | | | |
|---|---|---|---|---|
| | Mean Tides. | | Spring Tides. | |
| | Low Water. Feet. | High Water. Feet. | Low Water. Feet. | High Water. Feet. |
| Between the Capes at entrance to Hampton Roads, | 30. | 32.5 | 29.8 | 32.8 |
| Anchorage in Hampton Roads | 59. | 61.5 | 58.8 | 61.8 |
| From Hampton Roads to Sewall's Point | 25. | 27.5 | 24.8 | 27.8 |
| South of Sewall's Point 1½ miles | 21. | 23.5 | 20.8 | 23.8 |
| Up to Norfolk | 23. | 25.5 | 22.8 | 25.8 |
| From Hampton Roads to James River, entering north of Newport News Middle ground | 22. | 24.5 | 21.7 | 24.8 |
| Same—entering south of above | 27. | 29.5 | 26.7 | 29.8 |
| York River from abreast the tail of York Spit up to Yorktown | 33. | 35.5 | 32.7 | 35.8 |
| Elizabeth River between Norfolk and the Navy Yard | 25.5 | 28. | 25.3 | 28.3 |

The Potomac River is navigable for 110 miles above its entrance into Chesapeake Bay, 100 miles from the ocean. The head of navigation is Georgetown, in the Federal District. Washington, the Capital of the United States, is 2 miles lower down, and Alexandria, a flourishing Virginia city and port, is seven miles farther. These three cities are connected by canal, steam ferries and railway, and from them lines of steamers and sailing vessels of all kinds run to the numerous landings on the Potomac and the towns and cities of the bay and its tributaries; they also have a considerable coastwise and some foreign trade. Numerous lines of railways converge to these cities from all directions.

Alexandria is the terminus of the Alexandria and Washington Railway, giving connections to all points North and West; the Washington and Ohio, running through the fine Piedmont country and yet to run to the Ohio; the Washington City, Virginia Midland and Great Southern, part of the great South and Southwest system of railways; the Alexandria and Potomac, connecting with the South; the Baltimore and Ohio, with its numerous connections, runs to the opposite bank of the Potomac, and its cars are ferried across. There are numerous landings along the Potomac, giving great facilities for the shipment of produce and for communication with the extensive and excellent country, abounding in fine grain and fruit farms, along its shores. Alexandria and Georgetown are Ports of Entry.

The RAPPAHANNOCK is navigable to Fredericksburg, 92 miles from Chesapeake Bay, for steamers and sailing vessels drawing 8* feet. At Fredericksburg it is crossed by the great north and south line of railways from Baltimore and Washington to Richmond, and meets a nearly completed one from Gordonsville that will connect with the Chesapeake and Ohio and the Virginia Midland—most important lines, the trade from which will greatly benefit the city in question. The river was once improved above Fredericksburg, by locks and dams, as a canal; these are now used for water power. Port Royal, 22 miles below Fredericksburg, is a point to which vessels of larger draught can come; it is the port of a very fertile section. Tappahannock, the Port of Entry for the river, is 60 miles below Fredericksburg; vessels drawing 11½ feet can ascend to that place. Urbana is also an important port. Besides the places named, there are numerous landings on both banks, where the lines of steamers that run regularly from Fredericksburg to Baltimore stop for freight and passengers. The valley of the Rappahannock is a productive one, and its trade employs a good many sailing vessels.

The PIANKETANK is navigable for some 14 miles.

MOBJACK BAY and its tributary rivers give deep entrances to the fine Gloucester peninsula.

YORK river is a wide, deep and almost straight *belt* of water-reach over 40 miles long from the Bay to the junction of Pamunkey and Mattapony rivers, that form it, at West Point; those rivers are also navigable many miles for light draught vessels. Ships drawing 13 feet can go *to* West Point at all times, while the depth is 27 feet up to within a short distance. The Richmond, York River and Chesapeake Railroad connects West Point with Richmond and a daily line of steamers with Baltimore. There are numerous landings on the York, at which the steamers stop; the most important of these is Yorktown, the county town of York county, which

---

* United States Engineer's Report, 1871. It is proposed to deepen the channel to 10 feet, and appropriations have been made for the work.

has been selected as one of the deep water termini of the Chesapeake and Ohio Railroad—which is to be extended down The Peninsula by Williamsburg, the seat of William and Mary College. Yorktown is 16 miles* from the Bay.

There is a line of steamers from Yorktown to and from Norfolk, by way of Cherrystone, the Port of Entry for the Eastern shore peninsula, and Mathews Court-house; and the daily line to and from Baltimore touches here in going to and from West Point.

The MATTAPONY is navigable some 30 miles above the York to Aylett's and the PAMUNKEY 35 miles to Oyster Shell Landing. The valley of the York is celebrated for its fertility, and the river itself for its oysters and fish.

JAMES RIVER is navigable 110 miles, for vessels drawing 14 feet of water, to Richmond, the Capital of Virginia and a Port of Entry with a Custom House, where, at the head of its tides, it is crossed by the numerous lines of railway that radiate in all directions from that flourishing city. The navigation of the James is extended for 198 miles beyond Richmond by the water line of the James River and Kanawha Canal. Vessels drawing 15 feet can ascend at all times to City Point, 60 miles below Richmond, at the mouth of the Appomattox. It has at all times 30 feet of water and at high tide 32½ at its entrance, and Hampton Roads, the magnificent expansion of its mouth, has from 59 to 62 feet of depth in its anchorage, which is ample enough to float the marine of the world in its land-locked and well-defended limits. Numerous lines of steamers and sailing vessels run regularly to and from Richmond, touching at numerous landings on the James, connecting it directly with Norfolk, Baltimore, Philadelphia, New York and other places. Seventy-seven merchant ships belonged to the Richmond District in 1871. The James is acknowledged to be one of the finest navigable rivers of the Atlantic slope, and the fine lands—farming, planting, trucking forest, &c.—along it have great advantages in transportation at low rates. The branches of the James are the APPOMATTOX, navigable from City Point, 12 miles, to Petersburg, a thriving city, where lines of railway connect in all directions (one line to the deeper water at City Point); the CHICKAHOMINY, navigable for small steamers and vessels for many miles; PAGAN CREEK, a fine stream navigable to Smithfield; NANSEMOND river, navigable 15 miles to Suffolk and the railroads there—its lower reach a broad and deep estuary; ELIZABETH river, the noble stream on which the thriving seaport cities of Norfolk, Portsmouth and Gosport are situated, navigable 12 miles or more, with from 23 to 28 feet of water, and extended by ship canals to the bays of North Carolina. Eight miles from the James the Elizabeth expands into the noble harbor of Norfolk and Portsmouth, in which the depth of water is from 25.5 to 28.3 feet.

Norfolk and Portsmouth had, in 1871, belonging to their district, 335 merchant vessels. From these cities there is a *daily* line of steamers to Baltimore; another to Washington City and landings on the Potomac; another to Richmond and landings on the James; also regular steamers to Cherrystone, Mathews Courthouse and Yorktown; to Hampton and Fortress Monroe; by ship canal to Roanoke Island, Washington and Murfreesboro', North Carolina; to Boston, to Philadelphia and to New York, and to Liverpool, England. They have, besides, lines of sailing vessels

---

*English statute miles are the only ones used in this Summary.

of various kinds running not only to all parts of Tidewater Virginia, of which Norfolk is the commercial capital, but also to all portions of the trading world.

Norfolk, by the completion of railway connections and other transportation routes, is vindicating, by results, the advantages she possesses for commercial operations. In* 1858 this city received 6,174 bales of cotton; in 1873–'4 she received 467,561, and became the third cotton port of the United States (not far below Savannah, the second). In 1866 Norfolk exported to Europe but 733 bales; in 1873–'4 the export was 20,346 and for the first quarter of 1874–'5 it was 40,799 bales sent direct to Europe.

Hampton, the seat of the flourishing Hampton Normal and Agricultural Institute, and Newport's News, near the end of "The Peninsula," are on the splendid roadstead of Hampton Roads. The Chesapeake and Ohio Railway will no doubt have one of its deep water termini near these places, when they will become great shipping points.

There are numerous other navigable streams in Tidewater Virginia; and it may be again repeated that every portion of it is accessible, at all seasons, to craft of some description, and that from no section of the United States can the productions of the country be more readily and cheaply sent to market.

---

*Report of President Mahone to State, 1874.

## CHAPTER XI.

### THE FORM OF GOVERNMENT OF VIRGINIA.

The State of Virginia is an independent Republic, except in regard to powers which she, in common with the other states of the Union, has conferred upon the General Government of the United States for the common defence and general welfare of all the states, by a written constitution.

All the powers not expressly given to the Government of the Union are reserved to the states, and each one of these is independent in the exercise of these reserved powers.

The principle that underlies the foundation of the government of Virginia (as well as of all the different states of the Union and of the Union itself) is, that *Government is of the People* and *for the People;* is instituted for their common benefit, security and protection, and that they, or a majority of them, have a perfect right to frame, change or abolish it as they may judge most conducive to the public welfare.

The form adopted (and that has been most successfully and satisfactorily administered for a hundred years, 1876), is Republican; one in which the sovereign power is exercised by delegates and officers *elected* by the people, subject to the provisions and limitations of a written constitution, which has been adopted by the people as the organic law of the land.

The constitution of the State is prefaced by a "Bill of Rights," which sets forth the rights of the people, the State and the General Government. This Declaration is made part of the organic law. It declares "that all men are by nature equally free and independent;" "that they have inherent rights for the enjoyment of life and liberty," for "acquiring and possessing of property," and for "pursuing and obtaining happiness and safety." That the State is a member of the United States of America, and its people part of the American nation. That the constitution of the United States and the laws passed in pursuance of it are the *supreme* law of the land. That all power is vested in and derived from the people, and magistrates are their servants and trustees, and always amenable to them. That exclusive privileges belong to no man or set of men, and that no offices are hereditary. That the object of government is the common good of all, and that form is best that produces the greatest happiness and safety and is best secured against mal-administration. That the people have a *perfect* right to reform or abolish the form of government, as they shall judge best for the public welfare. That the legislative, executive and judicial powers should be kept separate, and that at fixed periods all officers should be remanded to private station, so they may feel and share the burthens of the people—all vacancies to be filled by "frequent, certain and regular elections." That all elections ought to be free, and all men having an interest in the community should have the right of suffrage, and cannot be taxed or bound by any law without their personal or representative consent, expressed at a popular election—the will of the majority governing.

That laws, or their execution, should not be suspended but by consent of the people's representatives. That in all criminal prosecutions a man may demand the cause and nature of charges made against him; that he shall be confronted by his accusers and witnesses; may call for witnesses in his favor; shall have a speedy trial by an impartial jury of his vicinage, "without whose unanimous consent he cannot be found guilty;" that he cannot be compelled to give evidence against himself, or be deprived of liberty but by law or the judgment of his peers. That excessive bail shall not be required, excessive fines imposed or cruel or unusual punishment inflicted. That general warrants of search shall not be granted on suspicion merely, without evidence of deeds done, or persons seized, unless by name and offence described and supported by evidence. That trial by jury is preferable in controversies about property and in suits between man and man, and should be held sacred. That the freedom of the press cannot be restrained or the right of any citizen to speak, write or publish his sentiments on all subjects--being responsible for the abuse of that liberty. That the body of the people trained to arms are the proper and safe defence of a free state. That standing armies, in peace, should be avoided, and that the military should always be subordinate to the civil power. That the people have a right to a uniform government, and that none independent of that of Virginia should be set up within her limits. That free governments can only be preserved by a "firm adherence to justice, moderation, temperance and virtue, and by a frequent recurrence to fundamental principles." That there should be perfect toleration in matters of religion, all men being free to follow the dictates of conscience, at the same time recognizing the duty of mutual forbearance. That there shall be no involuntary servitude, except as imprisonment for crime. That all citizens of the State possess equal civil and political rights and public privileges. And finally, that the enumeration of rights does not limit other rights of the people because not enumerated.

The Government of the State is entrusted to three departments—the LEGISLATIVE, the EXECUTIVE and the JUDICIAL, each with distinct and separate powers and officers.

### LEGISLATIVE.

The LEGISLATIVE, or Law-making, power of the State is vested in a GENERAL ASSEMBLY, consisting of two bodies—a Senate and a House of Delegates.

The HOUSE OF DELEGATES consists of 132 members, apportioned among the cities and counties of the Commonwealth, in proportion to population; elected to serve for two years, the election being held for the whole State every two years, on the Tuesday after the first Monday in November.

The SENATE consists of 43 members, the whole State being divided into that many districts (embracing cities, towns and counties), as nearly equal in population as may be. The districts are numbered, and those having even numbers elect biennially a senator for four years at one of the elections above mentioned, and those bearing odd numbers at the next succeeding election, so that although all the senators are elected for four years, one-half of them go out of office every two years. The State is districted anew after each decennial census of the United States for senatorial and delegate districts.

Any person resident in the district, and a qualified voter for members of the Senate or House of Delegates, may be elected a member of either body; he must continue a resident while he represents.

The Senate is presided over by the Lieutenant-Governor of the State, or, in his absence, by a President *pro tempore;* the House of Delegates is presided over by a Speaker elected by the body from among its own members.

Bills and resolutions may originate in either house, to be approved or rejected by the other. In order that any bill may become a law, it must have passed the Senate and House of Delegates and be approved by the Governor of the State. If the Governor does not approve of the proposed law he returns it, with his objections, and it can only become a law then by having two-thirds of the members of each house agree to it by a recorded vote. No bill can become a law until it has been read on three different days in the house in which it originated, unless two-thirds of the members determine otherwise. Each house is required to keep a journal of its proceedings and publish the same from time to time. No law can embrace more than one object. The House of Delegates alone has the power to prosecute for impeachment, and the Senate the power to try such cases.

The General Assembly is forbidden the power to legislate in a number of cases—in that it cannot pass a bill of attainder, an *ex post facto* law, a law impairing the obligation of contracts, one taking private property for public use without just compensation, one abridging the freedom of speech or of the press. It cannot compel any one to frequent or support any religious worship or molest him in any way on account of his religious belief; nor can matters of religion in any way affect one's civil capacities. The General Assembly cannot prescribe any religious test, confer any peculiar privileges on any sect, or authorize any society or the people of any district to levy on themselves or others a tax for any church purposes, leaving each one free to select his own religious instructor as he may please and provide for him by private contract. It cannot grant a charter of incorporation to any church or sect, but can secure the title to church property to a limited extent. The General Assembly has no power to establish a lottery, or to form new counties except under restriction; and it must confer upon the courts the power to grant divorces, change names, direct sales of estates of infants, &c., avoiding special legislation where courts, &c., have jurisdiction. The manner of conducting elections, making returns, filling vacancies in office, &c., is provided for by law.

## Executive.

The *Executive* power is vested in a Governor, elected for four years, and ineligible for the next four years after his term of service expires. The people choose the Governor at the election in November, before mentioned; he must be a citizen of the United States, and if foreign born, must have been one for ten years; must be 30 years old, and have been a resident of the State 3 years preceding his election. The Governor must reside at the seat of government. His duties are to take care that the laws are faithfully executed; communicate to the General Assembly at every session the condition of the Commonwealth; recommend such measures for their consideration as he may deem expedient; call extra sessions of the General Assembly when he shall consider that the interests of the Commonwealth demand it, or when requested to do so by two-thirds of the members. He is Commander-in-Chief of the land and naval forces of the State, and has power to embody the militia to repel invasion, suppress insurrection and enforce the laws, &c. The Governor holds intercourse with other and foreign states; fills vacancies in offices when not otherwise provided for; he has also the pardoning power, the granting of reprieves, remission of fines, &c., under provisions of law. He attests the commissions and grants of the State, and has a veto upon the acts of the General Assembly, as before recited.

A Lieutenant-Governor is elected at the same time and for the same term as the Governor and having the same qualifications; he is President of the Senate, having a vote only in case of an equal division. In the event of the removal from office, death, &c., of the Governor, he becomes the Executive of the State.

A *Secretary of the Commonwealth*, a *Treasurer* and an *Auditor of public accounts* are elected every two years, by the General Assembly, to discharge the duties pertaining to such offices, and in addition, there may be established in the office of the Secretary of State a bureau of agricultural chemistry and geology. Power is also granted to the General Assembly to establish a bureau of agriculture and immigration.

A *Board of Public Works*, composed of the Governor, Auditor and Treasurer, is provided, having charge of the Internal Improvement interests of the State.

A *Board of Education*, composed of the Governor, Superintendent of Public Instruction and Attorney General, has charge of the Public School System of the State; the *Superintendent of Public Instruction*, the Executive of this Board, is elected by the General Assembly, and holds office for four years.

A *Board of Immigration*, consisting of the Governor, the Speaker of the House of Delegates, the Secretary of the Commonwealth, the Auditor and the Treasurer, is charged with certain duties in collecting and disseminating information about the State.

### Judiciary Department.

There are provided a *Supreme Court of Appeals*, consisting of five judges; *Circuit Courts*, of which there are sixteen judges, the State being divided into that many judicial districts; and *County Courts*, presided over by judges—one for each of the counties of the State (except that counties with less than 8,000 inhabitants are attached to adjoining counties).

The *Judges of the Court of Appeals* are chosen by the General Assembly for a term of twelve years; they must have held judicial position or have practiced law for five years in the United States when chosen. This court is one of "appeal" only, except in cases of *habeas corpus*, *mandamus* and prohibition. It can only consider civil cases where the matter involved has a value of $500 or more, *except* in controversies concerning the title or boundaries of land; the probate of a will; the appointment, &c., of a guardian, committee, &c.; or concerning a mill, roadway, ferry or landing; the right of a corporation or county to levy taxes or tolls.

This court decides the constutionality of laws; but it requires the assent of a majority of all the judges elected to the court to declare any law null and void because of its repugnance to the constitution of the State or that of the United States. This court must state the reasons for its decisions, in writing, to be filed with the records of the case. The Court of Appeals meets annually at Richmond, Staunton, Wytheville and Winchester, appeals from certain portions of the State being made to the court when sitting at either of these places.

An Attorney-General is elected, at every election of Governor, by the qualified voters of the State. He is the representative attorney for the State in all cases in which the Commonwealth is a party.

The *Judges* of the *Circuit Courts* are chosen by the General Assembly for eight years; they must have the same qualifications as the judges of the Court of Appeals, and must reside in the districts for which they are judges. Three terms of the Circuit Court are held yearly in each county. Courts of the same grade are also provided for the cities and towns having over 5,000 inhabitants. These courts have general jurisdiction in all matters of law and chancery, but appeals may be taken from their decisions, with certain limitations, to the Supreme Court of Appeals. They are also courts of appeal from the decision of the County Courts. The judges of the Circuit Courts are authorized to grant charters and incorporate companies for any purpose, except the construction of a canal or railway, under legal restrictions.

The *Judges* of the *County Courts* are chosen by the General Assembly for a term of six years. They must be "men learned in the law of the State." The jurisdiction of this court is such as may be by law provided; its powers are, at this time, 1873, limited, making it a court of probate and giving it jurisdiction of all presentments, informations and indictments for misdemeanors; it has power in all matters specially referred to it by statute. Terms of this court are held every month. This court has charge of the clerk's offices, in which deeds, contracts, &c., are recorded.

The voters of each county elect every three years a Sheriff, County Treasurer and Commonwealth's Attorney and a Superintendent of the Poor, and every six years a County Clerk (and in counties having over 15,000 inhabitants a separate Circuit Court Clerk). These are officers of both the County and Circuit Courts.

The counties of the State are divided into districts, not less than three in any county, in which are elected, biennially, a Supervisor and an Overseer of the Poor. These hold office for two years. They also elect, biennially, three Justices of the Peace and three Constables for a term of three years—there being three of these officers in each district. A Commissioner of the Revenue is elected for four years.

The Supervisors of each township form a County Board that audits the accounts of the county, examines the books of the assessors, regulates and equalizes the valuation of property for purposes of taxation, fixes and apportions the county levy, &c.

There are also School Districts in each township. (The details of the School System have been given under the head of Education).

Each district is divided into Road Districts, each in charge of an Overseer of Roads appointed by the County Court, under whose direction the roads of that district are kept in repair at the public expense.

Cities and towns are provided with separate governments suited to their wants, having a mayor, a council, special courts, &c.

## Militia.

All able-bodied males between 18 and 45, except those exempted by law, form the militia of the State, and the General Assembly has power to arm, equip and train them by provisions of law; the militia are simply enrolled as a reserve, and perform no service of any kind in time of peace, being only liable to service in times of danger. There are volunteer military companies, to which the State grants special privileges. The volunteers constitute the active militia.

## Taxation and Finance.

Taxation of all kinds must be equal and uniform, and all property is taxed in equal proportion to its value, ascertained as prescribed by law, *except* that no tax can be imposed on citizens of the State for the privilege of taking oysters, with tongs, from their natural beds, but the sales of such oysters may be taxed in proportion to their value; property used exclusively for state, city or county, religious, educational, charitable, and such like purposes, may be exempted; incomes in excess of $600 a year may be taxed; licenses for selling liquors, for shows, &c., and all business that cannot be reached by an *ad valorem* system, may be taxed specially; capital invested is taxed as other property; stocks are assessed at market value; a capitation tax, not exceeding one dollar per annum, can be levied on all males 21 and over for public school purposes, and corporations and counties are limited to a capitation tax that shall not exceed 50 cents a year for all purposes. The lands in the State are valued every five years by properly appointed assessors, and provisions are made to secure a fair valuation. The State cannot contract a debt except to meet casual deficits in the revenue, pay former liabilities, or for the defence of the State, and every law creating a debt must provide for its payment by a sinking fund; so also a sinking fund is provided to pay past indebtedness. The same bonds of the State are everywhere to bear the same rate of interest, and the bonds are to bear, in redemption, a value not exceeding that established for them by law when issued. No money can be paid from the treasury of the State except it has been appropriated by law, and the prohibition is positive against the payment of any debt created for aiding rebellion against the State or General Government. It requires a majority of all the members of each house of the General Assembly to make an appropriation, and the ayes and noes of the vote must be recorded.

The credit of the State cannot be granted in aid of any person, association or corporation; and no bonds, &c., can be given by which the State may become indebted except to pay former debts or as permitted by the constitution. The State cannot become a party in any company, interested in or carry on any work of internal improvement, except in the expenditure of grants made to it for such purposes.

Every law imposing a tax must state what the tax is for. The State is forbidden to pay the debts of counties, boroughs or cities, or to lend them its credit; and it must publish with its laws, every year, an accurate statement of receipts and expenditures of the public money and of the State's indebtedness. The taxes must be limited to an amount necessary for the expenses of the State and to pay its indebtedness. The State is forbidden to release any incorporated company or institution from the payment of money due to the State.

### Homestead and Other Exemptions.

Every householder or head of a family can hold a homestead, valued at not over $2,000, free from seizure for debt, &c., except for the purchase money of the property; the services of a laboring man or mechanic; for liabilities as a public officer, fiduciary, &c.; for taxes, legal fees, for rents, or for mortgage, &c., on the same. By law many household articles are also exempt from seizure. The laws in relation to homesteads must be construed liberally.

The passage of any law staying the collection of debts is prohibited. The rights of ecclesiastical bodies to property, conveyed to them according to law, are guaranteed.

To make any changes in the constitution it is necessary for two successive General Assemblies to agree to the amendments proposed and then for the voters of the State to assent.

All the provisions of government and law that have been mentioned are constitutional—therefore of permanent and binding force upon the government and people of the State until changed as just stated or by a convention that may be called by a vote of the electors of the State in 1888, or any 20th year thereafter; so there can be no sudden changes of the organic law.

All the laws of the State are obliged to conform to these general provisions, and any one having a good idea of these foundation principles may readily understand what the body of the laws of the State, or the Code, must be.

### Laws of General Interest.

There are some provisions of law that a stranger to the State would wish to have the salient features of more in detail; some such are selected from the "Code of 1873."

Citizens of the State are: all persons born in the State; all persons born in other states of the United States that become residents of the State; all aliens naturalized under the laws of the United States that become residents of the State; all persons that have by law acquired citizenship; all children, wherever born, whose father, or if he be dead, whose mother, is a citizen of the State at the time of such birth.

Citizenship may be relinquished by deed or declaration to a court of record where the person desiring to relinquish resides, if the party leaves the country; or when a person 21 years of age voluntarily becomes a citizen of another state he loses his citizenship in this; only this cannot be done as to a foreign state during a war with any foreign power.

Immigrants may make contracts in a foreign country, for not less than two years, for labor in this State, and have them attested before a United States Consul or commercial agent at the port where such immigrant shall embark, and the same can be fully enforced in Virginia. The contract must be made in duplicate—the original in the vernacular of the immigrant, which he holds, and which binds him; the copy must be in English, and recorded by the employer in the County Court clerk's office within 10 days after the arrival of the immigrant, to make it binding on him. The immigrant may require security for the payment of his wages by application to a Justice of the Peace, and if discharged without good and sufficient cause, may recover what is due for past services and damages not exceeding three months' wages; and if the person employed leaves his employer without cause he becomes liable for an amount equal to three months' wages.

The State has made provision for publication, setting forth its resources, advantages, &c., and inviting the population of other states to settle and capitalists and manufacturers to invest and erect establishments in the State. The Board of Immigration—the Governor being its President—has charge of this.

Aliens may hold Real Estate in Virginia under the following law, viz: "Any alien, not an enemy, may acquire by purchase or descent and hold real estate in this State; and the same shall be transmitted in the same manner as real estate held by citizens." It is also provided that "Alienage in any person claiming a distributive share of the personal estate shall be no impediment to his receiving the same share that he would have been entitled to if he had been a citizen;" and again, "In making title by descent, it shall be no bar to a party that any ancestor (whether living or dead), through whom he derives his descent from the intestate, is or hath been an alien." An alien may also purchase, transfer or locate land warrants, provided he within two years becomes a citizen or transfers his rights to a citizen.

The State of Virginia is divided into nine Congressional districts, from each of which is biennially elected by the voters a member of the House of Representatives of the United States. Every four years the General Assembly elects a member of the Senate of the United States, to be one of the two representing the State of Virginia in that body.

The Qualifications of a Voter in Virginia are: that he shall be a male citizen of the United States, 21 years old, who has been a resident of Virginia for one year, and of the county, city or town where he offers to vote for three months next preceding any election and is a registered voter and resident in the election district in which he offers to vote. No soldier, sailor or officer of the United States army or navy is made a resident by being stationed in the State. The following are also excluded from voting, viz: idiots, lunatics, persons convicted of bribery in any election, embezzlement of public funds, treason or felony, or any one that, while a citizen of the State, has since July 6th, 1869, fought a duel or in any way assisted in fighting one.

Every precaution has been taken by provisions of law, with penalties, to secure perfectly fair elections and give to every voter an opportunity to express his preference. No intoxicating liquors are allowed to be sold or distributed from sunset of the day before to sunrise of the day after any election in a county, corporation or district, under a penalty of a fine of $1,000 and imprisonment for a year. Voting is by secret ballot.

No one can hold office in Virginia that, being a citizen, has been engaged in a duel since 26th of January, 1870, or that holds any office of any kind under or has any emolument from the United States Government, except that members of Congress may act as justices, as visitors of the University and Military Institute, or as militia officers; nor does it apply to pensioners on account of wounds received in war, or those recompensed for military service. No one convicted of felony can hold office; nor can any one that buys or sells or proposes to farm out an office, in whole or in part, *except the sheriffalty*.

The Common Law of England, when not repugnant to the Bill of Rights and the Constitution of the State, is in full force and is the rule of decision, unless altered by law; and the same is true of all writs, remedial and judicial, of a general nature, made in aid of the common law of England prior to the reign of James the First.

The Justices of the Peace have concurrent jurisdiction with the County and Corporation Courts of all petit larcenies, and in cases of assault and battery not felonious; they are general conservators of the peace and may adjudicate any claim for damages where the amount claimed does not exceed $20. An appeal can be taken from the justice's decisions to the county or corporation court.

The overseers of the poor are required to arrest all vagrants and beggars and take them to the poor-house, and compel those that are able to work; it is the duty of the same officer to provide for the destitute on proper application and proof of want.

Ample provisions are made for chartering companies of all kinds and giving to them such privileges as are needful for the proper transaction of any business they may carry on, the State especially desiring to foster and encourage all productive industries and all institutions that promote those industries.

Provision is made by law for the preservation of the public health.

To secure a proper care of tobacco, one of the important staples of the State, provision is made for the erection of warehouses, in which tobacco can be safely stored, and where it can be exposed for sale. Two inspectors are annually appointed for each of these warehouses, one by the Governor of the State and one by the owners of the warehouse, whose duty it is to examine and decide the condition, quality, &c., of all tobacco brought to be inspected, and certify the same to the owner. Tobacco unmanufactured cannot be exported until it has been inspected, nor can tobacco be conveyed in a boat from one part of the State to another except in hogsheads or casks. These provisions do not apply to Alexandria county. A penalty is attached to the use of false brands on manufactured tobacco.

Provision is made for the inspection of flour, corn meal, bread, fish, pork, beef, pitch, tar, turpentine, salt, lumber, hemp, butter, lard, &c., to the end that the brand on the same, or that which contains them, may indicate the quality and quantity of the article exposed for sale or shipped from the State, thus giving the seal of authority to the good article and condemning the bad.

Weights and measures must conform to the standards provided by the State.

Live stock sold by weight for the shambles at Richmond must be weighed at the public scales by the weigh-master.

Commissioners of wrecks are appointed for the counties on the sea or bay shore, who are charged with assisting vessels threatened with shipwreck and caring for those that may be wrecked. The State also sees that those acting as pilots in her navigable waters are properly qualified, and her commission is a guarantee of fitness. Ballast must be discharged under the direction of the ballast-master of the county or corporation where the discharge is made. The usual regulations for seaports and officers to enforce them are provided for by law. No one can obstruct a highway, and vehicles meeting must bear to the right, so each can pass safely. Lawful fences are those that are five feet high; but numerous rivers in the State are by law declared lawful fences. The owners of stock are liable to fine and damages whenever such stock shall enter grounds enclosed by a lawful fence. Provision is made by which counties may adopt a "fence law," which requires the owners of stock to keep such stock from running at large, and so does away with the necessity for fences. Some counties have adopted this law.

To preserve deer it is required by law that no one shall run them with dogs or kill them between the 15th of January and the 15th of the following July. A fine is imposed upon any one that hunts or shoots upon the enclosed lands of another without his consent, and for a second offence and conviction security may be required for good behavior for a year, and if not given the offender may be sent to jail for a month, unless the security is sooner given; and still more stringent laws are in force in parts of Fairfax, Stafford and King George counties. It is left discretionary with counties to adopt the more stringent laws that apply to hunting, shooting, &c., in a town or village, in the streets or lots of the same.

The State claims jurisdiction all over tide waters, and reserves the fishing and hunting of the same for its own residents. Wild fowl can only be shot or killed from the land during the night, and in some counties at no time from a boat, unless the marsh belongs to the one shooting or he is shooting for game for his own use, on the Potomac, below Alexandria county. In some counties it is unlawful to kill partridges, pheasants, woodcock or wild turkeys from the 1st of February to the 1st of October in any year; and any county may adopt the regulation. Fishing at certain seasons and places, and in certain ways, is also prohibited, in order that the growth of fish may be protected; and non-residents are not allowed to take fish to convert into oil or manure. The fishing season for shad and herrings in the waters of the Potomac begins the 1st day of March and ends the 1st day of June each year. The owners of dams are required in some counties to provide for the passage of fish over the same.

There are many provisions of law in relation to the taking of oysters, since they rank among the most valuable and important products of the State. The bays, rivers, creeks, &c., of the State, where no grants have been made by law, are considered the property of the State, and all the people of the State are privileged, under regulations, to fish, fowl, take oysters or other shell fish from them. But where waters are included in estates they belong to them, as do also their products; and where parties desire to plant oysters they can secure the right.

# APPENDIX A.

## *RAILROADS, CANALS, &c.*

### ATLANTIC, MISSISSIPPI AND OHIO RAILROAD* (A. M. & O.)

| STATIONS. | Miles between Stations. | Miles from Norfolk. | Feet above Tide. |
|---|---|---|---|
| Norfolk | ..... | ..... | ..... |
| Tucker's | 10.50 | 10.50 | ..... |
| Suffolk | 12.50 | 23. | 58.0 |
| Windsor | 11. | 34. | 84.3 |
| Zuni | 7. | 41. | 27.6 |
| Ivor | 4. | 45. | 87.4 |
| Wakefield | 7. | 52. | 99.5 |
| Waverley | 8. | 60. | 114.0 |
| Disputanta | 8. | 68. | 117.0 |
| Well's Siding | 7. | 75. | ..... |
| Petersburg | 6. | 81. | 93.0 |
| Sutherland's | 11. | 92. | ..... |
| Church Road | 3. | 95. | 302.5 |
| Ford's | 6. | 101. | 306.6 |
| Wilson's | 7. | 108. | 367.0 |
| Wellville | 4. | 112. | 420.0 |
| Blacks and Whites | 6. | 118. | 425.0 |
| Nottoway | 6. | 124. | 421.3 |
| Burkeville | 9. | 133. | 527.9 |
| Rice's | 8. | 141. | 396.0 |
| High Bridge | 4. | 145. | ..... |
| Farmville | 4. | 149. | 316.4 |
| Tuggle's Tank | 6. | 155. | ..... |
| Prospect | 6. | 161. | 575.0 |
| Pamplin's | 8. | 169. | 678.4 |
| Evergreen | 6. | 175. | ..... |
| Appomattox | 6. | 181. | 834.5 |
| Spout Spring | 5. | 186. | 847.6 |
| Concord | 5. | 191. | 833.1 |
| Lynchburg | 13. | 204. | 515.8 |
| Halsey's | 3.75 | 207.75 | ..... |
| Clay's | 4. | 211.75 | 851. |
| Forest | 2.75 | 214.50 | 865.0 |
| Goode's | 6. | 220.50 | 715.6 |
| Lowry's | 2.50 | 223. | 778.8 |
| Liberty | 5.50 | 228.50 | 947.0 |
| Thaxton's | 5.50 | 234. | 949.8 |
| Lisbon | 3. | 237. | ...... |
| Buford's | 4. | 241. | 1,002.4 |
| Blue Ridge | 5. | 246. | 1,285.7 |
| Bonsack's | 5.25 | 251.25 | 983.3 |
| Gish's | 3.50 | 254.75 | 910.0 |
| Big Lick | 2.75 | 257.50 | 912.8 |
| Salem | 6.75 | 264.25 | 1,006.5 |
| Dyerle's | 4.75 | 269.00 | ...... |
| Big Spring | 8.50 | 277.50 | 1,250.3 |
| Alleghany | 3. | 280.50 | 1,267.9 |
| Big Tunnel (Montgomery White Sulphur Springs) | 4. | 284.50 | 1,917.9 |
| Christiansburg | 5.50 | 290. | 2,000.0 |
| Vicker's | 5. | 295. | ...... |
| Central | 5.50 | 300.50 | 1,772.5 |
| New River | 1.50 | 302. | 1,745.2 |

* Furnished by Major Henry Fink, Superintendent Transportation.

## ATLANTIC, MISSISSIPPI AND OHIO RAILROAD—Continued.

| STATIONS. | Miles between Stations. | Miles from Norfolk. | Feet above Tide. | STATIONS. | Miles between Stations. | Miles from Norfolk. | Feet above Tide. |
|---|---|---|---|---|---|---|---|
| Dublin | 6.50 | 308.50 | 2,054.2 | Marion | 6. | 364. | 2,123.5 |
| Martin's | 7.50 | 316. | 1,906.6 | Seven-Mile Ford | 7. | 371. | 1,976.2 |
| Clark's | 7. | 323. | ...... | Glade Spring | 9. | 380. | 2,075.6 |
| Max Meadows | 5.50 | 328.50 | 2,015.5 | Emory & Henry College | 4. | 384. | 2,084.2 |
| Kent's | 3.75 | 332.25 | ...... | Abingdon | 9.25 | 393.25 | 2,056.8 |
| Wytheville | 4.25 | 336.50 | 2,230.4 | Montgomery's | 5.75 | 399. | ....... |
| Grubb's | 5. | 341.50 | ...... | Wallace's | 3.50 | 402.50 | ....... |
| Crockett's | 2.50 | 344. | ...... | Bristol-Goodson | 5.50 | 408. | 1,676.5 |
| Rural Retreat | 5.50 | 349.50 | 2,502.9 | SALTVILLE BRANCH. | | | |
| Hall's | 3. | 352.50 | ...... | Glade Spring | .... | 380. | 2,075.6 |
| Atkin's | 5.50 | 358. | ...... | Saltville | 9.5 | 389.5 | 1,712. |

---

## WASHINGTON CITY, VIRGINIA MIDLAND AND GREAT SOUTHERN RAILROAD.*

| STATIONS. | Miles between Stations. | Miles from Alexandria. | Feet above Tide. | STATIONS. | Miles between Stations. | Miles from Alexandria. | Feet above Tide. |
|---|---|---|---|---|---|---|---|
| Alexandria | ... | ... | 19 | Gordonsville | 5 | 88½ | 499 |
| Cameron | 3¾ | 3¾ | ... | Lindsay's | 4¾ | 93¼ | 477 |
| A. and F. Crossing | 1 | 4¾ | ... | Cobham | 2¼ | 95½ | 401 |
| Springfield | 4 | 8¾ | 240 | Campbell's | 3 | 98½ | ... |
| Burke's | 5¼ | 14 | 258 | Keswick | 3¾ | 102¼ | 435 |
| Fairfax | 3¾ | 17¾ | 382 | Shadwell | 3¼ | 105½ | 303 |
| Clifton | 3½ | 21¼ | 170 | Charlottesville | 4 | 109½ | 451 |
| Manassas Junction | 5¾ | 27 | 317 | Lynchburg Junction | 1 | 110½ | ... |
| Bristoe | 4¼ | 31¼ | 190 | Red Hill | 8½ | 119 | ... |
| Nokesville | 3 | 34¼ | 270 | North Garden | 2 | 121 | ... |
| Catlett's | 4½ | 38¾ | 250 | Covesville | 5½ | 126½ | ... |
| Warrenton Junction | 2¼ | 41 | 265 | Faber's | 4¾ | 131¼ | ... |
| Midland | 3½ | 44½ | 321 | Rockfish | 1¾ | 133 | ... |
| Bealeton | 3 | 47½ | 290 | Elmington | 4 | 137 | ... |
| Rappahannock | 3½ | 51 | 275 | Lovingston | 3½ | 140½ | ... |
| Brandy | 5 | 56 | 359 | Arrington | 4½ | 145 | ... |
| Culpeper | 6 | 62 | 403 | Tye River | 3½ | 148½ | ... |
| Mitchell's | 7 | 69 | 350 | New Glasgow | 3 | 151½ | ... |
| Rapid Anne | 4¾ | 73¾ | 306 | Amherst Courthouse | 5 | 156½ | ... |
| Orange Courthouse | 5½ | 79¼ | 506 | McIvor's | 6 | 162½ | ... |
| Madison | 4¼ | 83½ | 395 | Burford's | 3 | 165½ | ... |

* Furnished by Colonel J. S. Barbour, President.

## WASHINGTON CITY, VIRGINIA MIDLAND AND GREAT SOUTHERN RAILROAD—Continued.

| STATIONS. | Miles between Stations. | Miles from Alexandria. | Feet above Tide. | STATIONS. | Miles between Stations. | Miles from Manassas. | Feet above Tide. |
|---|---|---|---|---|---|---|---|
| Lynchburg.............. | 5 | 170½ | 529 | Thoroughfare............ | 3½ | 13 | 399 |
| Lucado.................. | 6 | 176½ | 633 | Broad Run............... | 5 | 16½ | 395 |
| Lawyer's Road.......... | 5 | 181½ | 739 | Plains..................... | 4½ | 21½ | 565 |
| Evington................ | 6 | 187½ | 724 | Salem..................... | 6 | 26 | 633 |
| Otter River.............. | 4 | 191½ | 665 | Rectortown............... | 3½ | 32 | 444 |
| Lynch's.................. | 3 | 194½ | 730 | Delaplane (Piedmont).... | 4 | 35½ | 455 |
| Staunton River.......... | 4 | 198½ | 560 | Markham................. | 5 | 39½ | 552 |
| Sycamore................ | 6½ | 205 | 733 | Linden (Manassas Gap).. | 4 | 44½ | 916 |
| Ward's Springs.......... | 3½ | 208½ | 797 | Happy Creek............. | 2½ | 48½ | 790 |
| Whittle's................. | 6 | 214½ | 812 | Front Royal.............. | 2 | 51 | 546 |
| Chatham................. | 5 | 219½ | 624 | River (S.Fk. Shenandoah) | 4 | 53 | 493 |
| Dry Fork................. | 4¾ | 224¼ | 624 | Buckton................... | 1 | 57 | 508 |
| Fall Creek............... | 5¼ | 229½ | 535 | Water Lick............... | 4 | 58 | 550 |
| Danville.................. | 6½ | 236 | 413 | Strasburg................ | 1 | 62 | 637 |
| Dundee................... | ½ | 336½ | ... | Strasburg Junction...... | .. | 63 | 694 |
| MANASSAS BRANCH. | | From Manassas. | | WARRENTON BRANCH. | | From Alexandria. | |
| Manassas................ | 9 | .. | 317 | Warrenton Junction..... | .. | 41 | ... |
| Gainesville.............. | 2 | 9 | 357 | Melrose.................. | 3 | 44 | ... |
| Haymarket.............. | 2 | 11 | 337 | Warrenton............... | 6 | 50 | ... |

## CHESAPEAKE AND OHIO RAILROAD.*

| STATIONS. | Miles between Stations. | Miles from Richmond. | Feet above Tide. | STATIONS. | Miles between Stations. | Miles from Richmond. | Feet above Tide. |
|---|---|---|---|---|---|---|---|
| James River............. | .... | .... | .... | Hewlett's................ | 4.68 | 35.38 | 276. |
| Richmond................ | 5.50 | .... | 36. | Beaver Dam.............. | 2.82 | 40.06 | 282. |
| Hunslett.................. | 3.35 | 5.50 | 100. | Green Bay................ | 2.12 | 42.88 | .... |
| Atlee's.................... | 3.56 | 8.85 | 201. | Bumpass'................. | 1.94 | 45.00 | 329. |
| Ashcake.................. | 2.35 | 12.41 | 199. | Buckner's................ | 3.27 | 46.94 | .... |
| Peake's................... | 3.48 | 14.76 | 194. | Frederick's Hall......... | 6.10 | 50.21 | 348. |
| Hanover (C. H.).......... | 2.71 | 18.24 | 82. | Tolersville.............. | 5.77 | 56.31 | 461. |
| Wickham's............... | 1.81 | 20.95 | 76. | Louisa Courthouse....... | 4.41 | 62.08 | 452. |
| South Anna.............. | 4.78 | 22.76 | .... | Trevilian's............... | 3.21 | 66.49 | 524. |
| Hanover Junction....... | 2.85 | 27.54 | 134. | Green Springs............ | 2.91 | 69.70 | .... |
| Anderson's............... | 2.95 | 30.39 | 221. | Melton's.................. | 3.20 | 72.61 | .... |
| Noel's..................... | 2.04 | 33.34 | 254. | Gordonsville............. | 4.88 | 75.81 | 498. |

* Furnished by Engineers St. John and Whitcomb.

## CHESAPEAKE AND OHIO RAILROAD—Continued.

| STATIONS. | Miles between Stations. | Miles from Richmond. | Feet above Tide. |
|---|---|---|---|
| Lindsay's | 2.21 | 80.69 | 477. |
| Cobham | 2.93 | 82.90 | 401. |
| Campbell | 3.75 | 85.83 | .... |
| Keswick | 3.38 | 89.58 | 435. |
| Shadwell | 3.85 | 92.96 | 303. |
| Charlottesville | .87 | 96.81 | 451. |
| Lynchburg Junction | 6.18 | 97.68 | .... |
| Ivy | 2.96 | 104.30 | 516. |
| Mechum's River | 7.69 | 107.26 | 550. |
| Greenwood | 4.76 | 114.95 | .... |
| Afton | 4.19 | 119.71 | .... |
| Blue Ridge Summit | .... | .... | 1,646.92 |
| Waynesboro' | 5.05 | 123.90 | 1,284.42 |
| Fishersville | 7.43 | 128.95 | 1,321. |
| Staunton | 7.93 | 136.38 | 1,387. |
| Swoope's | 2.95 | 144.31 | 1,653. |
| Buffalo Gap | 2.24 | 147.26 | 1,885. |
| North Mountain | 2.47 | 149.50 | 2,060. |
| Variety Springs | 1.36 | 151.97 | 1,905. |
| Elizabeth Furnace | 1.82 | 153.33 | 1,812. |
| Pond Gap | 4.20 | 155.15 | 1,677. |
| Craigsville | 5.09 | 159.35 | 1,516. |
| Bell's Valley | 4.00 | 164.44 | 1,507.50 |
| Goshen | 3.06 | 168.44 | 1,410. |
| Panther Gap | 4.01 | 171.50 | 1,590. |
| Millboro' | 1.88 | 175.51 | 1,679.50 |
| Mason's Tunnel | 4.11 | 177.39 | 1,550. |
| Crane's | 4.50 | 181.50 | 1,361. |
| Griffith's | 2.14 | 186.00 | 1,165. |
| Longdale | 1.56 | 188.14 | 1,150. |
| Peter's (Longdale Junc.) | 1.80 | 189.70 | 1,175. |
| Clifton Forge | 1.12 | 191.50 | 1,047.50 |
| Williamson's | 2.45 | 192.62 | 1,053. |
| Jackson's River | 1.68 | 195.07 | 1,135. |
| Lowmoor Junction | 3.32 | 196.75 | 1,155. |
| Steele's | 5.34 | 200.07 | 1,210. |
| Covington | 5.45 | 205.41 | 1,245. |
| Callaghan's | 4.50 | 210.86 | 1,427. |
| Backbone | 6.34 | 215.36 | 1,690. |
| Alleghany | 5.45 | 221.70 | 2,050. |
| White Sulphur Springs* | 5.45 | 227.15 | 1,917. |
| Caldwell | 5.30 | 232.60 | 1,765. |
| Ronceverte | 6.42 | 237.90 | 1,660. |
| Fort Spring | 6.82 | 244.32 | 1,625. |
| Alderson | 8.14 | 251.14 | 1,550. |
| Mason's Mill | 1.47 | 259.28 | 1,527. |
| Lowell's | 1.75 | 260.75 | 1,510. |
| Talcott | 5.50 | 262.50 | 1,510. |
| 268 Mile Post | 4.69 | 268.00 | 1,434. |
| Hinton | 8.89 | 272.69 | 1,368. |
| New River Falls | 3.42 | 281.58 | 1,290. |
| Meadow Creek | 4.60 | 285.00 | 1,265. |
| Pawpaw | 4.66 | 289.60 | 1,237. |
| Quinnimont | 3.43 | 294.26 | 1,196. |
| Siding | 2.79 | 297.69 | 1,150. |
| Buffalo | 6.98 | 300.48 | 1,109. |
| Dimmock | 5.35 | 307.46 | 1,045. |
| Sewell | 4.05 | 312.81 | 1,004. |
| Nutallburg | 1.89 | 316.86 | 948. |
| Fern Spring | .50 | 318.75 | 914. |
| Fayette Station | 4.84 | 319.25 | 908. |
| Hawk's Nest | 2.11 | 324.09 | 828. |
| Cotton Hill | 7.11 | 326.20 | 696. |
| Kanawha Falls | 3.87 | 333.31 | 672. |
| Loup Creek | 5.51 | 337.18 | 647. |
| Cannelton | 5.46 | 342.69 | 636. |
| Paint Creek | 2.22 | 348.15 | 622. |
| Blacksburg | 2.39 | 350.37 | 626. |
| Coalburg | 3.34 | 352.76 | 625. |
| Lewiston | 3.73 | 356.10 | 616. |
| Brownstown | 3.70 | 359.83 | 608. |
| Alden | 2.47 | 363.53 | 605. |
| Salton (Kanawha City) | 3.17 | 366.00 | 608. |
| Charleston | 5.68 | 369.17 | 602. |
| Spring Hill | 6.06 | 374.85 | 600. |
| St. Alban's (Coalsmouth) | 3.78 | 380.91 | 594. |
| Scary | 3.87 | 384.69 | 590. |
| Scott | 5.99 | 388.56 | 683. |
| Hurricane | 5.62 | 394.55 | 683. |
| Milton | 3.10 | 401.17 | 586. |
| Thorndyke | 5.82 | 404.27 | 640. |
| Barboursville | 6.60 | 410.09 | 580. |
| Guyandotte | 1.25 | 416.69 | 560. |
| Junction Switch | 3.09 | 417.94 | 560. |
| Huntington | .... | 421.03 | 566.50 |

* This and all stations below are in West Virginia.

# PIEDMONT AIR-LINE.

*Richmond and Danville and Piedmont Railroad.**

| STATIONS. | Miles between Stations. | Miles from Rich-mond. | Feet above Tide. | STATIONS. | Miles between Stations. | Miles from Rich-mond. | Feet above Tide. |
|---|---|---|---|---|---|---|---|
| Richmond................ | ... | .... | 25 | Sutherlin's Mill.......... | 3.0 | 129.9 | ... |
| Manchester.............. | 0.7 | 0.7 | 35 | Ringgold................. | 5.3 | 135.2 | ... |
| R., F. & P. Junction... .. | 0.7 | 1.4 | .. | Dundee.................. | 4.8 | 140.0 | ... |
| Rockfield ................ | 1.2 | 2.6 | .. | Danville.................. | 0.6 | 140.6 | 410 |
| Granite .................. | 1.9 | 4.5 | .. | Va. & N. C. State line.... | .... | .... | 653 |
| Powhite.................. | 3.4 | 7.9 | .. | Pelham†.................. | 8.7 | 149.3 | 730 |
| Robio's .................. | 2.6 | 10.5 | .. | Ruffin.................... | 6.3 | 155.6 | 707 |
| Coalfield................. | 2.5 | 13.0 | 320 | Reidsville................ | 9.1 | 164.7 | 828 |
| Tomahawk .............. | 4.5 | 17.5 | 254 | Benaja.................... | 8.9 | 173.6 | ... |
| Powhatan................ | 4.7 | 22.2 | 317 | Brown's Summit......... | 3.5 | 177.1 | 600 |
| Mattoax.................. | 4.6 | 26.8 | 220 | Morehead.............. . | 3.7 | 180.8 | ... |
| Chula..................... | 3.6 | 30.4 | 277 | Greensboro'.............. | 8.2 | 189.0 | 829 |
| Amelia Courthouse...... | 5.5 | 35.9 | 358 | Salem Junction.......... | 2.9 | 191.9 | .... |
| Jetersville............... | 7.4 | 43.3 | 443 | Jamestown .............. | 7.3 | 199.2 | .... |
| Jennings' Ordinary...... | 6.4 | 49.7 | 495 | High Point............... | 5.0 | 204.2 | .... |
| Burkeville............... | 3.7 | 53.4 | 520 | Thomasville.............. | 6.6 | 210.8 | .... |
| Green Bay............... | 7.5 | 60.9 | 586 | Lexington................ | 10.8 | 221.6 | .... |
| Meherrin ................ | 4.0 | 64.9 | 586 | Linwood.................. | 6.2 | 227.8 | .... |
| Keysville ................ | 8.5 | 73.4 | 625 | Holtsburg... ............ | 3.5 | 231.3 | .... |
| Drake's Branch.......... | 7.6 | 81.0 | 375 | Salisbury ................ | 7.1 | 238.4 | .... |
| Mossingford............. | 2.8 | 83.8 | 357 | China Grove............. | 9.4 | 247.8 | .... |
| Roanoke.................. | 5.9 | 89.7 | 331 | Coleman's.... ........... | 4.0 | 251.8 | .... |
| Staunton River.......... | 0.8 | 90.5 | ... | Concord.................. | 9.0 | 260.8 | .... |
| Clover .................... | 3.7 | 94.2 | 488 | Harrisburg............... | 7.8 | 268.6 | .... |
| Scottsburg............... | 6.4 | 100.6 | 339 | Query..................... | 4.2 | 272.8 | .... |
| Wolf Trap............... | 3.9 | 104.5 | 346 | Air-Line Junction........ | 7.7 | 280.5 | .... |
| Boston.................... | 4.4 | 108.9 | 322 | C. C. Crossing............ | 0.5 | 281.0 | .... |
| New's Ferry.............. | 8.5 | 117.4 | 337 | Charlotte................ | 1.0 | 282.0 | .... |
| Barksdale's.............. | 9.5 | 126.9 | 354 | | | | |

* Furnished by General R. Lindsay Walker, Master of Roadway.

† The stations from this are in the State of North Carolina.

## RICHMOND, FREDERICKSBURG AND POTOMAC RAILROAD.*

| STATIONS. | Miles between Stations. | Miles from Richmond. | Feet above Tide. | STATIONS. | Miles between Stations. | Miles from Richmond. | Feet above Tide. |
|---|---|---|---|---|---|---|---|
| Richmond (Byrd Street).. | .... | .... | 83 | Milford .................. | 4.75 | 39.75 | 100 |
| Elba...................... | 1.25 | 1.25 | 183 | Woodford.............. | 6.75 | 46.50 | 125 |
| Boulton................. | 0.75 | 2.00 | 199 | Guiney's................ | 2.40 | 48.90 | 121 |
| Hungary................ | 6.32 | 8.32 | 214 | Summit.................. | 4.49 | 53.39 | 219 |
| Kilby .................... | 5.12 | 13.44 | 212 | Fredericksburg.......... | 7.97 | 61.36 | 42 |
| Ashland................. | 3.25 | 16.69 | 221 | Potomac Run............ | 6.14 | 67.52 | 85 |
| Taylorsville............. | 4.96 | 21.65 | 119 | Brooke.................. | 2.65 | 70.17 | 66 |
| Hanover Junction........ | 2.23 | 23.88 | 135 | Richland. ............... | 6.43 | 76.60 | 10 |
| Rutherglen.............. | 5.18 | 29.06 | 216 | Y ......................... | 4.27 | 80.87 | .. |
| Penola.................. | 5.94 | 35.00 | 94 | Quantico................ | 0.85 | 81.70 | .. |

## BALTIMORE AND POTOMAC RAILROAD.†

| STATIONS. | Miles between Stations. | Miles from Richmond. | Feet above Tide. | STATIONS. | Miles between Stations. | Miles from Richmond. | Feet above Tide. |
|---|---|---|---|---|---|---|---|
| ALEX. AND FRED'G: | | | | WASH. AND ALEX.: | | | |
| Quantico............... | 3.9 | 81.7 | 16 | Alexandria ............ | 1.7 | 109.0 | 38 |
| Cherry Hill............ | 2.0 | 85.6 | 7 | St. Asaph Junction.... | .2 | 110.7 | 45 |
| Neabsco............... | 3.4 | 87.6 | 30 | W. & O. Junction ..... | .6 | 110.9 | 47 |
| Mount Pleasant........ | 1.4 | 91.0 | 11 | Four Mile Run......... | 1.4 | 111.5 | 10 |
| Wood Bridge.......... | 3.1 | 92.4 | 73 | Waterloo .............. | .3 | 112.9 | 50 |
| Telegraph Road....... | 3.2 | 95.5 | 82 | Fort Runyon........... | .3 | 113.2 | 27 |
| Long Branch........... | 3.5 | 98.7 | 82 | S. end Long Bridge.... | 2.1 | 114.0 | 12 |
| Franconia............. | 6.8 | 102.2 | 234 | Washington........... | 17.1 | 116.1 | 10 |
| | | | | Bowie.................. | 25.5 | 133.2 | 153 |
| | | | | Baltimore (B. & P. Stat'n) | ... | 158.7 | 68 |

## RICHMOND AND PETERSBURG RAILROAD.‡

| STATIONS. | Miles between Stations. | Miles from Richmond. | Feet above Tide. | STATIONS. | Miles between Stations. | Miles from Richmond. | Feet above Tide. |
|---|---|---|---|---|---|---|---|
| Richmond................ | .. | .. | 82. | Halfway.................. | 3 | 11 | 114. |
| Shops.................... | 1 | 1 | .... | Chester.................. | 2 | 13 | 143.4 |
| Manchester Crossing.... | 1 | 2 | 105. | Port Walthall........... | 4 | 17 | 87.4 |
| Temple's................. | 3 | 5 | 85.5 | Petersburg.............. | 6 | 23 | 17.1 |
| Drewry's Bluff.......... | 3 | 8 | 118.7 | | | | |

* Furnished by E. T. D. Myers, General Superintendent.
† Furnished by the Superintendent, through Assistant Engineer Joseph Wood.
‡ Furnished by A. Shaw, Superintendent.

## PETERSBURG RAILROAD.*

| STATIONS. | Miles between Stations. | Miles from Petersburg. | Feet above Tide. | STATIONS. | Miles between Stations. | Miles from Petersburg. | Feet above Tide. |
|---|---|---|---|---|---|---|---|
| Petersburg (Depot on Appomattox......... | | | 10 | Bellefield ............... | 10 | 42 | 131 |
| Petersburg (Depot on Washington Street... | .. | .. | 70 | Pleasant Hill............. | 10 | 52 | 145 |
| | | | | Garysburg .............. | 9 | 61 | 178 |
| Reams' Station.......... | 10 | 10 | 173 | Roanoke River Bridge... | .. | .. | 47 |
| Stony Creek............. | 11 | 21 | 91 | Weldon, N. C........... | 4 | 65 | 62 |
| Jarratt's................ | 11 | 32 | 177 | | | | |

## SEABOARD AND ROANOKE RAILROAD.†

| STATIONS. | Miles between Stations. | Miles from Portsmouth. | Feet above Tide. | STATIONS. | Miles between Stations. | Miles from Portsmouth. | Feet above Tide. |
|---|---|---|---|---|---|---|---|
| Portsmouth.............. | 0 | 0 | .. | Handsome.............. | 2 | 44 | .. |
| Pea Ridge............... | 5 | 5 | .. | Newsom's............... | 6 | 50 | .. |
| Bower's Hill............. | 3 | 8 | .. | Boykin's................ | 4 | 54 | .. |
| Stever's.................. | 6 | 14 | .. | Branchville.............. | 3 | 57 | .. |
| Suffolk.................. | 3 | 17 | .. | Margarettsville......... | 6 | 63 | .. |
| Purvis.................... | 9 | 26 | .. | Seaboard ............... | 7 | 70 | .. |
| Carrsville................ | 5 | 31 | .. | Gary's................... | .. | .. | .. |
| Franklin................. | 6 | 37 | .. | Weldon.......... ....... | 10 | 80 | .. |
| Nottoway................ | 5 | 42 | .. | | | | |

## RICHMOND, YORK RIVER AND CHESAPEAKE RAILROAD.‡

| STATIONS. | Miles between Stations. | Miles from Richmond. | Feet § above Tide. | STATIONS. | Miles between Stations. | Miles from Richmond. | Feet above Tide. |
|---|---|---|---|---|---|---|---|
| Richmond................ | 0 | 0 | 16 | White House............ | 4 | 24 | 16 |
| Fair Oaks................ | 7 | 7 | 161 | Fish Haul............... | 2 | 26 | 42 |
| Meadow.................. | 4 | 11 | 87 | Cohoke ................ | 2 | 28 | 38 |
| Dispatch................. | 2 | 13 | 65 | Sweet Hall.............. | 3 | 31 | 33 |
| Summit.................. | 2 | 15 | 130 | Romancoke............. | 3 | 34 | 42 |
| Tunstall's................ | 5 | 20 | 58 | West Point............. | 4 | 38 | 7 |

* Furnished by R. M. Sully, General Freight Agent.

† Furnished by E. G. Ghio, Superintendent.

‡ Furnished by Col. H. T. Douglas, Supt.

§ Datum line 16 feet above high tide.

## WASHINGTON AND OHIO RAILROAD.*

| STATIONS. | Miles between Stations. | Miles from Alexandria. | Feet above Tide. | STATIONS. | Miles between Stations. | Miles from Alexandria. | Feet above Tide. |
|---|---|---|---|---|---|---|---|
| Alexandria | ... | ... | 15 | Guilford | 3.75 | 27. | 415 |
| Junction | 1.5 | 1.5 | | Farmwell | 4. | 31. | 320 |
| Carlin's Spring | 5. | 6.5 | ... | Leesburg | 6.5 | 37.5 | 321 |
| East Falls Church | 2.5 | 9. | ... | Clark's Gap | 4. | 41.5 | 578 |
| Falls Church | 1.5 | 10.5 | ... | Hamilton | 3.5 | 45. | 454 |
| Vienna | 4.5 | 15. | 395 | Purcellville | 3.5 | 48.5 | 553 |
| Hunter's | 3. | 18. | 345 | Round Hill | 3. | 51.5 | 553 |
| Thornton | 3. | 21. | ... | Snickersville | 3. | 58.5 | 680 |
| Herndon | 2.25 | 23.25 | 395 | | | | |

---

## VALLEY RAILROAD.†

*Branch of the Baltimore and Ohio Railroad.*

| STATIONS. | Miles between Stations. | Miles from Staunton. | Feet ‡ above Tide. | STATIONS. | Miles between Stations. | Miles from Staunton. | Feet above Tide. |
|---|---|---|---|---|---|---|---|
| Staunton | ... | ... | 1,379 § | Maurertown | 4¼ | 69 | 788 |
| Verona | 5½ | 5½ | 1,272 | Tom's Brook | 1¾ | 70¾ | 745 |
| Fort Defiance | 3¾ | 9¼ | 1,247 | Strasburg Junction | 4¼ | 75 | 663 |
| Mt. Sidney | 1¾ | 11 | 1,258 | Strasburg | 1¼ | 76¼ | 637 |
| Weyer's Cave (Station) | 3 | 14 | 1,152 | Capon Road | 1 | 76 | 701 |
| Mt. Crawford (Station) | 4¼ | 18¼ | 1,171 | Cedar Creek | 4 | 80 | 591 |
| Pleasant Valley | 3 | 21¼ | 1,248 | Middletown | 2 | 82 | 660 |
| Harrisonburg | 4¾ | 26 | 1,338 | Newtown | 4¾ | 86¾ | 731 |
| Linville | 6¼ | 32¼ | 1,242 | Kernstown | 3½ | 90¼ | 744 |
| Cowan's | 3¾ | 36 | 1,107 | Winchester | 3¾ | 94 | 717 |
| Broadway | 2½ | 38½ | 1,038 | Stephenson's | 5 | 99 | 499 |
| Timberville | 2½ | 41 | 1,018 | Wadesville | 4½ | 103½ | 495 |
| New Market (Station) | 4 | 45 | 971 | Summit Point | 4½ | 108 | 623 |
| Forest | 4 | 49 | 953 | Cameron | 4½ | 112½ | 547 |
| Mt. Jackson | 3¼ | 52¼ | 916 | Charlestown | 3½ | 116 | 513 |
| Bellew's | 4 | 56¼ | 895 (?) | Halltown | 4 | 120 | 339 |
| Edinburg | 3½ | 59¾ | 845 | Harper's Ferry | 6 | 126 | 277 ‖ |
| Narrow Passage Bridge | ... | ... | 858 | Washington | ... | ... | ... |
| Woodstock | 5 | 64¾ | 820 | Baltimore | ... | 205 | ... |

* Furnished by R. H. Havener, General Superintendent.

† From Chief Eng. J. L. Randolph, through Asst. W. F. Elmer.

‡ The elevations are the sub-grade A. M. T.; the top of the rail is 22 inches higher.

§ At crossing of C. & O.R. R.

‖ Abutment of B. & O. R. R. bridge.

# JAMES RIVER AND KANAWHA CANAL.*

| PLACES. | Miles between Places. | Miles from Richmond. | Feet above Tide. |
|---|---|---|---|
| Tidewater | ... | ... | ...... |
| Richmond—Basin | 1.5 | 1.5 | 84. |
| Rutherford's Mills | 2.0 | 3.5 | ...... |
| Lock No. 1 | ... | ... | 94.75 |
| Lock No. 2 | 1.0 | 4.5 | 105.50 |
| Lock No. 3 | 2.5 | 7.0 | 115.50 |
| Rein's Island—River Lock | 0.5 | 7.5 | 115.00 |
| Westham | 1.0 | 8.5 | 115.00 |
| Bosher's Dam—Locks 4 and G | 2.5 | 11.0 | 124.25 |
| Lock No. 5 | ... | .... | 134.00 |
| Lock No. 6 | ... | .... | 142.75 |
| Ellerslie | 1.5 | 12.5 | 142.75 |
| Tuckahoe Railroad Basin | 1.0 | 13.5 | 145.75 |
| Tuckahoe Aqueduct | 0.5 | 14.0 | 142.75 |
| Tuckahoe | 0.5 | 14.5 | 142.75 |
| Powell's Bridge | 1.5 | 16.0 | 142.75 |
| Manakintown Ferry Road | 2.0 | 18.0 | 142.75 |
| Manakin | 0.5 | 18.5 | 142.75 |
| Sampson's Lock | 1.0 | 19.5 | 143.25 |
| Dover Mills and Aqueduct | 2.0 | 21.5 | 143.25 |
| Sabbot Hill | 1.0 | 22.5 | 143.25 |
| Dover | 0.5 | 23.0 | 143.25 |
| Jude's Ferry Road | 0.5 | 23.5 | 143.25 |
| Contention | 3.0 | 26.5 | 143.25 |
| Beaver Dam Aqueduct† | 1.5 | 28.0 | 143.25 |
| Maiden's Adventure Dam | 1.0 | 29.0 | 143.25 |
| Michaux's Ferry | 3.0 | 32.0 | 143.25 |
| Cedar Point Locks, No. 7 | ... | .... | 156.25 |
| Cedar Point Locks, No. 8 | 2.0 | 34.0 | 159.25 |
| Lickinghole Aqueduct—Lock No. 9 | 1.5 | 35.5 | 167.25 |
| Bolling Hall | 1.0 | 36.5 | 167.25 |
| Lock No. 10 | 2.5 | 39.0 | 167.25 |
| Jefferson Ferry Road | 1.5 | 40.5 | 177.25 |
| Rock Castle | 1.0 | 41.5 | 177.25 |
| Lock No 11 (Loch Lomond) | ... | .... | 185.25 |
| Bolling Island | 4.0 | 45.5 | 185.25 |
| Pemberton—Lock No. 12‡ | 2.5 | 48.0 | 192.25 |
| Lock No. 13 | 2.5 | 50.5 | 200.25 |
| Elk Hill | 2.0 | 52.5 | 200.25 |
| Lock No. 14 | 3.5 | 56.0 | 208.25 |
| Columbia | 2.0 | 58.0 | 208.25 |
| Galt's Quarry | 1.5 | 59.5 | 208.25 |
| Lock No. 15 | 3.5 | 63.0 | 215.25 |
| Lock No. 16 | 2.0 | 65.0 | ...... |
| New Canton | 2.5 | 67.5 | 223.25 |
| Lock No. 17 | 0.5 | 68.0 | 223.25 |
| Bremo | 1.5 | 69.5 | 233.75 |
| Middleton's Mills | 2.0 | 71.5 | 233.75 |
| Lock No. 18 and G | 0.5 | 72.0 | 241.75 |
| Lock No. 19 (7-Islands) | 0.5 | 72.5 | 250.50 |
| Virgin Mills | 1.0 | 73.5 | 250.50 |
| Lock No. 20 | 0.5 | 74.0 | 259.16 |
| Lock No. 21 | 0.5 | 74.5 | 267.82 |
| Bolling's Landing | 1.0 | 75.5 | 267.82 |
| Lock No. 22 | 3.0 | 78.5 | 274.50 |
| Scottsville | 2.0 | 80.5 | 274.50 |
| Lock No. 23 | 1.0 | 81.5 | 282.20 |
| Lock No. 24 | 2.5 | 84.0 | 290.50 |
| Warren—Lock No. 25 | 2.5 | 86.5 | 298.50 |
| Lock No. 26 | 1.5 | 88.0 | 306.50 |
| Lock No. 27 | 2.5 | 90.5 | 314.50 |
| Howardsville—Lock No 28 | 1.5 | 92.0 | 322.50 |
| Lock No. 29 | 4.5 | 96.5 | 331.25 |
| Lock No. 30 | 2.0 | 98.5 | 340.00 |
| Warminster | 1.5 | 100.0 | 340.00 |
| Lock No. 31 | 1.0 | 101.0 | 348.25 |
| Midway Mills | 1.5 | 102.5 | 346.25 |
| Hardwicksville—Lock No. 32 | 2.0 | 104.5 | 358.25 |
| New Market (Norwood) | 4.5 | 109.0 | 358.25 |
| Locks Nos. 33 and 34 | ... | ..... | 375.25 |
| Lock No. 35 | 3.5 | 112.5 | 383.25 |
| Lock No. 36 | 1.5 | 114.0 | 391.25 |
| Greenway | 0.5 | 114.5 | 391.25 |
| Lock No. 37 | 2.0 | 116.5 | 399.25 |
| Bent Creek—Lock No. 38 | 1.5 | 118.0 | 407.25 |
| Lock No. 39 | 2.0 | 120.0 | 415.25 |
| Elk Creek Mills | 1.0 | 121.0 | 415.25 |
| Lock No. 40 | 2.0 | 123.0 | 423.25 |
| Lock No. 41 | 0.5 | 123.5 | 431.25 |

* Furnished by Colonel C. S. Carrington, President. † Issaquena. ‡ Cartersville.

## JAMES RIVER AND KANAWHA CANAL—Continued.

| PLACES. | Miles between Places. | Miles from Richmond. | Feet above Tide. |
|---|---|---|---|
| Lock No. 42 | 3.0 | 126.5 | 439.25 |
| Lock No. 43 | 2.0 | 128.5 | 447.25 |
| Lock No. 44 | 2.5 | 131.0 | 455.25 |
| Staples' Mills | 1.0 | 132.0 | 455.25 |
| Lock No. 45 | 1.0 | 133.0 | 463.25 |
| Galt's Mills | 0.5 | 133.5 | 463.25 |
| Joshua Falls Dam | 2.0 | 135.5 | 463.25 |
| Crossing of James River—Locks 46 & 47 | 2.0 | 137.5 | 479.75 |
| Lock No. 48 | 0.5 | 138.0 | 487.75 |
| Lock No. 49 | 3.0 | 141.0 | 495.75 |
| Beaver Creek | 0.5 | 141.5 | 495.75 |
| Lock No. 50 | 0.5 | 142.0 | 503.75 |
| Lock No. 51 | 3.5 | 145.5 | 513 |
| Lynchburg | 2.0 | 147.5 | 513 |
| Lynchburg Water-works Dam | 1.0 | 148.5 | 513 |
| Lock No. 1—Second Division | 1.5 | 150.0 | 525.75 |
| Lock No. 2 | 1.0 | 151.0 | 538.50 |
| Judith's Dam—Lock No. 1 G | 1.0 | 152.0 | 539.75 |
| Bethel—Lock No. 3 | 4.0 | 156.0 | 557.75 |
| Bald Eagle Dam—Lock No. 2 G | 1.0 | 157.0 | 557.75 |
| Lock No. 4 (Holcomb's Rock) | 2.5 | 159.5 | 570.75 |
| Pedler Dam—Lock No. 3 G | 0.5 | 160.0 | 571.87 |
| Tumbling Run—Lock No. 5 | 2.0 | 162.0 | 587.87 |
| Coleman's Fall Dam—Lock No. 4 G | 0.5 | 162.5 | 587.87 |
| Read Creek—Lock No. 6 | 3.0 | 165.5 | 604.87 |
| Big Island Dam—Lock No. 5 G | 1.0 | 166.5 | 605.87 |

| PLACES. | Miles between Places. | Miles from Richmond. | Feet above Tide. |
|---|---|---|---|
| Lock No. 7 | 1.0 | 167.5 | 618.87 |
| Lock No. 8 | 0.5 | 168.0 | 626.87 |
| Lock No. 9 | 0.5 | 168.5 | 634.87 |
| Lock No. 10 | 1.0 | 169.5 | 643.87 |
| Cushaw Dam—Locks Nos. 11 and 6 G | 1.0 | 170.5 | 648.87 |
| Rope Ferry—Lock No. 12 | 0.5 | 171.0 | 660.87 |
| Lock No. 13 | 0.5 | 171.5 | 672.87 |
| Lock No. 14 | 1.0 | 172.5 | 680.87 |
| Lock No. 15 | 1.0 | 173.5 | 688.87 |
| Lock No. 16 | ... | ..... | 696.87 |
| Lock No. 17 | 0.5 | 174.0 | 705.87 |
| Cement Mills—Lock No. 7 G | 1.5 | 175.5 | 705.87 |
| North River Bridge—Mouth of North River | 0.5 | 176.0 | 705.87 |
| Lock No. 18 | 2.0 | 178.0 | 720.37 |
| Quarry Falls Dam—Lock No. 8 G | 0.5 | 178.5 | 720.37 |
| Lock No. 19 | 2.0 | 180.5 | 734.37 |
| Lock No. 20 | ... | ..... | 741.37 |
| Lock No. 21 | 2.0 | 182.5 | 749.37 |
| Lock No. 22 | 1.0 | 183.5 | 759.37 |
| Varney's Falls Dam—Lock No. 9 G | 2.0 | 185.5 | 759.37 |
| Lock No. 23 | 3.0 | 188.5 | 774.62 |
| Lock No. 24 | ... | ..... | 782.62 |
| Indian Rock Dam—Lock 10 G | 1.0 | 189.5 | 785.62 |
| Lock No. 25 | 3.0 | 192.5 | 802.12 |
| Lock No. 26 | 0.5 | 193.0 | 811.72 |
| Wasp Rock Dam—Lock No. 11 G | 1.0 | 194.0 | 811.72 |
| Buchanan | 4.0 | 198.0 | 811.72 |

## NORTH RIVER IMPROVEMENT.

*Branch of the James River and Kanawha Canal.*

| PLACES. | Miles between Places. | Miles from Richmond. | Feet above Tide. |
|---|---|---|---|
| North River Bridge—Mouth of North River | ... | 176.0 | 705.67 |
| Mouth of Buffalo Creek | 4.5 | 180.5 | ...... |
| Thompson's Landing | 3.0 | 183.5 | ...... |
| Hart's Bottom | 2.0 | 185.5 | ...... |
| Bensalem | 4.0 | 189.5 | ...... |
| Mouth of South River | 2.0 | 191.5 | ...... |
| Lexington | 4.5 | 196.0 | 893.87 |

# APPENDIX B.

## TABLE II.—POPULATION OF THE STATE OF VIRGINIA, BY COUNTIES.

(As in the United States Census of 1870).

| COUNTIES. | AGGREGATE. | | | | | | | | |
|---|---|---|---|---|---|---|---|---|---|
| | 1870. | 1860. | 1850. | 1840. | 1830. | 1820. | 1810. | 1800. | 1790. |
| Total | 1225,163 | 1219,630 | 1119,348 | a9,967<br>1015,260 | a9,573<br>1034,481 | *210<br>a9,703<br>928,348 | a8,552<br>869,131 | a5,949<br>801,608 | 691,737 |
| Variances from former official totals | ........ | ........ | ........ | ........ | ........ | ........ | b—22 | ........ | ........ |
| Accomac | 20,409 | 18,586 | 17,890 | 17,096 | 16,656 | 15,966 | 15,743 | 15,693 | 13,959 |
| Albemarle | 27,544 | 26,625 | 25,800 | 22,924 | 22,618 | *3<br>19,747 | 18,268 | 16,439 | 12,585 |
| Alexandria | 16,755 | 12,652 | 10,008 | a9,967 | a9,573 | a9,703 | a8,552 | a5,949 | ........ |
| Alleghany | 3,674 | 6,765 | 3,515 | 2,749 | 2,816 | ........ | ........ | ........ | ........ |
| Amelia | 9,878 | 10,741 | 9,770 | 10,320 | 11,036 | *110<br>10,994 | 10,594 | 9,432 | c18,097 |
| Amherst | 14,900 | 13,742 | 12,699 | 12,576 | 12,071 | 10,423 | 10,548 | 16,801 | 13,703 |
| Appomattox | 8,950 | 8,889 | 9,193 | ........ | ........ | ........ | ........ | ........ | ........ |
| Augusta | 28,763 | 27,749 | 24,610 | 19,628 | 19,926 | 16,742 | 14,308 | 11,712 | 10,886 |
| Bath | 3,795 | 3,676 | 3,426 | 4,300 | 4,002 | *6<br>5,231 | 4,837 | 5,508 | ........ |
| Bedford | 25,327 | 25,068 | 24,080 | 20,203 | 20,246 | 19,305 | 16,148 | 14,125 | 10,531 |
| Bland (d) | 4,000 | ........ | ........ | ........ | ........ | ........ | ........ | ........ | ........ |
| Botetourt | 11,329 | 11,516 | 14,908 | 11,679 | 16,354 | 13,589 | 13,301 | 10,427 | 10,524 |
| Brunswick | 13,427 | 14,809 | 13,894 | 14,346 | 15,767 | 16,687 | 15,411 | 16,339 | 12,827 |
| Buchanan | 3,777 | 2,793 | ........ | ........ | ........ | ........ | ........ | ........ | ........ |
| Buckingham | 13,371 | 15,212 | 13,837 | 18,786 | 18,351 | 17,569 | 20,059 | 13,389 | 9,779 |
| Campbell | 28,384 | 26,197 | 23,245 | 21,030 | 20,350 | 16,569 | 11,001 | 9,866 | 7,685 |
| Caroline | 15,128 | 18,464 | 18,456 | 17,813 | 17,760 | *26<br>17,982 | 17,544 | 17,438 | 17,489 |
| Carroll | 9,147 | 8,012 | 5,909 | ........ | ........ | ........ | ........ | ........ | ........ |
| Charles City | 4,975 | 5,609 | 5,200 | 4,774 | 5,500 | 5,255 | 5,186 | 5,365 | 5,588 |
| Charlotte | 14,513 | 14,471 | 13,955 | 14,595 | 15,252 | 13,290 | 13,161 | 11,912 | 10,078 |
| Chesterfield | 18,470 | 19,016 | 17,489 | 17,148 | 18,637 | 18,003 | 9,979 | 14,488 | 14,214 |

## TABLE II.—Continued.

| COUNTIES. | AGGREGATE. | | | | | | | | |
|---|---|---|---|---|---|---|---|---|---|
| | 1870. | 1860. | 1850. | 1840. | 1830. | 1820. | 1810. | 1800. | 1790. |
| Clarke | 6,670 | 7,146 | 7,352 | 6,353 | ........ | ........ | ........ | ........ | ........ |
| Craig | 2,942 | 3,553 | ....... | ........ | ........ | ........ | ........ | ........ | ........ |
| Culpeper | 12,227 | 12,063 | 12,282 | 11,393 | 24,027 | *2 20,942 | 18,967 | 18,100 | 22,105 |
| Cumberland | 8,142 | 9,961 | 9,751 | 10,399 | 11,690 | 11,023 | 9,992 | 9,839 | 8,153 |
| Dinwiddie | 30,702 | 30,198 | 25,118 | 22,558 | 21,901 | 20,482 | 18,190 | 15,374 | 13,934 |
| Elizabeth City | 8,303 | 5,798 | 4,586 | 3,706 | 5,053 | 3,789 | 3,608 | 2,778 | 3,450 |
| Essex | 9,927 | 10,469 | 10,206 | 11,309 | 10,521 | 9,909 | 9,376 | 9,508 | 9,122 |
| Fairfax | 12,952 | 11,834 | 10,682 | 9,370 | 9,204 | 11,404 | 13,111 | 13,317 | 12,320 |
| Fauquier | 19,690 | 21,706 | 20,868 | 21,897 | 26,086 | 23,103 | 22,689 | 21,329 | 17,892 |
| Floyd | 9,824 | 8,236 | 6,458 | 4,453 | ........ | ........ | ........ | ........ | ........ |
| Fluvanna | 9,875 | 10,353 | 9,487 | 8,812 | 8,221 | 6,704 | 4,775 | 4,623 | 3,921 |
| Franklin | 18,264 | 20,098 | 17,430 | 15,832 | 14,911 | 12,017 | 10,724 | 9,302 | 6,842 |
| Frederick | 16,596 | 16,546 | 15,975 | 14,242 | 26,046 | 24,706 | 22,574 | 24,744 | 19,681 |
| Giles (*d*) | 5,875 | 6,883 | 6,570 | 5,307 | 5,274 | 4,521 | 3,745 | ........ | ........ |
| Gloucester | 10,211 | 10,956 | 10,527 | 10,715 | 10,608 | 9,678 | 10,427 | 8,181 | 13,498 |
| Goochland | 10,313 | 10,656 | 10,352 | 9,760 | 10,369 | 10,007 | 10,203 | 9,696 | 9,053 |
| Grayson | 9,587 | 8,252 | 6,677 | 9,087 | 7,675 | 5,598 | 4,941 | 3,912 | ........ |
| Greene | 4,634 | 5,022 | 4,400 | 4,232 | ........ | ........ | ........ | ........ | ........ |
| Greensville | 6,362 | 6,374 | 5,639 | 6,366 | 7,117 | 6,858 | 6,853 | 6,727 | 6,362 |
| Halifax | 27,828 | 26,520 | 25,962 | 25,936 | 28,034 | 19,060 | 22,133 | 19,377 | 14,722 |
| Hanover | 16,455 | 17,222 | 15,153 | 14,968 | 16,253 | 15,267 | 15,082 | 14,403 | 14,754 |
| Henrico | 66,179 | 61,616 | 43,572 | 33,076 | 28,797 | 23,667 | 19,680 | 14,886 | 12,000 |
| Henry | 12,303 | 12,105 | 8,872 | 7,335 | 7,100 | 5,624 | 5,611 | 5,259 | 8,479 |
| Highland | 4,151 | 4,319 | 4,227 | ........ | ........ | ........ | ........ | ........ | ........ |
| Isle of Wight | 8,320 | 9,977 | 9,353 | 9,972 | 10,517 | *21 10,118 | 9,186 | 9,342 | 9,028 |
| James City | 4,425 | 5,798 | 4,020 | 3,779 | 3,838 | 4,563 | 4,094 | 3,931 | 4,070 |
| King and Queen | 9,709 | 10,328 | 10,319 | 10,862 | 11,644 | 11,798 | 10,988 | 9,879 | 9,377 |
| King George | 5,742 | 6,571 | 5,971 | 5,927 | 6,397 | 6,116 | 6,454 | 6,749 | 7,366 |
| King William | 7,515 | 8,530 | 8,779 | 9,258 | 9,812 | 9,697 | 9,285 | 9,055 | 8,128 |
| Lancaster | 5,355 | 5,151 | 4,708 | 4,628 | 4,801 | 5,517 | 5,592 | 5,375 | 5,638 |
| Lee | 13,268 | 11,032 | 10,267 | 8,441 | 6,461 | 4,256 | 4,694 | 3,538 | ........ |
| Loudoun | 20,929 | 21,774 | 22,079 | 20,431 | 21,939 | 22,702 | 21,338 | 20,523 | 18,962 |
| Louisa | 16,332 | 16,701 | 16,691 | 15,433 | 16,151 | 13,746 | 11,900 | 11,892 | 8,467 |
| Lunenburg | 10,403 | 11,983 | 11,692 | 11,055 | 11,957 | 10,662 | 12,265 | 10,381 | 8,959 |
| Madison | 8,670 | 8,854 | 9,331 | 8,107 | 9,236 | 8,490 | 8,381 | 8,322 | ........ |
| Mathews | 6,200 | 7,091 | 6,714 | 7,442 | 7,664 | 6,920 | 4,227 | 5,806 | ........ |
| Mecklenburg | 21,318 | 20,096 | 20,630 | 20,724 | 20,477 | 19,786 | 18,453 | 17,008 | 14,733 |
| Middlesex | 4,981 | 4,364 | 4,394 | 4,392 | 4,122 | 4,057 | 4,414 | 4,203 | 4,140 |
| Montgomery | 12,556 | 10,617 | 8,359 | 7,405 | 12,306 | 8,733 | 8,409 | 9,044 | 13,228 |
| Nansemond | 11,576 | 13,693 | 12,283 | 10,795 | 11,784 | 10,494 | 10,324 | 11,127 | 9,010 |

## TABLE II.—CONTINUED.

| COUNTIES. | AGGREGATE. | | | | | | | | |
|---|---|---|---|---|---|---|---|---|---|
| | 1870. | 1860. | 1850. | 1840. | 1830. | 1820. | 1810. | 1800. | 1790. |
| Nelson | 13,898 | 13,015 | 12,758 | 12,287 | 11,254 | 10,137 | 9,684 | ........ | ........ |
| New Kent | 4,381 | 5,884 | 6,064 | 6,230 | 6,458 | 6,030 | 6,478 | 6,303 | 6,239 |
| Norfolk | 46,702 | 36,227 | 33,036 | 27,569 | 24,806 | *7 23,936 | 22,872 | 19,419 | 14,524 |
| Northampton | 8,046 | 7,832 | 7,498 | 7,715 | 8,641 | 7,705 | 7,474 | 6,763 | 6,889 |
| Northumberland | 6,803 | 7,531 | 7,346 | 7,924 | 7,953 | 8,016 | 8,308 | 7,803 | 9,163 |
| Nottoway | 9,291 | 8,836 | 8,437 | 9,719 | 10,130 | *2 9,656 | 9,278 | 9,401 | (c) |
| Orange | 10,396 | 10,851 | 10,067 | 9,125 | 14,637 | *33 12,880 | 12,323 | 11,449 | 9,921 |
| Page | 8,462 | 8,109 | 7,600 | 6,194 | ........ | ........ | ........ | ........ | ........ |
| Patrick | 10,161 | 9,359 | 9,609 | 8,032 | 7,395 | 5,089 | 4,695 | 4,331 | ........ |
| Pittsylvania | 31,343 | 32,104 | 28,796 | 26,398 | 26,034 | 21,323 | 17,172 | 12,697 | 11,579 |
| Powhatan | 7,667 | 8,392 | 8,178 | 7,924 | 8,517 | 8,292 | 8,073 | 7,769 | 6,822 |
| Prince Edward | 12,004 | 11,844 | 11,857 | 14,069 | 14,107 | 12,577 | 12,409 | 10,962 | 8,107 |
| Prince George | 7,820 | 8,411 | 7,596 | 7,175 | 8,367 | 8,030 | 8,050 | 7,425 | 8,173 |
| Princess Anne | 8,273 | 7,714 | 7,669 | 7,285 | 9,102 | 8,768 | 9,498 | 8,859 | 7,793 |
| Prince William | 7,504 | 8,565 | 8,129 | 8,144 | 9,330 | 9,419 | 11,311 | 12,733 | 11,615 |
| Pulaski | 6,538 | 5,416 | 5,118 | 3,739 | ........ | ........ | ........ | ........ | ........ |
| Rappahannock | 8,261 | 8,850 | 9,782 | 9,257 | ........ | ........ | ........ | ........ | ........ |
| Richmond | 6,503 | 6,856 | 6,448 | 5,965 | 6,055 | 5,706 | 6,214 | e13,744 | 6,985 |
| Roanoke | 9,350 | 8,048 | 8,477 | 5,499 | ........ | ........ | ........ | ........ | ........ |
| Rockbridge | 16,058 | 17,248 | 16,045 | 14,284 | 14,244 | 11,945 | 10,318 | 8,945 | 6,548 |
| Rockingham | 23,668 | 23,408 | 20,294 | 17,344 | 20,683 | 14,784 | 12,753 | 10,374 | 7,449 |
| Russell | 11,103 | 10,280 | 11,919 | 7,878 | 6,714 | 5,536 | 6,319 | 4,808 | 3,338 |
| Scott | 13,036 | 12,072 | 9,829 | 7,303 | 5,724 | 4,263 | ........ | ........ | ........ |
| Shenandoah | 14,936 | 13,896 | 13,768 | 11,618 | 19,750 | 18,926 | 13,646 | 13,823 | 10,510 |
| Smyth | 8,898 | 8,952 | 8,162 | 6,522 | ........ | ........ | ........ | ........ | ........ |
| Southampton | 12,285 | 12,915 | 13,521 | 14,525 | 16,074 | 14,170 | 13,497 | 13,925 | 12,864 |
| Spotsylvania | 11,728 | 16,076 | 14,911 | 15,161 | 15,134 | 14,254 | 13,296 | 13,002 | 11,252 |
| Stafford | 6,420 | 8,555 | 8,044 | 8,454 | 9,362 | 9,517 | 9,830 | 9,971 | 9,588 |
| Surry | 5,585 | 6,133 | 5,679 | 6,480 | 7,109 | 6,594 | 6,855 | 6,535 | 6,227 |
| Sussex | 7,885 | 10,175 | 9,820 | 11,229 | 12,720 | 11,884 | 11,362 | 11,062 | 10,549 |
| Tazewell (d) | 10,791 | 9,920 | 9,942 | 6,290 | 5,749 | 3,916 | 3,007 | 2,127 | ........ |
| Warren | 5,716 | 6,442 | 6,607 | 5,627 | ........ | ........ | ........ | ........ | ........ |
| Warwick | 1,672 | 1,740 | 1,546 | 1,456 | 1,570 | 1,608 | 1,835 | 1,659 | 1,690 |
| Washington | 16,816 | 16,892 | 14,612 | 13,001 | 15,614 | 12,444 | 12,156 | 9,536 | 5,625 |
| Westmoreland | 7,682 | 8,282 | 8,080 | 8,019 | 8,396 | 6,901 | 8,102 | (e) | 7,722 |
| Wise | 4,785 | 4,508 | ........ | ........ | ........ | ........ | ........ | ........ | ........ |
| Wythe (d) | 11,611 | 12,305 | 12,024 | 9,375 | 12,163 | 9,692 | 8,356 | 6,380 | ........ |
| York | 7,198 | 4,949 | 4,460 | 4,720 | 5,354 | 4,384 | 5,187 | 3,231 f48 | 5,233 |

TABLE II.—CONTINUED.

| COUNTIES. | WHITE. | | | | | | | | |
|---|---|---|---|---|---|---|---|---|---|
| | 1870. | 1860. | 1850. | 1840. | 1830. | 1820. | 1810. | 1800. | 1790. |
| Total | 712,089 | 691,773 | 616,069 | a6,731<br>537,952 | a6,411<br>537,216 | a6,556<br>482,849 | a5,734<br>458,159 | a4,394<br>443,386 | 391,524 |
| Variances from former official totals | ........ | ........ | ........ | b—110 | ........ | b—11 | b—20 | ........ | ........ |
| Accomac | 12,567 | 10,661 | 9,608 | 9,618 | 9,458 | 9,386 | 9,341 | 9,723 | 8,976 |
| Albemarle | 12,550 | 12,103 | 11,875 | 10,512 | 10,455 | 8,715 | 8,642 | 8,796 | 6,835 |
| Alexandria | 9,444 | 9,851 | 7,217 | a6,731 | a6,411 | a6,556 | a5,734 | a4,394 | ........ |
| Alleghany | 3,095 | 5,643 | 2,763 | 2,142 | 2,197 | ........ | ........ | ........ | ........ |
| Amelia | 3,055 | 2,897 | 2,785 | 3,074 | 3,293 | 3,407 | 3,253 | 2,789 | c6,684 |
| Amherst | 8,184 | 7,167 | 6,352 | 6,426 | 5,883 | 4,610 | 5,143 | 9,205 | 8,286 |
| Appomattox | 4,414 | 4,118 | 4,209 | ........ | ........ | ........ | ........ | ........ | ........ |
| Augusta | 22,026 | 21,547 | 18,983 | 15,072 | 15,257 | 12,963 | 11,232 | 9,671 | 9,260 |
| Bath | 2,906 | 2,652 | 2,434 | 3,170 | 2,797 | 3,965 | 3,906 | 4,830 | ........ |
| Bedford | 14,557 | 14,388 | 13,586 | 11,016 | 11,123 | 10,953 | 9,789 | 9,826 | 7,725 |
| Bland | 3,783 | ........ | ........ | ........ | ........ | ........ | ........ | ........ | ........ |
| Botetourt | 8,166 | 8,441 | 10,746 | 8,877 | 11,798 | 10,493 | 10,726 | 8,773 | 9,241 |
| Brunswick | 4,525 | 4,992 | 4,885 | 4,978 | 5,397 | 5,889 | 5,665 | 6,647 | 5,919 |
| Buchanan | 3,730 | 2,762 | ........ | ........ | ........ | ........ | ........ | ........ | ........ |
| Buckingham | 5,669 | 6,041 | 5,426 | 7,323 | 7,177 | 7,345 | 7,780 | 6,824 | 5,496 |
| Campbell | 14,041 | 13,588 | 11,533 | 10,213 | 9,905 | 8,447 | 5,370 | 5,893 | 4,946 |
| Caroline | 7,077 | 6,948 | 6,891 | 6,725 | 6,499 | 6,497 | 6,452 | 6,492 | 6,994 |
| Carroll | 8,819 | 7,719 | 5,726 | ........ | ........ | ........ | ........ | ........ | ........ |
| Charles City | 1,822 | 1,806 | 1,664 | 1,671 | 1,782 | 1,750 | 1,776 | 1,954 | 2,084 |
| Charlotte | 4,930 | 4,981 | 4,615 | 5,030 | 5,583 | 5,005 | 5,354 | 5,506 | 5,199 |
| Chesterfield | 9,730 | 10,019 | 8,406 | 7,859 | 7,709 | 7,543 | 3,692 | 6,317 | 6,358 |
| Clarke | 4,511 | 3,707 | 3,614 | 2,867 | ........ | ........ | ........ | ........ | ........ |
| Craig | 2,712 | 3,103 | ........ | ........ | ........ | ........ | ........ | ........ | ........ |
| Culpeper | 6,058 | 4,959 | 5,112 | 4,933 | 12,046 | 11,136 | 10,391 | 10,479 | 13,809 |
| Cumberland | 2,709 | 2,946 | 3,092 | 3,263 | 4,054 | 3,966 | 3,715 | 3,945 | 3,577 |
| Dinwiddie | 13,017 | 13,678 | 10,942 | 9,847 | 8,635 | 8,470 | 7,010 | 6,347 | 6,039 |
| Elizabeth City | 2,832 | 3,180 | 2,341 | 1,954 | 2,704 | 2,076 | 1,799 | 1,238 | 1,556 |
| Essex | 3,277 | 3,296 | 3,035 | 3,955 | 3,647 | 3,499 | 3,411 | 3,465 | 3,543 |
| Fairfax | 8,667 | 8,046 | 6,835 | 5,469 | 4,892 | 6,224 | 6,626 | 7,035 | 7,611 |
| Fauquier | 11,834 | 10,430 | 9,875 | 10,501 | 12,950 | 11,429 | 11,984 | 12,444 | 11,157 |
| Floyd | 8,827 | 7,745 | 6,001 | 4,123 | ........ | ........ | ........ | ........ | ........ |
| Fluvanna | 4,778 | 5,093 | 4,539 | 4,445 | 4,223 | 3,375 | 2,576 | 2,659 | ,430 |
| Franklin | 12,268 | 13,642 | 11,638 | 10,500 | 9,728 | 8,227 | 7,966 | 7,701 | 5,735 |
| Frederick | 13,863 | 13,079 | 12,769 | 11,119 | 17,361 | 16,557 | 15,547 | 18,628 | 15,315 |
| Giles | 5,272 | 6,038 | 5,858 | 4,684 | 4,760 | 4,174 | 3,478 | ........ | ........ |
| Gloucester | 4,782 | 4,517 | 4,290 | 4,412 | 4,314 | 4,008 | 4,183 | 3,237 | 6,225 |
| Goochland | 3,711 | 3,814 | 3,863 | 3,570 | 3,857 | 3,793 | 4,230 | 4,480 | 4,140 |

TABLE II.—Continued.

| COUNTIES. | WHITE. | | | | | | | | |
|---|---|---|---|---|---|---|---|---|---|
| | 1870. | 1860. | 1850. | 1840. | 1830. | 1820. | 1810. | 1800. | 1790. |
| Grayson | 8,833 | 7,653 | 6,142 | 8,542 | 7,161 | 5,170 | 4,641 | 3,741 | ........ |
| Greene | 3,182 | 3,015 | 2,667 | 2,447 | ........ | ........ | ........ | ........ | ........ |
| Greensville | 2,155 | 1,974 | 1,731 | 1,928 | 2,104 | 2,056 | 2,254 | 2,398 | 2,530 |
| Halifax | 11,562 | 11,060 | 10,976 | 11,145 | 12,916 | 8,758 | 12,117 | 11,168 | 8,931 |
| Hanover | 7,893 | 7,482 | 6,539 | 6,262 | 6,526 | 6,130 | 6,219 | 5,952 | 6,291 |
| Henrico | 35,148 | 37,966 | 23,826 | 16,900 | 13,471 | 11,763 | 9,182 | 6,836 | 5,600 |
| Henry | 6,722 | 6,773 | 5,324 | 4,243 | 4,058 | 3,321 | 3,641 | 3,715 | 6,763 |
| Highland | 3,803 | 3,890 | 3,837 | ........ | ........ | ........ | ........ | ........ | ........ |
| Isle of Wight | 4,874 | 5,037 | 4,710 | 4,918 | 5,023 | 4,883 | 4,447 | 4,735 | 4,786 |
| James City | 1,985 | 2,167 | 1,489 | 1,325 | 1,283 | 1,551 | 1,354 | 1,374 | 1,519 |
| King and Queen | 4,221 | 3,801 | 4,094 | 4,426 | 4,714 | 5,460 | 4,718 | 4,335 | 4,159 |
| King George | 2,927 | 2,510 | 2,301 | 2,209 | 2,475 | 2,349 | 2,381 | 2,598 | 3,123 |
| King William | 2,943 | 2,589 | 2,701 | 3,150 | 3,155 | 3,449 | 3,294 | 3,139 | 2,893 |
| Lancaster | 2,198 | 1,981 | 1,802 | 1,903 | 1,976 | 2,388 | 2,276 | 2,090 | 2,259 |
| Lee | 12,263 | 10,185 | 9,440 | 7,829 | 5,830 | 3,885 | 4,337 | 3,292 | ........ |
| Loudoun | 15,288 | 15,021 | 15,081 | 13,840 | 15,497 | 16,144 | 15,577 | 15,200 | 14,749 |
| Louisa | 6,269 | 6,183 | 6,423 | 6,047 | 6,468 | 5,967 | 5,253 | 5,768 | 3,880 |
| Lunenburg | 4,344 | 4,421 | 4,314 | 4,132 | 4,479 | 3,873 | 4,933 | 4,372 | 4,547 |
| Madison | 4,959 | 4,360 | 4,456 | 3,729 | 4,289 | 3,800 | 4,323 | 4,836 | ........ |
| Mathews | 4,104 | 3,865 | 3,642 | 3,909 | 3,994 | 3,616 | 2,118 | 2,985 | ........ |
| Mecklenburg | 7,162 | 6,778 | 7,256 | 7,754 | 7,471 | 7,710 | 7,696 | 7,779 | 7,555 |
| Middlesex | 2,459 | 1,863 | 1,903 | 2,041 | 1,868 | 1,756 | 1,811 | 1,603 | 1,531 |
| Montgomery | 9,674 | 8,251 | 6,822 | 5,825 | 10,224 | 7,447 | 7,253 | 8,037 | 12,394 |
| Nansemond | 6,059 | 5,732 | 5,424 | 4,858 | 5,143 | 4,575 | 4,593 | 5,809 | 4,713 |
| Nelson | 7,586 | 6,649 | 6,478 | 6,168 | 5,186 | 4,395 | 4,897 | ........ | ........ |
| New Kent | 2,005 | 2,145 | 2,222 | 2,472 | 2,586 | 2,537 | 2,445 | 2,523 | 2,391 |
| Norfolk | 24,380 | 24,357 | 20,329 | 15,444 | 13,314 | 13,260 | 12,221 | 11,401 | 8,928 |
| Northampton | 3,198 | 2,998 | 3,105 | 3,341 | 3,574 | 3,369 | 3,216 | 2,931 | 3,181 |
| Northumberland | 3,808 | 3,870 | 3,072 | 4,034 | 4,029 | 4,134 | 4,162 | 3,679 | 4,506 |
| Nottoway | 2,241 | 2,270 | 2,234 | 2,490 | 2,965 | 2,805 | 2,730 | 3,311 | (c) |
| Orange | 4,938 | 4.553 | 3,962 | 3,575 | 6,456 | 5,219 | 5,711 | 6,160 | 5,436 |
| Page | 7,476 | 6,875 | 6,332 | 5,197 | ........ | ........ | ........ | ........ | ........ |
| Patrick | 7,836 | 7,158 | 7,187 | 6,087 | 5,496 | 3,776 | 3,696 | 3,552 | ........ |
| Pittsylvania | 15,259 | 17,105 | 15,263 | 14,283 | 14,694 | 12,636 | 10,710 | 8,503 | 8,538 |
| Powhatan | 2,552 | 2,580 | 2,513 | 2,432 | 2,661 | 2,492 | 2,484 | 2,393 | 2,286 |
| Prince Edward | 4,106 | 4,037 | 4,177 | 4,923 | 5,039 | 4,627 | 5,264 | 4,978 | 4,082 |
| Prince George | 2,774 | 2,899 | 2,670 | 2,692 | 3,069 | 3,119 | 3,101 | 2,795 | 3,387 |
| Princess Anne | 4,369 | 4,333 | 4,280 | 3,996 | 5,025 | 4,812 | 5,305 | 5,200 | 4,527 |
| Prince William | 5,691 | 5,690 | 5,079 | 4,867 | 5,127 | 4,761 | 5,733 | 6,975 | 6,744 |
| Pulaski | 4,729 | 3,814 | 3,613 | 2,768 | ........ | ........ | ........ | ........ | ........ |
| Rappahannock | 5,195 | 5,018 | 5,642 | 5,307 | ........ | ........ | ........ | ........ | ........ |

## TABLE II.—CONTINUED.

| COUNTIES. | WHITE. | | | | | | | | |
|---|---|---|---|---|---|---|---|---|---|
| | 1870. | 1860. | 1850. | 1840. | 1830. | 1820. | 1810. | 1800. | 1790. |
| Richmond | 3,475 | 3,570 | 3,463 | 3,092 | 2,975 | 2,749 | 2,775 | e5,334 | 2,918 |
| Roanoke | 6,218 | 5,250 | 5,812 | 3,845 | ........ | ........ | ........ | ........ | ........ |
| Rockbridge | 12,162 | 12,841 | 11,484 | 10,448 | 10,465 | 9,038 | 8,445 | 7,778 | 5,825 |
| Rockingham | 21,152 | 20,489 | 17,496 | 14,944 | 17,814 | 12,646 | 11,049 | 9,266 | 6,677 |
| Russell | 9,936 | 9,130 | 10,866 | 7,152 | 6,002 | 4,989 | 5,897 | 4,443 | 3,143 |
| Scott | 12,512 | 11,530 | 9,322 | 6,911 | 5,378 | 3,992 | ........ | ........ | ........ |
| Shenandoah | 14,260 | 12,827 | 12,565 | 10,320 | 16,869 | 16,708 | 12,461 | 12,947 | 9,979 |
| Smyth | 7,654 | 7,732 | 6,898 | 5,539 | ........ | ........ | ........ | ........ | ........ |
| Southampton | 5,468 | 5,713 | 5,940 | 6,171 | 6,573 | 6,127 | 5,982 | 6,461 | 6,312 |
| Spotsylvania | 7,069 | 7,716 | 6,894 | 6,786 | 6,384 | 5,939 | 5,596 | 5,875 | 5,171 |
| Stafford | 4,935 | 4,922 | 4,415 | 4,489 | 4,713 | 4,788 | 5,319 | 5,435 | 5,465 |
| Surry | 2,393 | 2,334 | 2,215 | 2,557 | 2,865 | 2,642 | 2,751 | 2,777 | 2,762 |
| Sussex | 2,962 | 3,118 | 3,086 | 3,584 | 4,118 | 4,155 | 4,436 | 4,532 | 4,771 |
| Tazewell | 9,193 | 8,625 | 8,807 | 5,466 | 4,911 | 3,435 | 2,061 | 1,895 | ........ |
| Warren | 4,611 | 4,583 | 4,493 | 3,851 | ........ | ........ | ........ | ........ | ........ |
| Warwick | 620 | 662 | 599 | 604 | 633 | 620 | 697 | 614 | 667 |
| Washington | 14,156 | 14,095 | 12,369 | 10,731 | 12,785 | 10,393 | 10,581 | 8,250 | 5,167 |
| Westmoreland | 3,531 | 3,387 | 3,376 | 3,466 | 3,710 | 3,031 | 3,401 | (e) | 3,183 |
| Wise | 4,717 | 4,416 | ........ | ........ | ........ | ........ | ........ | ........ | ........ |
| Wythe | 9,269 | 9,986 | 9,618 | 7,632 | 9,952 | 8,111 | 7,180 | 5,538 | ........ |
| York | 2,507 | 2,342 | 1,825 | 1,958 | 2,129 | 1,588 | 1,798 | 1,166 f8 | 2,115 |
| | FREE COLORED. | | | | | | | | |
| Total | 512,841 | 55,269 | 51,251 | a1,862 46,809 | a1,548 45,181 | a1,290 35,470 | a977 29,292 | a383 19,598 | 12,254 |
| Variances from former official totals | ........ | ........ | ........ | b—10 | ........ | b—6 | ........ | ........ | ........ |
| Accomac | 7,842 | 3,418 | 3,295 | 2,848 | 2,544 | 2,100 | 1,860 | 1,541 | 721 |
| Albemarle | 14,994 | 606 | 587 | 603 | 484 | 373 | 400 | 207 | 171 |
| Alexandria | 7,310 | 1,415 | 1,409 | a1,862 | a1,548 | a1,290 | a977 | a383 | ........ |
| Alleghany | 579 | 132 | 58 | 60 | 48 | ........ | ........ | ........ | ........ |
| Amelia | 6,823 | 189 | 166 | 223 | 220 | 187 | 155 | 58 | c106 |
| Amherst | 6,704 | 297 | 394 | 373 | 263 | 246 | 198 | 134 | 121 |
| Appomattox | 4,536 | 171 | 185 | ........ | ........ | ........ | ........ | ........ | ........ |
| Augusta | 6,737 | 586 | 574 | 421 | 404 | 267 | 196 | 95 | 59 |
| Bath | 889 | 78 | 45 | 83 | 65 | 64 | 49 | 17 | ........ |
| Bedford | 10,770 | 504 | 463 | 323 | 341 | 311 | 212 | 202 | 52 |
| Bland | 217 | ........ | ........ | ........ | ........ | ........ | ........ | ........ | ........ |
| Botetourt | 3,163 | 306 | 426 | 377 | 386 | 290 | 300 | 135 | 24 |
| Brunswick | 8,902 | 671 | 553 | 563 | 612 | 717 | 378 | 270 | 132 |

## TABLE II.—Continued.

| COUNTIES. | FREE COLORED. | | | | | | | | |
|---|---|---|---|---|---|---|---|---|---|
| | 1870. | 1860. | 1850. | 1840. | 1830. | 1820. | 1810. | 1800. | 1790. |
| Buchanan | 47 | 1 | ........ | ........ | ........ | ........ | ........ | ........ | ........ |
| Buckingham | 7,711 | 360 | 250 | 449 | 245 | 285 | 604 | 229 | 115 |
| Campbell | 14,343 | 1,029 | 846 | 772 | 859 | 677 | 263 | 302 | 251 |
| Caroline | 8,038 | 844 | 904 | 774 | 520 | 486 | 328 | 365 | 203 |
| Carroll | 328 | 31 | 29 | ........ | ........ | ........ | ........ | ........ | ........ |
| Charles City | 3,153 | 856 | 772 | 670 | 761 | 538 | 387 | 398 | 363 |
| Charlotte | 9,613 | 252 | 352 | 305 | 236 | 161 | 210 | 123 | 63 |
| Chesterfield | 8,733 | 643 | 467 | 587 | 591 | 947 | 272 | 319 | 369 |
| Clarke | 2,159 | 64 | 124 | 161 | ........ | ........ | ........ | ........ | ........ |
| Craig | 230 | 30 | ........ | ........ | ........ | ........ | ........ | ........ | ........ |
| Culpeper | 6,169 | 429 | 487 | 391 | 564 | 338 | 264 | 273 | 70 |
| Cumberland | 5,433 | 310 | 340 | 355 | 327 | 244 | 175 | 183 | 142 |
| Dinwiddie | 17,664 | 3,746 | 3,296 | 2,764 | 2,890 | 1,833 | 1,565 | 674 | 561 |
| Elizabeth City | 5,471 | 201 | 97 | 44 | 131 | 70 | 75 | 18 | 18 |
| Essex | 6,650 | 477 | 409 | 598 | 467 | 364 | 306 | 276 | 139 |
| Fairfax | 4,284 | 672 | 597 | 448 | 311 | 507 | 543 | 204 | 135 |
| Fauquier | 7,856 | 821 | 643 | 688 | 613 | 507 | 344 | 131 | 93 |
| Floyd | 997 | 16 | 14 | 9 | ........ | ........ | ........ | ........ | ........ |
| Fluvanna | 5,097 | 266 | 211 | 221 | 203 | 123 | 57 | 44 | 25 |
| Franklin | 5,996 | 105 | 66 | 174 | 195 | 143 | 86 | 27 | 34 |
| Frederick | 2,733 | 1,208 | 912 | 821 | 1,265 | 970 | 610 | 453 | 116 |
| Giles | 598 | 67 | 55 | 49 | 49 | 42 | 25 | ........ | ........ |
| Gloucester | 5,429 | 703 | 680 | 612 | 603 | 462 | 446 | 35 | 210 |
| Goochland | 6,601 | 703 | 644 | 690 | 796 | 685 | 509 | 413 | 257 |
| Grayson | 754 | 52 | 36 | 53 | 52 | 83 | 30 | 1 | ........ |
| Greene | 1,452 | 23 | 34 | 45 | ........ | ........ | ........ | ........ | ........ |
| Greensville | 4,207 | 233 | 123 | 136 | 332 | 290 | ........ | 213 | 212 |
| Halifax | 16,266 | 563 | 534 | 575 | 500 | 422 | 353 | 298 | 226 |
| Hanover | 8,562 | 257 | 221 | 312 | 449 | 381 | 409 | 259 | 240 |
| Henrico | 31,031 | 3,590 | 3,637 | 2,939 | 3,045 | 2,100 | 1,904 | 1,149 | 581 |
| Henry | 5,581 | 314 | 208 | 240 | 174 | 125 | 215 | 129 | 165 |
| Highland | 348 | 27 | 26 | ........ | ........ | ........ | ........ | ........ | ........ |
| Isle of Wight | 3,446 | 1,370 | 1,248 | 1,268 | 1,222 | 938 | 698 | 578 | 375 |
| James City | 2,440 | 1,045 | 663 | 507 | 572 | 552 | 420 | 168 | 146 |
| King and Queen | 5,488 | 388 | 461 | 499 | 416 | 297 | 267 | 164 | 75 |
| King George | 2,815 | 388 | 267 | 276 | 287 | 263 | 197 | 164 | 86 |
| King William | 4,455 | 416 | 347 | 328 | 347 | 238 | 203 | 172 | 84 |
| Lancaster | 3,157 | 301 | 266 | 247 | 193 | 185 | 204 | 159 | 143 |
| Lee | 1,005 | 13 | 40 | 32 | 19 | 5 | 21 | 3 | ........ |
| Londonn | 5,691 | 1,252 | 1,357 | 1,318 | 1,079 | 829 | 604 | 333 | 168 |
| Louisa | 10,063 | 324 | 404 | 376 | 301 | 219 | 157 | 132 | 14 |

TABLE II.—Continued.

| COUNTIES. | FREE COLORED. | | | | | | | | |
|---|---|---|---|---|---|---|---|---|---|
| | 1870. | 1860. | 1850. | 1840. | 1830. | 1820. | 1810. | 1800. | 1790. |
| Lunenburg | 6,059 | 257 | 191 | 216 | 245 | 126 | 177 | 133 | 80 |
| Madison | 3,711 | 97 | 151 | 70 | 71 | 78 | 88 | 50 | ........ |
| Mathews | 2,096 | 218 | 149 | 164 | 189 | 118 | 41 | 17 | ........ |
| Mecklenburg | 14,156 | 898 | 912 | 1,055 | 889 | 674 | 493 | 553 | 416 |
| Middlesex | 2,522 | 126 | 149 | 142 | 116 | 135 | 127 | 84 | 51 |
| Montgomery | 2,882 | 147 | 66 | 87 | 56 | 31 | 57 | 39 | 6 |
| Nansemond | 5,517 | 2,480 | 2,144 | 1,407 | 1,698 | 1,398 | 1,269 | 910 | 480 |
| Nelson | 6,312 | 128 | 138 | 152 | 122 | 82 | 108 | ........ | ........ |
| New Kent | 2,361 | 364 | 432 | 373 | 342 | 334 | 308 | 218 | 148 |
| Norfolk | 22,320 | 2,803 | 2,307 | 2,390 | 1,898 | 1,491 | 1,179 | 559 | 251 |
| Northampton | 4,848 | 962 | 745 | 754 | 1,333 | 1,013 | 908 | 654 | 464 |
| Northumberland | 3,054 | 222 | 519 | 647 | 567 | 614 | 299 | 221 | 197 |
| Nottoway | 7,050 | 98 | 153 | 158 | 223 | 175 | 180 | 107 | (c) |
| Orange | 5,458 | 187 | 184 | 186 | 198 | 143 | 96 | 47 | 64 |
| Page | 986 | 384 | 311 | 216 | ........ | ........ | ........ | ........ | ........ |
| Patrick | 2,325 | 131 | 98 | 103 | 117 | 100 | 275 | 130 | ........ |
| Pittsylvania | 16,084 | 659 | 735 | 557 | 341 | 203 | 150 | 61 | 62 |
| Powhatan | 5,115 | 409 | 388 | 363 | 384 | 324 | 498 | 345 | 211 |
| Prince Edward | 7,898 | 466 | 488 | 570 | 475 | 334 | 149 | 63 | 32 |
| Prince George | 5,046 | 515 | 518 | 469 | 700 | 588 | 463 | 250 | 267 |
| Princess Anne | 2,902 | 195 | 259 | 202 | 343 | 251 | 267 | 85 | 64 |
| Prince William | 1,813 | 519 | 552 | 510 | 361 | 278 | 358 | 342 | 167 |
| Pulaski | 1,809 | 13 | 34 | 17 | ........ | ........ | ........ | ........ | ........ |
| Rappahannock | 3,066 | 312 | 296 | 287 | ........ | ........ | ........ | ........ | ........ |
| Richmond | 3,028 | 820 | 708 | 510 | 450 | 293 | 261 | c584 | 83 |
| Roanoke | 3,132 | 155 | 155 | 101 | ........ | ........ | ........ | ........ | ........ |
| Rockbridge | 3,890 | 422 | 364 | 326 | 381 | 295 | 149 | 97 | 41 |
| Rockingham | 2,516 | 532 | 467 | 501 | 548 | 267 | 213 | 56 | ........ |
| Russell | 1,167 | 51 | 71 | 26 | 33 | 21 | 36 | 13 | 5 |
| Scott | 524 | 52 | 34 | 48 | 16 | 13 | ........ | ........ | ........ |
| Shenandoah | 676 | 316 | 292 | 265 | 458 | 317 | 147 | 85 | 19 |
| Smyth | 1,244 | 183 | 200 | 145 | ........ | ........ | ........ | ........ | ........ |
| Southampton | 6,795 | 1,794 | 1,826 | 1,799 | 1,745 | 1,306 | 1,109 | 839 | 559 |
| Spotsylvania | 4,659 | 574 | 536 | 785 | 697 | 591 | 565 | 297 | 148 |
| Stafford | 1,485 | 319 | 318 | 309 | 495 | 361 | 316 | 193 | 87 |
| Surry | 3,192 | 1,284 | 985 | 1,070 | 866 | 612 | 664 | 500 | 368 |
| Sussex | 4,923 | 673 | 742 | 811 | 866 | 684 | 582 | 542 | 391 |
| Tazewell | 1,508 | 93 | 75 | 88 | 18 | 18 | 18 | 13 | ........ |
| Warren | 1,105 | 284 | 366 | 342 | ........ | ........ | ........ | ........ | ........ |
| Warwick | 1,052 | 59 | 42 | 21 | 27 | 34 | 18 | 21 | 33 |
| Washington | 2,653 | 249 | 112 | 212 | 261 | 153 | 127 | 386 | 8 |

## TABLE II.—Continued.

| COUNTIES. | FREE COLORED. | | | | | | | | |
|---|---|---|---|---|---|---|---|---|---|
| | 1870. | 1860. | 1850. | 1840. | 1830. | 1820. | 1810. | 1800. | 1790. |
| Westmoreland | 4,151 | 1,191 | 1,147 | 963 | 847 | 477 | 621 | (c) | 114 |
| Wise | 63 | 26 | ........ | ........ | ........ | ........ | ........ | ........ | ........ |
| Wythe | 2,342 | 157 | 221 | 125 | 117 | 48 | 19 | 11 | ........ |
| York | 4,691 | 682 | 454 | 650 | 627 | 631 | 458 | 45 | 358 |
| | SLAVE. | | | | | | | | |
| Total | ........ | 472,494 | 452,028 | a1,374<br>430,499 | a1,614<br>452,084 | a1,857<br>410,029 | a1,841<br>351,680 | a1,172<br>338,624 | 287,959 |
| Variances from former official totals | ........ | ........ | ........ | b—100 | ........ | b—5 | b—2 | ........ | ........ |
| Accomac | ........ | 4,507 | 4,987 | 4,630 | 4,654 | 4,480 | 4,542 | 4,429 | 4,262 |
| Albemarle | ........ | 13,916 | 13,238 | 11,809 | 11,679 | 10,659 | 9,226 | 7,436 | 5,579 |
| Alexandria | ........ | 1,386 | 1,382 | a1,374 | a1,614 | a1,857 | a1,841 | a1,172 | ........ |
| Alleghany | ........ | 990 | 694 | 547 | 571 | ........ | ........ | ........ | ........ |
| Amelia | ........ | 7,655 | 6,819 | 7,023 | 7,523 | 7,400 | 7,186 | 6,585 | c11,307 |
| Amherst | ........ | 6,278 | 5,953 | 5,777 | 5,925 | 5,507 | 5,207 | 7,462 | 5,296 |
| Appomattox | ........ | 4,600 | 4,799 | ........ | ........ | ........ | ........ | ........ | ........ |
| Augusta | ........ | 5,616 | 5,053 | 4,135 | 4,265 | 3,512 | 2,880 | 1,946 | 1,567 |
| Bath | ........ | 946 | 947 | 1,047 | 1,140 | 1,202 | 882 | 661 | ........ |
| Bedford | ........ | 10,176 | 10,061 | 8,864 | 8,782 | 8,041 | 6,147 | 4,097 | 2,754 |
| Bland | ........ | ........ | ........ | ........ | ........ | ........ | ........ | ........ | ........ |
| Botetourt | ........ | 2,769 | 3,736 | 2,925 | 4,170 | 2,806 | 2,275 | 1,519 | 1,259 |
| Brunswick | ........ | 9,146 | 8,456 | 8,805 | 9,758 | 10,081 | 9,368 | 9,422 | 6,776 |
| Buchanan | ........ | 30 | ........ | ........ | ........ | ........ | ........ | ........ | ........ |
| Buckingham | ........ | 8,811 | 8,161 | 11,014 | 10,929 | 9,939 | 11,675 | 6,336 | 4,168 |
| Campbell | ........ | 11,580 | 10,866 | 10,045 | 9,496 | 7,445 | 5,368 | 3,671 | 2,488 |
| Caroline | ........ | 10,672 | 10,661 | 10,314 | 10,741 | 10,999 | 10,764 | 10,581 | 10,292 |
| Carroll | ........ | 262 | 154 | ........ | ........ | ........ | ........ | ........ | ........ |
| Charles City | ........ | 2,947 | 2,764 | 2,433 | 2,957 | 2,967 | 3,023 | 3,013 | 3,141 |
| Charlotte | ........ | 9,238 | 8,988 | 9,260 | 9,433 | 8,124 | 7,597 | 6,283 | 4,816 |
| Chesterfield | ........ | 8,354 | 8,616 | 8,702 | 10,337 | 9,513 | 6,015 | 7,852 | 7,487 |
| Clarke | ........ | 3,375 | 3,614 | 3,325 | ........ | ........ | ........ | ........ | ........ |
| Craig | ........ | 420 | ........ | ........ | ........ | ........ | ........ | ........ | ........ |
| Culpeper | ........ | 6,675 | 6,683 | 6,069 | 11,417 | 9,468 | 8,312 | 7,348 | 8,226 |
| Cumberland | ........ | 6,705 | 6,329 | 6,781 | 7,309 | 6,813 | 6,102 | 5,711 | 4,434 |
| Dinwiddie | ........ | 12,774 | 10,880 | 9,947 | 10,356 | 10,179 | 9,615 | 8,303 | 7,334 |
| Elizabeth City | ........ | 2,417 | 2,148 | 1,708 | 2,218 | 1,643 | 1,734 | 1,522 | 1,876 |
| Essex | ........ | 6,696 | 6,762 | 6,756 | 6,407 | 6,046 | 5,659 | 5,767 | 5,440 |
| Fairfax | ........ | 3,116 | 3,250 | 3,453 | 4,001 | 4,673 | 5,942 | 6,078 | 4,574 |
| Fauquier | ........ | 10,455 | 10,350 | 10,708 | 12,523 | 11,167 | 10,361 | 8,754 | 6,642 |

TABLE II.—CONTINUED.

| COUNTIES. | SLAVE. | | | | | | | | |
|---|---|---|---|---|---|---|---|---|---|
| | 1870. | 1860. | 1850. | 1840. | 1830. | 1820. | 1810. | 1800. | 1790. |
| Floyd | ........ | 475 | 443 | 321 | ........ | ........ | ........ | ........ | ........ |
| Fluvanna | ........ | 4,994 | 4,737 | 4,146 | 3,795 | 3,206 | 2,142 | 1,920 | 1,466 |
| Franklin | ........ | 6,351 | 5,726 | 5,158 | 4,988 | 3,647 | 2,672 | 1,574 | 1,073 |
| Frederick | ........ | 2,259 | 2,294 | 2,302 | 7,420 | 7,179 | 6,417 | 5,663 | 4,250 |
| Giles | ........ | 778 | 657 | 574 | 465 | 305 | 242 | ........ | ........ |
| Gloucester | ........ | 5,736 | 5,557 | 5,691 | 5,691 | 5,208 | 5,798 | 4,909 | 7,063 |
| Goochland | ........ | 6,139 | 5,845 | 5,500 | 5,716 | 5,526 | 5,464 | 4,803 | 4,656 |
| Grayson | ........ | 547 | 499 | 492 | 462 | 345 | 270 | 170 | ........ |
| Greene | ........ | 1,984 | 1,699 | 1,740 | ........ | ........ | ........ | ........ | ........ |
| Greensville | ........ | 4,167 | 3,785 | 4,302 | 4,681 | 4,512 | 4,599 | 4,116 | 3,620 |
| Halifax | ........ | 14,897 | 14,452 | 14,216 | 14,528 | 9,880 | 9,663 | 7,911 | 5,565 |
| Hanover | ........ | 9,483 | 8,393 | 8,394 | 9,278 | 8,756 | 8,454 | 8,192 | 8,223 |
| Henrico | ........ | 20,041 | 16,109 | 13,237 | 12,281 | 9,804 | 8,594 | 6,901 | 5,819 |
| Henry | ........ | 5,018 | 3,340 | 2,852 | 2,868 | 2,178 | 1,755 | 1,415 | 1,551 |
| Highland | ........ | 402 | 364 | ........ | ........ | ........ | ........ | ........ | ........ |
| Isle of Wight | ........ | 3,570 | 3,395 | 3,786 | 4,272 | 4,297 | 4,041 | 4,029 | 3,867 |
| James City | ........ | 2,586 | 1,868 | 1,947 | 1,983 | 2,460 | 2,320 | 2,389 | 2,405 |
| King and Queen | ........ | 6,139 | 5,764 | 5,937 | 6,514 | 6,041 | 6,003 | 5,380 | 5,143 |
| King George | ........ | 3,673 | 3,403 | 3,382 | 3,685 | 3,504 | 3,876 | 3,987 | 4,157 |
| King William | ........ | 5,525 | 5,731 | 5,780 | 6,310 | 6,010 | 5,788 | 5,744 | 5,151 |
| Lancaster | ........ | 2,869 | 2,640 | 2,478 | 2,632 | 2,944 | 3,112 | 3,126 | 3,236 |
| Lee | ........ | 824 | 787 | 580 | 612 | 366 | 336 | 243 | ........ |
| Loudoun | ........ | 5,501 | 5,641 | 5,273 | 5,363 | 5,729 | 5,157 | 4,990 | 4,030 |
| Louisa | ........ | 10,194 | 9,864 | 9,010 | 9,382 | 7,560 | 6,490 | 5,992 | 4,573 |
| Lunenburg | ........ | 7,305 | 7,187 | 6,707 | 7,233 | 6,663 | 7,155 | 5,876 | 4,332 |
| Madison | ........ | 4,397 | 4,724 | 4,308 | 4,876 | 4,612 | 3,970 | 3,436 | ........ |
| Mathews | ........ | 3,008 | 2,923 | 3,309 | 3,481 | 3,186 | 2,068 | 2,804 | ........ |
| Mecklenburg | ........ | 12,420 | 12,462 | 11,915 | 12,117 | 11,402 | 10,264 | 8,676 | 6,762 |
| Middlesex | ........ | 2,375 | 2,342 | 2,209 | 2,138 | 2,166 | 2,476 | 2,516 | 2,558 |
| Montgomery | ........ | 2,219 | 1,471 | 1,493 | 2,026 | 1,255 | 1,099 | 968 | 828 |
| Nansemond | ........ | 5,481 | 4,715 | 4,530 | 4,943 | 4,526 | 4,462 | 4,408 | 3,817 |
| Nelson | ........ | 6,238 | 6,142 | 5,967 | 5,946 | 5,660 | 4,679 | ........ | ........ |
| New Kent | ........ | 3,374 | 3,410 | 3,385 | 3,530 | 3,759 | 3,725 | 3,622 | 3,700 |
| Norfolk | ........ | 9,004 | 10,400 | 9,735 | 9,504 | 9,185 | 9,472 | 7,459 | 5,345 |
| Northampton | ........ | 3,872 | 3,648 | 3,620 | 3,734 | 3,323 | 3,350 | 3,178 | 3,244 |
| Northumberland | ........ | 3,439 | 3,755 | 3,243 | 3,357 | 3,268 | 3,547 | 3,903 | 4,460 |
| Nottoway | ........ | 6,468 | 6,050 | 7,071 | 6,942 | 6,676 | 6,368 | 5,983 | (c) |
| Orange | ........ | 6,111 | 5,921 | 5,364 | 7,983 | 7,518 | 6,516 | 5,242 | 4,421 |
| Page | ........ | 850 | 957 | 781 | ........ | ........ | ........ | ........ | ........ |
| Patrick | ........ | 2,070 | 2,324 | 1,842 | 1,782 | 1,213 | 724 | 649 | ........ |
| Pittsylvania | ........ | 14,340 | 12,798 | 11,558 | 10,999 | 8,484 | 6,312 | 4,133 | 2,979 |

## TABLE II.—Continued.

| COUNTIES. | SLAVE. | | | | | | | | |
|---|---|---|---|---|---|---|---|---|---|
| | 1870. | 1860. | 1850. | 1840. | 1830. | 1820. | 1810. | 1800. | 1790. |
| Powhatan | ........ | 5,403 | 5,282 | 5,129 | 5,472 | 5,476 | 5,091 | 5,031 | 4,325 |
| Prince Edward | ........ | 7,341 | 7,192 | 8,576 | 8,593 | 7,616 | 6,996 | 5,921 | 3,986 |
| Prince George | ........ | 4,997 | 4,408 | 4,014 | 4,598 | 4,323 | 4,486 | 4,380 | 4,519 |
| Princess Anne | ........ | 3,186 | 3,130 | 3,087 | 3,734 | 3,705 | 3,926 | 3,574 | 3,202 |
| Prince William | ........ | 2,356 | 2,498 | 2,767 | 3,842 | 4,380 | 5,220 | 5,416 | 4,704 |
| Pulaski | ........ | 1,589 | 1,471 | 954 | ........ | ........ | ........ | ........ | ........ |
| Rappahannock | ........ | 3,520 | 3,844 | 3,663 | ........ | ........ | ........ | ........ | ........ |
| Richmond | ........ | 2,466 | 2,277 | 2,363 | 2,630 | 2,064 | 3,178 | *e*7,826 | 3,984 |
| Roanoke | ........ | 2,643 | 2,510 | 1,553 | ........ | ........ | ........ | ........ | ........ |
| Rockbridge | ........ | 3,985 | 4,197 | 3,510 | 3,398 | 2,612 | 1,724 | 1,070 | 682 |
| Rockingham | ........ | 2,387 | 2,331 | 1,899 | 2,321 | 1,671 | 1,491 | 1,052 | 772 |
| Russell | ........ | 1,099 | 982 | 700 | 679 | 526 | 386 | 352 | 190 |
| Scott | ........ | 490 | 473 | 344 | 330 | 258 | ........ | ........ | ........ |
| Shenandoah | ........ | 753 | 911 | 1,033 | 2,428 | 1,901 | 1,038 | 791 | 512 |
| Smyth | ........ | 1,037 | 1,064 | 838 | ........ | ........ | ........ | ........ | ........ |
| Southampton | ........ | 5,408 | 5,755 | 6,555 | 7,756 | 6,737 | 6,406 | 6,625 | 5,993 |
| Spotsylvania | ........ | 7,760 | 7,481 | 7,590 | 8,053 | 7,724 | 7,135 | 6,830 | 5,933 |
| Stafford | ........ | 3,314 | 3,311 | 3,596 | 4,164 | 4,368 | 4,195 | 4,343 | 4,036 |
| Surry | ........ | 2,515 | 2,479 | 2,853 | 3,378 | 8,340 | 3,440 | 3,258 | 3,097 |
| Sussex | ........ | 6,384 | 5,992 | 6,834 | 7,736 | 7,045 | 6,344 | 5,988 | 5,387 |
| Tazewell | ........ | 1,202 | 1,060 | 786 | 820 | 463 | 328 | 219 | ........ |
| Warren | ........ | 1,575 | 1,748 | 1,434 | ........ | ........ | ........ | ........ | ........ |
| Warwick | ........ | 1,019 | 905 | 831 | 910 | 954 | 1,120 | 1,024 | 990 |
| Washington | ........ | 2,547 | 2,131 | 2,058 | 2,568 | 1,898 | 1,448 | 900 | 450 |
| Westmoreland | ........ | 3,704 | 3,557 | 3,590 | 3,639 | 3,393 | 4,080 | (*e*) | 4,425 |
| Wise | ........ | 66 | ........ | ........ | ........ | ........ | ........ | ........ | ........ |
| Wythe | ........ | 2,162 | 2,185 | 1,618 | 2,094 | 1,533 | 1,157 | 831 | ........ |
| York | ........ | 1,925 | 2,181 | 2,112 | 2,598 | 2,165 | 2,931 | 2,020<br>*f*40 | 2,760 |

| | CHINESE. | | | | | | | | |
|---|---|---|---|---|---|---|---|---|---|
| Total | 4 | ........ | ........ | ........ | ........ | ........ | ........ | ........ | ........ |
| Variances from former official totals | ........ | ........ | ........ | ........ | ........ | ........ | ........ | ........ | ........ |
| Alexandria | 1 | ........ | ........ | ........ | ........ | ........ | ........ | ........ | ........ |
| Fairfax | 1 | ........ | ........ | ........ | ........ | ........ | ........ | ........ | ........ |
| Princess Anne | 2 | ........ | ........ | ........ | ........ | ........ | ........ | ........ | ........ |

TABLE II.—CONTINUED.

| COUNTIES. | INDIAN. | | | | | | | | |
|---|---|---|---|---|---|---|---|---|---|
| | 1870. | 1860. | 1850. | 1840. | 1830. | 1820. | 1810. | 1800. | 1790. |
| Total | 229 | 94 | ........ | ........ | ........ | ........ | ........ | ........ | ........ |
| Variances from former official totals | ........ | ........ | ........ | ........ | ........ | ........ | ........ | ........ | ........ |
| Amherst | 12 | ........ | ........ | ........ | ........ | ........ | ........ | ........ | ........ |
| Caroline | 13 | ........ | ........ | ........ | ........ | ........ | ........ | ........ | ........ |
| Chesterfield | 7 | ........ | ........ | ........ | ........ | ........ | ........ | ........ | ........ |
| Dinwiddie | 21 | ........ | ........ | ........ | ........ | ........ | ........ | ........ | ........ |
| Giles | 5 | ........ | ........ | ........ | ........ | ........ | ........ | ........ | ........ |
| Goochland | 1 | ........ | ........ | ........ | ........ | ........ | ........ | ........ | ........ |
| Henrico | ........ | 19 | ........ | ........ | ........ | ........ | ........ | ........ | ........ |
| King William | 117 | ........ | ........ | ........ | ........ | ........ | ........ | ........ | ........ |
| Lee | ........ | 10 | ........ | ........ | ........ | ........ | ........ | ........ | ........ |
| New Kent | 15 | 1 | ........ | ........ | ........ | ........ | ........ | ........ | ........ |
| Norfolk | 2 | 63 | ........ | ........ | ........ | ........ | ........ | ........ | ........ |
| Northumberland | 1 | ........ | ........ | ........ | ........ | ........ | ........ | ........ | ........ |
| Rockbridge | 6 | ........ | ........ | ........ | ........ | ........ | ........ | ........ | ........ |
| Southampton | 22 | ........ | ........ | ........ | ........ | ........ | ........ | ........ | ........ |
| Washington | 7 | 1 | ........ | ........ | ........ | ........ | ........ | ........ | ........ |

(*) All other persons, except Indians, not taxed.

(a) Then in the District of Columbia.

(b) These are variances from the totals of Virginia, including West Virginia. They result from errors too numerous to be here specified.

(c) Amelia and Nottoway tabulated together, and here placed opposite Amelia.

(d) In 1861 Bland from Giles, Tazewell, and Wythe.

(e) Richmond and Westmoreland tabulated together, opposite Richmond.

(f) Lacking to complete the official totals. Possibly the result of typographical errors. There are no manuscript returns with which to compare the printed census, which has totals of columns but no totals of any horizontal lines, therefore these deficiencies cannot be located in any civil division of the State.

# INDEX.

## ABBREVIATIONS.

App.—Appalachia grand division.
A. M. & O.—Atlantic, Miss. and Ohio R'd.
A. & F.—Alexandria and Fredericksburg R'd.
A. & W.—Alexandria and Washington R'd.
B. R.—Blue Ridge grand division.
B. & P.—Baltimore and Potomac R'd.
B. & O.—Baltimore and Ohio R'd.
C. & O.—Chesapeake and Ohio R'd.
Div.—Grand Divisions of Virginia.
J. R. & K.—James River and Kanawha Canal.
M.—Manassas Branch R'd.
Mid.—Middle or Midland grand division.
P.—Petersburg R'd.
Pied.—Piedmont grand division.
Rich.—Richmond.
R'd or R'y—Railroad.
R. & D.—Richmond and Danville R'd.
R. F. & P.—Richmond, Fredericksburg and Potomac R'd.
R. & P.—Richmond and Petersburg R'd.
R., Y. R. & C.—Richmond, York River and Chesapeake R'd.
St.—Station of R'd.
Tr.—Tidewater grand division.
U. S.—United States.
Val.—The Valley grand division.
Va.—Virginia.
Va. Mid.—Virginia Midland R'd.
V.—Valley Railroad.
W. & O.—Washington and Ohio R'd.

40

# ERRATA.

Page 23—Ninth line from bottom, for *Miocence* read *Miocene.*

Page 33—Sixth line from bottom, omit "Tertiary *limestones* are frequent and furnish a very good building material."

Page 37—In table of analyses, in No. 5, for 0.22 of titanic acid read 0.12.

Page 40—Fourteenth line from bottom, for Page read Rockingham.

Page 84—Eighth line from top, for Latukiah read Latakiah.

Page 86—Third line from bottom. for Greenesville read Greensville.

Page 130—The lbs. after Confectionery put after Tallow in next line.

Page 140—For Quantity of Castings, 1872, put 3,550 for 3,350.

Page 165—Put 100,615 in last blank of No. 3.

Page 193—Seventeenth line from bottom, for too read two, and put and after curses.

Page 209—First line from top, for Statistics in, put Statistics of.

Page 221—Twenty-first line from top, for Covington read Evington.

Page 227—Eighteenth line from bottom, for Fall's read Falls.

Page 230—For Alexandria and Potomac, read Alexandria and Fredericksburg.

Page 230—Put 1,623.5 for miles of completed railroad. See Appendix A, giving information to January, 1876.

Page 230—Last column of table, for 427 read 426.5, for 123 read 162.7, for 106 read 108, for 52 read 58.5, and for 207 read 205. *Official changes.*

Page 232—The General Assembly chartered a railroad from Buchanan to Clifton Forge.

Page 233—Ninth line from top, for Connelville read Connelsville.

Page 237—Eighteenth line from bottom, for Urbana read Urbanna.

Page 237—Second line from bottom, for Engineer's read Engineers.

Page 238—Twentieth line from bottom, insert comma after trucking.

Page 248—Erase 15th line from bottom, after owner. Law repealed 1876.

Page 257—Change page to 258, to agree with index. Page transposed.

Page 258—Change page to 257, to agree with index. Page transposed.

Page 258—After Wadesville put West Virginia. Put distance from Staunton to Washington 180 miles.

Page 257—Third line from bottom, for 58 read 55.

Page 280—Put Making, below Bread, over Inspection.

Page 301—After Slaves, under Northumberland, for 237 put 270.

www.ingramcontent.com/pod-product-compliance
Lightning Source LLC
Chambersburg PA
CBHW021127270326
41929CB00009B/1079
*9783337373764*